SAMUEL L. CLEMENS

Life As I Find It

A Treasury of Mark Twain Rarities

Edited by
Charles Neider

Cooper Square Press

Published by Cooper Square Press,
An Imprint of Rowman & Littlefield Publishers, Inc.
150 Fifth Avenue, Suite 911
New York, New York 10011

Distributed by National Book Network

Library of Congress Cataloging-in-Publication Data
Twain, Mark, 1835-1910.
   [Mark Twain]
   Life as I find it : a treasury of Mark Twain Rarities / edited by Charles Neider.— 1st
Cooper Square Press ed.
     p.   cm.
   "Unabridged republication of the edition titled Mark Twain: life as I find it, first
published in Garden City, New York in 1961"— T.p. verso.
   Includes indexes
   Contents: Essays, sketches, and tales— Selected interviews.
   ISBN 0-8154-1027-1 (alk. paper)
   1. Humorous stories, American. 2. United States— Social life and customs— Fiction. 3.
Twain, Mark, 1835-1910— Interviews. I. Neider, Charles, 1915- II. Title.

PS1302 . N4 2000
818'.409— dc21   99-050204

ACKNOWLEDGMENTS

I wish especially to thank Frederick Anderson of the University of California in Berkeley for help in the making of this book. I also wish to thank Donald Gallup of Yale University, and Harold Kuebler and Jane Klemer of Doubleday. I am indebted to several libraries for generous assistance: the New York Public Library, the Berg Collection of the New York Public Library, the library of the New York Historical Society, the Buffalo Public Library, the Library of Congress, the libraries of Harvard University, Yale University, and Columbia University, the public libraries of St. Louis and Hartford, and the library of the University of California in Berkeley. Permission to reprint a number of the newspaper interviews was kindly granted by the New York *Times*, the New York *Journal-American*, the New York *Sun* Corporation (for the New York *Herald*), and by Thomas W. Dewart (for the New York *Sun*).

C. N.

To Daniel Levine

CONTENTS

Part II: SELECTED INTERVIEWS

FOREWORD
MARK TWAIN UNCENSORED

Harper & Brothers published *The Autobiography of Mark Twain* in February 1959. Forty years later, in April 1999, a panel of Modern Library judges selected the *Autobiography* for a list of the hundred best nonfiction books in English of the twentieth century. The list included British books. The *Autobiography* was a comfortable number 43. An English friend, Clive Sinclair, called from St. Albans and congratulated me. He would have preferred to congratulate Mark Twain, but Clemens was gone somewhere. For the moment I was his stand-in. Clemens once said, "Chaucer is dead. Shakespeare is dead. And I'm not feeling too good myself." It's an honest question as to whether too many stogies, which he had bought by the barrel, had carried him off with angina before his time. "All lists are suspect," I remarked to Sinclair, hoping he'd contradict. Being a friend, he said drily, "Better to be on it than not on it." I heartily agree. I've written the following essay to mark the occasion of the *Autobiography*'s inclusion in the list, and to share some of the interesting, even important, by-products of the book's first public appearance.

In arranging and editing *The Autobiography of Mark Twain* I ran into complications from the start: from my editors and from Mark Twain's daughter, Clara Clemens Samossoud, and her Russian-born husband, Jacques. When I asked her for permission to include in the *Autobiography* her father's reflections on religion, which he had dictated in the rented Upton house, located on a slope of Mount Monadnock near Dublin, New Hampshire, during five, windy, spectral days in June 1906, she declined. She and her husband feared their publication would mar Mark Twain's reputation around the world and would give aid and comfort to the communistic, atheistic Soviet

Union. Also, Mrs. Samossoud was in her eighties and her health was precarious. Her husband was afraid that the publication of the chapters would release a deluge of fanatical mail upon her.

There was perhaps another reason for her suppressing the chapters, one which she didn't mention to me: the offense she must have taken because of her father's acidulous comments on Mary Baker Eddy in the chapters. Mrs. Samossoud was a devout Christian Scientist. In the chapter written on Friday, June 22, 1906 he wrote, "At this very day there are thousands upon thousands of Americans of average intelligence who fully believe in *Science and Health*, although they can't understand a line of it, and who also worship the sordid and ignorant old purloiner of that gospel—Mrs. Mary Baker G. Eddy, whom they do absolutely believe to be a member by adoption of the Holy Family and on the way to push the Savior to third place and assume the occupancy of His present place and continue that occupancy during the rest of eternity."

I had a lengthy, amiable correspondence with Mrs. Samossoud. On March 28, 1959 I met with her at the Bahia Hotel in Mission Beach, California, a suburb of San Diego, and was impressed by her physical and mental vigor though she was bent with age and had pathetically thin, small hands. I remembered that she had once been an accomplished pianist. Her husband had been a symphony conductor. Her dark eyes were lively now despite pain she was feeling from an old neuritis, which caused her occasionally to press a hand against the left side of her breastbone.

We chatted almost affectionately for more than an hour. Part of the time her husband and her young physician were present. I expressed as diplomatically as I could the hope that she wouldn't consider the matter of the religious chapters closed because the *Autobiography* had recently been issued, but would reconsider the advantages of allowing them to be made public, perhaps in a second edition of the *Autobiography*. To no avail. However, as this narrative will show, she had an important change of mind and heart as a consequence of a widely publicized controversy I had later that year with a Russian critic about the *Autobiography*, a controversy with large political and cultural overtones, in which the suppression of the chapters played a major role.

As for my editors. They feared the book proposed by me would lose money, whereas I cockily (crossing my fingers that I was right) predicted both its financial and critical success. We had a lengthy correspondence punctuated by many phone calls. At one point, losing heart, I backed out. The editors relaxed only when, while still in galleys, to their great surprise (and mine, too) the *Autobiography* became an alternate selection of the Book of the Month Club. The book was very widely and very favorably reviewed. And then, toward the end of August 1959, some six months after its publication, a little cloud appeared above the sunny horizon.

The director of an organization that monitored Slavic journals sent a letter to the "Advertising Director" of Harper & Brothers, which said that a recent issue of the Russian newspaper *Literary Gazette* had carried a highly critical review of the *Autobiography*, and that the review charged the book to be a "disembowelled" and "lixiviated" autobiography, whose editor "tries to pass off the defects of his work for virtues and in so doing doesn't blush with shame." My editor at Harper scrawled on a photocopy of the letter, "Charles—this may amuse you," and mailed it to me. I was amused. And piqued.

The director of the organization, in his letter to the advertising director, offered to provide a translation at his minimum charge of three cents a word, but I was put off by "lixiviated" because I had never used it in my whole life and doubted that the director had ever used it. After looking it up in Webster, I merely ordered a copy of the issue of the *Literary Gazette*, known in the Soviet Union as *Literaturnaya Gazeta*, the official organ of the Union of Writers in the USSR.

I received the newspaper in late September. It was a four-page paper, huge by American standards. The front page, with its six columns of cyrillic type, was 23½ × 16⅝ inches. The upper right-hand corner had an exterior photograph of a vast industrial plant of some kind, in which construction was still ongoing. The lower left-hand corner had a photo of two young women, one a Caucasian, the other Asiatic, broadly smiling at each other. The criticism of Mark Twain's book and me appeared on page four. It was marked with two strokes of an orange pencil for any American's benefit. The only thing that wasn't Greek to me was a footnote in English: "*The Autobiography of Mark Twain*; including chapters now published for the first time. Harper & Brothers, New York, 1959." This was during the Cold War, when the rambunctious Soviet Premier Khrushchev predicted the Russians would soon bury the Americans. (His son became a U.S. citizen in 1999.) To be attacked in the monolithic, controlled Soviet Union press seemed like an impossibly remote event, as if it had occurred on Mars.

Unable to read Russian (born in Odessa, Russia, I came to the United States in December 1920, just under the age of six, and soon forgot the Russian language), I asked a friend, Robert L. Belknap, who taught Russian literature at Columbia University, to do an oral translation for me. He obliged one jolly evening in his ground-floor apartment (we lived in the same Manhattan building), with some friends, family, and lots of beer present. It was a sort of Event. It wasn't every day that somebody in our neighborhood got mauled in a prominent Soviet newspaper. The Russian writer's criticism was so vehement and so outlandish that I responded with belly laughs as if it were a wild joke. Two or three days later, Belknap, at my request, produced a written translation. Here are two excerpts:

Mark Twain on the Bed of Procrustes

Shortly before the opening of the American exhibit in Moscow, the correspondents of the *Literary Gazette* who were getting acquainted with its proposed exposition were amazed to notice that among the books selected for display at the exhibit there were neither any new editions of the works of Mark Twain nor any interesting new publications about his works. Obviously the organizers of the exhibit caught themselves in time, and recently on one of the bookshelves in the Sokolniki [Park] there stood *The Autobiography of Mark Twain*, newly edited in New York.

Still, that initial forgetfulness expresses fairly accurately the relationship of official America to its greatest writer. They try to forget him. And if they have to take notice of him anyway, then in that case everything possible is done to crop the great writer's hair, to deflower the blazing and furious colors of his satire, to eat away the socially unmasking resonance of Twain's work and, in the last analysis, to make him up as a benevolent and simple-minded scoffer. The new edition of the *Autobiography* is the logical fruit of these efforts at literary hairdressing. . . .

Procrustes, as is well known, either stretched his victim to the desired length or else cut off those parts of the body which seemed superfluous to him. Charles Neider uses both methods. On the one hand, he actually introduces into the volume he has edited several items which had no place in previous editions. On the other hand, he excludes from it a large part of the material which went into the editions of 1924 and especially of 1940; moreover, the principle upon which he bases his selection is so interesting that it is fitting to discuss it more fully.

Who does not know Twain's famous pronouncements about American "democracy," his indignant notes about the predatory wars which the United States carried on half a century ago, his satirical sketches, cutting as a slap in the face, of the oil king, Rockefeller, Senator Clark, General Wood, President Theodore Roosevelt, and other knights and henchmen of American expansionism. All these materials (except for an insignificant part which came out in the 1924 edition) came out in the 1940 edition. True, even then an effort was made to soften Twain's more than unambiguous remarks about the bosses of political life in the America of his time. Bernard DeVoto, the editor of that edition, expressed, in part, a naive amazement that Mark Twain, who had once called himself "an unwashed son of labor," could not accept in Rockefeller and T. Roosevelt fellow "sons of labor." But the debunking voice of Mark Twain cuts through the most stifling editorial comments. In 1959 Charles Neider found the precautions of his predecessors insufficient, and he decided without superfluous ceremony to "shut Twain's trap," blotting out from his edition all the notes mentioned above. This is a supreme example of scholarly ill faith and of that very political tendentiousness whose pretended absence certain American men of letters so love to boast on occasion.

Y. Bereznitsky

The gist of Bereznitzky's argument was that the United States had an official line on Mark Twain, that the nation tried to suppress or forget him, that his editors had followed the line carefully, and that I was probably the worst offender in this respect. Since I had been dealing with materials in my own language and had had access to the original manuscripts and typescripts, and inasmuch as my volume had enjoyed a critical success in my own country (facts available to Bereznitsky), it seemed to me that his self-confidence was presumptuous. Still, I was encountering the official Soviet literary line regarding the United States, so I wasn't surprised by the content of the criticism or by its harsh and self-righteous tone.

During the next several days the attack on me and the book increasingly struck me as unfunny. Normally, I didn't reply to criticisms of my books. This one, however, offered a special and complex challenge. It was obviously "protected." It struck through me at the society of which I was a member. And it seemed to discount the possibility of free literary endeavor in my country. I got to wondering, and thought it was a pity it wasn't possible to answer the Soviet critic in his own paper. As far as I knew, it was unheard of for an American writer to defend himself in a Soviet journal. I didn't think I'd get very far writing to the *Literary Gazette*, so I took a stab in the dark and on October 13, 1959 wrote a two-sentence letter directly to Premier

Khrushchev, who had recently visited the United States and had been in an expansive mood. He and President Eisenhower, meeting at Camp David, had indicated a desire for a cultural rapprochement between their nations.

"On August 18th I was severely criticized in the Moscow *Literary Gazette* for my editing of *The Autobiography of Mark Twain*," I wrote. "In the interest of cultural relations between our two countries will you please ask the *Literary Gazette* to open its pages to me for a reply?" I didn't really expect anything to happen. Still. . . .

I addressed the letter, "Premier Nikita Khrushchev, The Kremlin, Moscow, USSR." I was living with my wife Joan and very young daughter Susy in the Columbia University neighborhood and was well known in the small post office on Amsterdam Avenue near 116th Street. Being uncertain what it cost to send an airmail letter to Moscow, I went to the post office to buy the stamp. (I had to go there anyway.) Embarrassed, I hoped no one would notice the name on the envelope. A middle-aged male clerk with bushy eyebrows did notice it, however.

"What? Khrushchev? Are you *crazy*?" he exclaimed, then laughed loudly, causing people to stare. I couldn't blame him.

My sending the letter was so quixotic, a case of one hand clapping, that I didn't mention it to my friends. I didn't hear from Khrushchev, but to my astonishment, in the late afternoon of November 16th, I received a reply in English from Boris Leontyev, foreign editor of the *Literary Gazette*. Dated November 9th, it was brief: "We received your letter and although we have no reason to change our opinion about your book, we shall gladly open our pages to you for a statement on the subject."

I thought, "It will be interesting to see what happens in a paper as politically homogenized as the *Literary Gazette* when an American accuses one of their writers of using unscholarly, devious methods; in short, of not playing fair with his readers."

I received the *Gazette* on a Monday. I wrote my reply the following morning and mailed it the same day. I thanked Khrushchev in a separate letter, and, as a pressure lever, enclosed a copy of my article. To keep the record straight and the pressure lever in position, I noted in my response to Leontyev, the foreign editor, that I was keeping Khrushchev up to date.

While I was composing my reply, my friend Max Eastman, an early and harsh critic of communism and the Soviet regime, called and asked what I was up to. I explained. He asked if I had informed *The New York Times* and *The New York Herald Tribune* about the letter from the *Literary Gazette*. I replied that I didn't think the letter was that important. He said an invitation to an American to defend himself in a Soviet journal, in this case the official literary journal, was unprecedented, adding that if I didn't phone the papers, he would. Skeptical, I called the *Times*, asked for the city desk, and explained the situation to a very busy-sounding man.

"Are you positive?" the man asked. "Yes." "Describe the envelope and its contents." I did. "Are you at home?" "Yes." "A reporter and a photographer will be there promptly." I got a similar response at the *Herald Tribune*. My study was soon crowded with journalists who said their story would probably appear on tomorrow's front page.

Late that evening of November 18th, I walked in a light snow to Broadway and 116th Street, bought the two morning papers, and was impressed by journalistic cleverness. The photo of me on the front page of the *Times* showed what struck me as a snarling face. I couldn't recall having snarled during the interview. The photo on the front page of the *Herald Tribune* showed me as I liked to envision myself: mellow, benign. The *Herald Tribune* ran an editorial on the subject. *The New York Post* published both a story and a "close-up" column. The AP and the UPI sent the story and its sequel over their wires.

My reply to the Soviet critic appeared on page four of the *Literary Gazette* of December 12, 1959, together with a new criticism, on the same page, by Bereznitsky, whose latest attack was twice the length of his first. An editorial note mentioned my having appealed to Premier Khrushchev. The publication of my reply apparently marked the first time a Soviet literary journal published the uncensored comments by an American writer who had been attacked in its pages. It represented what was thought at the time to be a significant breakthrough in Soviet-American cultural relations. Long articles about my appearance in the *Gazette* and about Bereznitsky's new criticism were published in the *Times* and the *Herald Tribune* the next day. The Moscow correspondent of the *Times*, Osgood Caruthers, wrote to me from Moscow on the day my rebuttal appeared:

"Enclosed is the page from *Literaturnaya Gazeta* containing your excellent letter and the Soviet critic's answer. I found both extremely interesting—yours for having very ably tried to straighten out some of the thinking here and Mr. Bereznitsky's for his refusal to be straightened out. This, as you may realize, is an experience we go through here in every contact in every field. I think, however, that if you were able to talk to Mr. Bereznitsky or his like privately, you would come across less polemics, even though the whole premise of accepting Twain and others is so dogmatically based. They just won't give up on old Dreiser, for instance."

The following are some excerpts of my reply. Belknap assured me the Russian translation was complete and accurate.

On August 18th the *Literary Gazette* published a rather severe criticism of the so-called American attitude toward Mark Twain, as well as of my editing of the recently published *Autobiography of Mark Twain*. I should like to say a few words about this criticism, which was signed by Y. Bereznitsky. . . .

The article charged that my predecessors as editors of Mark Twain's *Autobiography* took "precautions" through "stifling editorial comments," as well as other means, to follow the "official" line. Yet it carefully failed to state what every student of Mark Twain knows. The first editor, Albert Bigelow Paine, Twain's friend and literary executor, slavishly followed Twain's requests in the matter of the *Autobiography* and by no means undertook "stifling editorial comments." On the other hand Bernard DeVoto, the second editor, broke Twain's own injunctions in publishing his edition, and did so at the request of and with the approval of the Mark Twain Estate. I too broke Twain's injunctions as expressed in his manuscripts. And so if anyone is to blame for the slowness with which the *Autobiography* has been made public, it is Mark Twain himself, who wanted it that way. The article also failed to state that far from suppressing anything, DeVoto freely published Mark Twain's "political" utterances of some thirty-five years previous: the attacks on Theodore Roosevelt, General Wood, Senator Clark, and others. . . .

My intention was to make a volume designed for the general reader, not the scholar, a volume culled from the autobiographical manuscript as a whole, published as well as unpublished parts (for there were still sections unpublished). It was my hope to unburden the excellent parts from the dated, dull, trivial, and journalese sections of the work. And finally I hoped to concentrate less on opinion and second-hand recollection and more on the truly autobiographical, the more purely literary, and the more characteristically humorous material. For me Mark Twain is essentially a great fabulist and not a great maker of political utterances. The reason that I omitted his attacks on the politicians was that I found them dull and dated. Besides, anyone who cared to look them up could easily do so by referring to the earlier editions, as well as to various editions of his works. What is more, I listed for my readers the contents of the previous editions, so that ready comparisons could be made and my own omissions noted. . . .

Finally, Mr. Bereznitsky wrote: "It is plain that the bitter prophecy which Twain made in the midst of work on his *Autobiography* in a letter to William Dean Howells is coming true." And then he quoted from the letter. I should like to quote the letter again, for to do so is relevant to an illumination of Mr. Bereznitsky's critical methods. "Tomorrow I mean to dictate a chapter which will get my heirs and assigns burned alive if they venture to print it this side of A.D. 2006—which I judge they won't. There'll be lots of such chapters if I live 3 or 4 years longer. The edition of A.D. 2006 will make a stir when it comes out. I shall be hovering around taking notice, along with other dead pals. You are invited."

Now this letter referred to the first of five chapters which Twain dictated on the subject of religion. On the title pages of two of the chapters is a penned note in his hand: "Not to be exposed to any eye until the edition of A.D. 2406. S.L.C." The meaning is clear. Writing to Howells, Twain dared his heirs and assigns to print the chapters a century hence. But on his own manuscripts he specifically prohibited his heirs and assigns from publishing the chapters until *five* centuries hence. . . .

The following are some excerpts of Belknap's translation of Bereznitsky's second article.

THE QUESTION IS SIGNIFICANTLY MORE PROFOUND
A Letter to Charles Neider

. . . . The basis of your objections, as I recall, involved in your eyes an insufficiently respectful attitude on my part toward the work which was performed by you as editor of the third edition of *The Autobiography of Mark Twain*. No, you did great work—I would even say difficult work—as far as you are concerned. You quite successfully coped with this work as you wanted to. In your edition Twain actually appears as you are trying to present him. And you are trying to present him as a "great fabulist" (from your letter) or a master of "anecdote" (from your Introduction.) But is the real Twain like that? Let us try to remember what he himself said about this. This citation is doubtless well known to you. I am taking it from your edition of his *Autobiography:*

". . . . Within the compass of these forty years wherein I have been playing professional humorist before the public, I have had for company seventy-eight other American humorists. . . . Why have they perished? Because they were *merely humorists*. [Here and in the later quotations the italics are mine. Y.B.] Humorists of the "mere" sort cannot survive. . . . I have always preached. That is the reason that I have lasted thirty years. If the humor came of its own accord and uninvited I have allowed it a place in my sermon, but I was not writing the sermon for the sake of the humor."

The sermons about which Twain writes are just what constitute the social content of his work. The content is inseparable from the humor, just as the humor is inseparable from it. And you cut Twain's work in two and call the part which you don't like "dated, dull, and trivial." Yes, in your Introduction you listed just what you left out. "From the published parts I have omitted such matter as the . . . Morris incident . . . elongated remarks on Theodore Roosevelt, Andrew Carnegie, the Plutocracy, and so on." If it were only a matter of remarks (or "attacks" as you call them in your letter), it might really not be worth while building up a case. But in these "remarks" or "attacks" are expressed Twain's feelings, thoughts, interests; and this all helps re-establish the writer's countenance, a goal, which from your point of view, should also be sought by the autobiography of a great writer. . . .

The composers of numerous "digests" which offer *David Copperfield* and *Anna Karenina* in a form fit for "digestion" are sick with the same disease: they consider that only the bare bones of events are fit to interest the simple reader, and the "feelings and interests" which are "based" upon them are not in his power to digest. But it seems to me that the logical inconsistency of that part of your letter would strike even "a simple writer"; throwing light on my "critical methods," you refer to Twain's "demands" and "prohibitions." You claim credit for yourself and DeVoto for having "deliberately broken the great writer's injunctions," and right next to this, when it is a question of "the slowness with which the *Autobiography* has been made public," or of still unpublished chapters, you again refer to these same "demands" and "prohibitions." After all, if in some cases you break Twain's injunctions, it is hardly worth while to take refuge in it.

I would be sorry if you took all the above as only my comments, or even attacks, on your book, or your method of editorial work. No, the question is significantly more profound, and the dispute is going on actually not between you and me, but between two opposed tendencies in literary scholarship. . . .

This second article was notably different in tone from the first. Its tone could almost be described as reasonable. Far from being impersonal, the article was couched in the form of an open letter to me, and even contained remarks complimentary to me. On December 21, 1959 I airmailed my reply to it. Eight weeks later I received a letter from the foreign editor of the *Literary Gazette* which said, "It seems that you and Mr. Bereznitsky expressed your views about Mark Twain and his works in full. That is why we do not consider it necessary to continue this discussion any longer." The following are some excerpts of my second response.

> I am delighted to see in Mr. Bereznitsky's second criticism, of December 12th, a tacit admission that no official point of view regarding Mark Twain exists in America. I am also delighted to find that he recognizes the existence of a multitude of literary points of view in the United States. . . .
>
> Mr. Bereznitsky arrives at the conclusion, somewhat to my astonishment, that it is only "events" which interest me in Mark Twain's *Autobiography*. This is news to me, for events are perhaps what I am least interested in in the *Autobiography*. . . . What I am interested in primarily are psychology, humor, emotions, reflections, and reminiscences—all those matters which cannot easily be referred to as didactic—and I am interested in them because it happens that when he is dealing with them Mark Twain is at his best as a stylist and creator. . . .
>
> In our discussion it is well to remember that I regard an autobiography as capable of being a work of art, and that I come to it with certain aesthetic expectations, even requirements. . . . The aesthetic element for me is a primary one when it comes to literature. I am content to believe that it is the first function and value of the artist to perceive and to create works of beauty. That is what he specializes in, from my view. . . .
>
> Among the finest didactic chapters of the *Autobiography* are the five chapters on religion which my book unfortunately did not include, and which still await the first fine light of publication. It was painful for me to have to exclude them, but Mr. Bereznitsky will recall that in my Introduction I placed the responsibility for their exclusion where it rightly belongs, on Mark Twain's daughter. She has the legal right to keep them from being published, a right her father conferred on her in his will, and no person or agency in America can force her to publish them. . . .
>
> As for his comparison of my edition with digests of such books as *David Copperfield* and *Anna Karenina*, let me point out that this is hardly an accurate or fruitful comparison. These books are novels, not works of nonfiction. They were published during their authors' supervision. And they are both finished works. . . .

Criticisms such as those in the *Literary Gazette* were not isolated ones, nor were they new. The attacks on *The Autobiography of Mark Twain* followed an old Soviet line on Mark Twain, which consisted in general of this: that he was primarily significant as a social and political observer; that the objects of his criticisms were chiefly aspects of the American scene; and that the United States officially and unofficially suppressed or distorted his criticisms of his own country. This notion of America's being a monolithic structure, with control stemming from the top, struck most Americans as a curious one.

Even more curious, perhaps, was the way in which Soviet literary spokesmen viewed us as if we were a mirror image of themselves, and this despite their protestations we were so different from them. *They* lived under an official line and censorship; *they* were primarily social and political critics; and it followed that we closely resembled them. One wondered what the mass of Soviet readers thought. Could they digest the official line? And were they as humorless as their literary spokesmen often gave the impression of being? I like to believe they weren't, and that Mark Twain's great popularity among them was an indication not so much that the official line had been getting through as that Mark Twain had.

It could be argued that he was primarily a humorist. If he had never possessed his humorous gift, if he had written only his social criticism, he would probably not have been read by millions of Russians and it would have been useless for Soviet literary spokesmen to point to him as the arch critic of democratic morals. He was also primarily a writer of fiction. It was through those two great gifts that he made the reputation which is so well sustained almost ninety years after his death. His American readers on the whole had no difficulty in comprehending this simple fact, and I liked to think that most Russian readers had the same common sense, that they read him basically not for the lessons he taught of the inherent "evils" of the nation across what would later be called the Iron Curtain, but because he enlarged their lives imaginatively through a flow of pleasure. Great humor, after all, being so rare, is a very exportable commodity. When blended with wisdom and humanitarianism, it is irresistible.

If one were exposed only to the official Soviet line, one might have thought that Mark Twain spent most of his time in severely criticizing aspects of his own country. His voice, it may be mentioned in passing, although justly loud, was by no means the loudest or sternest when it came to social criticism. He wasn't a muckraker at a time when muckrakers flourished. Nor did he limit himself to matters of social or personal injustice, but took as his province the whole realm of cant, hypocrisy, corruption, and humbug. He was a freewheeler with the remembered spirit of the frontier, whose basis was a vigorous if rough-hewn egalitarianism. He took a fresh and saucy view of many things. If he didn't write much concerning his love of his country, it was not only because professed patriotism embarrassed him, it was also and chiefly because love of his country was implicit in everything he wrote. He was, after all, *the* American writer close to the native soil, and the American writer who in *The Innocents Abroad* forever put out of fashion the literary habit of fawning on Europe while finding little worth back home. In both these respects he resembled Dostoyevsky, just as his opposite number, Henry James, resembled Turgenev the Francophile.

From the way official Soviet critics sometimes spoke of him, one might have imagined that, if he were still alive, he would have been delighted to take up residence in Moscow. If he had been unpredictable enough to do such a thing, he would soon have complained about the quality of the borscht there. It was not the sort they served up in Missouri or Nevada or the California of his day, or even in Connecticut or New York. And he would have been forcefully instructed that criticizing Moscow borscht was strictly forbidden in the Soviet Union, a lesson that Boris Pasternak learned to his sorrow.

Mark Twain was useful to the Soviet spokesmen, and to most Americans as well, as a critic of certain aspects of American life. What the spokesmen failed to acknowledge was that his criticism of America was a department of a larger criticism, his criticism of mankind. In those days of the Cold War, Americans were better prepared to value self-criticism than the citizens of a nation that still remained an autocracy. Democracy for all its shortcomings prizes self-criticism as it cannot be prized in an autocracy. Democracy flourishes under self-criticism, whereas an autocracy dies by it.

On returning home from Bermuda on March 18, 1960, I found in my mail a curious item. It was an appendage to my affair with the *Literary Gazette* and assumed the form of a treasurer's check for $49 drawn on the Morgan Guaranty Trust Company of New York by order of the Bank for Foreign Trade of the USSR in Moscow. Under the amount of the check was an explanation. "B/O Redaktzia Literaturnoi Gazety—Author's Fee." I was pleasantly astonished by the check. Both the *Times* and the *Herald Tribune* published stories about it on March 20, for it was well known that literary dollars rarely left the Soviet Union.

As I noted earlier, my highly publicized controversy with Bereznitsky had an important consequence. It made it possible for me, from time to time, to make the point to Mrs. Samossoud that the suppression of the chapters on religion was giving the very aid and comfort to the Russians which she and her husband had feared their publication would give them. On the occasion of the appearance of the English edition of *The Autobiography of Mark Twain* in 1960, shortly before the 125th anniversary of Clemens's birth on November 30th of that year, I once again asked Mrs. Samossoud to change her mind. This time she consented. She went even further and lifted the ban on all her father's unpublished work. The first important literary result was the publication of *Letters from the Earth* (1962), which DeVoto had unsuccessfully tried to publish.

My controversy with Bereznitsky was published as a pamphlet, *Mark Twain and the Russians* (Hill & Wang, New York, 1960.) The "Reflections on Religion" appeared in *The Hudson Review* (October 1963) and in book form as part of *The Outrageous Mark Twain* (Doubleday, 1987).

CHARLES NEIDER
Princeton, New Jersey
September 1999

INTRODUCTION

With one exception, none of the items in this book, although many are of considerable importance, was included in the august and expensive version of Mark Twain's collected works subtitled the "Definitive Edition" and issued more than a decade after his death. Whether they were included in any of the earlier and less comprehensive editions I have not troubled myself to discover, but I have seen enough of those editions to doubt it. The exception was "The Indignity Put Upon the Remains . . . ," which A. B. Paine rescued from the files of *The Galaxy* magazine and which he reprinted as one of the many appendixes of his official biography of Clemens, issued almost half a century ago and later included in the Definitive Edition.

The Definitive Edition is eccentric in a few other respects. Volume XIX contains "Speech on the Babies" (pp. 397–401) and "Speech on the Weather" (pp. 402–6). Volume XXVIII contains the same speeches but with abbreviated titles: "The Weather" (pp. 53–57) and "The Babies" (pp. 58–62). These are only examples, not the complete record.

It is a curious fact of Mark Twain scholarship and publishing that fifty years after his death it is possible to put together a volume such as the present one, in which a large majority of the items make their first appearance in book form.

A glance at my sources will show the reader that I have revived many of the items which Mark Twain wrote for *The Galaxy*. *The Galaxy* was a literary monthly which flourished from 1866 to 1878 and which ended its career by merging with—or rather, being absorbed by—the *Atlantic Monthly*. The being absorbed by the *Atlantic* was not without its irony, inasmuch as the original intention of the founders of *The Galaxy* was to establish a New York rival to the prestigious Boston *Atlantic*. Boston in those days was dominant in the field of American letters, and published the leading quarterly, the *North American Review,* as well as the leading monthly, the *Atlantic.* The *Atlantic* habitually devoted a large part of its space to New England writers and matters and was regarded in certain quarters as having an exclusive attitude toward New York.

In its time *The Galaxy* published many of the interesting writers of the day, including Henry James, Walt Whitman, Trollope, Turgenev, and Bret Harte. Despite its several attempts it failed to persuade James Russell Lowell, that *Atlantic* lion, to contribute. The magazine was founded and edited by two New York brothers. It first appeared in 1866, and by the spring of 1870 was able to boast of having Mark Twain as a monthly contributor. Clemens conducted a humorous department which he called "Memoranda." It is worth noting that his department appeared near the end of each issue and was in double columns per page, whereas most of each issue was in single columns. It was not a good billing for one who was already enormously popular as a result of the publication of *The Innocents Abroad.* Mark Twain's first contribution appeared in May 1870 and his final one in April 1871. In the latter he wrote in explanation: "For the last eight months, with hardly an interval, I have had for my fellows and comrades, night and day, doctors and watchers of the sick! During these eight months death has taken two members of my home circle and malignantly threatened two others. All this I have experienced, yet all the time been under contract to furnish 'humorous' matter once a month for this magazine. . . ." It was only part of the story. He was being pressed for time, he wanted to devote himself to writing the more profitable books, and he was hoping to leave journalism as a regular occupation.

The Galaxy's editors continued the humorous department under the name of "Galaxy Club-Room." It became a miscellany of material supplied by several writers. In 1873 the magazine abandoned its attempt at a special department of humor.

A number of the pieces in the present volume appeared in a book of limited circulation issued in 1919, whose title was *The Curious Republic of Gondour and Other Whimsical Sketches.* I have reprinted them because in some instances the text of this book is at variance with that of the original published text, and because the pieces deserve to be better known.

"Open Letter to Commodore Vanderbilt" is a brilliant example of Mark Twain's early social criticism and personal invective. It appeared in *Packard's Monthly* in 1869 and has been reprinted only once, I believe, as a pamphlet of very limited circulation. Its facts may at times be vulnerable—as a reader wrote to *Packard's* in defense of the Commodore—but this probably did not disturb Clemens and need not bother us much now. I am happy to be able to print the piece in book form for the first time—in the English language. I must add "in the English language" because it is possible that it is already in volume form in the Soviet Union. When I spoke last November with a Professor Mendelson of Moscow, a Russian scholar interested in Mark Twain, he informed me that "Open Letter to Commodore Vanderbilt" would be included in the new Soviet twelve-volume edition of Mark Twain's works. One could see that the Russians had been busy looking up the uncollected pieces with the desire to add to the canon of Mark Twain's criticism of America.

I was informed that the Soviet edition would include "quite a few works" that have not appeared in American editions, among them "The Curious Republic of Gondour" and "King Leopold's Soliloquy." Professor Mendelson was in a position to give me accurate information, for he was a member of the editorial board in charge of publishing the twelve-volume edition, for which there are 300,000 subscribers. Eight volumes have already been published, he said. About one third of the final volume will be devoted to the *Autobiography* and will include chapters from my edition of this work. Although my edition was blasted in Moscow, with the charge that the hitherto unpublished chapters which it contained were of "poor quality," these same chapters were judged fit to print in the collected works, after having been published in *Krokodil*, a Russian magazine of large circulation, and in *Hammer and Sickle*, an Estonian magazine —without, of course, a kopeck of royalty either to me or to the Mark Twain Estate. The Russians refuse to sign a copyright treaty with us. I wonder if the twelve-volume edition will contain any of the fiery articles on copyright which Clemens got off in his lifetime. I doubt it.

Professor Mendelson and I were conversing over the long-distance telephone on the 125th anniversary of Mark Twain's birth, November 30, 1960. He informed me that a Mark Twain stamp had been issued in the Soviet to commemorate the day, and added that since the October Revolution of 1917, 272 books by Mark Twain have been published in the Soviet Union, in 26 languages, with a circulation of 12,309,000. The Russians are proud of their Mark Twain— the anti-American Mark Twain, as they seem to believe he was, and as any of his countrymen know better. I might add that the telephone call had been arranged by the Committee for Cultural Relations with Foreign Countries (of the Soviet), as a result of a cable I had sent to Premier Khrushchev. The purpose of the call was to discuss Mark Twain, in the interest of improved cultural relations between the Soviet Union and the United States. The bill, which I gladly footed, came to $118.80.

"Goldsmith's Friend Abroad Again" is a story which deserves to be much better known. I cannot understand why Mark Twain never included it in his volumes of stories and sketches. "The Noble Red Man" is a peppery bit of satire which has never been reprinted and which is easily as good as many of the essays or articles in the collected works. "The Coming Man" is—— But let the reader judge for himself whether these stories, sketches, and articles are worth preserving in this volume.

"King Leopold's Soliloquy" was written as a savage protest against the excesses of King Leopold II's rule in the Congo territory. It appeared (1905) at a time when much of the Western world had already been aroused to the consequences of Leopold's personal rule in the Congo, but Clemens' voice had a stature that sharply focused general attention on the evident injustices. The pamphlet elicited countercharges from Brussels that it contained inaccuracies, which was no doubt true, but truer was the long and unexampled exploitation of a primitive people for the enrichment of a modern sovereign who claimed to be a devoted Christian. Eventually Belgium took over the administration of the Congo and instituted various reforms. The current confusion, violence, and hatred of whites in the Congo has a background of Belgian colonization and rule, abetted by the great powers (including the United States), which it is not pleasant to contemplate.

The illustrated pamphlet sold for 25¢. It had a gray cover containing a motif of a crucifix and a butcher's knife crossed, with the motto, "By this sign we prosper." The proceeds of the sale of the pamphlet were donated by Clemens to the Congo Reform Association. An Englishman connected with the association, E. D. Morel, had, in 1904, brought to Clemens' attention the deteriorating situation in the Congo. Morel wrote a few years later: "I can see him now, pacing up and down his bedroom in uncontrollable indignation, breaking out ever and again with his favourite exclamation, 'By George!'; or with some rapid, searching question."

With the exception of the present volume's title piece, the items are arranged in chronological sequence, and in alphabetical order in any given year. The dates printed at the end of the items are the years of first publication, as far as I have been able to ascertain them.

I have included a sampling of newspaper interviews, with the full knowledge that Mark Twain was on the whole distrustful of interviews. They are obviously not to be regarded in the same light as his signed work. Nevertheless, many of them sound authentic, some were dictated or signed, and a number contain valuable information. All of them amuse, and they bring back those days in which Mark Twain played a conspicuous part. I believe this is the first collection of interviews to be published. I have not attempted to be inclusive or to go far afield. I have merely tried to show something of what the old files contain.

CHARLES NEIDER

New York

PART I

Essays, Sketches, and Tales

LIFE AS I FIND IT

The man lives in Philadelphia, who, when young and poor, entered a bank, and says he: "Please sir, don't you want a boy?" And the stately personage said: "No, little boy, I don't want a little boy."

The little boy, whose heart was too full for utterance, chewing a piece of licorice stick he had bought with a cent stolen from his good and pious aunt, with sobs plainly audible, and with great globules of water running down his cheeks, glided silently down the marble steps of the bank. Bending his noble form, the bank man dodged behind a door, for he thought the little boy was going to shy a stone at him. But the little boy picked up something, and stuck it in his poor but ragged jacket.

"Come here, little boy," and the little boy did come here; and the bank man said: "Lo, what pickest thou up?" And he answered and replied: "A pin." And the bank man said: "Little boy, are you good?" and he said he was. And the bank man said: "How do you vote?—excuse me, do you go to Sunday school?" and he said he did.

Then the bank man took down a pen made of pure gold, and flowing with pure ink, and he wrote, on a piece of paper: "St. Peter," and he asked the little boy what it stood for, and he said: "Salt Peter." Then the bank man said it meant "Saint Peter." Then the little boy said: "Oh!"

Then the bank man took the little boy into partnership, and gave him half the profits and all the capital, and he married the bank man's daughter, and now all he has is all his, and all his own, too.

My uncle told me this story, and I spent six weeks in picking up pins in front of a bank. I expected the bank man would call me in and say: "Little boy, are you good?" and I was going to say "Yes"; and when he asked me what "St. John" stood for, I was going to say "Salt John." But the bank man wasn't anxious to have a partner, and I guess the daughter was a son, for one day says he to me; "Little

boy, what's that you're picking up?" Says I, awful meekly, "Pins."
Says he: "Let's see 'em." And he took 'em, and I took off my cap all
ready to go in the bank and become a partner, and marry his daughter. But I didn't get an invitation. He said: "Those pins belong to the
bank, and if I catch you hanging around here any more I'll set the
dog on you!" Then I left, and the mean old cuss kept the pins. Such
is life as I find it.

1874

THE FACTS IN THE CASE OF THE SENATE
DOORKEEPER

Since this case has excited so much attention in diplomatic circles, and has provoked so much comment in the newspapers, both of this country and Europe, I will make a plain, simple statement of the facts in the matter, and leave the public to judge between myself and the Administration. When I resigned the office of Page of the House of Representatives, the best men of the nation were alarmed for the welfare of the Republic. That this alarm was well founded, I cannot undertake to say. It would be indelicate in me to do more than call passing attention to the fact, that while I was connected with the Government in the capacity already named, the affairs of the Government prospered, and no cloud darkened the political horizon. I had no sooner resigned my office than the negotiations with England for the settlement of the Alabama claims came to an abrupt and unsatisfactory termination. This may have been a result of my resignation; it may not have been. I shall express no opinion in the premises.

However, as before stated, the best men of the nation were alarmed. They visited me in my self-imposed exile and begged me to come to the rescue, and take again the helm of the ship of state. They urged that the foreign complications likely to grow out of the new order of things, rendered my re-entry into the Cabinet imperatively necessary; that to me the country turned for succor in this season of peril; that if I would live in the hearts of the people, I must not desert them at a time like this. Thus importuned, I consigned to oblivion my grievous wrongs, my bitterness of spirit, and rejoined Mr. Johnson's Administration as Doorkeeper of the Senate.

I surely thought that by this time persecution had tired of hunting its victim. Was I right? The facts will show. On the first morning of my occupation of my new post, I locked all the entrances to the Senate Chamber but one, and took my station there. Presently a gentleman approached, and tried to pass in. I stopped him, and said:

"Well, sir, what do *you* want?"

"I want to go in, of course."

"You want to go in. That is all right, no doubt, but we will consider on it a moment, if you have the time to spare. Who are you?"

"You are insolent, sir! I am the President of the Senate."

"President of the Senate. Ah—what might your name be?"

"I will just see, out of curiosity, how far you will venture to carry this thing. My name is Wade—Benjamin F. Wade."

"Wade—Wade. I don't remember hearing of you before. Is that your regular name, or is it a *nom de plume?*"

"It is my regular name, as you call it, of course."

"Where are you from, Mr. Wade?"

"From Ohio."

"About how old might you be, friend?"

"Fifty-two in January."

"Fifty-two. You look—you look rather older than that, Wade. I should say—well, I should say you look as much as a hundred and thirty, or a hundred and forty, or along there. But age isn't anything —it is blood that tells. Give me blood, above everything. That is my sentiment. But about this business of President of the Senate. Have you got your little credentials along with you?"

He had them. Considering that he was the ring-master of the circus, I let him in free. But I had trouble with the others. Some of them had no credentials, and had to stay out. I taxed the balance fifty cents admission, and as soon as they got a quorum they passed a resolution of instruction to the Sergeant-at-arms, and I was arrested and compelled to disgorge. This high-handed usurpation of power came near making another split between myself and the Government, but I submitted, and resolved to bide my time.

During the afternoon one of the Senators addressed the Chair, and said he wished to offer a resolution recognizing his Majesty King Theodorus as a belligerent.

I said: "Your Highness, I rise to a point of order. This old gentleman that has just taken his seat—"

"Silence! The Doorkeeper will resume his station by the door."

This from the man—and the only man—that I had passed in free! My heart was too full for utterance. From this time forward, for three days, I could never get the floor. I was snubbed every time I attempted to speak; whenever a *viva voce* vote was taken, my voice did not affect the result; when there was a division, I was not counted, either when I stood up or sat down; when there was a call of the house, my name was studiously omitted by the secretary and his minions. I frequently voted on both sides of the same question, purposely to catch the secretary, and I succeeded. During all this time the galleries were filled with people from all parts of the country, who were anxious to hear me speak. No matter—their feelings were not respected—the venomous persecution went on.

On the fourth day, at one o'clock, the ring-master announced the special order of the day—the Senate bill for the recognition of General Garibaldi as a Roman General, an Italian Deputy, and an American citizen. Here was my opportunity. I had been waiting, just waiting, to catch the house on a special order. I arose and said:

"Your Imperial Highness, I hold in my hand an Act entitled an Act supplementary to an Act entitled an Act amendatory of an Act to Confer Universal Suffrage upon Women. Woman! your Royal Highness—Oh, woman! in our hours of ease, uncertain, coy, and hard to please—"

"Silence!" It is not worth while to repeat more of the tirade uttered by the individual whom the fortuitous accident of a majority vote has elevated to the position of President of the Senate. I was subjugated. That is sufficient.

I waited one hour. A Senator from some obscure Indian reservation was tiring everybody to death with a stupid harangue about Garibaldi and several other incendiary Frenchmen, and it was plain that the crowd in the galleries was growing impatient. I arose and said:

"Your Royal Highness, woman! Oh, woman, in our hours of ease, uncertain—"

It was as far as I could get. A storm of malignant outcries assailed me, and for a time it seemed that I was going to be subjected to personal violence. The Sergeant-at-arms was ordered to put me in my seat and keep me there. In this humiliating position I remained for full two hours. I leave my countrymen to imagine what my feelings were. A spectacle was here presented to the nation such as has no parallel in history—the spectacle of a Senate degrading and trampling upon one of its own members. I could not long bear this. Every fibre of my being, every emotion of my nature, revolted at it. In the midst of some solemn, sentimental bosh by the Chair, concerning one of the new Senators from Walrussia, who had lost his way in the wilds of his native land, and had had nothing to eat for eighteen days but an iceberg, I emerged from the impressive silence, and thundered forth:

"Woman! Oh, woman! in—"

The door was in the way, and that is how it got broken down. The Senatorial mob did it. I fell in the hall, and in a single instant the aggregated wisdom of the nation was piled above me. Let us drop the curtain upon the disgraceful scene.

I approach the last chapter in the sad record of my official career. Its events transpired the next day. They culminated in a report of the Judiciary Committee—or rather two reports. Five members of it— a majority—brought in a wild document, which they styled "Articles of Impeachment Against the Doorkeeper of the United States Senate." The minority, of four members, reported against impeachment. The curious document first mentioned set forth that I had rendered my impeachment a just and righteous measure for the following specific reasons—viz:

In that I had transcended the powers vested in me by the Constitution of the United States by charging divers and sundry Senators fifty cents admission to their own department of the Capitol.

In that I had voted, during a regular session of the United States Senate, by word of mouth, and upon a division, and also upon the yeas and nays, in direct violation of a clause of the Constitution of the United States, which expressly forbids the Doorkeeper of the Senate to vote upon any question whatever which that body may have under consideration.

In that I had frequently risen to points of order, questions of privilege, etc., and had at divers and sundry times interrupted the Senate with attempts to deliver a speech upon a subject which was not before the house at the time, and always commencing with the same tiresome formula of "Woman! Oh, woman," etc.—all of which was in direct violation of that clause in the Constitution of the United States which expressly decrees that the Doorkeeper of the Senate shall at no time take part in the deliberations of that body.

In that I had attempted to introduce Female Suffrage at a time when the Hero of Italy was the special order of the day—which was in direct violation of that article of the Constitution of the United States which expressly stipulates that special orders of the day shall at all times take precedence of other matters.

In that, after disrupting and disorganizing the Senate time and again by repetitions of the beforementioned speech, commencing "Woman! Oh, woman!" I incited the said Senate to rebellion and insurrection by still another attempt to inflict that speech upon them, and thus materially retarded the reconstruction of the aforesaid Senate at the period of its most promising progress—all of which, when taken in connection with the aforementioned charge of fifty cents admission to the Senate, is in flagrant violation of that article of the Constitution of the United States which decrees that for the Doorkeeper of the Senate to levy war or collect taxes on his individual responsibility is high treason and punishable with death.

The infamy of the Senate is complete. Their work is done, and I stand before my country to-day a Doorkeeper on Sufferance! But firm as a rock I stand at my post and await the verdict.

MARK TWAIN, Doorkeeper *ad interim*
1867

FEMALE SUFFRAGE

Editors Missouri Democrat:

I have read the long list of lady petitioners in favor of female suffrage, and as a husband and a father I want to protest against the whole business. It will never do to allow women to vote. It will never do to allow them to hold office. You know, and I know, that if they were granted these privileges there would be no more peace on earth. They would swamp the country with debt. They like to hold office too well. They like to be Mrs. President Smith of the Dorcas society, or Mrs. Secretary Jones of the Hindoo aid association, or Mrs. Treasurer of something or other. They are fond of the distinction of the thing, you know; they revel in the sweet jingle of the title. They are always setting up sanctified confederations of all kinds, and then running for president of them. They are even so fond of office that they are willing to serve without pay. But you allow them to vote and to go to the Legislature once, and then see how it will be. They will go to work and start a thousand more societies, and cram them full of salaried offices. You will see a state of things then that will stir your feelings to the bottom of your pockets. The first fee bill would exasperate you some. Instead of the usual schedule for judges, State printer, Supreme court clerks, &c., the list would read something like this:

OFFICES AND SALARIES.

President Dorcas society	$4,000
Subordinate officers of same, each	2,000
President Ladies' Union prayer meeting	3,000
President Pawnee Educational society	4,000
President of Ladies' society for Dissemination of Belles Lettres among the Shoshones	5,000
State Crinoline Directress	10,000
State Superintendent of waterfalls	10,000

State Hair Oil inspectress............................ 10,000
State milliner 50,000

You know what a state of anarchy and social chaos that fee bill would create. Every woman in the commonwealth of Missouri would let go everything and run for State Milliner. And instead of ventilating each other's political antecedents, as men do, they would go straight after each other's private moral character. (I know them—they are all like my wife.) Before the canvass was three days old it would be an established proposition that every woman in the State was "no better than she ought to be." Only think how it would lacerate me to have an opposition candidate say that about my wife. That is the idea, you know—having other people say these hard things. Now, I know that my wife isn't any better than she ought to be, poor devil—in fact, in matters of orthodox doctrine, she is particularly shaky—but still I would not like these things aired in a political contest. I don't really suppose that that woman will stand any more show hereafter than—however, she may improve—she may even become a beacon light for the saving of others—but if she does, she will burn rather dim, and she will flicker a good deal, too. But, as I was saying, a female political canvass would be an outrageous thing.

Think of the torch-light processions that would distress our eyes. Think of the curious legends on the transparencies:

"Robbins forever! Vote for Sallie Robbins, the only virtuous candidate in the field!"

And this:

"Chastity, modesty, patriotism! Let the great people stand by Maria Sanders, the champion of morality and progress, and the only candidate with a stainless reputation!"

And this: "Vote for Judy McGinniss, the incorruptible! Nine children—one at the breast!"

In that day a man shall say to his servant, "What is the matter with the baby?" And the servant shall reply, "It has been sick for hours." "And where is its mother?" "She is out electioneering for Sallie Robbins." And such conversations as these shall transpire between ladies and servants applying for situations: "Can you cook?" "Yes." "Wash?" "Yes." "Do general housework?" "Yes." "All right; who is your choice for State milliner?" "Judy McGinniss." "Well, you can tramp." And women shall talk politics instead of discussing the fashions; and they shall neglect the duties of the household to go out and take a drink with candidates; and men shall nurse the baby while their wives travel to the polls to vote. And also in that day the man who hath beautiful whiskers shall beat the homely man of wisdom for Governor, and the youth who waltzes with exquisite grace shall be Chief of Police, in preference to the man of practiced sagacity and determined energy.

Every man, I take it, has a selfish end in view when he pours out eloquence in behalf of the public good in the newspapers, and such is the case with me. I do not want the privileges of women extended, because my wife already holds office in nineteen different infernal female associations and I have to do all her clerking. If you give the women full sweep with the men in political affairs, she will proceed to run for every confounded office under the new dispensation. That will finish me. It is bound to finish me. She would not have time to do anything at all then, and the one solitary thing I have shirked up to the present time would fall on me and my family would go to destruction; for I am *not* qualified for a wet nurse.

MARK TWAIN

A VOLLEY FROM THE DOWN-TRODDEN

A DEFENSE

Editors Missouri Democrat:

I should think you would be ashamed of yourselves. I would, anyway—to publish the vile, witless drivelings of that poor creature who degrades me with his name. I say you ought to be ashamed of yourselves. Two hundred noble, Spartan women cast themselves into the breach to free their sex from bondage, and instead of standing with bowed heads before the majesty of such a spectacle, you permit this flippant ass, my husband, to print a weak satire upon it. The wretch! I combed him with a piano stool for it. And I mean to comb every newspaper villain I can lay my hands on. They are nothing but villains anyhow. They published our names when nobody asked them to, and therefore they are low, mean and depraved, and fit for any crime however black and infamous.

Mr. Editor, I have not been appointed the champion of my sex in this matter; still, if I could know that any argument of mine in favor of female suffrage which has been presented in the above communication will win over any enemy to our cause, it would soften and soothe my dying hour; ah, yes, it would soothe it as never another soother could soothe it.

MRS. MARK TWAIN
President Afghanistan Aid Association, Secretary of the Society for introducing the Gospel into New Jersey, etc., etc., etc.

[The old woman states a case well, don't she? She states a case mighty well, for a woman of her years? She even soars into moving eloquence in that place where she says: "two hundred noble Spartan women cast themselves into the breeches," etc. And those "arguments" of hers afford her a prodigious satisfaction, don't they? She may possibly die easy on account of them, but she won't if I am around to stir her up in her last moments. That woman has made my life a burthen to me, and I mean to have a hand in soothing her myself when her time is up.—MARK TWAIN]

MORE DEFENSE

Editors Missouri Democrat:
I have read the article in your paper on female suffrage, by the atrocious scoundrel Mark Twain. But do not imagine that such a thing as that will deter us from demanding and enforcing our rights. Sir, we will have our rights, though the heavens fall. And as for this wretch, he had better find something else to do than meddling with matters he is incapable of understanding. I suppose he votes—such is law!—such is justice!—he is allowed to vote, but women a thousand times his superiors in intelligence are ruled out!—he!—a creature who don't know enough to follow the wires and find the telegraph office. Comment is unnecessary. If I get my hands on that whelp I will snatch hair out of his head till he is as bald as a phrenological bust.

Mr. Editor, I may not have done as much good for my species as I ought, in my time, but if any of the arguments I have presented in this article in favor of female suffrage shall aid in extending the privileges of woman, I shall die happy and content.

MRS. ZEB. LEAVENWORTH
Originator and President of the Association for the Establishment of a Female College in Kamschatka.

[I perceive that I have drawn the fire of another heavy gun. I feel as anxious as any man could to answer this old Kamschatkan, but I do not know where to take hold. Her "arguments" are too subtle for me. If she can die happy and content on that mild sort of gruel, though, let her slide.—MARK TWAIN]

MORE YET

Editors Missouri Democrat:
The depths of my heart of hearts are stirred. Gentle chiding from those that love me has ever fallen upon my wounded spirit like soothing moonlight upon a troubled sea, but harsh words from wretches is more than I can bear. I am not formed like others of my sex. All with me is ideal—is romance. I live in a world of my own that is peopled with the fairy creatures of fancy. When that is rudely invaded, my ethereal soul recoils in horror. For long years I have collected buttons, and door-plates and dictionaries, and all such things as I thought would make the poor savages of the South seas contented with their lot and lift them out of their ignorance and degradation—and no longer than a month ago I sent them Horace Greeley's speeches and some other cheerful literature, and the pure delight I felt was only marred by the reflection that the poor creatures could not read them—and yet I may not vote! Our petition for our rights is humanly attacked by one who has no heart, no soul, no gentle emotions, no poesy! In tuneful numbers I will bid this cold world adieu, and perchance when I am gone, Legislatures will drop a tear over one whose budding life they blighted, and be torn with vain regrets when it is all too late:

> In sorrow I sorrow, O sorrowful day!
> In grief-stricken tears O joy speed away!
> I weep and I wail, and I waft broken sighs,
> And I cry in my anguish, O Woman arise!

> But I shout it in vain! for Demons have come,
> Who drown my appeal with foul blasphemous tongue;
> Yes, in sorrow I fade, and flicker and die!
> Lo! a martyr to Suffrage in the tomb let me lie!

If I dared to hope that any argument I have here presented may be the means of securing justice to my down-trodden sex, I could lay me down and pass away as peacefully as the sighing of a breeze in summer forests.

Miss Augusta Josephine Maitland,
Secretary of the Society for the Dissemination
of Poetry among the Pawnees.

[Now, this old maid is a little spooney, of course, but she does not abuse me as much as the others, and it really touches me to know that she is going to fade, and flicker out. Her "arguments" are a little vague, but that is of no consequence. I haven't anything in the world against her, except that inspired atrocity of inflicting Horace Greeley's speeches on the poor heathen of the South Seas. What harm have they ever done her, that she should want to * * * * ?

You must excuse me. I see a procession of ladies filing in at my street door with tar-buckets and feather-beds, and other arrangements. I do not wish to crowd them. I will go out the back way. But I will singe that pestilent old wild-cat, my wife, for leading them. —Mark Twain]

"MARK TWAIN" GETS AN OVERHAULING FROM "COUSIN JENNIE"

"A. L." PITCHES IN, TOO

Dear Mark:

I have just read the article in the Democrat wherein your views on "Female Suffrage" are so *characteristically* set forth. I am sorry you did not apprise me of your intentions previous to placing yourself before the public in such a light, for, as your cousin, I would, and as a woman I could have told you just how such an article would be received, and thus your good name might have been allowed to preserve untarnished its *sparkling* lustre. As you did not take me into your confidence, I have no right to respect your feelings by scolding you through the postoffice—you shall hear me through your own chosen medium.

And, in the first place, I venture the assertion that you yourself do not believe a word you say. Doubtless you are anxious it should be received as veritable truth. There are many who, when truth and justice give them the challenge, in their heart of hearts are with woman in her endeavors to do all and to be all, that she can do and be, still preserving her womanly dignity and integrity; yet through a selfish, unmanly fear—a fear that certain honors, and pleasant emoluments would be worthily worn and enjoyed by her, are loud and bitter in their denunciations against such endeavors.

As for voting, they are confident that for every stupid, thick brained man who is *sent* to the polls, a dozen clear thinking, unbiased women might *go*. As for offices, they know there is many a one that could as well, *fully as well*, be filled by even a weak woman as by a strong man. And as for the "jingle," Mark, they dare not say it is less sweet to their ears than to ours. Many a page of history will have to be obliterated, and many a memory clouded, before that will be received for truth. Then be honest, cousin Mark—confess that all light is not concealed in man's brain—admit that there is a ray or two in woman's, and after a while you will be prepared to see that mother nature has been as kind to her as to you, to say the least.

Of course, man's natural vanity and I-am-ism will suffer some in the contest. He has been taught that, although the other part of humanity is very beautiful and very lovely, it is every way unquestionably *weak*; and it is his enviable prerogative to fashion the laws and rules which shall regulate the life of that weak part. No wonder then his fancied superiority, and no wonder now, when the light that has been struggling for years to be admitted is seen and believed in, that many of the *strong* party are somewhat crestfallen. We are strong enough to see *that*, cousin Mark, and we see, too, a very good thing that may spring out of your disappointment—for we take it you *are* disappointed—since you see we are just as smart as you, you will bestir yourselves lest we outstrip you; for the opportunity given us, we will soar as high as we can. In this way, many a talent which is now folded away in a napkin, will be brought to light and polished. There is the "sweet" in the "bitter" for you, Mark Twain.

COUSIN JENNIE,
(*not one of the "signers"*)

THE DUTY OF MAN

Editors Missouri Democrat:
I am exceedingly curious to know why no one ever sees fit to write anything about the duty of man, when every issue of the press contains some lengthy article on woman's duty. Is it because man is so superior to the other sex, and created so perfect that his duties are

always promptly and perfectly performed, leaving no room for advice or comment? or, is it because he is so inferior and insignificant that neither Creator nor creature ever saw fit to assign any duties for his performance? The press would have us believe the latter case, for how frequently it gives us illustrations of his weakness, in publishing the alarming numbers of drunkard's and suicide's graves, caused by some dereliction of woman's duty—say, for instance, a "missing button"; and then again it speaks of the drinking saloons, gambling halls, and worse places, being filled by men driven from their homes through woman's neglect. To give another instance, say an overdone joint, or a cup of weak coffee; and how many of the lords of creation are annually driven to insanity by the cruel treatment of their wives in having failed (perhaps but once) to meet their husbands with a smile; but no one seems to write anything about the cause of that smile's absence. Perhaps that very missing button might have had something to do with it. Might she not have been for many weary hours busy with her needle, not only for her husband but for their six or dozen children, and satisfied at last that she has all their garments in apple pie order; but when her "lord" comes to don a clean shirt preparatory to his club meeting, and draws from the very bottom of two dozen or more in *perfect* order one minus a button, with what heartache must that wife listen to cruel taunts and harsh fault-finding—harsher than even the most flagrant fault would justify. I don't wonder that "Mark Twain" and the male sex in general *should tremble in their shoes* at the *very idea* of having female influence extended, for if they wield such a mighty and almost miraculous influence *now* within the small sphere granted to them by the lords of creation, limited to the supervision of pots, kettles, buttons and babies, permitted to occupy the position of housekeeper and "wet nurse" for their victuals and clothes, what imagination could depict the unbounded influence she would exert if allowed to "*swing 'round the whole circle.*" We are truly grateful to man for condescending to admit that woman possesses such mighty power, but we don't altogether thank him for the impression he would convey that that same power is exerted *entirely for evil.* At the same time we pity him sincerely from the very bottom of our hearts for being so contemptibly weak as to allow his evil nature to yield to temptation; and what a miserable existence would be his but for his many comforts—*cards, liquor, tobacco, etc.* Alas for man's *strength of mind* and superiority. "*I don't see it.*"

A.L.

THE INIQUITOUS CRUSADE AGAINST MAN'S
REGAL BIRTHRIGHT MUST BE CRUSHED

ANOTHER LETTER FROM MARK TWAIN

Dear Cousin Jennie:

I did not know I had a cousin named Jennie, but I am proud to claim such a relationship with you. I have no idea who you are, but you talk well—you talk exceedingly well. You seem inclined to treat the question of female suffrage seriously, and for once I will drop foolishness, and speak with the gravity the occasion demands. You fully understand the difference between justice and expediency? I am satisfied you do. You know very well that it would have been a just and righteous act if we had rescued struggling Poland four or five years ago, but you know also that it would not have been good policy to do it. No one will say that it is not just and right that women should vote; no one will say that an educated American woman would not vote with fifty times the judgment and independence exercised by stupid, illiterate newcomers from foreign lands; I will even go so far myself as to say that in my experience only third-rate intelligence is sent to Legislatures to make laws, because the first-rate article will not leave important private interests go unwatched to go and serve the public for a beggarly four or five dollars a day, and a miserably trivial distinction, while it is possible that a talented matron, unincumbered with children, might go with no great detriment to the affairs of her household. We know also that between constable and United States Senator, the one thousand offices of mere honor (though burdened with high responsibilities) are held by third-rate ability because first-rate ability can only afford to hold offices of great emolument—and we know that first-rate female talent *could* afford to hold those offices of mere honor without making business sacrifices. You see I have made a very strong argument for your side; and I repeat that no one will deny the truth of any of the above propositions; but behold that matter of expediency comes in here—policy!

Now, you think I am going to string out a long argument on my own side, but I am not. I only say this: The ignorant foreign women would vote with the ignorant foreign men—the bad women would vote with the bad men—the good women would vote with the good men. The same candidate who would be elected now would be elected then, the only difference being that there might be twice as many votes polled then as now. Then in what respect is the condition of things improved? I cannot see.

So, I conceive that if nothing is to be gained by it, it is inexpedient to extend the suffrage to women. That must be a benefit beyond the power of figures to estimate, which can make us consent to take the High Priestess we reverence at the sacred fireside and send her forth to electioneer for votes among a mangy mob who are unworthy to touch the hem of her garment. A lady of my acquaintance came very near putting my feeling in this matter into words the other day, Jennie, when she said she was opposed to female suffrage, because she was not willing to see her sex reduced to a level with negroes and men!

Female suffrage would do harm, my dear—it would actually do harm. A very large proportion of our best and wisest women would still cling to the holy ground of the home circle, and refuse to either vote or hold office—but every grand rascal among your sex would work, bribe and vote with all her might; and, behold, mediocrity and dishonesty would be appointed to conduct the affairs of government more surely than ever before. You see the policy of the thing is bad, very bad. It would augment the strength of the bad vote. I consider it a very strong point on our side of the question.

I think I could write a pretty strong argument in favor of female suffrage, but I do not want to do it. I never want to see women voting, and gabbling about politics, and electioneering. There is something revolting in the thought. It would shock me inexpressibly for an angel to come down from above and ask me to take a drink with him (though I should doubtless consent); but it would shock me still more to see one of our blessed earthly angels peddling election tickets among a mob of shabby scoundrels she never saw before.

There is one insuperable obstacle in the way of female suffrage, Jennie; I approach the subject with fear and trembling, but it must out: A woman would never vote, because she would have to tell her age at the polls. And even if she did dare to vote once or twice when she was just of age, you know what dire results would flow from "putting this and that together" in after times. For instance, in an unguarded moment, Miss A. says she voted for Mr. Smith. Her auditor, who knows it has been seven years since Smith ran for anything, easily ciphers out that she is at least seven years over age, instead of the tender young pullet she has been making herself out to be. No, Jennie, this new fashion of registering the name, age, residence and occupation of every voter, is a fatal bar to female suffrage.

Women will never be permitted to vote or hold office, Jennie, and it is a lucky thing for me, and for many other men, that such is the decree of fate. Because, you see, there are some few measures they would all unite on—there are one or two measures that would bring out their entire voting strength, in spite of their antipathy to making themselves conspicuous; and there being vastly more women than men in this State, they would trot those measures through the Legislature with a velocity that would be appalling. For instance, they would enact:

1. That all men should be at home by ten P.M., without fail.

2. That married men should bestow considerable attention on their own wives.

3. That it should be a hanging offense to sell whisky in saloons, and that fine and disfranchisement should follow the drinking of it in such places.

4. That the smoking of cigars to excess should be forbidden, and the smoking of pipes utterly abolished.

5. That the wife should have a little of her own property when she married a man who hadn't any.

Jennie, such tyranny as this, we could never stand. Our free souls could never endure such degrading thraldom. Women, go your ways! Seek not to beguile us of our imperial privileges. Content yourself with your little feminine trifles—your babies, your benevolent societies and your knitting—and let your natural bosses do the voting. Stand back—you will be wanting to go to war next. We will let you teach school as much as you want to, and we will pay you half wages for it, too, but beware! we don't want you to crowd us too much.

If I get time, Cousin Jennie, I will furnish you a picture of a female legislature that will distress you—I know it will, because you cannot disguise from me the fact that you are no more in favor of female suffrage, really, than I am.

In conclusion, honesty compels me to tell you that I have been highly complimented a dozen times on *my* articles signed "Cousin Jennie" and "A.L." The same honesty, though, compelled me to confess that I did not write either of those articles.

MARK TWAIN

P.S. That tiresome old goose, my wife, is prancing around like a lunatic, up stairs, rehearsing a speech in favor of female suffrage which she is going to deliver before a mass meeting of seditious old maids in my back parlor to-night. (She is a vigorous speaker, but you can smell her eloquence further than you can hear it; it is on account of gin, I think.) It is a pity those old skeletons have chosen my back parlor, because I have concluded to touch off a keg of powder under there to-night, and I am afraid the noise may disturb their deliberations some.

M.T.

ANOTHER FROM A.L.

Editors Missouri Democrat:

I think Cousin Jennie has handled the late popular subject pretty cleverly; but I think she has perpetrated somewhat of an "Irish bull," in calling upon "Mark Twain" to "confess that all light was not concealed in man's brain"; or, perhaps she was only cunningly contriving to have Mark commit himself and his sex irretrievably by strenuously maintaining that such was really the case. For so far as the light of man's brain *exists*—"that's just what's the matter"—it is always so *completely concealed,* that it never by any chance emits a single ray. Man runs away with the *fact* that by actual measurement the weight of his brain exceeds that of woman's, and he immediately builds up his everlasting reputation for intellect on that flimsy foundation, forgetting that quantity cannot make up for quality: when his very love for the "jingle" should have taught him that an ounce of gold is worth more than a pound of lead.

A.L.

1867

PRIVATE HABITS OF HORACE GREELEY

An intimate acquaintance with a distant relative of the editor of the *Tribune** puts it in my power to furnish the public with the last—positively the very last—link necessary to perfect the chain of knowledge already in its possession concerning Mr. Greeley: I mean his private habits. We know *all* about him as regards every other department of his life and service. Because, whenever a magazinist or a bookmaker is employed to write, and cannot think of a subject, he writes about Horace Greeley. Even the boys in the schools have quit building inspired "compositions" on "The Horse," and have gone to doing Horace Greeley instead; and when declamation-day comes around, their voices are no longer "still for war" and Patrick Henry, but for peace and Horace Greeley. Now, the natural result of all this is that the public have come at last to think that this man has no life but public life, no nature but a public nature, no habits but public habits. This is all wrong. Mr. Greeley *has* a private life. Mr. Greeley *has* private habits.

Mr. Greeley gets up at three o'clock in the morning; for it is one of his favorite maxims that only early rising can keep the health unimpaired and the brain vigorous. He then wakes up all the household and assembles them in the library, by candle-light: and, after quoting the beautiful lines,

> "Early to bed and early to rise
> Make a man healthy, wealthy, and wise,"

he appoints each individual's task for the day, sets him at it with encouraging words, and goes back to bed again. I mention here, in no fault-finding spirit, but with the deference justly due a man who is

* That is, Horace Greeley, editor of the New York *Tribune*. Mark Twain knew Greeley. In *Roughing It*, issued four years later, he had fun with Greeley's horrific handwriting. The present article originally appeared in *The Spirit of the Times*, a weekly which was a sister publication of the *Police Gazette* and which was characterized as "a chronicle of the turf, field sports and the stage."

older and wiser and worthier than I, that he snores awfully. In a moment of irritation, once, I was rash enough to say I never would sleep with him until he broke himself of the unfortunate habit. I have kept my word with bigoted and unwavering determination.

At half-past eleven o'clock Mr. Greeley rises again. He shaves himself. He considers that there is great virtue and economy in shaving himself. He does it with a dull razor, sometimes humming a part of a tune (he knows part of a tune and takes an innocent delight in regarding it as the first half of Old Hundred; but parties familiar with that hymn have felt obliged to confess that they could not recognize it, and, therefore, the noise he makes is doubtless an unconscious original composition of Mr. Greeley's) and sometimes, when the razor is especially dull, he accompanies himself with a formula like this: "Damn the damned razor, and the damned outcast who made it."—H.G.

He then goes out into his model garden, and applies his vast store of agricultural knowledge to the amelioration of his cabbage: after which he writes an able agricultural article for the instruction of American farmers, his soul cheered the while with the reflection that if cabbages were worth eleven dollars apiece his model farm would pay.

He next goes to breakfast, which is a frugal, abstemious meal with him, and consists of nothing but just such things as the market affords, nothing more. He drinks nothing but water—nothing whatever but water and coffee, and tea, and Scotch ale, and lager beer and lemonade with a fly in it—sometimes a house fly, and sometimes a horse fly, according to the amount of inspiration required to warm him up to his daily duties. During breakfast he reads the *Tribune* all through, and enjoys the satisfaction of knowing that all the brilliant things in it, written by Young and Cooke and Hazard, and myself, are attributed to *him* by a confiding and infernal public.

After breakfast he writes a short editorial, and puts a large dash at the beginning of it, thus (——), which is the same as if he put H.G. after it, and takes a savage pleasure in reflecting that none of us understrappers can use that dash, except in profane conversation when chaffing over the outrage. He writes this editorial in his own handwriting. He does it because he is so vain of his penmanship. He always did take an inordinate pride in his penmanship. He hired out once, in his young days, as a writing master, but the enterprise failed. The pupils could not translate his marks with any certainty. His first copy was "Virtue is its own reward," and they got it "Washing with soap is wholly absurd," and so the trustees discharged him for attempting to convey bad morals, through the medium of worse penmanship. But, as I was saying, he writes his morning editorial. Then he tries to read it over, and can't do it, and so sends it to the printers, and *they* try to read it, and can't do it; and so they set it up at random, as you may say, putting in what words they can make out, and when they get aground on a long word they put in "reconstruction" or "universal suffrage," and spar off the paddle ahead, and next morning, if the degraded public can tell what it is all about, they say H.G. wrote it, and if they can't, they say it is one of those imbecile understrappers, and that is the end of it.

On Sundays Mr. Greeley sits in a prominent pew in Mr. Chaplin's church and lets on that he is asleep, and the congregation regard it as an eccentricity of genius.

When he is going to appear in public, Mr. Greeley spends two hours on his toilet. He is the most painstaking and elaborate man about getting up his dress that lives in America. This is his chiefest and his pleasantest foible. He puts on a soiled shirt, saved from the wash, and leaves one end of the collar unbuttoned. He puts on his most dilapidated hat, turns it wrong side before, cants it onto the back of his head, and jams an extra dent in the side of it. He puts on his most atrocious boots, and spends fifteen minutes tucking the left leg of his pants into his boottop in what shall seem the most careless and unstudied way. But his cravat—it is into the arrangement of his cravat that he throws all his soul, all the powers of his great mind. After fixing at it for forty minutes before the glass it is perfect—it is askew in every way—it overflows his coat-collar on one side and sinks into oblivion on the other—it climbs and it delves around about his neck —the knot is conspicuously displayed under his left ear, and it stretches one of its long ends straight out horizontally, and the other goes after his eye, in the good old Toodles fashion—and then, completely and marvelously appareled, Mr. Greeley strides forth, rolling like a sailor, a miracle of astounding costumery, the awe and wonder of the nations!

But I haven't time to tell the rest of his private habits. Suffice it that he is an upright and an honest man—a practical, great-brained man—a useful man to his nation and his generation—a famous man who has justly earned his celebrity—and withal the worst-dressed man in this or any other country, even though he *does* take so thundering much pains and put on so many frills about it.

1868

YE CUBAN PATRIOT:
A CALM INSPECTION OF HIM

Just at this time our souls are wrenched with sympathy for the Cuban
"patriot," and with hatred for his inhuman oppressor. Our journals
are filled with the struggles, the sufferings and the noble deeds of this
patriot, and nothing on earth can get our attention for a moment unless it has something to do with him. The tears that are shed over his
misfortunes every day would float a navy; the daily ink that is lavished upon the limning of his virtues would float another one, and
a month of the prayers that are offered for his lifting up, if concentrated upon the world's dead, might precipitate the final resurrection.
We are bound up, heart and soul, in our Cuban "patriot." We live
but for him, we should die if he were taken from us. Daily we cry,
"Holy, holy, holy, and perfect and beautiful, is Heaven's beloved, the
sublime Cuban 'patriot!'"

And how grand a character he is! How gallant, how lofty, how
magnanimous! His career, from the moment his heart is first stirred
with patriotic emotions, till that heart ceases to beat, is a chivalrous
romance. He begins by shouting "Down with the Spaniard!" in the
streets of Havana. Then he and a hundred of his fellows are captured
by a handful of soldiers and thrown into prison. Here they take the
oath to the government, hire out to it as spies upon other patriots,
and finish by denouncing a hundred of their personal friends to the
government at so much a head. Those parties are duly shot, garroted,
hanged in the public plaza, or otherwise made away with according
to the peculiar taste of the commandant in the matter of executions.

Next, the patriot escapes to the country and resumes patriotism
once more. A few hundreds of them band together, and then we hear
of gallant deeds! They pounce upon deserted plantations and burn up
the sugar crop and the negro quarter—and forthwith our journals
shriek the tidings of "Another Grand Patriot Victory!"

Then the government troops capture half the knightly gang and shut them up in a barn and burn them alive. And instantly our great journals, and our Congressmen, and ourselves, rage about the brutal inhumanity of Spain—and with all our hearts we hate those Spaniards for burning up those pure patriots, and we know we are sincere, too, notwithstanding we cannot somehow help feeling rather glad they did it.

Pretty soon the great journals tell us, in thundering display lines, how the patriot warrior Don Aguilar Jesus Maria Jose y John the Baptist Bustamente made a brilliant dash upon the plantation of Señor Madre de Dios el Calderon Gewhillikins de Valladolid and burned up the whole concern, considering it best on the whole to do this, inasmuch as Señor Valladolid's political opinions were exactly of the universal Cuban pattern and could never by any possibility be depended upon to remain in one shape two hours at a time unless the holder of the same were asleep or dead. And further, the papers tell us how the patriot Bustamente and his six hundred followers next marched Valladolid and his family down the road some thirteen miles, on foot, and with ropes around their necks for convenience in steering them, and then, while the helpless parents and children knelt and pleaded piteously for life, boldly carved them to pieces with bowie knives. And all America shouts, "Hurrah for Gallant Cuba!— down with her hated oppressor!" And fiercely we besiege Congress to "recognize" the struggling patriots and reward their singlehearted virtues with our appreciative protection.

Right away we hear that the Spanish troops and Bustamente's army have met and fought a tremendous battle. We gloat over the particulars. We thrill from head to heel as we read how that the battle raged furiously from eight in the morning till six in the evening, resulting in the complete destruction of eleven barns, two plantations, three sawmills, one hospital and its patients, and the total rout of the enemy, with a loss of sixteen wounded, and also one killed by being run over by a wagon. But we grieve sore to hear that the patriot Bustamente was taken prisoner by the brutal Spanish horde, and our hearts sink, and suffer and break when we hear that his captors lassoed him and dragged him three miles to the military prison at the heels of a galloping horse, and then decided it was just as cheap to confine what was left of him in a coffin. And how we do abuse the uncivilized sort of war those Spaniards wage!

But soon we rejoice once more, when we hear that the unconquerable patriots, from a safe hiding-place in the hills, have sent out emissaries and fomented a conspiracy among the slaves which has resulted in a gentle midnight massacre, by the blacks, of a couple of dozen slumbering families of white people, accompanying the deed with the usual Cuban impartiality as to whether the families were "patriots" or friends of the government.

And while we are still rejoicing over this victory, we learn how the patriot instigators of it, being close pressed, laid down their arms, took the oath to serve Spain, and then for a consideration informed on and helped to capture all those slaves and furnish each of them with twelve hundred trifling lashes on the bare back with ox-whips, in the course of which entertainment some of the slaves died—and the rest followed suit the next day. But ah, they died in a glorious cause. They died to free their country from the oppressor. It is sweet to die for one's native land. Those poor humble blacks will live in history, for nearly a year.

In his self-sacrificing struggles for his country's freedom, the Cuban patriot makes valorous use of every method and every contrivance that can aid the good cause. Murder, theft, burglary, arson, assassination, rape, poison, treachery, mendacity, fratricide, homicide, parricide, and all sides but suicide, are instruments in his hands for the salvation of his native land—and the same are instruments in the hands of his "oppressors" for the damnation *of the same*. Both parties, patriots and government servants alike, stand ready at any moment, apparently, to sell out body, soul and boots, politics, religion and principles, to anybody that will buy—and they seem equally ready to give the same away for nothing whenever their lives are in peril. Both sides massacre their prisoners; both sides are as proud of burning a deserted plantation or conquering, capturing, scalping and skinning a crippled blind idiot, as any civilized army would be of taking a fortified city; both sides make a grand school-boy pow-wow over it every time they fight all day long and kill a couple of sick women and disable a jackass; both sides lie, and brag, and betray, and rob, and destroy; a happy majority of both sides are fantastic in costume, grotesque in manner, half civilized, unwashed, ignorant, bigoted, selfish, base, cruel, swaggering, plantation-burning semi-devils, and it is devoutly to be hoped that an all-wise Providence will permit them to go on eating each other up until there isn't enough left of the last ragamuffin of the lot to hold an inquest on. Amen.

Now there you have a sober, quiet, opinion of the idolized Cuban "patriot" and his cause, and one which is impartial and full of charity. I have read about the Cuban "patriot" and the Cuban "oppressor," and the ghastly atrocities they are pleased to call "warfare," till I seem almost to have got enough. Everybody knows that the Cuban "oppressor" is a very devil incarnate, and if thoroughly impartial news-accounts of the doings in Cuba were furnished us everybody would see that the Cuban "patriot" is another devil incarnate just exactly like him. They are of the same breed, the same color, they speak the same language, they dishonor the same religion, and verily their instincts are precisely and unvaryingly the same. I do not love the Cuban patriot or the Cuban oppressor either, and I never want to see our government "recognize" anything of theirs but their respective corpses. If the *Buffalo Express** thinks differently, let it say it in its editorials, but not over the signature of yours, with emotion.

MARK TWAIN

1869

* This piece was written for the *Express* at a time when Mark Twain owned a third interest in the paper and when he wrote regularly for it.

LAST WORDS OF GREAT MEN

Marshal Neil's last words were: "L'armée francaise!" (The French army.)—*Exchange.*

What a sad thing it is to see a man close a grand career with a plagiarism in his mouth. Napoleon's last words were: "Tête d'armée." (Head of the army.) Neither of those remarks amounts to anything as "last words," and reflects little credit upon the utterer. A distinguished man should be as particular about his last words as he is about his last breath. He should write them out on a slip of paper and take the judgment of his friends on them. He should never leave such a thing to the last hour of his life, and trust to an intellectual spirit at the last moment to enable him to say something smart with his latest gasp and launch into eternity with grandeur. No—a man is apt to be too much fagged and exhausted, both in body and mind, at such a time, to be reliable; and maybe the very thing he wants to say, he cannot think of to save him; and besides there are his weeping friends bothering around; and worse than all as likely as not he may have to deliver his last gasp before he is expecting to. A man cannot always expect to think of a natty thing to say under such circumstances, and so it is pure egotistic ostentation to put it off. There is hardly a case on record where a man came to his last moment unprepared and said a good thing—hardly a case where a man trusted to that last moment and did not make a solemn botch of it and go out of the world feeling absurd.

Now there was Daniel Webster. Nobody could tell him anything. *He* was not afraid. *He* could do something neat when the time came. And how did it turn out? Why, his will had to be fixed over; and then all the relations came; and first one thing and then another interfered, till at last he only had a chance to say, "I still live," and up he went. Of course he didn't still live, because he died—and so he might as well have kept his last words to himself as to have gone and made such a failure of it as that. A week before that fifteen minutes of calm reflection would have enabled that man to contrive some last words that would have been a credit to himself and a comfort to his family for generations to come.

And there was John Quincy Adams. Relying on his splendid abilities and his coolness in emergencies, *he* trusted to a happy hit at the last moment to carry him through, and what was the result? Death smote him in the House of Representatives, and he observed, casually, "This is the last of earth." The last of earth! Why "the last of earth" when there was so much more left? If he had said it was the last rose of summer or the last run of shad, it would have had as much point in it. What he meant to say was, "Adam was the first and Adams is the last of earth," but he put it off a trifle too long, and so he had to go with that unmeaning observation on his lips.

And there we have Napoleon's "Tête d'armée." That don't mean anything. Taken by itself, "Head of the army," is no more important than "Head of the police." And yet that was a man who could have said a good thing if he had barred out the doctor and studied over it a while. Marshal Neil, with half a century at his disposal, could not dash off anything better in his last moments than a poor plagiarism of another man's words, which were not worth plagiarizing in the first place. "The French army." Perfectly irrelevant—perfectly flat—utterly pointless. But if he had closed one eye significantly, and said, "The subscriber has made it lively for the French army," and then thrown a little of the comic into his last gasp, it would have been a thing to remember with satisfaction all the rest of his life. I do wish our great men would quit saying these flat things just at the moment they die. Let us have their next-to-the-last words for a while, and see if we cannot patch up from them something that will be more satisfactory. The public does not wish to be outraged in this way all the time.

But when we come to call to mind the last words of parties who took the trouble to make the proper preparation for the occasion, we immediately notice a happy difference in the result.

There was Chesterfield. Lord Chesterfield had labored all his life to build up the most shining reputation for affability and elegance of speech and manners the world has ever seen. And could you suppose he failed to appreciate the efficiency of characteristic "last words," in the matter of seizing the successfully driven nail of such a reputation and clinching on the other side for ever? Not he. He prepared himself. He kept his eye on the clock and his finger on his pulse. He awaited his chance. And at last, when he knew his time was come, he pretended to think a new visitor had entered, and so, with the rattle in his throat emphasised for dramatic effect, he said to the servant, "Shin around, John, and get the gentleman a chair." And so he died, amid thunders of applause.

Next we have Benjamin Franklin. Franklin, the author of Poor Richard's quaint sayings; Franklin the immortal axiom-builder, who used to sit up at nights reducing the rankest old threadbare platitudes to crisp and snappy maxims that had a nice, varnished, original look in their regimentals; who said, "Virtue is its own reward"; who said, "Procrastination is the thief of time"; who said, "Time and tide wait for no man" and "Necessity is the mother of invention"; good old Franklin, the Josh Billings of the eighteenth century—though, sooth to say, the latter transcends him in proverbial originality as much as he falls short of him in correctness of orthography. What sort of tactics did Franklin pursue? He pondered over his last words for as much as two weeks, and then when the time came, he said, "None but the brave deserve the fair," and died happy. He could not have said a sweeter thing if he had lived till he was an idiot.

Byron made a poor business of it, and could not think of anything to say, at the last moment but, "Augusta-sister-Lady Byron—tell Harriet Beecher Stowe"—etc., etc.,—but Shakespeare was ready and said, "England expects every man to do his duty!" and went off with splendid eclat.

And there are other instances of sagacious preparation for a felicitous closing remark. For instance:

Joan of Arc said, "Tramp, tramp, tramp the boys are marching."

Alexander the Great said, "Another of those Santa Cruz punches, if you please."

The Empress Josephine said, "Not for Jo—" and could get no further.

Cleopatra said, "The Old Guard dies, but never surrenders."

Sir Walter Raleigh said, "Executioner, can I take your whetstone a moment, please?" though what for is not clear.

John Smith said, "Alas, I am the last of my race."

Queen Elizabeth said, "Oh, I would give my kingdom for one moment more—I have forgotten my last words."

And Red Jacket, the noblest Indian brave that ever wielded a tomahawk in defence of a friendless and persecuted race, expired with these touching words upon his lips, "*Wawkawampanoosuc, winnebagowallawsagamoresaskatchewan.*" There was not a dry eye in the wigwam.

Let not this lesson be lost upon our public men. Let them take a healthy moment for preparation, and contrive some last words that shall be neat and to the point. Let Louis Napoleon say,

"I am content to follow my uncle—still, I do not wish to improve upon his last word. Put me down for 'Tête d'armée.'"

And Garret Davis, "Let me recite the unabridged dictionary."

And H.G., "I desire, now, to say a few words on political economy."

And Mr. Bergh, "Only take part of me at a time, if the load will be fatiguing to the hearse horses."

And Andrew Johnson, "I have been an Alderman, Member of Congress, Governor, Senator, Pres—adieu, you know the rest."

And Seward, "Alas!-ka."

And Grant, "O."

All of which is respectfully submitted, with the most honorable intentions.

M.T.

P.S.—I am obliged to leave out the illustrations. The artist finds it impossible to make a picture of people's last words.

1869

THE LATE RELIABLE CONTRABAND

Our estimable contributor, Mark Twain, is at present busy at Hartford, crowding his new book, "The New Pilgrim's Progress,"* through the press. *How* busy, will be apparent in the fact that he could not find time to eat a Delmonico Dinner with the members of the New York Press Club. With his usual sagacity, however, he saw the advantage of being represented; and so, when he found it impossible to go, he sent on his speech, to be orated by another—the very identical speech, he writes, which he should *extemporaneously* have "expelled from his system" had he been present. As the proceedings of the Press Club are never made public, this document, like other as brilliant lucubrations of the evening, would have been doomed to the darkness of silence but for the timely aid of that ubiquitous "Reliable Contraband," who, though dead enough for an eulogy and an epitaph, is sufficiently alive to serve his old friends when he knows them. So this *morceau* was rescued from oblivion and the hands of the reporters for exclusive publication in PACKARD'S MONTHLY.

TOAST
To one whose eminent services in time of great national peril we gratefully acknowledge; whose memory we revere; whose death we deplore; the journalist's truest friend—the late "RELIABLE CONTRABAND."

SPEECH
Mr. President and Gentlemen.

It is my painful duty to mar these festivities with the announcement of the death of one who was dear to us all—our tried and noble friend, the "Reliable Contraband." To the world at large this event will bring no sorrow, for the world never comprehended him, never knew him as we did, never had such cause to love him; but unto

* An early title of *The Innocents Abroad*, issued in 1869. In 1867, just prior to embarking on the Quaker City excursion, which was to become the basis of *The Innocents Abroad*, Clemens had published his first book, *The Celebrated Jumping Frog of Calaveros County*.

us the calamity brings unutterable anguish—for it heralds the loss of one whose great heart beat for us alone, whose tireless tongue vibrated in our interest only, whose fervent fancy wrought its miracles solely for our enrichment and renown.

In his time what did he not do for us? When marvels languished and sensation dispatches grew tame, who was it that laid down the shovel and the hoe and came with healing on his wings? The Reliable Contraband. When armies fled in panic and dismay, and the great cause seemed lost beyond all hope of succor, who was it that turned the tide of war and gave victory to the vanquished? The Reliable Contraband. When despair hung its shadows about the hearts of the people, and sorrow sat on every face, who was it that braved every danger to bring cheering and incomprehensible news from the front? The Reliable Contraband. Who took Richmond the first time? The Reliable Contraband. Who took it the second time? The Reliable Contraband. Who took it *every* time until the last, and then felt the bitterness of hearing a nation applaud the man more who took it once than that greater man who had taken it six times before? The Reliable Contraband. When we needed a bloodless victory to whom did we look to win it? The Reliable Contraband. When we needed news to make the people's bowels yearn, and their knotted and combined locks to stand on end like quills upon the fretful porcupine, to whom did we look to fetch it? The Reliable Contraband. When we needed *any* sort or description of news, upon *any* sort or description of subject, who was it that stood always ready to steal a horse and bring that news along? The Reliable Contraband.

My friends, he was the faithfulest vassal that ever fought, bled and lied in the glorious ranks of journalism. Thunder and lightning never stopped him; annihilated railroads never delayed him; the telegraph never overtook him; military secrecy never crippled his knowledge; strategic feints never confused his judgment; cannon balls couldn't kill him; clairvoyance couldn't find him; Satan himself couldn't catch him. His information comprised all knowledge, possible and impossible; his imagination was utterly boundless; his capacity to make mighty statements, and so back them up as to make an inch of truth cover an acre of ground, without appearing to stretch or tear, was a thing that appalled even the most unimpressible with its awful grandeur.

The Reliable Contraband is no more! Born of the war, and a necessity of the war, and of the war only, he watched its progress, took notes of its successes and reverses, manufactured and recorded the most thrilling features of its daily history, and then, when it died, his great mission was fulfilled, his occupation gone, and he died likewise.

No journalist here present can lay his hand upon his heart and say he had not cause to love this faithful creature, over whose unsentient form we drop these unavailing tears—for no journalist among us all can lay his hand upon his heart and say he ever lied with such pathos, such unction, such exquisite symmetry, such sublimity of conception and such felicity of execution, as when he did it through and by the inspiration of this regally gifted marvel of mendacity, the lamented RELIABLE CONTRABAND. Peace to his ashes!

Respectfully,

MARK TWAIN

1869

A MYSTERY CLEARED UP

Ex-Secretary Stanton had an interview with Secretary Fish, yesterday.—

Sensation Telegram of Associated Press.

I was present at that interview. The subject of it was Warts.

Ex-Secretary Stanton said that when he was a boy, he had sixteen on his left hand, one or two on his right thumb, and one on his elbow. He said he used to always hunt for old hollow stumps, with rain-water standing in them, to soak his warts in.

Secretary Fish said he had a million of warts when he was a boy, and sometimes he split a bean and tied it over his wart, and then took that bean and buried it in the cross roads at midnight in the dark of the moon.

Ex-Secretary Stanton said he had tried that, but it never worked.

Secretary Fish said he could not remember that it worked—he only remembered trying it a good many times, and in the most unquestioning good faith.

Ex-Secretary Stanton said his usual plan was to run a needle through the wart, and then hold the end of the needle in the candle till it warmed the wart to that degree that it would never take an interest in this world's follies and vanities any more forever.

Secretary Fish said he thought likely he was the wartiest boy that ever——

At this opportune moment ex-Secretary Stanton's carriage was announced, and he arose and took his leave. The next Associated Press dispatch that distressed the people through the columns of every single newspaper in America read as follows:

"The subject of the interview between ex-Secretary Stanton and Secretary Fish has not transpired. There are various flying rumors. It is generally believed that it referred to the Alabama question, and was very important."

And yet they were only talking about Warts.

Hereafter, when I see vague, dreadful Associated Press dispatches, stating that Jones called on the Secretary of the Interior last night, or Smith had an interview with the Attorney General, or Brown was closeted with the President until a late hour yesterday evening, I shall feel certain that they were only talking about Warts, or something like that. They can never fire my interest again with one of those dispatches, unless they state *what* the interview was about.

1869

OPEN LETTER TO COMMODORE VANDERBILT*

How my heart goes out in sympathy to you! how I do pity you, Commodore Vanderbilt! Most men have at least a few friends, whose devotion is a comfort and a solace to them, but you seem to be the idol of only a crawling swarm of small souls, who love to glorify your most flagrant unworthinesses in print; or praise your vast possessions worshippingly; or sing of your unimportant private habits and sayings and doings, as if your millions gave them dignity; friends who applaud your superhuman stinginess with the same gusto that they do your most magnificent displays of commercial genius and daring, and likewise your most lawless violations of commercial honor—for these infatuated worshippers of dollars not their own seem to make no distinctions, but swing their hats and shout hallelujah every time you do *anything*, no matter what it is. I do pity you. I would pity any man with such friends as these. I should think you would hate the sight of a newspaper. I should think you would not dare to glance at one, for fear you would find in it one of these distressing eulogies of something you had been doing, which was either infinitely trivial or else a matter you ought to be ashamed of. Unacquainted with you as I am, my honest compassion for you still gives me a right to speak in this way. Now, have you ever thought calmly over your newspaper reputation? Have you ever dissected it, to see what it was made of? It would interest you. One day one of your subjects comes out with a column or two detailing your rise from penury to affluence, and praising you as if you were the last and noblest work of God, but un-consciously telling how exquisitely mean a man has to be in order to achieve what you have achieved. Then another subject tells how you drive in the Park, with your scornful head down, never deigning to look to the right or the left, and make glad the thousands who

* Mark Twain had a remarkable gift of invective, which he liberally displayed in his *Autobiography*, written in his later years. The present essay is a brilliant early example.

covet a glance of your eye, but driving straight ahead, heedlessly and recklessly, taking the road by force, with a bearing which plainly says, "Let these people get out of the way if they can; but if they can't, and I run over them, and kill them, no matter, I'll pay for them." And then how the retailer of the pleasant anecdote does grovel in the dust and glorify you, Vanderbilt! Next, a subject of yours prints a long article to show how, in some shrewd, under-handed way, you have "come it" over the public with some Erie dodge or other, and added another million or so to your greasy greenbacks; and behold! *he* praises you, and never hints that immoral practices, in so prominent a place as you occupy, are a damning example to the rising commercial generation—more, a damning thing to the whole nation, while there are insects like your subjects to make virtues of them in print. Next, a subject tells a most laughable joke in *Harpers* of how a lady laid a wager of a pair of gloves that she could touch your heart with the needs of some noble public charity, which unselfish people were building up for the succoring of the helpless and the unfortunate, and so persuade you to spare a generous billow to it from your broad ocean of wealth, and how you listened to the story of want and suffering, and then—then what?— gave the lady a paltry dollar (the act in itself an insult to your sister or mine, coming from a stranger) and said. "Tell your opponent you have won the gloves." And, having told his little anecdote, how your loving subject did shake his sides at the bare idea of *your* having generosity enough to be persuaded by any tender womanly pleader into giving a manly lift to any helpless creature under the sun! What precious friends you do have, Vanderbilt! And next, a subject tells how when you owned the California line of steamers you used to have your pursers make out false lists of passengers, and thus carry some hundreds more than the law allowed—in this way breaking the laws of your country and jeopardizing the lives of your passengers by overcrowding them during a long, sweltering voyage over tropical seas, and through a disease-poisoned atmosphere. And this shrewdness was duly glorified too. But I remember how those misused passengers used to revile you and curse you when they got to the Isthmus—and especially the women and young girls, who were forced to sleep on your steerage floors, side by side with strange men, who were the offscourings of creation, and even in the steerage beds with them, if the poor wretches told the truth; and I do assure you that nobody who lived in California at that time disbelieved them—O, praised and envied Vanderbilt! These women were nothing

to you and me; but if they had been, we might have been shamed
and angered at this treatment, mightn't we? We cannot rightly judge
of matters like these till we sit down and try to fancy these women
related to us by ties of blood and affection, but *then* the rare joke of
it melts away, and the indignant tides go surging through our veins,
poor little Commodore!

There are other anecdotes told of you by your glorifying subjects,
but let us pass them by, they only damage you. They only show
how unfortunate and how narrowing a thing it is for a man to have
wealth who makes a god of it instead of a servant. They only show
how soulless it can make him—like that pretty anecdote that tells
how a young lawyer charged you $500 for a service, and how you
deemed the charge too high, and so went shrewdly to work and
won his confidence, and persuaded him to borrow money and put it
in Erie, when you knew the stock was going down, and so held
him in the trap till he was a ruined man, and then you were revenged;
and you gloated over it; and, as usual, your admiring friends told the
story in print, and lauded you to the skies. No, let us drop the
anecdotes. I don't remember ever reading anything about you which
you oughtn't be ashamed of.

All I wish to urge upon you now is, that you crush out your native
instincts and go and do something *worthy* of praise—go and do
something you need not blush to see in print—do something that may
rouse one solitary good impulse in the breasts of your horde of worshippers; prove one solitary good example to the thousands of young
men who emulate your energy and your industry; shine as one solitary
grain of pure gold upon the heaped rubbish of your life. Do this, I
beseech you, else through your example we shall shortly have in our
midst five hundred Vanderbilts, which God forbid! Go, now please
go, and do one worthy act. Go, boldly, grandly, nobly, and give four
dollars to some great public charity. It will break your heart, no doubt;
but no matter, you have but a little while to live, and it is better to
die suddenly and nobly than live a century longer the same Vanderbilt you are now. Do this, and I declare *I* will praise you too.

Poor Vanderbilt. How I do pity you; and this is honest. You are
an old man, and ought to have some rest; and yet you have to
struggle and struggle, and deny yourself, and rob yourself of restful
sleep and peace of mind, because you need money so badly. I always
feel for a man who is so poverty ridden as you. Don't misunderstand
me, Vanderbilt. I know you own seventy millions; but then you
know and I know that it isn't what a man has that constitutes

wealth. No—it is to be *satisfied* with what one has; that is wealth. As long as one sorely *needs* a certain additional amount, that man isn't rich. Seventy times seventy millions can't make him rich as long as his poor heart is breaking for more. I am just about rich enough to buy the least valuable horse in your stable, perhaps, but I cannot sincerely and honestly take an oath that I need any more now. And so I am rich. But you! you have got seventy millions, and you *need* five hundred millions, and are really suffering for it. Your poverty is something appalling. I tell you truly that I do not believe I could live twenty-four hours with the awful weight of four hundred and thirty millions of abject want crushing down upon me. I should die under it. My soul is so wrought upon by your hapless pauperism, that if you came by me now I would freely put ten cents in your tin cup, if you carry one, and say, "God pity you, poor unfortunate!"

Now, I pray you take kindly all that I have said, Vanderbilt, for I assure you I have meant it kindly, and it is said in an honester spirit than you are accustomed to find in what is said to you or about you. And *do* go, now, and do something that isn't shameful. Do go and do something worthy of a man possessed of seventy millions—a man whose most trifling act is remembered and imitated all over the country by younger men than you. Do not be deceived into the notion that everything you do and say is wonderful, simply because those asses who publish you so much make it appear so. Do not deceive yourself. Very often an idea of yours is possessed of no innate magnificence, but is simply shining with the reflected splendor of your seventy millions. Now, think of it. I have tried to imitate you and become famous; all the young men do it; but, bless you, my performances attracted no attention. I gave a crippled beggar girl a two-cent piece and humorously told her to go to the Fifth Avenue Hotel and board a week; but nobody published it. If you had done that it would have been regarded as one of the funniest things that ever happened; because you *can* say the flattest things that ever I heard of, Vanderbilt, and have them magnified into wit and wisdom in the papers. And the other day, in Chicago, I talked of buying the entire Union Pacific Railroad, clear to the Rocky Mountains, and running it on my own hook. It was as splendid an idea and as bold an enterprise as ever entered that overpraised brain of yours, but did it excite any newspaper applause? No. If you had conceived it, though, the newspaper world would have gone wild over it. No, sir; other men think and talk as brilliantly as you do, but they don't do it in the glare of seventy millions; so pray do not be deceived by the laudation you receive; more of it belongs to your millions than to you. I say this to warn you against becoming vainglorious on a false basis, and an unsound one—for if your millions were to pass from you you might be surprised and grieved to notice what flat and uncelebrated things you were capable of saying and doing forever afterwards.

You observe that I don't say anything about your soul, Vanderbilt. It is because I have evidence that you haven't any. It would be impossible to convince me that a man of your matchless financial ability would overlook so dazzling an "operation," if you had a soul to save, as the purchasing of millions of years of Paradise, and rest, and peace, and pleasure, for so trifling a sum as ten years blamelessly lived on earth—for you probably haven't longer than that to live now, you know, you are very old. Well, I don't know, after all, possibly you *have* got a soul. But I know you, Vanderbilt— I know you well. You will try to get the purchase cheaper. You will want those millions of years of rest and pleasure, and you will try to make the trade and get the superb stock; but you will wait till you are on your death-bed, and then offer *an hour and forty minutes* for it. I know you so well, Vanderbilt! Still worse men than you do this. The people we hang always send for a priest at the last moment.

I assure you, Vanderbilt, that I mean what I am saying for your good—not to make you mad. Why, the way you are going on, you are no better than those Astors. No, I won't say that; for it is better to be a mean *live* man than a stick—even a gold-headed stick. And now my lesson is done. It is bound to refresh you and make you feel good; for you must necessarily get sick of puling flattery and syco- phancy sometimes, and sigh for a paragraph of honest criticism and abuse for a change. And in parting, I say that, surely, standing as you do upon the pinnacle of moneyed magnificence in America you must certainly feel a vague desire in you sometimes to do some splendid deed in the interest of commercial probity, or of human charity, or of manly honor and dignity, that shall flash into instant celebrity over the whole nation, and be rehearsed to ambitious boys by their mothers a century after you are dead. I say you must feel so sometimes, for it is only natural, and therefore I urge you to congeal that thought into an act. Go and surprise the whole country by doing something right. Cease to do and say unworthy things, and excessively *little* things, for those reptile friends of yours to magnify in the papers. Snub them thus, or else throttle them.

Yours truly,

MARK TWAIN

1869

TO THE CALIFORNIA PIONEERS*

To the California Pioneers:

Gentlemen: Circumstances render it out of my power to take advantage of the invitation extended to me through Mr. Simonton, and be present at your dinner at New York. I regret this very much, for there are several among you whom I would have a right to join hands with on the score of old friendship, and I suppose I would have a sublime general right to shake hands with the rest of you on the score of kinship in California ups and downs in search of fortune.

If I were to tell some of my experience, you would recognize California blood in me; I fancy the old, old story would sound familiar no doubt. I have the usual stock of reminiscences. For instance: I went to Esmeralda early. I purchased largely in the "Wide West," "Winnemucca," and other fine claims, and was very wealthy. I fared sumptuously on bread when flour was $200 a barrel and had beans for dinner every Sunday, when none but bloated aristocrats could afford such grandeur. But I finished by feeding batteries in a quartz mill at $15 a week, and wishing I was a battery myself and had somebody to feed me. My claims in Esmeralda are there yet. I suppose I could be persuaded to sell.

I went to Humboldt District when it was new; I became largely interested in the "Alba Nueva" and other claims with gorgeous names, and was rich again—in prospect. I owned a vast mining property there. I would not have sold out for less than $400,000 at that time. But I will now. Finally I walked home—200 miles—partly for exercise, and partly because stage fare was expensive. Next I entered upon an affluent career in Virginia City, and by a judicious investment of labor and the capital of friends, became the owner of about all the

---

* A letter written in reply to an invitation from the New York Society of California Pioneers to attend a banquet to be given to the visiting members of the Society of California Pioneers of the Pacific Coast. The letter was read at the banquet in New York and was published in the Buffalo *Express* on October 19, 1869.

worthless wild cat mines there were in that part of the country. Assessments did the business for me there. There were a hundred and seventeen assessments to one dividend, and the proportion of income to outlay was a little against me. My financial barometer went down to 32 Fahrenheit, and the subscriber was frozen out.

I took up extensions on the main lead—extensions that reached to British America in one direction, and to the Isthmus of Panama in the other—and I verily believe I would have been a rich man if I had ever found those infernal extensions. But I didn't. I ran tunnels till I tapped the Arctic Ocean, and I sunk shafts till I broke through the roof of perdition; but those extensions turned up missing every time. I am willing to sell all that property and throw in the improvements.

Perhaps you remember that celebrated "North Ophir?" I bought that mine. It was very rich in pure silver. You could take it out in lumps as large as a filbert. But when it was discovered that those lumps were melted half dollars, and hardly melted at that, a painful case of "salting" was apparent, and the undersigned adjourned to the poorhouse again.

I paid assessments on "Hale and Norcross" until they sold me out, and I had to take in washing for a living—and the next month that infamous stock went up to $7000 a foot.

I own millions and millions of feet of affluent silver leads in Nevada—in fact the entire undercrust of that country nearly, and if Congress would move that State off my property so that I could get at it, I would be wealthy yet. But no, there she squats—and here am I. Failing health persuades me to sell. If you know of any one desiring a permanent investment, I can furnish one that will have the virtue of being eternal.

I have been through the California mill, with all its "dips, spurs and angles, variations and sinuosities." I have worked there at all the different trades and professions known to the catalogues. I have been everything, from a newspaper editor down to a cowcatcher on a locomotive, and I am encouraged to believe that if there had been a few more occupations to experiment on, I might have made a dazzling success at last, and found out what mysterious designs Providence had in creating me.

But you perceive that although I am not a Pioneer, I have had a sufficiently variegated time of it to enable me to talk Pioneer like a native, and feel like a Forty-Niner. Therefore, I cordially welcome you to your old remembered homes and your long deserted firesides, and close this screed with the sincere hope that your visit here will be a happy one, and not embittered by the sorrowful surprises that absence and lapse of years are wont to prepare for wanderers; surprises which come in the form of old friends missed from their places; silence where familiar voices should be; the young grown old; change and decay everywhere; home a delusion and a disappoint-ment; strangers at hearthstone; sorrow where gladness was; tears for laughter; the melancholy pomp of death where the grace of life has been!

With all good wishes for the Returned Prodigals, and regrets that I cannot partake of a small piece of the fatted calf (rare and no gravy,)
I am yours, cordially,

MARK TWAIN
1869

THE WILD MAN INTERVIEWED

There has been so much talk about the mysterious "wild man" out there in the West for some time, that I finally felt it was my duty to go out and interview him. There was something peculiarly and touchingly romantic about the creature and his strange actions, according to the newspaper reports. He was represented as being hairy, long-armed, and of great strength and stature; ugly and cumbrous; avoiding men, but appearing suddenly and unexpectedly to women and children; going armed with a club, but never molesting any creature, except sheep, or other prey; fond of eating and drinking, and not particular about the quality, quantity, or character of the beverages and edibles; living in the woods like a wild beast, but never angry; moaning, and sometimes howling, but never uttering articulate sounds. Such was "Old Shep" as the papers painted him. I felt that the story of his life must be a sad one—a story of suffering, disappointment, and exile—a story of man's inhumanity to man in some shape or other—and I longed to persuade the secret from him.

"Since you say you are a member of the press," said the wild man, "I am willing to tell you all you wish to know. Bye and bye you will comprehend why it is that I wish to unbosom myself to a newspaper man when I have so studiously avoided conversation with other people. I will now unfold my strange story. I was born with the world we live upon, almost. I am the son of Cain."

"What?"

"I was present when the flood was announced."

"Which?"

"I am the father of the Wandering Jew."

"Sir?"

I moved out of range of his club, and went on taking notes, but keeping a wary eye on him all the while. He smiled a melancholy smile and resumed:

"When I glance back over the dreary waste of ages, I see many a glimmering and mark that is familiar to my memory. And oh, the leagues I have travelled! the things I have seen! the events I have helped to emphasise! I was at the assassination of Caesar. I marched upon Mecca with Mahomet. I was in the Crusades, and stood with Godfrey when he planted the banner of the cross on the battlements of Jerusalem. I—."

"One moment, please. Have you given these items to any other journal? Can I—"

"Silence. I was in the Pinta's shrouds with Columbus when America burst upon his vision. I saw Charles I beheaded. I was in London when the Gunpowder Plot was discovered. I was present at the trial of Warren Hastings. I was on American soil when the battle of Lexington was fought—when the declaration was promulgated—when Cornwallis surrendered—when Washington died. I entered Paris with Napoleon after Elba. I was present when you mounted your guns and manned your fleets for the war of 1812—when the South fired upon Sumter—when Richmond fell—when the President's life was taken. In all the ages I have helped to celebrate the triumphs of genius, the achievements of arms, the havoc of storm, fire, pestilence, famine."

"Your career has been a stirring one. Might I ask how you came to locate in these dull Kansas woods, when you have been so accustomed to excitement during what I might term so protracted a period, not to put too fine a point on it?"

"Listen. Once I was the honoured servitor of the noble and illustrious" (here he heaved a sigh, and passed his hairy hand across his eyes) "but in these degenerate days I am become the slave of quack doctors and newspapers. I am driven from pillar to post and hurried up and down, sometimes with stencil-plate and paste-brush to defile the fences with cabalistic legends, and sometimes in grotesque and extravagant character at the behest of some driving journal. I attended to that Ocean Bank robbery some weeks ago, when I was hardly rested from finishing up the pow-wow about the completion of the Pacific Railroad; immediately I was spirited off to do an atrocious murder for the benefit of the New York papers; next to attend the wedding of a patriarchal millionaire; next to raise a hurrah about the great boat race; and then, just when I had begun to hope that my old bones would have a rest, I am bundled off to this howling wilderness to strip, and jibber, and be ugly and hairy, and pull down fences and waylay sheep, and waltz around with a club, and play 'Wild Man' generally—and all to gratify the whim of a bedlam of crazy newspaper scribblers? From one end of the continent to the other, I am described as a gorilla, with a sort of human seeming about me—and all to gratify this quill-driving scum of the earth!"

"Poor old carpet bagger!"

"I have been served infamously, often, in modern and semi-modern times. I have been compelled by base men to create fraudulent history, and to perpetrate all sorts of humbugs. I wrote those crazy Junius letters, I moped in a French dungeon for fifteen years, and wore a ridiculous Iron Mask; I poked around your Northern forests, among your vagabond Indians, a solemn French idiot, personating the ghost of a dead Dauphin, that the gaping world might wonder if we had 'a Bourbon among us'; I have played sea-serpent off Nahant, and Woolly-Horse and What-is-it for the museums; I have interviewed politicians for the Sun, worked up all manner of miracles for the Herald, ciphered up election returns for the World, and thundered Political Economy through the Tribune. I have done all the extravagant things that the wildest invention could contrive, and done them well, and *this* is my reward—playing Wild Man in Kansas without a shirt!"

"Mysterious being, a light dawns vaguely upon me—it grows apace —what—what is your name?"

"Sensation!"

"Hence, horrible shape!"

It spoke again:

"Oh pitiless fate, my destiny hounds me once more. I am called. I go. Alas, is there no rest for me?"

In a moment the Wild Man's features seemed to soften and refine, and his form to assume a more human grace and symmetry. His club changed to a spade, and he shouldered it and started away sighing profoundly and shedding tears.

"Whither, poor shade?"

"To dig up the Byron family!"

Such was the response that floated back upon the wind as the sad spirit shook its ringlets to the breeze, flourished its shovel aloft, and disappeared beyond the brow of the hill.

All of which is in strict accordance with the facts.

1869

ABOUT SMELLS

In a recent issue of the "Independent," the Rev. T. De Witt Talmage, of Brooklyn, has the following utterance on the subject of "Smells":

I have a good Christian friend who, if he sat in the front pew in church, and a working man should enter the door at the other end, would smell him instantly. My friend is not to blame for the sensitiveness of his nose, any more than you would flog a pointer for being keener on the scent than a stupid watch-dog. The fact is, if you had all the churches free, by reason of the mixing up of the common people with the uncommon, you would keep one-half of Christendom sick at their stomach. If you are going to kill the church thus with bad smells, I will have nothing to do with this work of evangelization.

We have reason to believe that there will be laboring men in heaven; and also a number of negroes, and Esquimaux, and Terra del Fuegans, and Arabs, and a few Indians, and possibly even some Spaniards and Portuguese. All things are possible with God. We shall have all these sorts of people in heaven; but, alas! in getting them we shall lose the society of Dr. Talmage. Which is to say, we shall lose the company of one who could give more real "tone" to celestial society than any other contribution Brooklyn could furnish. And what would eternal happiness be without the Doctor? Blissful, unquestionably—we know that well enough—but would it be *distingué*, would it be *recherché* without him? St. Matthew without stockings or sandals; St. Jerome bareheaded, and with a coarse brown blanket robe dragging the ground; St. Sebastian with scarcely any raiment at all—these we should see, and should enjoy seeing them; but would we not miss a spike-tailed coat and kids, and turn away regretfully, and say to parties from the Orient: "These are well enough, but you ought to see Talmage of Brooklyn." I fear me that in the better world we shall not even have Dr. Talmage's "good

Christian friend." For if he were sitting under the glory of the Throne, and the keeper of the keys admitted a Benjamin Franklin or other laboring man, that "friend," with his fine natural powers infinitely augmented by emancipation from hampering flesh, would detect him with a single sniff, and immediately take his hat and ask to be excused.

To all outward seeming, the Rev. T. De Witt Talmage is of the same material as that used in the construction of his early predecessors in the ministry; and yet one feels that there must be a difference somewhere between him and the Saviour's first disciples. It may be because here, in the nineteenth century, Dr. T. has had advantages which Paul and Peter and the others could not and did not have. There was a lack of polish about them, and a looseness of etiquette, and a want of exclusiveness, which one cannot help noticing. They healed the very beggars, and held intercourse with people of a villainous odor every day. If the subject of these remarks had been chosen among the original Twelve Apostles, he would not have associated with the rest, because he could not have stood the fishy smell of some of his comrades who came from around the Sea of Galilee. He would have resigned his commission with some such remark as he makes in the extract quoted above: "Master, if thou art going to kill the church thus with bad smells, I will have nothing to do with this work of evangelization." He is a disciple, and makes that remark to the Master; the only difference is, that he makes it in the nineteenth instead of the first century.

Is there a choir in Mr. T.'s church? And does it ever occur that they have no better manners than to sing that hymn which is so suggestive of laborers and mechanics:

> "Son of the Carpenter! receive
> This humble work of mine?"

Now, can it be possible that in a handful of centuries the Christian character has fallen away from an imposing heroism that scorned even the stake, the cross, and the axe, to a poor little effeminacy that withers and wilts under an unsavory smell? We are not prepared to believe so, the reverend Doctor and his friend to the contrary notwithstanding.

1870

THE APPROACHING EPIDEMIC

One calamity to which the death of Mr. Dickens dooms this country has not awakened the concern to which its gravity entitles it. We refer to the fact that the nation is to be lectured to death and read to death all next winter, by Tom, Dick, and Harry, with poor lamented Dickens for a pretext. All the vagabonds who can spell will afflict the people with "readings" from Pickwick and Copperfield, and all the insignificants who have been ennobled by the notice of the great novelist or transfigured by his smile will make a marketable commodity of it now, and turn the sacred reminiscence to the practical use of procuring bread and butter. The lecture rostrums will fairly swarm with these fortunates. Already the signs of it are perceptible. Behold how the unclean creatures are wending toward the dead lion and gathering to the feast:

"Reminiscences of Dickens." A lecture. By John Smith, who heard him read eight times.

"Remembrances of Charles Dickens." A lecture. By John Jones, who saw him once in a street car and twice in a barber shop.

"Recollections of Mr. Dickens." A lecture. By John Brown, who gained a wide fame by writing deliriously appreciative critiques and rhapsodies upon the great author's public readings; and who shook hands with the great author upon various occasions, and held converse with him several times.

"Readings from Dickens." By John White, who has the great delineator's style and manner perfectly, having attended all his readings in this country and made these things a study, always practising each reading before retiring, and while it was hot from the great delineator's lips. Upon this occasion Mr. W. will exhibit the remains of a cigar which he saw Mr. Dickens smoke. This Relic is kept in a solid silver box made purposely for it.

"Sights and Sounds of the Great Novelist." A popular lecture.

By John Gray, who waited on his table all the time he was at the Grand Hotel, New York, and still has in his possession and will exhibit to the audience a fragment of the Last Piece of Bread which the lamented author tasted in this country.

"Heart Treasures of Precious Moments with Literature's Departed Monarch." A lecture. By Miss Serena Amelia Tryphenia McSpadden, who still wears, and will always wear, a glove upon the hand made sacred by the clasp of Dickens. Only Death shall remove it.

"Readings from Dickens." By Mrs. J. O'Hooligan Murphy, who washed for him.

"Familiar Talks with the Great Author." A narrative lecture. By John Thomas, for two weeks his valet in America.

And so forth, and so on. This isn't half the list. The man who has a "Toothpick once used by Charles Dickens" will have to have a hearing; and the man who "once rode in an omnibus with Charles Dickens"; and the lady to whom Charles Dickens "granted the hospitalities of his umbrella during a storm"; and the person who "possesses a hole which once belonged in a handkerchief owned by Charles Dickens." Be patient and long-suffering, good people, for even this does not fill up the measure of what you must endure next winter. There is no creature in all this land who has had any personal relations with the late Mr. Dickens, however slight or trivial, but will shoulder his way to the rostrum and inflict his testimony upon his helpless countrymen. To some people it is fatal to be noticed by greatness.

1870

BREAKING IT GENTLY

"Yes, I remember that anecdote," the Sunday school superintendent said, with the old pathos in his voice and the old sad look in his eyes. "It was about a simple creature named Higgins, that used to haul rock for old Maltby. When the lamented Judge Bagley tripped and fell down the court-house stairs and broke his neck, it was a great question how to break the news to poor Mrs. Bagley. But finally the body was put into Higgins's wagon and he was instructed to take it to Mrs. B., but to be very guarded and discreet in his language, and not break the news to her at once, but do it gradually and gently. When Higgins got there with his sad freight, he shouted till Mrs. Bagley came to the door. Then he said:

"Does the widder Bagley live here?"

"The *widow* Bagley? *No*, Sir!"

"I'll bet she does. But have it your own way. Well, does *Judge* Bagley live here?"

"Yes, Judge Bagley lives here."

"I'll bet he don't. But never mind—it ain't for me to contradict. Is the Judge in?"

"No, not at present."

"I jest expected as much. Because, you know—take hold o' suthin, mum, for I'm a-going to make a little communication, and I reckon maybe it'll jar you some. There's been an accident, mum. I've got the old Judge curled up out here in the wagon—and when you see him you'll acknowledge, yourself, that an inquest is about the only thing that could be a comfort to *him!*"

1870

A COUPLE OF SAD EXPERIENCES*

When I published a squib recently, in which I said I was going to edit an Agricultural Department in this magazine, I certainly did not desire to deceive anybody. I had not the remotest desire to play upon any one's confidence with a practical joke, for he is a pitiful creature indeed who will degrade the dignity of his humanity to the contriving of the witless inventions that go by that name. I purposely wrote the thing as absurdly and as extravagantly as it could be written, in order to be sure and not mislead hurried or heedless readers: for I spoke of launching a triumphal *barge* upon a *desert,* and planting a *tree* of prosperity *in a mine*—a tree whose *fragrance* should *slake the thirst* of the *naked,* and whose *branches* should spread abroad till they *washed the shores* of, etc., etc. I thought that manifest lunacy like that would protect the reader. But to make assurance absolute, and show that I did not and could not seriously mean to attempt an *Agricultural* Department, I stated distinctly in my postcript that I *did not know anything about Agriculture.* But alas! right there is where I made my worst mistake—for that remark seems to have recommended my proposed Agriculture more than anything else. It lets a little light in on me, and I fancy I perceive that the farmers feel a little bored, sometimes, by the oracular profundity of agricultural editors who "know it all." In fact, one of my correspondents suggests this (for that unhappy squib has deluged me with letters about potatoes, and cabbages, and hominy, and vermicelli, and maccaroni, and all the other fruits, cereals, and vegetables that ever grew on earth; and if I get done answering questions about the best way of raising these things before I go raving crazy, I shall be thankful, and shall never write obscurely for fun any more).

* This is the preface to his "The Petrified Man" and "My Famous 'Bloody Massacre,'" both reprinted in *Sketches New and Old,* 1875, and included in my *The Complete Humorous Sketches and Tales of Mark Twain.* The preface is reprinted for the first time.

Shall I tell the real reason why I have unintentionally succeeded in fooling so many people? It is because some of them only read a little of the squib I wrote and jumped to the conclusion that it was serious, and the rest did not read it at all, but heard of my agricultural venture at second-hand. Those cases I could not guard against, of course. To write a burlesque so wild that its pretended facts will not be accepted in perfect good faith by somebody, is very nearly an impossible thing to do. It is because, in some instances, the reader is a person who never tries to deceive anybody himself, and therefore is not expecting any one to wantonly practise a deception upon *him*; and in this case the only person dishonored is the man who wrote the burlesque. In other instances the "nub" or moral of the burlesque —if its object be to enforce a truth—escapes notice in the superior glare of something in the body of the burlesque itself. And very often this "moral" is tagged on at the bottom, and the reader, not knowing that it is the key of the whole thing and the only important paragraph in the article, tranquilly turns up his nose at it and leaves it unread. One can deliver a satire with telling force through the insidious medium of a travesty, if he is careful not to overwhelm the satire with the extraneous interest of the travesty, and so bury it from the reader's sight and leave him a joked and defrauded victim, when the honest intent was to add to either his knowledge or his wisdom. I have had a deal of experience in burlesques and their unfortunate aptness to deceive the public, and this is why I tried hard to make that agricultural one so broad and so perfectly palpable that even a one-eyed potato could see it; and yet, as I speak the solemn truth, it fooled one of the ablest agricultural editors in America!

1870

CURIOUS RELIC FOR SALE

"For sale, for the benefit of the Fund for the Relief of the Widows and Orphans of Deceased Firemen, a Curious Ancient Bedouin Pipe procured at the city of Endor in Palestine, and believed to have once belonged to the justly-renowned Witch of Endor. Parties desiring to examine this singular relic with a view to purchasing, can do so by calling upon Daniel S., 119 and 121 William street, New York."

As per advertisement in the "Herald." A curious old relic indeed, as I had a good personal right to know. In a single instant of time, a long drawn panorama of sights and scenes in the Holy Land flashed through my memory—town and grove, desert, camp, and caravan clattering after each other and disappearing, leaving me with a little of the surprised and dizzy feeling which I have experienced at sundry times when a long express train has overtaken me at some quiet curve and gone whizzing, car by car, around the corner and out of sight. In that prolific instant I saw again all the country from the Sea of Galilee and Nazareth clear to Jerusalem, and thence over the hills of Judea and through the Vale of Sharon to Joppa, down by the ocean. Leaving out unimportant stretches of country and details of incident, I saw and experienced the following-described matters and things. Immediately three years fell away from my age, and a vanished time was restored to me—September, 1867. It was a flaming Oriental day—this one that had come up out of the past and brought along its actors, its stage-properties, and scenic effects—and our party had just ridden through the squalid hive of human vermin which still holds the ancient Biblical name of Endor; I was bringing up the rear on my grave four-dollar steed, who was about beginning to compose himself for his usual noon nap. My! only fifteen minutes before how the black, mangy, nine-tenths naked, ten-tenths filthy, ignorant, bigoted, besotted, hungry, lazy, malignant, screeching, crowding, struggling, wailing, begging, cursing, hateful spawn of the original Witch had swarmed out of the caves in the rocks and the holes and crevices in the earth, and blocked our horses' way, besieged us, threw themselves in the animals' path, clung to their manes, saddle-furniture, and tails, asking, beseeching, demanding "bucksheesh! *buocksheesh!* BUCKSHEESH!" We had rained small copper Turkish coins among them, as fugitives fling coats and hats to pursuing wolves, and then had spurred our way through as they stopped to scramble for the largess. I was fervently thankful when we had gotten well up on the desolate hillside and outstripped them and left them jawing and gesticulating in the rear. What a tempest had seemingly gone roaring and crashing by me and left its dull thunders pulsing in my ears!

I was in the rear, as I was saying. Our pack-mules and Arabs were far ahead, and Dan, Jack, Moult, Davis, Denny, Church, and Birch (these names will do as well as any to represent the boys) were following close after them. As my horse nodded to rest, I heard a sort of panting behind me, and turned and saw that a tawny youth from the village had overtaken me—a true remnant and representative of his ancestress the Witch—a galvanized scurvy, wrought into the human shape and garnished with ophthalmia and leprous scars—an airy creature with an invisible shirt-front that reached below the pit of his stomach, and no other clothing to speak of except a tobacco-pouch, an ammunition-pocket, and a venerable gun, which was long enough to club any game with that came within shooting distance, but far from efficient as an article of dress.

I thought to myself, "Now this disease with a human heart in it is going to shoot me." I smiled in derision at the idea of a Bedouin daring to touch off his great-grandfather's rusty gun and getting his head blown off for his pains. But then it occurred to me, in simple school-boy language, "Suppose he should take deliberate aim and 'haul off' and fetch me with the butt-end of it?" There was wisdom in that view of it, and I stopped to parley. I found he was only a friendly villain who wanted a trifle of bucksheesh, and after begging what he could get in that way, was perfectly willing to trade off everything he had for more. I believe he would have parted with his last shirt for bucksheesh if he had had one. He was smoking the "humblest" pipe I ever saw—a dingy, funnel-shaped, red-clay thing, streaked and grimed with oil and years of tobacco, and with all the different kinds of dirt there are, and thirty per cent of them peculiar and indigenous to Endor and perdition. And rank? I never smelt anything like it. It withered a cactus that stood lifting its prickly hands aloft beside the trail. It even woke up my horse. I said I would take that. It cost me a franc, a Russian kopek, a brass button, and a slate pencil; and my spendthrift lavishness so won upon the son of the desert that he passed over his pouch of most unspeakably villainous tobacco to me as a free gift. What a pipe it was, to be sure! It had a rude brass-wire cover to it, and a little coarse iron chain suspended from the bowl, with an iron splinter attached to loosen up the tobacco and pick your teeth with. The stem looked like the half of a slender walking-stick with the bark on.

I felt that this pipe had belonged to the original Witch of Endor as soon as I saw it; and as soon as I smelt it, I knew it. Moreover, I asked the Arab cub in good English if it was not so, and he answered in good Arabic that it was. I woke up my horse and went my way, smoking. And presently I said to myself reflectively, "If there *is* anything that could make a man deliberately assault a dying cripple, I reckon may be an unexpected whiff from this pipe would do it." I smoked along till I found I was beginning to lie, and project murder, and steal my own things out of one pocket and hide them in another; and then I put up my treasure, took off my spurs and put them under my horse's tail, and shortly came tearing through our caravan like a hurricane. From that time forward, going to Jerusalem, the Dead Sea, and the Jordan, Bethany, Bethlehem, and everywhere, I loafed contentedly in the rear and enjoyed my infamous pipe and revelled in imaginary villainy. But at the end of two weeks we turned our faces toward the sea and journeyed over the Judean hills, and through rocky defiles, and among the scenes that Samson knew in his youth, and by and by we touched level ground just at night, and trotted off cheerily over the plain of Sharon. It was perfectly jolly for three hours, and we whites crowded along together, close after the chief Arab muleteer (all the pack animals and the other Arabs were miles in the rear), and we laughed, and chatted, and argued hotly about Samson, and whether suicide was a sin or not, since Paul speaks of Samson distinctly as being saved and in heaven. But by and by the night air, and the duskiness, and the weariness of eight hours in the saddle, began to tell, and conversation flagged and finally died out utterly. The squeak-squeaking of the saddles grew very distinct; occasionally somebody sighed, or started to hum a tune and gave it up; now and then a horse sneezed. These things only emphasized the solemnity and the stillness. Everybody got so listless that for once I and my dreamer found ourselves in the lead. It was a glad, new sensation, and I longed to keep the place forevermore. Every little stir in the dingy cavalcade behind made me nervous. Davis and I were riding side by side, right after the Arab. About 11 o'clock it had become really chilly, and the dozing boys roused up and began to inquire how far it was to Ramlah yet, and to demand that the Arab hurry along faster. I gave it up then, and my heart sank within me, because of course they would come up to scold the Arab. I knew I had to take the rear again. In my sorrow I unconsciously took to my pipe, my only comfort. As I touched the match to it the whole company came lumbering up and crowding my horse's rump and flanks. A whiff of smoke drifted back over my shoulder, and—

"The suffering Moses!"

"Whew!"

"By George, who opened that graveyard?"

"Boys, that Arab's been swallowing something dead!"

Right away there was a gap behind us. Whiff after whiff sailed airily back, and each one widened the breach. Within fifteen seconds the barking, and gasping, and sneezing, and coughing of the boys, and their angry abuse of the Arab guide, had dwindled to a murmur, and Davis and I were alone with the leader. Davis did not know what the matter was, and don't to this day. Occasionally he caught a faint film of the smoke and fell to scolding at the Arab and wondering how long he had been decaying in that way. Our boys kept on dropping back further and further, till at last they were only in hearing, not in sight. And every time they started gingerly forward to reconnoitre—or shoot the Arab, as they proposed to do—I let them get within good fair range of my relic (she would carry seventy yards with wonderful precision), and then wafted a whiff among them that sent them gasping and strangling to the rear again. I kept my gun well charged and ready, and twice within the hour I decoyed the boys right up to my horse's tail, and then with one malarious blast emptied the saddles, almost. I never heard an Arab abused so in my life. He really owed his preservation to me, because for one entire hour I stood between him and certain death. The boys would have killed him if they could have got by me.

By and by, when the company were far in the rear, I put away my pipe—I was getting fearfully dry and crisp about the gills and rather blown with good diligent work—and spurred my animated trance up alongside the Arab and stopped him and asked for water. He unslung his little gourd-shaped earthenware jug, and I put it under my moustache and took a long, glorious, satisfying draught. I was going to scour the mouth of the jug a little, but I saw that I had brought the whole train together once more by my delay, and that they were all anxious to drink too—and would have been long ago if the Arab had not pretended that he was out of water. So I hastened to pass the vessel to Davis. He took a mouthful, and never said a word, but climbed off his horse and lay down calmly in the road. I felt sorry for Davis. It was too late now, though, and Dan was drinking. Dan got down too, and hunted for a soft place. I thought I heard Dan say, "That Arab's friends ought to keep him in alcohol or else take him out and bury him somewhere." All the boys took a drink and climbed down. It is not well to go into further particulars. Let us draw the curtain upon this act.

Well, now, to think that after three changing years I should hear from that curious old relic again, and see Dan advertising it for sale for the benefit of a benevolent object. Dan is not treating that present right. I gave that pipe to him for a keepsake. However, he probably finds that it keeps away custom and interferes with business. It is the most convincing inanimate object in all this part of the world, perhaps. Dan and I were room-mates in all that long "Quaker City" voyage, and whenever I desired to have a little season of privacy I used to fire up on that pipe and persuade Dan to go out; and he seldom waited to change his clothes, either. In about a quarter, or from that to three-quarters of a minute, he would be propping up the smoke-stack on the upper deck and cursing. I wonder how the faithful old relic is going to sell?

1870

A DARING ATTEMPT AT A SOLUTION OF IT

The Fenian invasion failed because George Francis Train was absent. There was no lack of men, arms, or ammunition, but there was sad need of Mr. Train's organizing power, his coolness and caution, his tranquillity, his strong good sense, his modesty and reserve, his secrecy, his taciturnity and above all his frantic and bloodthirsty courage. Mr. Train and his retiring and diffident private secretary were obliged to be absent, though the former must certainly have been lying at the point of death, else nothing could have kept him from hurrying to the front, and offering his heart's best blood for the Downtrodden People he so loves, so worships, so delights to champion. He *must* have been in a disabled condition, else nothing could have kept him from invading Canada at the head of his "children."

And indeed, this modern Samson, solitary and alone, with his formidable jaw, would have been a more troublesome enemy than five times the Fenians that did invade Canada, because *they* could be made to retire, but G.F. would never leave the field while there was an audience before him, either armed or helpless. The invading Fenians were wisely cautious, knowing that such of them as were caught would be likely to hang; but the Champion would have stood in no such danger. There is no law, military or civil, for hanging persons afflicted in his peculiar way.

He was not present, alas!—save in spirit. He could not and would not waste so fine an opportunity, though, to send some ecstatic lunacy over the wires, and so he wound up a ferocious telegram with this:

WITH VENGEANCE STEEPED IN WORMWOOD'S GALL!
D—D OLD ENGLAND, SAY WE ALL!
  And keep your powder dry.

GEO. FRANCIS TRAIN.
SHERMAN HOUSE,
CHICAGO, NOON, Thursday, May 26.

  P.S.—Just arrived and addressed grand Fenian meeting in Fenian Armory, donating $50.

This person could be made really useful by roosting him on some Hatteras lighthouse or other prominence where storms prevail, because it takes so much wind to keep him going that he probably moves in the midst of a dead calm wherever he travels.

1870

THE EUROPEAN WAR

First Day
THE EUROPEAN WAR!!!
NO BATTLE YET!!!
HOSTILITIES IMMINENT!!!
TREMENDOUS EXCITEMENT.
AUSTRIA ARMING!

BERLIN, Tuesday.

No battle has been fought yet. But hostilities may burst forth any week.

There is tremendous excitement here over news from the front that two companies of French soldiers are assembling there.

It is rumoured that Austria is arming—what with, is not known.

Second Day
THE EUROPEAN WAR
NO BATTLE YET!
FIGHTING IMMINENT.
AWFUL EXCITEMENT.
RUSSIA SIDES WITH PRUSSIA!
ENGLAND NEUTRAL!!
AUSTRIA NOT ARMING.

BERLIN, Wednesday.

No battle has been fought yet. However, all thoughtful men feel that the land may be drenched with blood before the Summer is over.

There is an awful excitement here over the rumour that two companies of Prussian troops have concentrated on the border. German confidence remains unshaken!!

There is news to the effect that Russia espouses the cause of Prussia and will bring 4,000,000 men to the field.

England proclaims strict neutrality.

The report that Austria is arming needs confirmation.

Third Day
THE EUROPEAN WAR
NO BATTLE YET!

BLOODSHED IMMINENT!!

ENORMOUS EXCITEMENT!!

INVASION OF PRUSSIA!!

INVASION OF FRANCE!!!

RUSSIA SIDES WITH FRANCE.

ENGLAND STILL NEUTRAL!

FIRING HEARD!

THE EMPEROR TO TAKE COMMAND.

PARIS, Thursday.

No battle has been fought yet. But Field Marshal McMahon telegraphs thus to the Emperor:

"If the Frinch airmy survoives until Christmas there'll be throuble. Forninst this fact it would be sagacious if the divil wint the rounds of his establishment to prepare for the occasion, and tuk the precaution to warrum up the Prussian depairtment a bit agin the day.

MIKE."

There is an enormous state of excitement here over news from the front to the effect that yesterday France and Prussia were simultaneously invaded by the two bodies of troops which lately assembled on the border. Both armies conducted their invasions secretly and are now hunting around for each other on opposite sides of the border.

Russia espouses the cause of France. She will bring 200,000 men to the field.

England continues to remain neutral.

Firing was heard yesterday in the direction of Blucherberg, and for a while the excitement was intense. However the people reflected that the country in that direction is uninhabitable, and impassable by anything but birds, they became quiet again.

The Emperor sends his troops to the field with immense enthusiasm. He will lead them in person, when they return.

Fourth Day
THE EUROPEAN WAR!
NO BATTLE YET!!

THE TROOPS GROWING OLD!

BUT BITTER STRIFE IMMINENT!

PRODIGIOUS EXCITEMENT!
THE INVASIONS SUCCESSFULLY ACCOMPLISHED
AND THE INVADERS SAFE!
RUSSIA SIDES WITH BOTH SIDES
ENGLAND WILL FIGHT BOTH!

LONDON, Friday.

No battle has been fought thus far, but a million impetuous soldiers are gritting their teeth at each other across the border, and the most serious fears entertained that if they do not die of old age first, there will be bloodshed in this war yet.

The prodigious patriotic excitement goes on. In Prussia, per Prussian telegrams, though contradicted from France. In France, per French telegrams, though contradicted from Prussia.

The Prussian invasion of France was a magnificent success. The military failed to find the French, but made good their return to Prussia without the loss of a single man. The French invasion of Prussia is also demonstrated to have been a brilliant and successful achievement. The army failed to find the Prussians, but made good their return to the Vaterland without bloodshed, after having invaded as much as they wanted to.

There is glorious news from Russia to the effect that she will side with both sides.

Also from England—she will fight both sides.

LONDON, Thursday evening.

I rushed over too soon. I shall return home on Tuesday's steamer and wait until the war begins.

1870

FAVORS FROM CORRESPONDENTS

An unknown friend in Cleveland sends me a printed paragraph, signed "Lucretia," and says: "I venture to forward to you the enclosed article taken from a news correspondence in a New Haven paper, feeling confident that for gushing tenderness it has never been equalled. Even that touching Western production which you printed in the June GALAXY by way of illustrating what Californian journalists term 'hogwash,' is thin when compared with the unctuous ooze of 'Lucretia.'" The Clevelander has a correct judgment, as "Lucretia's" paragraph, hereunto appended, will show:

One lovely morning last week, the pearly gates of heaven were left ajar, and white-robed angels earthward came, bearing on their snowy pinions a lovely babe. Silently, to a quiet home nest, where love and peace abide, the angels came and placed the infant softly on a young mother's arm, saying in sweet musical strains, "Lady, the Saviour bids you take this child and nurse it for him." The low-toned music died away as the angels passed upward to their bright home; but the baby girl sleeps quietly in her new-found home. We wish thee joy, young parents, in thy happiness.

This, if I have been rightly informed, is not the customary method of acquiring offspring, and for all its seeming plausibility it does not look to me to be above suspicion. I have lived many years in this world, and I never knew of an infant being brought to a party by angels, or other unauthorized agents, but it made more or less talk in the neighborhood. It may be, Miss Lucretia, that the angels consider New Haven a more eligible place to raise children in than the realms of eternal day, and are capable of deliberately transferring infants from the one locality to the other; but I shall have to get you to excuse me. I look at it differently. It would be hard to get me to believe such a thing. And I will tell you why. However, never mind. You know, yourself, that the thing does not stand to reason. Still, if you were present when the babe was brought so silently to that quiet home nest, and placed in that soft manner on the young mother's arm, and if you heard the sweet musical strains which the messengers made, and could not recognize the tune, and feel justified in believing that it and likewise the messengers themselves were of super-sublunary origin, I pass. And so I leave the question open. But I will say, and do say, that I have not read anything sweeter than that paragraph for seventy or eighty years.

Another correspondent writes as follows from New York:

Having read your "Beef Contract" in the May GALAXY with a great deal of gratification, I showed it to a friend of mine, who after reading it said he did not believe a word of it, and that he was sure it was nothing but a *pack of lies*; that it was a libel on the Government, and the man who wrote it ought to be prosecuted. I thought this was as good as the "Contract" itself, and knew it would afford you some amusement.

Yours truly,   S.S.G.

That does amuse me, but does not surprise me. It is not possible to write a burlesque so broad that some innocent will not receive it in good faith as being a solemn statement of fact. Two of the lamest that ever were cobbled up by literary shoemakers went the rounds two or three months ago, and excited the wonder and led captive the faith of many unprejudiced people. One was a sickly invention about a remote valley in Arizona where all the lost hair-pins and such odds and ends as had disappeared from the toilet tables of the world for a generation, had somehow been mysteriously gathered together; and this poor little production wound up with a "prophecy" by an Apache squaw to the effect that "By'm'by heap muchee shake—big town muchee shake all down"; a "prophecy" which pointed inexorably at San Francisco and was awfully suggestive of its coming fate. The other shallow invention was one about some mud-turtle of a Mississippi diving-bell artist finding an ancient copper canoe, roofed and hermetically sealed, and believed to contain the remains of De Soto. Now, it could not have marred, but only symmetrically finished, so feeble an imposture as that, to have added that De Soto's name was deciphered upon a tombstone which was found tagging after the sunken canoe by a string. Plenty of people even believed that story of a South American doctor who had discovered a method of chopping off people's heads and putting them on again without discommoding the party of the second part, and who finally got a couple of heads mixed up and transposed, yet did the fitting of them on so neatly that even the experimentees themselves thought everything was right, until each found that his restored head was recalling, believing in, and searching after moles, scars, and other marks which had never existed upon his body, and at the same time refusing to remember or recognize similar marks which had always existed upon the said body. A "Bogus Proclamation" is a legitimate inspiration of genius, but any infant can contrive such things as those I have been speaking of. They really require no more brains than it does to be a "practical joker." Perhaps it is not risking too much to say that even the innocuous small reptile they call the "village wag" is able to build such inventions. . . . Before I end this paragraph and subject, I wish to remark that maybe the gentleman who said my "Beef Contract" article was a libel upon the Government was right —though I had certainly always thought differently about it. I wrote that article in Washington, in November, 1867, during Andrew Johnson's reign. It was suggested by Senator Stewart's account of a tedious, tiresome, and exasperating search which he had made through the Land Office and the Treasury Department, among no end of lofty and supercilious clerks, to find out something which he ought to have been able to find out at ten minutes' notice. I mislaid the MS. at the time, and never found it again until last April. It was not a libel on the Government in 1867. Mr. Stewart still lives to testify to that.

From Boston a correspondent writes as follows: "Please make a memorandum of this drop of comfort which I once heard a child-hating bachelor offer to his nieces at their FATHER's funeral: 'Remember, children, this happens only once in your lifetime, and don't cry—it can't possibly occur again!' "

From Alabama "A Friend" responds to our call for touching obituaries, with the following "from an old number of the 'Tuscaloosa Observer.'" The disease of this sufferer (as per third stanza) will probably never attack the author of his obituary—and for good and sufficient reasons:

> Farewell, thou earthy friend of mine,
> The messenger was sent, why do we repine,
> Why should we grieve and weep,
> In Jesus he fell asleep.

Around his bed his friends did stand,
Nursing with a willing hand;
Anxiety great with medical skill,
The fever raged he still was ill.

His recovery we prayed but in vain,
The disease located on his brain,
Death succeeded human skill,
Pulse ceased to beat, death chilled every limb.

Death did not distorture his pale face,
How short on earth was his Christian race
With tears flowing from the youth and furrowed face,
He was consigned to his last resting, resting place.

The lofty oaks spreading branches
Shades the grave of his dear sister Addie and sweet little Frances,
Three children now in Heaven rest,
Should parents grieve? Jesus called and blest.

1870

A GENERAL REPLY

When I was sixteen or seventeen years old, a splendid idea burst upon me—a bran-new one, which had never occurred to anybody before: I would write some "pieces" and take them down to the editor of the "Republican," and ask him to give me his plain, unvarnished opinion of their value! Now, as old and threadbare as the idea was, it was fresh and beautiful to me, and it went flaming and crashing through my system like the genuine lightning and thunder of originality. I wrote the pieces. I wrote them with that placid confidence and that happy facility which only want of practice and absence of literary experience can give. There was not one sentence in them that cost half an hour's weighing and shaping and trimming and fixing. Indeed, it is possible that there was no one sentence whose mere wording cost even one-sixth of that time. If I remember rightly, there was not one single erasure or interlineation in all that chaste manuscript. [I have since lost that large belief in my powers, and likewise that marvellous perfection of execution.] I started down to the "Republican" office with my pocket full of manuscripts, my brain full of dreams, and a grand future opening out before me. I knew perfectly well that the editor would be ravished with my pieces. But presently——

However, the particulars are of no consequence. I was only about to say that a shadowy sort of doubt just then intruded upon my exaltation. Another came, and another. Pretty soon a whole procession of them. And at last, when I stood before the "Republican" office and looked up at its tall, unsympathetic front, it seemed hardly *me* that could have "chinned" its towers ten minutes before, and was now so shrunk up and pitiful that if I dared to step on the gratings I should probably go through.

At about that crisis the editor, the very man I had come to consult, came down stairs, and halted a moment to pull at his wristbands and settle his coat to its place, and he happened to notice that I was eyeing him wistfully. He asked me what I wanted. I answered, "Nothing!" with a boy's own meekness and shame; and, dropping my eyes, crept humbly round till I was fairly in the alley, and then drew a big grateful breath of relief, and picked up my heels and ran!

I was satisfied. I wanted no more. It was my first attempt to get a "plain unvarnished opinion" out of a literary man concerning my compositions, and it has lasted me until now. And in these latter days, whenever I receive a bundle of MS. through the mail, with a request that I will pass judgment upon its merits, I feel like saying to the author, "If you had only taken your piece to some grim and stately newspaper office, where you did not know anybody, you would not have so fine an opinion of your production as it is easy to see you have now."

Every man who becomes editor of a newspaper or magazine straightway begins to receive MSS. from literary aspirants, together with requests that he will deliver judgment upon the same. And after complying in eight or ten instances, he finally takes refuge in a general sermon upon the subject, which he inserts in his publication, and always afterward refers such correspondents to that sermon for answer. I have at last reached this station in my literary career. I now cease to reply privately to my applicants for advice, and proceed to construct my public sermon.

As all letters of the sort I am speaking of contain the very same matter, differently worded, I offer as a fair average specimen the last one I have received:

Oct. 3.

Mark Twain, Esq.

Dear Sir: I am a youth, just out of school and ready to start in life. I have looked around, but don't see anything that suits exactly. Is a literary life easy and profitable, or is it the hard times it is generally put up for? It *must* be easier than a good many if not most of the occupations, and I feel drawn to launch out on it, make or break, sink or swim, survive or perish. Now, what are the conditions of success in literature? You need not be afraid to paint the thing just as it is. I can't do any worse than fail. Everything else offers the same. When I thought of the law—yes, and five or six other professions—I found the same thing was the case every time, viz: *all full—overrun—every profession so crammed that success is rendered impossible—too many hands and not enough work.* But I must try *something,* and so I turn at last to literature. Something tells me that that is the true bent of my genius, if I have any. I enclose some of my pieces. Will you read them over and give me your candid, unbiassed opinion of them? And now I hate to trouble you, but you have been a young man yourself, and what I want is for you to get me a newspaper job of writing to do. You know many newspaper people, and I am entirely unknown. And will you make the best terms you can for me? though I do not expect what might be called high wages at first, of course. Will you candidly say what such articles as these I enclose are worth? I have plenty of them. If you should sell these and let me know, I can send you more, as good and may be better than these. An early reply, etc.

Yours truly, etc.

I will answer you in good faith. Whether my remarks shall have great value or not, or my suggestions be worth following, are problems which I take great pleasure in leaving entirely to you for solution. To begin: There are several questions in your letter which only a man's life experience can eventually answer for him—not another man's words. I will simply skip those.

1. Literature, like the ministry, medicine, the law, and *all other* occupations, is cramped and hindered for want of men to do the work, not want of work to do. When people tell you the reverse, they speak that which is not true. If you desire to test this, you need only hunt up a first-class editor, reporter, business manager, foreman of a shop, mechanic, or artist in any branch of industry, and *try to hire him*. You will find that he is already hired. He is sober, industrious, capable, and reliable, and is always in demand. He cannot get a day's holiday except by courtesy of his employer, or his city, or the great general public. But if you need idlers, shirkers, half-instructed, unambitious, and comfort-seeking editors, reporters, lawyers, doctors, and mechanics, apply anywhere. There are millions of them to be had at the dropping of a handkerchief.

2. No; I must not and will not venture any opinion whatever as to the literary merit of your productions. The public is the only critic whose judgment is worth anything at all. Do not take my poor word for this, but reflect a moment and take your own. For instance, if Sylvanus Cobb or T. S. Arthur had submitted their maiden MSS. to you, you would have said, with tears in your eyes, "Now please don't write any more!" But you see yourself how popular they are. And if it had been left to you, you would have said the "Marble Faun" was tiresome, and that even "Paradise Lost" lacked cheerfulness; but you know they sell. Many wiser and better men than you pooh-poohed Shakespeare, even as late as two centuries ago; but still

that old party has outlived those people. No, I will not sit in judgment upon your literature. If I honestly and conscientiously praised it, I might thus help to inflict a lingering and pitiless bore upon the public; if I honestly and conscientiously condemned it, I mght thus rob the world of an undeveloped and unsuspected Dickens or Shakespeare.

3. I shrink from hunting up literary labor for you to do and receive pay for. Whenever your literary productions have proved for themselves that they have a real value, you will never have to go around hunting for remunerative literary work to do. You will require more hands than you have now, and more brains than you probably ever will have, to do even half the work that will be offered you. Now, in order to arrive at the proof of value hereinbefore spoken of, one needs only to adopt a very simple and certainly very sure process; and that is, to *write without pay until somebody offers pay.* If nobody offers pay within three years, the candidate may look upon this circumstance with the most implicit confidence as the sign that sawing wood is what he was intended for. If he has any wisdom at all, then, he will retire with dignity and assume his heaven-appointed vocation.

In the above remarks I have only offered a course of action which Mr. Dickens and most other successful literary men had to follow; but it is a course which will find no sympathy with my client, perhaps. The young literary aspirant is a very, very curious creature. He knows that if he wished to become a tinner, the master smith would require him to prove the possession of a good character, and would require him to promise to stay in the shop three years—possibly four —and would make him sweep out and bring water and build fires all the first year, and let him learn to black stoves in the intervals; and for these good honest services would pay him two suits of cheap clothes and his board; and next year he would begin to receive instructions in the trade, and a dollar a week would be added to his emoluments; and two dollars would be added the third year, and three the fourth; and *then,* if he had become a first-rate tinner, he would get about fifteen or twenty, or may be thirty dollars a week, with never a possibility of getting seventy-five while he lived. If he wanted to become a mechanic of any other kind, he would have to undergo this same tedious, ill-paid apprenticeship. If he wanted to become a lawyer or a doctor, he would have fifty times worse; for he would get nothing at all during his long apprenticeship, and in addition would have to pay a large sum for tuition, and have the privilege of boarding and clothing himself. The literary aspirant knows all this, and yet he has the hardihood to present himself for reception into the literary guild and ask to share its high honors and emoluments, without a single twelvemonth's apprenticeship to show in excuse for his presumption! He would smile pleasantly if he were asked to make even so simple a thing as a ten-cent tin dipper without previous instruction in the art; but, all green and ignorant, wordy, pompously-assertive, ungrammatical, and with a vague, distorted knowledge of men and the world acquired in a back country village, he will serenely take up so dangerous a weapon as a pen, and attack the most formidable subject that finance, commerce, war, or politics can furnish him withal. It would be laughable if it were not so sad and so pitiable. The poor fellow would not intrude upon the tin-shop without an apprenticeship, but is willing to seize and wield with unpractised hand an instrument which is able to overthrow dynasties, change religions, and decree the weal or woe of nations.

If my correspondent will write free of charge for the newspapers of his neighborhood, it will be one of the strangest things that ever happened if he does not get all the employment he can attend to on those terms. And as soon as ever his writings are worth money, plenty of people will hasten to offer it.

And by way of serious and well-meant encouragement, I wish to urge upon him once more the truth that acceptable writers for the press are so scarce that book and periodical publishers are seeking them constantly, and with a vigilance that never grows heedless for a moment.

1870

GOLDSMITH'S FRIEND ABROAD AGAIN

NOTE.—No experience is set down in the following letters which had to be invented. Fancy is not needed to give variety to the history of a Chinaman's sojourn in America. Plain fact is amply sufficient.

LETTER I

SHANGHAI, 18—

Dear Ching-Foo: It is all settled, and I am to leave my oppressed and overburdened native land and cross the sea to that noble realm where all are free and all equal, and none reviled or abused—America! America, whose precious privilege it is to call herself the Land of the Free and the Home of the Brave. We and all that are about us here look over the waves longingly, contrasting the privations of this our birthplace with the opulent comfort of that happy refuge. We know how America has welcomed the Germans and the Frenchmen and the stricken and sorrowing Irish, and we know how she has given them bread and work and liberty, and how grateful they are. And we know that America stands ready to welcome all other oppressed peoples and offer her abundance to all that come, without asking what their nationality is, or their creed or color. And, without being told it, we know that the foreign sufferers she has rescued from oppression and starvation are the most eager of her children to welcome us, because, having suffered themselves, they know what suffering is, and having been generously succored, they long to be generous to other unfortunates and thus show that magnanimity is not wasted upon them.

AH SONG HI

LETTER II

At Sea, 18—

Dear Ching-Foo: We are far away at sea now, on our way to the beautiful Land of the Free and Home of the Brave. We shall soon be where all men are alike, and where sorrow is not known.

The good American who hired me to go to his country is to pay me $12 a month, which is immense wages, you know—twenty times as much as one gets in China. My passage in the ship is a very large sum—indeed, it is a fortune—and this I must pay myself eventually, but I am allowed ample time to make it good to my employer in, he advancing it now. For a mere form, I have turned over my wife, my boy, and my two daughters to my employer's partner for security for the payment of the ship fare. But my employer says they are in no danger of being sold, for he knows I will be faithful to him, and that is the main security.

I thought I would have twelve dollars to begin life with in America, but the American Consul took two of them for making a certificate that I was shipped on the steamer. He has no right to do more than charge the ship two dollars for *one* certificate for the *ship*, with the number of her Chinese passengers set down in it; but he chooses to force a certificate upon each and every Chinaman and put the two dollars in his pocket. As 1300 of my countrymen are in this vessel, the Consul received $2600 for certificates. My employer tells me that the Government at Washington know of this fraud, and are so bitterly opposed to the existence of such a wrong that they tried hard to have the extor——the fee, I mean, legalized by the last Congress;* but as the bill did not pass, the Consul will have to take the fee dishonestly until next Congress makes it legitimate. It is a great and good and noble country, and hates all forms of vice and chicanery.

We are in that part of the vessel always reserved for my countrymen. It is called the steerage. It is kept for us, my employer says, because it is not subject to changes of temperature and dangerous drafts of air. It is only another instance of the loving unselfishness of the Americans for all unfortunate foreigners. The steerage is a little crowded, and rather warm and close, but no doubt it is best for us that it should be so.

* Pacific and Mediterranean steamship bills.—M.T.

Yesterday our people got to quarrelling among themselves, and the captain turned a volume of hot steam upon a mass of them and scalded eighty or ninety of them more or less severely. Flakes and ribbons of skin came off some of them. There was wild shrieking and struggling while the vapor enveloped the great throng, and so some who were not scalded got trampled upon and hurt. We do not complain, for my employer says this is the usual way of quieting disturbances on board the ship, and that it is done in the cabins among the Americans every day or two.

Congratulate me, Ching-Foo! In ten days more I shall step upon the shore of America, and be received by her great-hearted people; and I shall straighten myself up and feel that I am a free man among freemen.

AH SONG HI

LETTER III

SAN FRANCISCO, 18—

Dear Ching-Foo: I stepped ashore jubilant! I wanted to dance, shout, sing, worship the generous Land of the Free and Home of the Brave. But as I walked from the gang-plank a man in a gray uniform* kicked me violently behind and told me to look out—so my employer translated it. As I turned, another officer of the same kind struck me with a short club and also instructed me to look out. I was about to take hold of my end of the pole which had mine and Hong-Wo's basket and things suspended from it, when a third officer hit me with his club to signify that I was to drop it, and then kicked me to signify that he was satisfied with my promptness. Another person came now, and searched all through our basket and bundles, emptying everything out on the dirty wharf. Then this person and another searched us all over. They found a little package of opium sewed into the artificial part of Hong-Wo's queue, and they took that, and also they made him prisoner and handed him over to an officer, who marched him away. They took his luggage, too, because of his crime, and as our luggage was so mixed together that they could not tell mine from his, they took it all. When I offered to help divide it, they kicked me and desired me to look out.

Having now no baggage and no companion, I told my employer that if he was willing, I would walk about a little and see the city

* Policeman.—M.T.

and the people until he needed me. I did not like to seem disappointed with my reception in the good land of refuge for the oppressed, and so I looked and spoke as cheerily as I could. But he said, wait a minute—I must be vaccinated to prevent my taking the small-pox. I smiled and said I had already had the small-pox, as he could see by the marks, and so I need not wait to be "vaccinated," as he called it. But he said it was the law, and I must be vaccinated anyhow. The doctor would never let me pass, for the law obliged him to vaccinate all Chinamen and charge them *ten dollars apiece* for it, and I might be sure that no doctor who would be the servant of that law would let a fee slip through his fingers to accommodate any absurd fool who had seen fit to have the disease in some other country. And presently the doctor came and did his work and took my last penny—my ten dollars which were the hard savings of nearly a year and a half of labor and privation. Ah, if the law-makers had only known there were plenty of doctors in the city glad of a chance to vaccinate people for a dollar or two, they would never have put the price up so high against a poor friendless Irish, or Italian, or Chinese pauper fleeing to the good land to escape hunger and hard times.

AH SONG HI

LETTER IV

SAN FRANCISCO, 18—

Dear Ching-Foo: I have been here about a month now, and am learning a little of the language every day. My employer was disappointed in the matter of hiring us out to service on the plantations in the far eastern portion of this continent. His enterprise was a failure, and so he set us all free, merely taking measures to secure to himself the repayment of the passage money which he paid for us. We are to make this good to him out of the first moneys we earn here. He says it is sixty dollars apiece.

We were thus set free about two weeks after we reached here. We had been massed together in some small houses up to that time, waiting. I walked forth to seek my fortune. I was to begin life a stranger in a strange land, without a friend, or a penny, or any clothes but those I had on my back. I had not any advantage on my side in the world—not one, except good health and the lack of any necessity to waste any time or anxiety on the watching of my baggage. No, I forget. I reflected that I had one prodigious advantage over paupers in other lands—I was in America! I was in the heaven-provided refuge of the oppressed and the forsaken!

Just as that comforting thought passed through my mind, some young men set a fierce dog on me. I tried to defend myself, but could do nothing. I retreated to the recess of a closed doorway, and there the dog had me at his mercy, flying at my throat and face or any part of my body that presented itself. I shrieked for help, but the young men only jeered and laughed. Two men in gray uniforms (policemen is their official title) looked on for a minute and then walked leisurely away. But a man stopped them and brought them back and told them it was a shame to leave me in such distress. Then the two policemen beat off the dog with small clubs, and a comfort it was to be rid of him, though I was just rags and blood from head to foot. The man who brought the policemen asked the young men why they abused me in that way, and they said they didn't want any of his meddling. And they said to him:

"This Ching divil comes till Ameriky to take the bread out o' dacent intilligent white men's mouths, and whin they try to defind their rights there's a dale o' fuss made about it."

They began to threaten my benefactor, and as he saw no friendliness in the faces that had gathered meanwhile, he went on his way. He got many a curse when he was gone. The policemen now told me I was under arrest and must go with them. I asked one of them what wrong I had done to any one that I should be arrested, and he only struck me with his club and ordered me to "hold my yop." With a jeering crowd of street boys and loafers at my heels, I was taken up an alley and into a stone-paved dungeon which had large cells all down one side of it, with iron gates to them. I stood up by a desk while a man behind it wrote down certain things about me on a slate. One of my captors said:

"Enter a charge against this Chinaman of being disorderly and disturbing the peace."

I attempted to say a word, but he said:

"Silence! Now ye had better go slow, my good fellow. This is two or three times you've tried to get off some of your d—d insolence. Lip won't do here. You've *got* to simmer down, and if you don't take to it paceable we'll see if we can't make you. Fat's your name?"

"Ah Song Hi."

"*Alias* what?"

I said I did not understand, and he said what he wanted was my *true* name, for he guessed I picked up this one since I stole my last chickens. They all laughed loudly at that.

Then they searched me. They found nothing, of course. They seemed very angry and asked who I supposed would "go my bail or pay my fine." When they explained these things to me, I said I had done nobody any harm, and why should I need to have bail or pay a fine? Both of them kicked me and warned me that I would find it to my advantage to try and be as civil as convenient. I protested that I had not meant anything disrespectful. Then one of them took me to one side and said:

"Now look here, Johnny, it's no use you playing softy wid us. We mane business, ye know; and the sooner ye put us on the scent of a V, the asier ye'll save yerself from a dale of trouble. Ye can't get out o' this for anny less. Who's your frinds?"

I told him I had not a single friend in all the land of America, and that I was far from home and help, and very poor. And I begged him to let me go.

He gathered the slack of my blouse collar in his grip and jerked and shoved and hauled at me across the dungeon, and then unlocking an iron cell-gate thrust me in with a kick and said:

"Rot there, ye furrin spawn, till ye lairn that there's no room in America for the likes of ye or your nation."

AH SONG HI

LETTER V

SAN FRANCISCO, 18—

Dear Ching-Foo: You will remember that I had just been thrust violently into a cell in the city prison when I wrote last. I stumbled and fell on some one. I got a blow and a curse; and on top of these a kick or two and a shove. In a second or two it was plain that I was in a nest of prisoners and was being "passed around"—for the instant I was knocked out of the way of one I fell on the head or heels of another and was promptly ejected, only to land on a third prisoner and get a new contribution of kicks and curses and a new destination. I brought up at last in an unoccupied corner, very much battered and bruised and sore, but glad enough to be let alone for a little while. I was on the flag-stones, for there was no furniture in the den except a long, broad board, or combination of boards, like a barn door, and this bed was accommodating five or six persons, and that was its full capacity. They lay stretched side by side, snoring—when not fighting. One end of the board was four inches higher than the other, and so the slant answered for a pillow. There were no blankets, and the night was a little chilly; the nights are always a little chilly in San Francisco, though never severely cold. The board was a deal more comfortable than the stones, and occasionally some flag-stone plebeian like me would try to creep to a place on it; and then the aristocrats would hammer him good and make him think a flag pavement was a nice enough place after all.

I lay quiet in my corner, stroking my bruises and listening to the revelations the prisoners made to each other—and to me—for some that were near me talked to me a good deal. I had long had an idea that Americans, being free, had no need of prisons, which are a contrivance of despots for keeping restless patriots out of mischief. So I was considerably surprised to find out my mistake.

Ours was a big general cell, it seemed, for the temporary accommodation of all comers whose crimes were trifling. Among us there were two Americans, two "Greasers" (Mexicans), a Frenchman, a German, four Irishmen, a Chilenean (and, in the next cell, only separated from us by a grating, two women), all drunk, and all more or less noisy; and as night fell and advanced, they grew more and more discontented and disorderly, occasionally shaking the prison bars and glaring through them at the slowly pacing officer, and cursing him with all their hearts. The two women were nearly middle-aged, and they had only had enough liquor to stimulate instead of stupefy them. Consequently they would fondle and kiss each other for some minutes, and then fall to fighting and keep it up till they were just two grotesque tangles of rags and blood and tumbled hair. Then they would rest awhile, and pant and swear. While they were affectionate they always spoke of each other as "ladies," but while they were fighting "strumpet" was the mildest name they could think of—and they could only make that do by tacking some sounding profanity to it. In their last fight, which was toward midnight, one of them bit off the other's finger, and then the officer interfered and put the "Greaser" into the "dark cell" to answer for it—because the woman that did it laid it on him, and the other woman did not deny it because, as she said afterward, she "wanted another crack at the huzzy when her finger quit hurting," and so she did not want her removed. By this time those two women had mutilated each other's clothes to that extent that there was not sufficient left to cover their nakedness. I found that one of these creatures had spent nine years in the county jail, and that the other one had spent about four or five years in the

same place. They had done it from choice. As soon as they were discharged from captivity they would go straight and get drunk, and
then steal some trifling thing while an officer was observing them.
That would entitle them to another two months in jail, and there
they would occupy clean, airy apartments, and have good food in
plenty, and being at no expense at all, they could make shirts for the
clothiers at half a dollar apiece and thus keep themselves in smoking
tobacco and such other luxuries as they wanted. When the two
months were up, they would go just as straight as they could walk to
Mother Leonard's and get drunk; and from there to Kearny street
and steal something; and thence to this city prison, and next day
back to the old quarters in the county jail again. One of them had
really kept this up for nine years and the other four or five, and
both said they meant to end their days in that prison.* Finally, both
these creatures fell upon me while I was dozing with my head against
their grating, and battered me considerably, because they discovered
that I was a Chinaman, and they said I was "a bloody interlopin'
loafer come from the divil's own country to take the bread out of
dacent people's mouths and put down the wages for work whin it was
all a Christian could do to kape body and sowl together as it was."
"Loafer" means one who will not work.

Ah Song Hi

LETTER VI

San Francisco, 18—

Dear Ching-Foo: To continue—the two women became reconciled
to each other again through the common bond of interest and sympathy created between them by pounding me in partnership, and
when they had finished me they fell to embracing each other again
and swearing more eternal affection like that which had subsisted between them all the evening, barring occasional interruptions. They
agreed to swear the finger-biting on the Greaser in open court, and
get him sent to the penitentiary for the crime of mayhem.

Another of our company was a boy of fourteen who had been
watched for some time by officers and teachers, and repeatedly detected in enticing young girls from the public schools to the lodgings
of gentlemen down town. He had been furnished with lures in the
form of pictures and books of a peculiar kind, and these he had

* The former of the two did.—M.T.

distributed among his clients. There were likenesses of fifteen of these young girls on exhibition (only to prominent citizens and persons in authority, it was said, though most people came to get a sight) at the police headquarters, but no punishment at all was to be inflicted on the poor little misses. The boy was afterward sent into captivity at the House of Correction for some months, and there was a strong disposition to punish the gentlemen who had employed the boy to entice the girls, but as that could not be done without making public the names of those gentlemen and thus injuring them socially, the idea was finally given up.

There was also in our cell that night a photographer (a kind of artist who makes likenesses of people with a machine), who had been for some time patching the pictured heads of well-known and respectable young ladies to the nude, pictured bodies of another class of women; then from this patched creation he would make photographs and sell them privately at high prices to rowdies and blackguards, averring that these, the best young ladies of the city, had hired him to take their likenesses in that unclad condition. What a lecture the police judge read that photographer when he was convicted! He told him his crime was little less than an outrage. He abused that photographer till he almost made him sink through the floor, and then he fined him a hundred dollars. And he told him he might consider himself lucky that he didn't fine him a hundred and twenty-five dollars. They are awfully severe on crime here.

About two or two and a half hours after midnight, of that first experience of mine in the city prison, such of us as were dozing were awakened by a noise of beating and dragging and groaning, and in a little while a man was pushed into our den with a "There, d—n you, soak there a spell!"—and then the gate was closed and the officers went away again. The man who was thrust among us fell limp and helpless by the grating, but as nobody could reach him with a kick without the trouble of hitching along toward him or getting fairly up to deliver it, our people only grumbled at him, and cursed him, and called him insulting names—for misery and hardship do not make their victims gentle or charitable toward each other. But as he neither tried humbly to conciliate our people nor swore back at them, his unnatural conduct created surprise, and several of the party crawled to him where he lay in the dim light that came through the grating, and examined into his case. His head was very bloody and his wits were gone. After about an hour, he sat up and stared around; then his eyes grew more natural and he began to tell how that he was going along with a bag on his shoulder and a brace of policemen ordered him to stop, which he did not do—was chased and caught, beaten ferociously about the head on the way to the prison and after arrival there, and finally thrown into our den like a dog. And in a few seconds he sank down again and grew flighty of speech. One of our people was at last penetrated with something vaguely akin to compassion, may be, for he looked out through the gratings at the guardian officer pacing to and fro, and said:

"Say, Mickey, this shrimp's goin' to die."

"Stop your noise!" was all the answer he got. But presently our man tried it again. He drew himself to the gratings, grasping them with his hands, and looking out through them, sat waiting till the officer was passing once more, and then said:

"Sweetness, you'd better mind your eye, now, because you beats have killed this cuss. You've busted his head and he'll pass in his checks before sun-up. You better go for a doctor, now, you bet you had."

The officer delivered a sudden rap on our man's knuckles with his club, that sent him scampering and howling among the sleeping forms on the flag-stones, and an answering burst of laughter came from the half dozen policemen idling about the railed desk in the middle of the dungeon.

But there was a putting of heads together out there presently, and a conversing in low voices, which seemed to show that our man's talk had made an impression; and presently an officer went away in a hurry, and shortly came back with a person who entered our cell and felt the bruised man's pulse and threw the glare of a lantern on his drawn face, striped with blood, and his glassy eyes, fixed and vacant. The doctor examined the man's broken head also, and presently said:

"If you'd called me an hour ago I might have saved this man, may be—too late now."

Then he walked out into the dungeon and the officers surrounded him, and they kept up a low and earnest buzzing of conversation for fifteen minutes, I should think, and then the doctor took his departure from the prison. Several of the officers now came in and worked a little with the wounded man, but toward daylight he died.

It was the longest, longest night! And when the daylight came filtering reluctantly into the dungeon at last, it was the grayest, dreariest, saddest daylight! And yet, when an officer by and by turned off the sickly yellow gas flame, and immediately the gray of dawn became fresh and white, there was a lifting of my spirits that acknowledged and believed that the night *was* gone, and straightway I fell to stretching my sore limbs, and looking about me with a grateful sense of relief and a returning interest in life. About me lay the evidences that what seemed now a feverish dream and a nightmare was the memory of a reality instead. For on the boards lay four frowsy, ragged, bearded vagabonds, snoring—one turned end-for-end and resting an unclean foot, in a ruined stocking, on the hairy breast of a neighbor; the young boy was uneasy, and lay moaning in his sleep; other forms lay half revealed and half concealed about the floor; in the furthest corner the gray light fell upon a sheet, whose elevations and depressions indicated the places of the dead man's face and feet and folded hands; and through the dividing bars one could discern the almost nude forms of the two exiles from the county jail twined together in a drunken embrace, and sodden with sleep.

By and by all the animals in all the cages awoke, and stretched themselves, and exchanged a few cuffs and curses, and then began to clamor for breakfast. Breakfast was brought in at last—bread and beefsteak on tin plates, and black coffee in tin cups, and no grabbing allowed. And after several dreary hours of waiting, after this, we were all marched out into the dungeon and joined there by all manner of vagrants and vagabonds, of all shades and colors and nationalities, from the other cells and cages of the place; and pretty soon our whole menagerie was marched upstairs and locked fast behind a high railing in a dirty room with a dirty audience in it. And this audience stared at us, and at a man seated on high behind what they call a pulpit in this country, and at some clerks and other officials seated below him—and waited. This was the police court.

The court opened. Pretty soon I was compelled to notice that a culprit's nationality made for or against him in this court. Overwhelming proofs were necessary to convict an Irishman of crime, and even then his punishment amounted to little; Frenchmen, Spaniards, and Italians had strict and unprejudiced justice meted out to them, in exact accordance with the evidence; negroes were promptly punished, when there was the slightest preponderance of testimony against them; but Chinamen were punished *always*, apparently. Now this gave me some uneasiness, I confess. I knew that this state of things must of necessity be accidental, because in this country all men were free and equal, and one person could not take to himself an advantage not accorded to all other individuals. I knew that, and yet in spite of it I was uneasy.

And I grew still more uneasy, when I found that any succored and befriended refugee from Ireland or elsewhere could stand up before that judge and swear away the life or liberty or character of a refugee from China; but that by the law of the land *the Chinaman could not testify against the Irishman.* I was really and truly uneasy, but still my faith in the universal liberty that America accords and defends, and my deep veneration for the land that offered all distressed outcasts a home and protection, was strong within me, and I said to myself that it would all come out right yet.

AH SONG HI

LETTER VII

SAN FRANCISCO, 18—

Dear Ching-Foo: I was glad enough when my case came up. An hour's experience had made me as tired of the police court as of the dungeon. I was not uneasy about the result of the trial, but on the contrary felt that as soon as the large auditory of Americans present should hear how that the rowdies had set the dogs on me when I was going peacefully along the street, and how, when I was all torn and bleeding, the officers arrested *me* and put me in jail and let the rowdies go free, the gallant hatred of oppression which is part of the very flesh and blood of every American would be stirred to its utmost, and I should be instantly set at liberty. In truth I began to fear for the other side. There in full view stood the ruffians who had misused me, and I began to fear that in the first burst of generous anger occasioned by the revealment of what they had done, they might be harshly handled, and possibly even banished the country as having dishonored her and being no longer worthy to remain upon her sacred soil.

The official interpreter of the court asked my name, and then spoke it aloud so that all could hear. Supposing that all was now ready, I cleared my throat and began—in Chinese, because of my imperfect English:

"Hear, O high and mighty mandarin, and believe! As I went about my peaceful business in the street, behold certain men set a dog on me, and——"

"Silence!"

It was the judge that spoke. The interpreter whispered to me that I must keep perfectly still. He said that no statement would be received from me—I must only talk through my lawyer.

I had no lawyer. In the early morning a police court lawyer (termed, in the higher circles of society, a "shyster") had come into our den in the prison and offered his services to me, but I had been obliged to go without them because I could not pay in advance or give security. I told the interpreter how the matter stood. He said I must take my chances on the witnesses then. I glanced around, and my failing confidence revived.

"Call those four Chinamen yonder," I said. "They saw it all. I remember their faces perfectly. They will prove that the white men set the dog on me when I was not harming them."

"That won't work," said he. "In this country white men can testify against Chinamen all they want to, but *Chinamen ain't allowed to testify against white men!*"

What a chill went through me! And then I felt the indignant blood rise to my cheek at this libel upon the Home of the Oppressed, where all men are free and equal—perfectly equal—perfectly free and perfectly equal. I despised this Chinese-speaking Spaniard for his mean slander of the land that was sheltering and feeding him. I sorely wanted to sear his eyes with that sentence from the great and good American Declaration of Independence which we have copied in letters of gold in China and keep hung up over our family altars and in our temples—I mean the one about all men being created free and equal.

But woe is me, Ching-Foo, the man was right. He was right, after all. There were my witnesses, but I could not use them. But now came a new hope. I saw my white friend come in, and I felt that he had come there purposely to help me. I may almost say I knew it. So I grew easier. He passed near enough to me to say under his breath, "Don't be afraid," and then I had no more fear. But presently the rowdies recognized him and began to scowl at him in no friendly way, and to make threatening signs at him. The two officers that arrested me fixed their eyes steadily on his; he bore it well, but gave in presently, and dropped his eyes. They still gazed at his eyebrows, and every time he raised his eyes he encountered their winkless stare—until after a minute or two he ceased to lift his head at all. The judge had been giving some instructions privately to some one for a little while, but now he was ready to resume business. Then the trial so unspeakably important to me, and freighted with such prodigious consequence to my wife and children, began, progressed, ended, was recorded in the books, noted down by the newspaper reporters, and *forgotten* by everybody but me—all in the little space of two minutes!

"Ah Song Hi, Chinaman. Officers O'Flannigan and O'Flaherty, witnesses. Come forward, Officer O'Flannigan."

OFFICER—"He was making a disturbance in Kearny street."

JUDGE—"Any witnesses on the other side?"

No response. The white friend raised his eyes—encountered Officer O'Flaherty's—blushed a little—got up and left the courtroom, avoiding all glances and not taking his own from the floor.

JUDGE—"Give him five dollars or ten days."

In my desolation there was a glad surprise in the words; but it passed away when I found that he only meant that I was to be fined five dollars or imprisoned ten days longer in default of it.

There were twelve or fifteen Chinamen in our crowd of prisoners, charged with all manner of little thefts and misdemeanors, and their cases were quickly disposed of, as a general thing. When the charge came from a policeman or other white man, he made his statement and that was the end of it, unless the Chinaman's lawyer could find some white person to testify in his client's behalf; for, neither the accused Chinaman nor his countrymen being allowed to say anything, the statement of the officers or other white person was amply sufficient to convict. So, as I said, the Chinamen's cases were quickly disposed of, and fines and imprisonment promptly distributed among them. In one or two of the cases the charges against Chinamen were brought by Chinamen themselves, and in those cases Chinamen testified against Chinamen, through the interpreter; but the fixed rule of the court being that the *preponderance* of testimony in such cases should determine the prisoner's guilt or innocence, and there being nothing very binding about an oath administered to the lower orders of our people without the ancient solemnity of cutting off a chicken's head and burning some yellow paper at the same time, the interested parties naturally drum up a cloud of witnesses who are cheerfully willing to give evidence without ever knowing anything about the matter in hand. The judge has a custom of rattling through with as much of this testimony as his patience will stand, and then shutting off the rest and striking an average.

By noon all the business of the court was finished, and then several of us who had not fared well were remanded to prison; the judge went home; the lawyers, and officers, and spectators departed their several ways, and left the uncomely court-room to silence, solitude, and Stiggers, the newspaper reporter, which latter would now write up his items (said an ancient Chinaman to me), in the which he would praise all the policemen indiscriminately and abuse the Chinamen and dead people.

AH SONG HI
1870–71

"HOGWASH"

For five years I have preserved the following miracle of pointless imbecility and bathos, waiting to see if I could find anything in literature that was worse. But in vain. I have read it forty or fifty times, altogether, and with a steadily-increasing pleasurable disgust. I now offer it for competition as the sickliest specimen of sham sentimentality that exists. I almost always get it out and read it when I am low-spirited, and it has cheered many and many a sad hour for me. I will remark, in the way of general information, that in California, that land of felicitous nomenclature, the literary name of this sort of stuff is *"hogwash"*:

[From the "California Farmer."]
A TOUCHING INCIDENT.

Mr. Editor: I hand you the following for insertion, if you think it worthy of publication; it is a picture, though brief, of a living reality which the writer witnessed, within a little time since, in a luxurious city:

A beautiful lady sat beneath a verandah overshadowed by clustering vines; in her lap was a young infant, apparently asleep; the mother sat, as she supposed, unobserved, and lost in deep meditation. Richly-robed and surrounded with all the outward appearances of wealth and station, wife and mother and mistress of a splendid mansion and garden around it, it would have seemed as if the heart that could claim to be queen here should be a happy one. Alas! appearances are not always the true guide, for—

> That mother sat there like a statue awhile,
> When over her face beamed a sad, sad smile;
> Then she started and shudder'd as if terrible fears
> Were crushing her spirit—then came the hot tears.

And the wife and mother, with all that was seemingly joyous around her, gave herself up to the full sweep of agonizing sorrow. I gazed upon this picture for a little while, only, for my own tears fell freely and without any control; the lady was so truthful and innocent, to all outward appearances, that my own deepest sympathies went out instantly to her and her sorrows.

This is no fancy sketch, but a sad, sad reality. It occurred in the very heart of our city, and witnessing it with deep sorrow, I asked myself, how can these things be? But I remember that this small incident may only be a foreshadowing of some great sorrow deeply hidden in that mother's aching heart. The Bard of Avon says:

> "When sorrows come, they come not single spies,
> But in battalions."

I had turned away for a moment to look at some object that attracted my attention, when looking again, this child of sorrow was drying her eyes carefully and preparing to leave and go within—..

> "And *there* will canker sorrow eat her bud,
> And chase the native beauty from her cheek."

1870

INTRODUCTORY TO *MEMORANDA**

In taking upon myself the burden of editing a department in THE
GALAXY magazine, I have been actuated by a conviction that I was
needed, almost imperatively, in this particular field of literature. I
have long felt that while the magazine literature of the day had
much to recommend it, it yet lacked stability, solidity, weight. It
seemed plain to me that too much space was given to poetry and
romance, and not enough to statistics and agriculture. This defect
it shall be my earnest endeavor to remedy. If I succeed, the simple
consciousness that I have done a good deed will be a sufficient
reward.**

In this department of mine the public may always rely upon finding exhaustive statistical tables concerning the finances of the country,
the ratio of births and deaths, the percentage of increase of population,
etc., etc.—in a word, everything in the realm of statistics that can
make existence bright and beautiful.

Also, in my department will always be found elaborate conden-
sations of the Patent Office Reports, wherein a faithful endeavor
will at all times be made to strip the nutritious facts bare of that
effulgence of imagination and sublimity of diction which too often
mar the excellence of those great works.†

In my department will always be found ample excerpts from those
able dissertations upon Political Economy which I have for a long
time been contributing to a great metropolitan journal, and which,
for reasons utterly incomprehensible to me, another party has chosen
to usurp the credit of composing.

And, finally, I call attention with pride to the fact that in my

* This was Mark Twain's introduction to the humorous column he had agreed to
edit for *The Galaxy* and which he had entitled "Memoranda."
** Together with salary.—M.T.
† N. B.—No other magazine in the country makes a specialty of the Patent Office Reports.—M.T.

department of the magazine the farmer will always find full market reports, and also complete instructions about farming, even from the grafting of the seed to the harrowing of the matured crop. I shall throw a pathos into the subject of Agriculture that will surprise and delight the world.

Such is my programme; and I am persuaded that by adhering to it with fidelity I shall succeed in materially changing the character of this magazine. Therefore I am emboldened to ask the assistance and encouragement of all whose sympathies are with Progress and Reform.

In the other departments of the magazine will be found poetry, tales, and other frothy trifles, and to these the reader can turn for relaxation from time to time, and thus guard against overstraining the powers of his mind.

MARK TWAIN

P.S.—1. I have not sold out of the "Buffalo Express," and shall not; neither shall I stop writing for it. This remark seems necessary in a business point of view.

2. These MEMORANDA are not a "humorous" department. I would not conduct an exclusively and professedly humorous department for any one. I would always prefer to have the privilege of printing a serious and sensible remark, in case one occurred to me, without the reader's feeling obliged to consider himself outraged. We cannot keep the same mood day after day. I am liable, some day, to want to print my opinion on jurisprudence, or Homeric poetry, or international law, and I shall do it. It will be of small consequence to me whether the reader survive or not. I shall never go straining after jokes when in a cheerless mood, so long as the unhackneyed subject of international law is open to me. I will leave all that straining to people who edit professedly and inexorably "humorous" departments and publications.

3. I have chosen the general title of MEMORANDA for this department because it is plain and simple, and makes no fraudulent promises. I can print under it statistics, hotel arrivals, or anything that comes handy, without violating faith with the reader.

4. Puns cannot be allowed a place in this department. Inoffensive ignorance, benignant stupidity, and unostentatious imbecility will always be welcomed and cheerfully accorded a corner, and even the feeblest humor will be admitted, when we can do no better; but no

circumstances, however dismal, will ever be considered a sufficient excuse for the admission of that last and saddest evidence of intellectual poverty, the Pun.

M.T.
1870

A LITERARY "OLD OFFENDER"

In last month's MEMORANDA I published a sketch entitled "The Story of the Good Little Boy Who Did Not Prosper," and closed it with a dreadful nitro-glycerine explosion which destroyed the boy. He had unwittingly been sitting on a can of this compound and got his pantaloons greased with it; and when he got a reproving spank upon that portion of his system, the catastrophe instantly followed. There was something so stupendously grotesque about the "situation," that I was filled with admiration of it, and therefore borrowed it. I say "borrowed" it, for it was not my invention. I found it drifting about the sea of journalism, in the shape of a simple statement of the catastrophe in a single sentence, and attributed to a California paper. I thought, at the time, that in saying it was Californian unnecessary pains had been taken, for such a happy inspiration of extravagance as that could not well have originated elsewhere. I used it, and stated in a foot-note that I "borrowed it, without the unknown but most ingenious owner's permission." I naturally expected that so neat a compliment as that would resurrect the "ingenious unknown," and bring him to the light of day. Truly, it did produce a spectre, but not the one I was looking for. The party thus raised hails from Philadelphia, and in testimony that he is the "ingenious unknown," he encloses to me a half-column newspaper article, dated December 22, signed with his name, and being what he says is the original draft of the nitro-glycerine catastrophe.

The impulse to make pleasant mention of this person's name and give him the credit he claims, is crippled by the fact that I, or any one else acquainted with his literary history, would feel obliged to decline to accept any evidence coming from him, upon any matter, and especially upon a question of authorship. His simple word is worthless; and to embellish it with his oath would merely make it picturesque, not valuable. This person several of us know of our own personal knowledge to be a poor little purloiner of other men's ideas and handicraft. It would not be just to call him a literary pirate, for there is a sort of manliness about flaunting the black flag in the face of a world, and taking desperate chances against death and dishonor, that gives a sombre dignity to the pirate's calling but little suggestive of the creeping and stealthy ways of the smaller kind of literary rogues. But there is a sort of adventurers whom the police detect by a certain humble look in their faces, and who, when searched, yield abundance of spools, handkerchiefs, napkins, spoons, and such things, acquired by them when the trusting owners left the property openly in their company not thinking any harm. The police call this kind of adventurer a ——. However, upon second thought, I will not print the name, for it has almost too harsh a sound for polite ears; but the Philadelphia person I have spoken of will probably recognize a long-lost brother in the description. Anybody capturing the subject of these remarks and overhauling the catalogue of what he calls his "writings," will find in it two very good articles of mine, and if the rest were advertised as "strayed or stolen," they would doubtless be called for by journalists residing in all the different States of the Union. The effrontery of this person in appearing before me, through the U.S. mail, and claiming to have originated an idea, surpasses anything that has come under my notice lately. I cannot conceive of his being so reckless as to deliberately try to originate an idea—considering how he is built. He knows himself that it would rip, and tear, and rend him worse than the glycerine did the boy.

This sad person purloins all his literary materials, I fancy. And he spreads his damaged remnants before his customers with as happy an admiration as if they were bright and fresh from the intellectual loom. With due modesty I venture the prophecy that some day he will even ravish a dying speech from some poor fellow, and say with a flourish as he goes out of the world: "Fellow-citizens, I die innocent."

I do not print this party's name, because, knowing as I do upon what an exceedingly slender capital of merit, fame, or public invitation, two or three of the most widely popular lecturers of the day, of both sexes, got a foothold upon the rostrum, I might thus help to pave the way for him to transfer the report of somebody's speech from the papers to his portfolio, and step into the lecture arena upon a sudden and comfortable income of ten or fifteen thousand dollars a season.

I cannot take this person's evidence. Will the party from whom he pilfered the nitro-glycerine idea please send me a copy of the paper in which it first appeared, and with the date of the paper intact? I shall now soon find out who really invented the exploded boy.

1870

MAP OF PARIS*

I published my "Map of the Fortifications of Paris" in my own paper a fortnight ago, but am obliged to reproduce it in THE GALAXY, to satisfy the extraordinary demand for it which has arisen in military circles throughout the country. General Grant's outspoken commendation originated this demand, and General Sherman's fervent endorsement added fuel to it. The result is that tons of these maps have been fed to the suffering soldiers of our land, but without avail. They hunger still. We will cast THE GALAXY into the breach and stand by and await the effect.

The next Atlantic mail will doubtless bring news of a European frenzy for the map. It is reasonable to expect that the siege of Paris will be suspended till a German translation of it can be forwarded (it is now in preparation), and that the defence of Paris will likewise be suspended to await the reception of the French translation (now progressing under my own hands, and likely to be unique). King William's high praise of the map and Napoleon's frank enthusiasm concerning its execution will ensure its prompt adoption in Europe as the only authoritative and legitimate exposition of the present military situation. It is plain that if the Prussians cannot get into Paris with the facilities afforded by this production of mine they ought to deliver the enterprise into abler hands.

Strangers to me keep insisting that this map does *not* "explain itself." One person came to me with bloodshot eyes and a harassed look about him, and shook the map in my face and said he believed I was some new kind of idiot. I have been abused a good deal by other quick-tempered people like him, who came with similar complaints. Now, therefore, I yield willingly, and for the information

* Mark Twain's famous "Map of Paris" first appeared in the Buffalo *Express* on September 17, 1870. It was included by him in TOM SAWYER ABROAD, TOM SAWYER DETECTIVE AND OTHER STORIES (1896), but without the introductory note here printed, written for the map's appearance in *The Galaxy* of November 1870.

of the ignorant will briefly explain the present military situation as illustrated by the map. Part of the Prussian forces, under Prince Frederick William, are now boarding at the "farm-house" in the margin of the map. There is nothing between them and Vincennes but a rail fence in bad repair. Any corporal can see at a glance that they have only to burn it, pull it down, crawl under, climb over, or walk around it, just as the commander-in-chief shall elect. Another portion of the Prussian forces are at Podunk, under Von Moltke. They have nothing to do but float down the river Seine on a raft and scale the walls of Paris. Let the worshippers of that overrated soldier believe in him still, and abide the result—for me, I do not believe he will ever think of a raft. At Omaha and the High Bridge are vast masses of Prussian infantry, and it is only fair to say that they are likely to *stay* there, as that figure of a window-sash between them stands for a brewery. Away up out of sight over the top of the map is the fleet of the Prussian navy, ready at any moment to come cavorting down the Erie Canal (unless some new iniquity of an unprincipled Legislature shall put up the tolls and so render it cheaper to walk). To me it looks as if Paris is in a singularly close place. She never was situated before as she is in this map.

1870

A MEMORY

When I say that I never knew my austere father to be enamored of but one poem in all the long half century that he lived, persons who knew him will easily believe me; when I say that I have never composed but one poem in all the long third of a century that I have lived, persons who know me will be sincerely grateful; and finally, when I say that the poem which I composed was not the one which my father was enamored of, persons who may have known us both will not need to have this truth shot into them with a mountain howitzer before they can receive it. My father and I were always on the most distant terms when I was a boy—a sort of armed neutrality, so to speak. At irregular intervals this neutrality was broken, and suffering ensued; but I will be candid enough to say that the breaking and the suffering were always divided up with strict impartiality between us—which is to say, my father did the breaking, and I did the suffering. As a general thing I was a backward, cautious, unadventurous boy; but once I jumped off a two-story stable; another time I gave an elephant a "plug" of tobacco and retired without waiting for an answer; and still another time I pretended to be talking in my sleep, and got off a portion of a very wretched original conundrum in hearing of my father. Let us not pry into the result; it was of no consequence to any one but me.

But the poem I have referred to as attracting my father's attention and achieving his favor was "Hiawatha." Some man who courted a sudden and awful death presented him an early copy, and I never lost faith in my own senses until I saw him sit down and go to reading it in cold blood—saw him open the book, and heard him read these following lines, with the same inflectionless judicial frigidity with which he always read his charge to the jury, or administered an oath to a witness:

Take your bow, O Hiawatha,
Take your arrows, jasper-headed,
Take your war-club, Puggawaugun,
And your mittens, Minjekahwan,
And your birch canoe for sailing,
And the oil of Mishe-Nama.

Presently my father took out of his breast pocket an imposing "Warranty Deed," and fixed his eyes upon it and dropped into meditation. I knew what it was. A Texan lady and gentleman had given my half-brother, Orrin Johnson, a handsome property in a town in the North, in gratitude to him for having saved their lives by an act of brilliant heroism.

By and by my father looked toward me and sighed. Then he said:

"If I had such a son as this poet, here were a subject worthier than the traditions of these Indians."

"If you please, sir, where?"

"In this deed."

"In the—deed?"

"Yes—in this very deed," said my father, throwing it on the table. "There is more poetry, more romance, more sublimity, more splendid imagery hidden away in that homely document than could be found in all the traditions of all the savages that live."

"Indeed, sir? Could I—could I get it out, sir? Could I compose the poem, sir, do you think?"

"You!"

I wilted.

Presently my father's face softened somewhat, and he said:

"Go and try. But mind, curb folly. No poetry at the expense of truth. Keep strictly to the facts."

I said I would, and bowed myself out, and went up stairs.

"Hiawatha" kept droning in my head—and so did my father's remarks about the sublimity and romance hidden in my subject, and also his injunction to beware of wasteful and exuberant fancy. I noticed, just here, that I had heedlessly brought the deed away with me. Now, at this moment came to me one of those rare moods of daring recklessness, such as I referred to a while ago. Without another thought, and in plain defiance of the fact that I knew my father meant me to write the romantic story of my half-brother's adventure and subsequent good fortune, I ventured to heed merely the letter of his remarks and ignore their spirit. I took the stupid

"Warranty Deed" itself and chopped it up into Hiawathian blank verse, without altering or leaving out three words, and without transposing six. It required loads of courage to go down stairs and face my father with my performance. I started three or four times before I finally got my pluck to where it would stick. But at last I said I would go down and read it to him if he threw me over the church for it. I stood up to begin, and he told me to come closer. I edged up a little, but still left as much neutral ground between us as I thought he would stand. Then I began. It would be useless for me to try to tell what conflicting emotions expressed themselves upon his face, nor how they grew more and more intense as I proceeded; nor how a fell darkness descended upon his countenance, and he began to gag and swallow, and his hands began to work and twitch, as I reeled off line after line, with the strength ebbing out of me, and my legs trembling under me:

THE STORY OF A GALLANT DEED

THIS INDENTURE, made the tenth
Day of November, in the year
Of our Lord one thousand eight
Hundred six-and-fifty,

Between JOANNA S. E. GRAY
And PHILIP GRAY, her husband,
Of Salem City in the State
Of Texas, of the first part,

And O. B. Johnson, of the town
Of Austin, ditto, WITNESSETH:
That said party of first part,
For and in consideration

Of the sum of Twenty Thousand
Dollars, lawful money of
The U. S. of Americay,
To them in hand now paid by said

Party of the second part,
The due receipt whereof is here-
By confessed and acknowledg-ed,
Have Granted, Bargained, Sold, Remised,

Released and Aliened and Conveyed,
   Confirmed, and by these presents do
Grant and Bargain, Sell, Remise,
   Alien, Release Convey, and Con-

Firm unto the said aforesaid
   Party of the second part,
And to his heirs and assigns
   Forever and ever, ALL

That certain piece or parcel of
   LAND situate in city of
Dunkirk, county of Chautauqua,
   And likewise furthermore in York State,

Bounded and described, to-wit,
   As follows, herein, namely:
BEGINNING at the distance of
   A hundred two-and-forty feet,

North-half-east, north-east-by north,
   East-north-east and northerly
Of the northerly line of Mulligan street,
   On the westerly line of Brannigan street,

And running thence due northerly
   On Brannigan street 200 feet,
Thence at right angles westerly,
   North-west-by-west-and-west-half-west,

West-and-by-north, north-west-by-west,
   About——

I kind of dodged, and the boot-jack broke the looking-glass. I could have waited to see what became of the other missiles if I had wanted to, but I took no interest in such things.

1870

THE NOBLE RED MAN

In books he is tall and tawny, muscular, straight, and of kingly presence; he has a beaked nose and an eagle eye.

His hair is glossy, and as black as the raven's wing; out of its massed richness springs a sheaf of brilliant feathers; in his ears and nose are silver ornaments; on his arms and wrists and ankles are broad silver bands and bracelets; his buckskin hunting suit is gallantly fringed, and the belt and the moccasins wonderfully flowered with colored beads; and when, rainbowed with his war-paint, he stands at full height, with his crimson blanket wrapped about him, his quiver at his back, his bow and tomahawk projecting upward from his folded arms, and his eagle eye gazing at specks against the far horizon which even the paleface's field-glass could scarcely reach, he is a being to fall down and worship.

His language is intensely figurative. He never speaks of the moon, but always of "the eye of the night"; nor of the wind *as* the wind, but as "the whisper of the Great Spirit"; and so forth and so on. His power of condensation is marvellous. In some publications he seldom says anything but "Waugh!" and this, with a page of explanation by the author, reveals a whole world of thought and wisdom that before lay concealed in that one little word.

He is noble. He is true and loyal; not even imminent death can shake his peerless faithfulness. His heart is a well-spring of truth, and of generous impulses, and of knightly magnanimity. With him, gratitude is religion; do him a kindness, and at the end of a lifetime he has not forgotten it. Eat of his bread, or offer him yours, and the bond of hospitality is sealed—a bond which is forever inviolable with him.

He loves the dark-eyed daughter of the forest, the dusky maiden of faultless form and rich attire, the pride of the tribe, the all-beautiful. He talks to her in a low voice, at twilight, of his deeds on the war-path and in the chase, and of the grand achievements of his ancestors; and she listens with downcast eyes, "while a richer hue mantles her dusky cheek."

Such is the Noble Red Man in print. But out on the plains and in the mountains, not being on dress parade, not being gotten up to see company, he is under no obligation to be other than his natural self, and therefore:

He is little, and scrawny, and black, and dirty; and, judged by even the most charitable of our canons of human excellence, is thoroughly pitiful and contemptible. There is nothing in his eye or his nose that is attractive, and if there is anything in his hair that—however, that is a feature which will not bear too close examination. He wears no feathers in his hair, and no ornament or covering on his head. His dull-black, frowsy locks hang straight down to his neck behind, and in front they hang just to his eyes, like a curtain, being cut straight across the forehead, from side to side, and never parted on top. He has no pendants in his ears, and as for his—however, let us not waste time on unimportant particulars, but hurry along. He wears no bracelets on his arms or ankles; his hunting suit is gallantly fringed, but not intentionally; when he does not wear his disgusting rabbit-skin robe, his hunting suit consists wholly of the half of a horse blanket brought over in the Pinta or the Mayflower, and frayed out and fringed by inveterate use. He is not rich enough to possess a belt; he never owned a moccasin or wore a shoe in his life; and truly he is nothing but a poor, filthy, naked scurvy vagabond, whom to exterminate were a charity to the Creator's worthier insects and reptiles which he oppresses. Still, when contact with the white man has given to the Noble Son of the Forest certain cloudy impressions of civilization, and aspirations after a nobler life, he presently appears in public with one boot on and one shoe—shirtless, and wearing ripped and patched and buttonless pants which he holds up with his left hand—his execrable rabbit-skin robe flowing from his shoulders —an old hoop-skirt on, outside of it—a necklace of battered sardine-boxes and oyster-cans reposing on his bare breast—a venerable flint-lock musket in his right hand—a weather-beaten stove-pipe hat on, canted "gallusly" to starboard, and the lid off and hanging by a thread or two; and when he thus appears, and waits patiently around a saloon till he gets a chance to strike a "swell" attitude before a looking-glass, he is a good, fair, desirable subject for extermination if ever there was one.*

* This is not a fancy picture; I have seen it many a time in Nevada, just as it is here limned.—M.T.

There is nothing figurative, or moonshiny, or sentimental about his language. It is very simple and unostentatious, and consists of plain, straightforward lies. His "wisdom" conferred upon an idiot would leave that idiot helpless indeed.

He is ignoble—base and treacherous, and hateful in every way. Not even imminent death can startle him into a spasm of virtue. The ruling trait of all savages is a greedy and consuming selfishness, and in our Noble Red Man it is found in its amplest development. His heart is a cesspool of falsehood, of treachery, and of low and devilish instincts. With him, gratitude is an unknown emotion; and when one does him a kindness, it is safest to keep the face toward him, lest the reward be an arrow in the back. To accept of a favor from him is to assume a debt which you can never repay to his satisfaction, though you bankrupt yourself trying. To give him a dinner when he is starving, is to precipitate the whole hungry tribe upon your hospitality, for he will go straight and fetch them, men, women, children, and dogs, and these they will huddle patiently around your door, or flatten their noses against your window, day after day, gazing beseechingly upon every mouthful you take, and unconsciously swallowing when you swallow! The scum of the earth!

And the Noble Son of the Plains becomes a mighty hunter in the due and proper season. That season is the summer, and the prey that a number of the tribes hunt is crickets and grasshoppers! The warriors, old men, women, and children, spread themselves abroad in the plain and drive the hopping creatures before them into a ring of fire. I could describe the feast that then follows, without missing a detail, if I thought the reader would stand it.

All history and honest observation will show that the Red Man is a skulking coward and a windy braggart, who strikes without warning—usually from an ambush or under cover of night, and nearly always bringing a force of about five or six to one against his enemy; kills helpless women and little children, and massacres the men in their beds; and then brags about it as long as he lives, and his son and his grandson and great-grandson after him glorify it among the "heroic deeds of their ancestors." A regiment of Fenians will fill the whole world with the noise of it when they are getting ready to invade Canada; but when the Red Man declares war, the first intimation his friend the white man whom he supped with at twilight has of it, is when the war-whoop rings in his ears and the tomahawk sinks into his brain. In June, seven Indians went to a small station on the Plains where three white men lived, and asked for food; it was given them, and also tobacco. They stayed two hours, eating and smoking and talking, waiting with Indian patience for their customary odds of seven to one to offer, and as soon as it came they seized the opportunity; that is, when two of the men went out, they killed the other the instant he turned his back to do some solicited favor; then they caught his comrades separately, and killed one, but the other escaped.

The Noble Red Man seldom goes prating loving foolishness to a splendidly caparisoned blushing maid at twilight. No; he trades a crippled horse, or a damaged musket, or a dog, a gallon of grass-hoppers, and an inefficient old mother for her, and makes her work like an abject slave all the rest of her life to compensate him for the outlay. He never works himself. She builds the habitation, when they use one (it consists in hanging half a dozen rags over the weather side of a sage-brush bush to roost under); gathers and brings home the fuel; takes care of the raw-boned pony when they possess such grandeur; she walks and carries her nursing cubs while he rides. She wears no clothing save the fragrant rabbit-skin robe which her great-grandmother before her wore, and all the "blushing" she does can be removed with soap and a towel, provided it is only four or five weeks old and not caked.

Such is the genuine Noble Aborigine. I did not get him from books, but from personal observation.

By Dr. Keim's excellent book it appears that from June, 1868, to October, 1869, the Indians *massacred nearly* 200 *white persons and ravished over forty women captured in peaceful outlying settlements along the border, or belonging to emigrant trains traversing the settled routes of travel. Children were burned alive in the presence of their parents. Wives were ravished before their husbands' eyes. Husbands were mutilated, tortured, and scalped, and their wives compelled to look on.* These facts and figures are official, and they exhibit the misunderstood Son of the Forest in his true character— as a creature devoid of brave or generous qualities, but cruel, treacher-ous, and brutal. During the Pi-Ute war the Indians often dug the sinews out of the backs of white men before they were dead. (The sinews are used for bow-strings.) But their favorite mutilations can-not be put into print. Yet it is this same Noble Red Man who is always greeted with a wail of humanitarian sympathy from the Atlantic seaboard whenever he gets into trouble; the maids and matrons throw up their hands in horror at the bloody vengeance wreaked upon him, and the newspapers clamor for a court of inquiry to examine into the conduct of the inhuman officer who inflicted the little pleasantry upon the "poor abused Indian." (They always look at the matter from the abused-Indian point of view, never from that of the bereaved white widow and orphan.) But it is a great and unspeakable comfort to know that, let them be as prompt about it as they may, the inquiry has always got to come *after* the good officer has administered his little admonition.

1870

OUR PRECIOUS LUNATIC

New York, May 10.
The Richardson-McFarland jury had been out one hour and fifty minutes. A breathless silence brooded over court and auditory—a silence and a stillness so absolute, notwithstanding the vast multitude of human beings packed together there, that when some one far away among the throng under the northeast balcony cleared his throat with a smothered little cough it startled everybody uncomfortably, so distinctly did it grate upon the pulseless air. At that imposing moment the bang of a door was heard, then the shuffle of approaching feet, and then a sort of surging and swaying disorder among the heads at the entrance from the jury-room told them that the Twelve were coming. Presently all was silent again, and the foreman of the jury rose and said:

"Your Honor and Gentlemen: We, the jury charged with the duty of determining whether the prisoner at the bar, Daniel McFarland, has been guilty of murder, in taking by surprise an unarmed man and shooting him to death, or whether the prisoner is afflicted with a sad but irresponsible insanity which at times can be cheered only by violent entertainment with firearms, do find as follows, namely:

That the prisoner, Daniel McFarland, is insane as above described. Because:

1. His great grandfather's stepfather was tainted with insanity, and frequently killed people who were distasteful to him. Hence, insanity is hereditary in the family.

2. For nine years the prisoner at the bar did not adequately support his family. Strong circumstantial evidence of insanity.

3. For nine years he made of his home, as a general thing, a poor-house; sometimes (but very rarely) a cheery, happy habitation; frequently the den of a beery, drivelling, stupefied animal; but never,

as far as ascertained, the abiding place of a gentleman. These be evidences of insanity.

4. He once took his young unmarried sister-in-law to the museum; while there his hereditary insanity came upon him to such a degree that he hiccupped and staggered; and afterward, on the way home, even made love to the young girl he was protecting. These are the acts of a person not in his right mind.

5. For a good while his sufferings were so great that he had to submit to the inconvenience of having his wife give public readings for the family support; and at times, when he handed these shameful earnings to the barkeeper, his haughty soul was so torn with anguish that he could hardly stand without leaning against something. At such times he has been known to shed tears into his sustenance till it diluted to utter inefficiency. Inattention of this nature is not the act of a Democrat unafflicted in mind.

6. He never spared expense in making his wife comfortable during her occasional confinements. Her father is able to testify to this. There was always an element of unsoundness about the prisoner's generosities that is very suggestive at this time and before this court.

7. Two years ago the prisoner came fearlessly up behind Richardson in the dark, and shot him in the leg. The prisoner's brave and protracted defiance of an adversity that for years had left him little to depend upon for support but a wife who sometimes earned scarcely anything for weeks at a time, is evidence that he would have appeared in front of Richardson and shot him in the stomach if he had not been insane at the time of the shooting.

8. Fourteen months ago the prisoner told Archibald Smith that he was going to kill Richardson. This is insanity.

9. Twelve months ago he told Marshall P. Jones that he was going to kill Richardson. Insanity.

10. Nine months ago he was lurking about Richardson's home in New Jersey, and said he was going to kill Richardson. Insanity.

11. Seven months ago he showed a pistol to Seth Brown and said that that was for Richardson. He said Brown testified that at that time it seemed plain that something was the matter with McFarland, for he crossed the street diagonally nine times in fifty yards, apparently without any settled reason for doing so, and finally fell in the gutter and went to sleep. He remarked at the time that McFarland acted strange—believed he was insane. Upon hearing Brown's evidence, John W. Galen, M.D., affirmed at once that McFarland *was* insane.

12. Five months ago, McFarland showed his customary pistol, in his customary way, to his bed-fellow, Charles A. Dana, and told him he was going to kill Richardson the first time an opportunity offered. Evidence of insanity.

13. Five months and two weeks ago McFarland asked John Morgan the time of day, *and turned and walked rapidly away without waiting for an answer.* Almost indubitable evidence of insanity. And—

14. It is remarkable that exactly one week after this circumstance, the prisoner, Daniel McFarland, confronted Albert D. Richardson suddenly and without warning, and shot him dead. *This is manifest insanity.* Everything we know of the prisoner goes to show that if he had been sane at the time, he would have shot his victim from behind.

15. There is an absolutely overwhelming mass of testimony to show that *an hour before the shooting, McFarland was* ANXIOUS AND UNEASY, *and that five minutes after it he was* EXCITED. Thus the accumulating conjectures and evidences of insanity culminate in this sublime and unimpeachable *proof* of it. Therefore—

Your Honor and Gentlemen—We the jury pronounce the said Daniel McFarland INNOCENT OF MURDER, BUT CALAMITOUSLY INSANE."

The scene that ensued almost defies description. Hats, handkerchiefs and bonnets were frantically waved above the massed heads in the courtroom, and three tremendous cheers and a tiger told where the sympathies of the court and people were. Then a hundred pursed lips were advanced to kiss the liberated prisoner, and many a hand thrust out to give him a congratulatory shake—but presto! with a maniac's own quickness and a maniac's own fury the lunatic assassin of Richardson fell upon his friends with teeth and nails, boots and office furniture, and the amazing rapidity with which he broke heads and limbs, and rent and sundered bodies, till nearly a hundred citizens were reduced to mere quivering heaps of fleshy odds and ends and crimson rags, was like nothing in this world but the exultant frenzy of a plunging, tearing, roaring devil of a steam machine when it snatches a human being and spins him and whirls him till he shreds away to nothingness like a "Four o'clock" before the breath of a child.

The destruction was awful. It is said that within the space of eight minutes McFarland killed and crippled some six score persons and tore down a large portion of the City Hall building, carrying away and casting into Broadway six or seven marble columns fifty-four feet long and weighing nearly two tons each. But he was finally captured and sent in chains to the lunatic asylum for life. (By late telegrams it appears that this is a mistake.—Editor *Express*.)*

But the really curious part of this whole matter is yet to be told. And that is, that McFarland's most intimate friends believe that the very next time that it ever occurred to him that the insanity plea was not a mere politic pretense, was when the verdict came in. They think that the startling thought burst upon him then, that if twelve good and true men, able to comprehend all the baseness of perjury, *proclaimed under oath that he was a lunatic, there was no gainsaying such evidence and that he* UNQUESTIONABLY WAS INSANE!

Possibly that was really the way of it. It is dreadful to think that maybe the most awful calamity that can befall a man, namely, loss of reason, was precipitated upon this poor prisoner's head by a jury that could have hanged him instead, and so done him a mercy and his country a service.

M.T.

Postscript—Later

May 11—I do not expect anybody to believe so astounding a thing, and yet it is the solemn truth that instead of instantly sending the dangerous lunatic to the insane asylum (which I naturally supposed they would do, and so I prematurely *said* they had) the court has actually SET HIM AT LIBERTY. Comment is unnecessary.

M.T.
1870

* This article appeared in the Buffalo *Express*.

THE "PRESENT" NUISANCE

To be the editor of any kind of a newspaper, either country or metropolitan (but very especially the former), is a position which must be trying to a good-natured man. Because it makes him an object of charity whether or no. It makes him the object of a peculiar and humiliating, because an interested, charity—a charity thrust upon him with offensive assurance and a perfectly unconcealed taken-for-granted that it will be received with gratitude, and the donor accounted a benefactor; and at the very same time the donor's chief motive, his vulgar self-interest, is left as frankly unconcealed. The country editor offers his advertising space to the public at the trifle of one dollar and a half or two dollars a square, first insertion, and one would suppose his "patrons" would be satisfied with that. But they are not. They puzzle their thin brains to find out some still cheaper way of getting their wares celebrated—some way whereby they can advertise virtually for nothing. They soon hit upon that meanest and shabbiest of all contrivances for robbing a gentle-spirited scribbler, viz., the conferring upon him of a present and begging a "notice" of it—thus pitifully endeavoring to not only invade his sacred editorial columns, but get ten dollars' worth of advertising for fifty cents' worth of merchandise, and on top of that leave the poor creature burdened with a crushing debt of gratitude! And so the corrupted editor, having once debauched his independence and received one of these contemptible presents, wavers a little while the remnant of his self-respect is consuming, and at last abandons himself to a career of shame, and prostitutes his columns to "notices" of every sort of present that a stingy neighbor chooses to inflict upon him. The confectioner insults him with forty cents' worth of ice-cream— and he lavishes four "squares" of editorial compliments on him; the grocer insults him with a bunch of overgrown radishes and a dozen prize turnips—and gets an editorial paragraph perfectly putrid with gratitude; the farmer insults him with three dollars' worth of peaches, or a beet like a man's leg, or a watermelon like a channel-buoy, or a cabbage in many respects like his own head, and expects a third of a column of exuberant imbecility—and gets it. And these trivial charities are not respectfully and gracefully tendered, but are thrust insolently upon the victim, and with an air that plainly shows that the victim will be held to a strict accountability in the next issue of his paper.

I am not an editor of a newspaper, and shall always try to do right and be good, so that God will not make me one; but there are some persons who have got the impression, somehow, that I am that kind of character, and they treat me accordingly. They send me a new-fangled wheel-barrow, and ask me to "notice" it; or a peculiar boot-jack, and ask me to "notice" it; or a sample of coffee, and ask me to "notice" it; or an article of furniture worth eight or ten dollars, or a pair of crutches, or a truss, or an artificial nose, or a few shillings' worth of rubbish of the vegetable species; and here lately, all in one day, I receive a barrel of apples, a thing to milk cows with, a basket of peaches, a box of grapes, a new sort of wooden leg, and a patent "composition" grave-stone. "Notices" requested. A barrel of apples, a cow-milker, a basket of peaches, and a box of grapes, all put together, are not worth the bore of writing a "notice," nor a tenth part of the room the "notice" would take up in the paper, and so they remained unnoticed. I had no immediate use for the wooden leg, and would not have accepted a charity grave-stone if I had been dead and actually suffering for it when it came—so I sent those articles back.

I do not want any of these underhanded, obligation-inflicting presents. I prefer to cramp myself down to the use of such things as I can afford, and then pay for them; and then when a citizen needs the labor of my hands he can have it, and I will infallibly come on him for damages.

The ungraceful custom, so popular in the back settlements, of facetiously wailing about the barren pockets of editors, is the parent of this uncanny present-inflicting, and it is time that the guild that originated the custom and now suffer in pride and purse from it, reflected that decent and dignified poverty is thoroughly respectable; while the flaunting of either a real or pretended neediness in the public face, and the bartering of nauseating "puffs" for its legitimate fruit of charitable presents, are as thoroughly indelicate, unbecoming, and disreputable.

1870

THE RECEPTION AT THE PRESIDENT'S

After I had drifted into the White House with the flood tide of humanity that had been washing steadily up the street for an hour, I obeyed the orders of the soldier at the door and the policeman within, and banked my hat and umbrella with a colored man, who gave me a piece of brass with a number on it and said that that thing would reproduce the property at any time of the night. I doubted it, but I was on unknown ground now, and must be content to take a good many chances.

Another person told me to drop in with the crowd and I would come to the President presently. I joined, and we drifted along till we passed a certain point, and then we thinned out to double and single file. It was a right gay scene, and a right stirring and lively one; for the whole place was brightly lighted, and all down the great hall, as far as one could see, was a restless and writhing multitude of people, the women powdered, painted, jewelled, and splendidly upholstered, and many of the men gilded with the insignia of great naval, military, and ambassadorial rank. It was bewildering.

Our long line kept drifting along, and by and by we came in sight of the President and Mrs. Grant. They were standing up shaking hands and trading civilities with our procession. I grew somewhat at home little by little, and then I began to feel satisfied and contented. I was getting to be perfectly alive with interest by the time it came my turn to talk with the President. I took him by the hand and looked him in the eye, and said:

"Well, I reckon I see you at last, General. I have said as much as a thousand times, out in Nevada, that if ever I went home to the States I would just have the private satisfaction of going and saying to you by word of mouth that I thought you was considerable of a soldier, anyway. Now, you know, out there we——"

I turned round and said to the fellow behind me:

"Now, look here, my good friend, how the nation do you suppose

I can talk with any sort of satisfaction, with you crowding me this way? I am surprised at your manners."

He was a modest-looking creature. He said:

"But you see the whole procession's stopped, and they're crowding up on me."

I said:

"Some people have got more cheek. Just suggest to the parties behind you to have some respect for the place they are in and not try to shove in on a private conversation. What the General and me are talking about ain't of the least interest to them."

Then I resumed with the President:

"Well, well, well. Now this is fine. This is what I call something *like.* Gay? Well, I should say so. And so *this* is what you call a Presidential reception. I'm free to say that it just lays over anything that ever *I* saw out in the sage-brush. I have been to Governor Nye's Injun receptions at Honey Lake and Carson City, many and many a time—he that's Senator Nye now—*you* know him, of course. I never saw a man in all my life that Jim Nye didn't know—and not only that, but he could tell him *where* he knew him, and all about him, family included, even if it was forty years ago. Most remarkable man, Jim Nye—remarkable. He can tell a lie with that purity of accent, and that grace of utterance, and that convincing emotion——"

I turned again, and said:

"My friend, your conduct surprises me. I have come three thousand miles to have a word with the President of the United States upon subjects with which you are not even remotely connected, and by the living geewhillikins I can't proceed with any sort of satisfaction on account of your cussed crowding. Will you just please to go a little slow, now, and not attract so much attention by your strange conduct? If you had any eyes you could see how the bystanders are staring."

He said:

"But I tell you, sir, it's the people behind. They are just growling and surging and shoving, and I wish I was in Jericho, I do."

I said:

"I wish you was, myself. You might learn some delicacy of feeling in that ancient seat of civilization, maybe. Drat if you don't need it."

And then I resumed with the President:

"Yes, sir, I've been at receptions before, plenty of them—old Nye's Injun receptions. But they warn't as starchy as this by considerable.

No great long strings of high-fliers like these galoots here, you know, but old high-flavored Washoes and Pi-Utes, each one of them as powerful as a rag-factory on fire. Phew! Those were halcyon days. Yes, indeed, General; and madam, many and many's the time, out in the wilds of Nevada, I've been——"

"Perhaps you had better discontinue your remarks till another time, sir, as the crowd behind you are growing somewhat impatient," the President said.

"Do you hear that?" I said to the fellow behind me. "I suppose you will take *that* hint, anyhow. I tell you he is milder than *I* would be. If I was President, I would waltz you people out at the back door if you came crowding a gentleman this way, that *I* was holding a private conversation with."

And then I resumed with the President:

"I think that hint of yours will start them. I never saw people act so. It is really about all I can do to hold my ground with that mob shoving up behind. But don't you worry on my account, General —don't give yourself any uneasiness about me—I can stand it as long as they can. I've been through this kind of a mill before. Why, as I was just saying to you, many and many a time, out in the wilds of Nevada, I have been at Governor Nye's Injun receptions—and between you and me that old man was a good deal of a Governor, take him all round. I don't know what for Senator he makes, though I think you'll admit that him and Bill Steward and Tom Fitch take a bigger average of brains into that Capitol up yonder, by a hundred and fifty fold, than any other State in America, according to population. Now that is so. Those three men represent only twenty or twenty-five thousand people—bless you, the least little bit of a trifling ward in the city of New York casts two votes to Nevada's one—and yet those three men haven't their superiors in Congress for straight-out, simon pure brains and ability. And if you could just have been at one of old Nye's Injun receptions and seen those savages—not high-fliers like these, you know, but frowsy old bummers with nothing in the world on, in the summer time, but an old battered plug hat and a pair of spectacles—I tell you it was a swell affair, was one of Governor Nye's early-day receptions. Many and many's the time I have been to them, and seen him stand up and beam and smile on his children, as he called them in his motherly way—beam on them by the hour out of his splendid eyes, and fascinate them with his handsome face, and comfort them with his persuasive tongue—seen him stand up there and tell them anecdotes and lies, and quote Watts's hymns to them, until he just took the war spirit all out of them—and grim chiefs that came two hundred miles to tax the whites for whole wagon-loads of blankets and things or make eternal war if they didn't get them, he has sent away bewildered with his inspired mendacity and perfectly satisfied and enriched with an old hoop skirt or two, a lot of Patent Office reports, and a few sides of condemned army bacon that they would have to chain up to a tree when they camped, or the skippers would walk off with them. I tell you he is a rattling talker. Talk! It's no name for it. He—well, he is bound to launch straight into close quarters and a heap of trouble hereafter, of course—we all know that—but you can rest satisfied that he will take off his hat and put out his hand and introduce himself to the King of Darkness perfectly easy and comfortable, and let on that he has seen him somewhere before; and he will remind him of parties he used to know, and things that's slipped out of his memory—and he'll tell him a thousand things that he can't *help* taking an interest in, and every now and then he will just gently mix in an anecdote that will fetch him if there's any laugh in him—he will, indeed—and Jim Nye will chip in and help cross-question the candidates, and he will just hang around and hang around and hang around, getting more and more sociable all the time, and doing this, that, and the other thing in the handiest sort of way, till he has made himself perfectly indispensable— and then, the very first thing you know——"

I wheeled and said:

"My friend, your conduct grieves me to the heart. A dozen times at least your unseemly crowding has seriously interfered with the conversation I am holding with the President, and if the thing occurs again I shall take my hat and leave the premises."

"I wish to the mischief you would! Where did you come from anyway, that you've got the unutterable cheek to spread yourself here and keep fifteen hundred people standing waiting half an hour to shake hands with the President?"

An officer touched me on the shoulder and said:

"Move along, please; you're annoying the President beyond all patience. You have blocked the procession, and the people behind you are getting furious. Come, move along, please."

Rather than have trouble, I moved along. So I had no time to do more than look back over my shoulder and say: "Yes, sir, and the first thing they would know, Jim Nye would have that place, and the salary doubled! I do reckon he is the handiest creature about making the most of his chances that ever found an all-sufficient substitute for mother's milk in politics and sin. Now that is the kind of man old Nye is—and in less than two months he would talk every—— But I can't make you hear the rest, General, without hollering too loud."

1870

A ROYAL COMPLIMENT

The latest report about the Spanish crown is, that it will now be offered to Prince Alfonso, the second son of the King of Portugal, who is but five years of age. The Spaniards have hunted through all the nations of Europe for a King. They tried to get a Portuguese in the person of Dom Luis, who is an old ex-monarch; they tried to get an Italian, in the person of Victor Emanuel's young son, the Duke of Genoa; they tried to get a Spaniard, in the person of Espartero, who is an octogenarian. Some of them desired a French Bourbon, Montpensier; some of them a Spanish Bourbon, the Prince of Asturias; some of them an English prince, one of the sons of Queen Victoria. They have just tried to get the German Prince Leopold; but they have thought it better to give him up than take a war along with him. It is a long time since we first suggested to them to try an American ruler. We can offer them a large number of able and experienced sovereigns to pick from—men skilled in statesmanship, versed in the science of government, and adepts in all the arts of administration—men who could wear the crown with dignity and rule the kingdom at a reasonable expense. There is not the least danger of Napoleon threatening them if they take an American sovereign; in fact, we have no doubt he would be pleased to support such a candidature. We are unwilling to mention names—though *we have a man in our eye whom we wish they had in theirs.—New York Tribune.*

It would be but an ostentation of modesty to permit such a pointed reference to myself to pass unnoticed. This is the second time that "The Tribune" (no doubt sincerely looking to the best interests of Spain and the world at large) has done me the great and unusual honor to propose me as a fit person to fill the Spanish throne. Why "The Tribune" should single me out in this way from the midst of a dozen Americans of higher political prominence, is a problem which I cannot solve. Beyond a somewhat intimate knowledge of Spanish history and a profound veneration for its great names and illustrious deeds, I feel that I possess no merit that should peculiarly recommend me to this royal distinction. I cannot deny that Spanish history has always been mother's milk to me. I am proud of every Spanish achievement, from Hernando Cortes's victory at Thermopylae down to Vasco Nunez de Balboa's discovery at the Atlantic ocean; and of every splendid Spanish name, from Don Quixote and the Duke of Wellington down to Don Caesar de Bazan. However, these little graces of erudition are of small consequence, being more showy than serviceable.

In case the Spanish sceptre is pressed upon me—and the indications unquestionably are that it will be—I shall feel it necessary to have certain things set down and distinctly understood beforehand. For instance: My salary must be paid quarterly in advance. In these unsettled times it will not do to trust. If Isabella had adopted this plan, she would be roosting on her ancestral throne to-day, for the simple reason that her subjects never could have raised three months of a royal salary in advance, and of course they could not have discharged her until they had squared up with her. My salary must be paid in gold; when greenbacks are fresh in a country, they are too fluctuating. My salary has got to be put at the ruling market rate; I am not going to cut under on the trade, and they are not going to trail me a long way from home and then practise on my ignorance and play me for a royal North Adams Chinaman, by any means. As I understand it, imported kings generally get five millions a year and house-rent free. Young George of Greece gets that. As the revenues only yield two millions, he has to take the national note for considerable; but even with things in that sort of shape he is better fixed than he was in Denmark, where he had to eternally stand up because he had no throne to sit on, and had to give bail for his board, because a royal apprentice gets no salary there while he is learning his trade. England is the place for that. Fifty thousand dollars a year Great Britain pays on each royal child that is born, and this is increased from year to year as the child becomes more and more indispensable to his country. Look at Prince Arthur. At first he only got the usual birth-bounty; but now that he has got so that he can dance, there is simply no telling what wages he gets.

I should have to stipulate that the Spanish people wash more and endeavor to get along with less quarantine. Do you know, Spain keeps her ports fast locked against foreign traffic three-fourths of each year, because one day she is scared about the cholera, and the next about the plague, and next the measles, next the whooping cough, the hives, and the rash? but she does not mind leonine leprosy and elephantiasis any more than a great and enlightened civilization minds freckles. Soap would soon remove her anxious distress about foreign distempers. The reason arable land is so scarce in Spain is because the people squander so much of it on their persons, and then when they die it is improvidently buried with them.

I should feel obliged to stipulate that Marshal Serrano be reduced to the rank of constable, or even roundsman. He is no longer fit to be City Marshal. A man who refused to be king because he was too old and feeble, is ill qualified to help sick people to the station-house when they are armed and their form of delirium tremens is of the exuberant and demonstrative kind.

I should also require that a force be sent to chase the late Queen Isabella out of France. Her presence there can work no advantage to Spain, and she ought to be made to move at once; though, poor thing, she has been chaste enough heretofore—for a Spanish woman.

I should also require that——

I am at this moment authoritatively informed that "The Tribune" did not mean me, after all. Very well, I do not care two cents.

1870

THE "TOURNAMENT" IN A.D. 1870

Lately there appeared an item to this effect, and the same went the customary universal round of the press:

A telegraph station has just been established upon the traditional site of the Garden of Eden.

As a companion to that, nothing fits so aptly and so perfectly as this:

Brooklyn has revived the knightly tournament of the Middle Ages.

It is hard to tell which is the most startling, the idea of that highest achievement of human genius and intelligence, the telegraph, prating away about the practical concerns of the world's daily life in the heart and home of ancient indolence, ignorance, and savagery, or the idea of that happiest expression of the brag, vanity, and mockheroics of our ancestors, the "tournament," coming out of its grave to flaunt its tinsel trumpery and perform its "chivalrous" absurdities in the high noon of the nineteenth century, and under the patronage of a great, broad-awake city and an advanced civilization.

A "tournament" in Lynchburg is a thing easily within the comprehension of the average mind; but no commonly gifted person can conceive of such a spectacle in Brooklyn without straining his powers. Brooklyn is part and parcel of the city of New York, and there is hardly romance enough in the entire metropolis to re-supply a Virginia "knight" with "chivalry," in case he happened to run out of it. Let the reader, calmly and dispassionately, picture to himself "lists"—in Brooklyn; heralds, pursuivants, pages, garter king-at-arms —in Brooklyn; the marshalling of the fantastic hosts of "chivalry" in slashed doublets, velvet trunks, ruffles, and plumes—in Brooklyn;

mounted on omnibus and livery-stable patriarchs, promoted, and referred to in cold blood as "steeds," "destriers," and "chargers," and divested of their friendly, humble names—these meek old "Jims" and "Robs" and "Charleys," and renamed "Mohammed," "Bucephalus," and "Saladin"—in Brooklyn; mounted thus, and armed with swords and shields and wooden lances, and cased in pasteboard hauberks, morions, greaves, and gauntlets, and addressed as "Sir" Smith, and "Sir" Jones, and bearing such titled grandeurs as "The Disinherited Knight," the "Knight of Shenandoah," the "Knight of the Blue Ridge," the "Knight of Maryland," and the "Knight of the Secret Sorrow"—in Brooklyn; and at the toot of the horn charging fiercely upon a helpless ring hung on a post, and prodding at it intrepidly with their wooden sticks, and by and by skewering it and cavorting back to the judges' stand covered with glory—this in Brooklyn; and each noble success like this duly and promptly announced by an applauding toot from the herald's horn, and "the band playing three bars of an old circus tune"—all in Brooklyn, in broad daylight. And let the reader remember, and also add to his picture, as follows, to wit: when the show was all over, the party who had shed the most blood and overturned and hacked to pieces the most knights, or at least had prodded the most muffin-rings, was accorded the ancient privilege of naming and crowning the Queen of Love and Beauty— which naming had in reality been done *for* him by the "cut-and-dried" process, and long in advance, by a committee of ladies, but the crowning he did in person, though suffering from loss of blood, and then was taken to the county hospital on a shutter to have his wounds dressed—these curious things all occurring in Brooklyn, and no longer ago than one or two yesterdays. It seems impossible, and yet it is true.

This was doubtless the first appearance of the "tournament" up here among the rolling-mills and factories, and will probably be the last. It will be well to let it retire permanently to the rural districts of Virginia, where, it is said, the fine mailed and plumed, noble-natured, maiden-rescuing, wrong-redressing, adventure-seeking knight of romance is accepted and believed in by the peasantry with pleasing simplicity, while they reject with scorn the plain, unpolished verdict whereby history exposes him as a braggart, a ruffian, a fantastic vagabond, and an ignoramus.

All romance aside, what shape would our admiration of the heroes of Ashby de la Zouch be likely to take, in this practical age, if those worthies were to rise up and come here and perform again the chivalrous deeds of that famous passage of arms? Nothing but a New York jury and the insanity plea could save them from hanging, from the amiable Bois-Guilbert and the pleasant Front-de-Boeuf clear down to the nameless ruffians that entered the riot with unpictured shields and did their first murder and acquired their first claim to respect that day. The doings of the so-called "chivalry" of the Middle Ages were absurd enough, even when they were brutally and bloodily in earnest, and when their surroundings of castles and donjons, savage landscapes and half-savage peoples, were in keeping; but those doings gravely reproduced with tinsel decorations and mock pageantry, by bucolic gentlemen with broomstick lances, and with muffin-rings to represent the foe, and all in the midst of the refinement and dignity of a carefully-developed modern civilization, is absurdity gone crazy.

Now, for next exhibition, let us have a fine representation of one of those chivalrous wholesale butcheries and burnings of Jewish women and children, which the crusading heroes of romance used to indulge in in their European homes, just before starting to the Holy Land, to seize and take to their protection the Sepulchre and defend it from "pollution."

1870

UNBURLESQUABLE THINGS

There are some things which cannot be burlesqued, for the simple reason that in themselves they are so extravagant and grotesque that nothing is left for burlesque to take hold of. For instance, all attempts to burlesque the "Byron Scandal" were failures because the central feature of it, incest, was a "situation" so tremendous and so imposing that the happiest available resources of burlesque seemed tame and cheap in its presence. Burlesque could invent nothing to transcend incest, except by enlisting two crimes, neither of which is ever mentioned among women and children, and one of which is only mentioned in rare books of the law, and then as "the crime without a name"—a term with a shudder in it! So the reader never saw the "Byron Scandal" successfully travestied in print, and he may rest satisfied that he never will.

All attempts to burlesque the monster musical "Peace Jubilee" in Boston were mournful failures. The ten thousand singers, the prodigious organ, the hundred anvils, and the artillery accompaniment made up an unintentional, but complete, symmetrical and enormous burlesque, which shamed the poor inventions of the sketchers and scribblers who tried to be funny over it in magazines and newspapers. Even Cruikshank failed when he tried to pictorially burlesque the English musical extravaganza which probably furnished Mr. Gilmore with his idea.

There was no burlesquing the "situation" when the French Train, Henri Rochefort, brayed forth the proclamation that whenever he was arrested forty thousand *ouvriers* would be there to know the reason why—when, alas! right on top of it one single humble policeman took him and marched him off to prison through an atmosphere with never a taint of garlic in it.

There is no burlesquing the McFarland trial, either as a whole or piecemeal by selection. Because it was sublimated burlesque itself, in any way one may look at it. The court gravely tried the prisoner, *not* for murder, apparently, but as to his sanity or insanity. His counsel attempted the intellectual miracle of proving the prisoner's deed to have been a *justifiable homicide by an insane person*. The Recorder charged the jury to—well, there are different opinions as to what the Recorder wanted them to do, among those who have translated the charge from the original Greek, though his general idea seemed to be to scramble first to the support of the prisoner and then to the support of the law, and then to the prisoner again, and back again to the law, with a vaguely perceptible desire to help the prisoner a little the most without making that desire unofficially and ungracefully prominent. To wind up and put a final polish to the many-sided burlesque, the jury went out and devoted nearly two hours to trying for his life a man whose deed would not be accepted as a capital crime by the mass of mankind even though all the lawyers did their best to prove it such. It is hardly worth while to mention that the emotional scene in the court room, following the delivery of the verdict, when women hugged the prisoner, the jury, the reporters, and even the remorselessly sentimental Graham, is eminently un-burlesquable.

But first and last, the splendid feature of the McFarland comedy was the *insanity* part of it. Where the occasion was for dragging in that poor old threadbare lawyer-trick, is not perceptible, except it was to make a *show* of difficulty in winning a verdict that would have won itself without ever a lawyer to meddle with the case. Heaven knows insanity was disreputable enough, long ago; but now that the lawyers have got to cutting every gallows rope and picking every prison lock with it, it is become a sneaking villainy that ought to hang and keep on hanging its sudden possessors until evil-doers should conclude that the safest plan was to never claim to have it until they came by it legitimately. The very calibre of the people the lawyers most frequently try to save by the insanity subterfuge, ought to laugh the plea out of the courts, one would think. Any one who watched the proceedings closely in the McFarland-Richardson mockery will be-lieve that the insanity plea was a rather far-fetched compliment to pay the prisoner, inasmuch as one must first have brains before he can go crazy, and there was surely nothing in the evidence to show that McFarland had enough of the raw material to justify him in at-tempting anything more imposing than a lively form of idiocy.

Governor Alcorn, of Mississippi, recommends his Legislature to so alter the laws that as soon as the insanity plea is offered in the case of a person accused of crime, the case shall be sent up to a high State court and the insanity part of the matter inquired into and settled permanently, *by itself*, before the trial for the crime charged is touched at all. Anybody but one of this latter-day breed of "lunatics" on trial for murder will recognize the wisdom of the proposition at a glance.

There is one other thing which transcends the powers of burlesque, and that is a Fenian "invasion." First we have the portentous mystery that precedes it for six months, when all the air is filled with stage whisperings; when "Councils" meet every night with awful secrecy, and the membership try to see who can get up first in the morning and tell the proceedings. Next, the expatriated Nation struggles through a travail of national squabbles and political splits, and is finally delivered of a litter of "Governments," and Presidents Mc-This, and Generals O'That, of several different complexions, politically speaking; and straightway the newspapers teem with the new names, and men who were insignificant and obscure one day find themselves great and famous the next. Then the several "governments," and presidents, and generals, and senates get by the ears, and remain so until the customary necessity of carrying the American city elections with a minority vote comes around and unites them; then they begin to "sound the tocsin of war" again—that is to say, in solemn whisperings at dead of night they secretly plan a Canadian raid, and publish it in the "World" next morning; they begin to refer significantly to "Ridgway," and we reflect bodingly that there is no telling how soon that slaughter may be repeated. Presently the "invasion" begins to take tangible shape; and as no news travels so freely or so fast as the "secret" doings of the Fenian Brotherhood, the land is shortly in a tumult of apprehension. The telegraph announces that "last night, 400 men went north from Utica, but refused to disclose their destination—were extremely reticent—answered no questions—were not armed, or in uniform, but *it was noticed that they marched to the depot in military fashion*"—and so on. Fifty such despatches follow each other within two days, evidencing that squads of locomotive mystery have gone north from a hundred different points and rendezvoused on the Canadian border—and that, consequently, a horde of 25,000 invaders, at least, is gathered together; and then, hurrah! they cross the line; hurrah! they meet the enemy; hip, hip, hurrah! a battle ensues; hip—no, not hip nor hurrah—for the U. S. Marshal and one man seize the Fenian General-in-Chief on the battle-field, in the midst of his "army," and bowl him off in a carriage and lodge him in a common jail—and, presto! the illustrious "invasion" is at an end!

The Fenians have not done many things that seemed to call for pictorial illustration; but their first care has usually been to make a picture of any performance of theirs that would stand it as soon as possible after its achievement, and paint everything in it a violent green, and embellish it with harps and pickaxes, and other emblems of national grandeur, and print thousands of them in the severe simplicity of primitive lithography, and hang them above the National Palladium, among the decanters. Shall we have a nice picture of the battle of Pigeon Hill and the little accident to the Commander-in-Chief?

No, a Fenian "invasion" cannot be burlesqued, because it uses up all the material itself. It is harmless fun, this annual masquerading toward the border; but America should not encourage it, for the reason that it may some time or other succeed in embroiling the country in a war with a friendly power—and such an event as that would be ill compensated by the liberation of even so excellent a people as the Downtrodden Nation.

1870

A BRACE OF BRIEF LECTURES ON SCIENCE

I. PALEONTOLOGY

What a noble science is paleontology! And what really startling sagacity its votaries exhibit!

Immediately after the Nathan murder, twenty practiced detectives went and viewed the dead body; examined the marks on the throat and on the head; followed the bloody tracks; looked at the bloody clothes, the broken safe, and the curious, unusual, mysterious "dog." They took note of the stolen diamond studs and set a watch on the pawnbrokers, and they set watches upon all the known thieves and housebreakers, and upon their fast women. They had the detectives of all the wide world to help them watch and work, and the telegraph to facilitate communication. They had the testimony of fifty witnesses in point and conveniently at hand for reference, a knowledge of everything that transpired about the Nathan mansion during the entire eventful night with the exception of the single hour during which the murder was committed. Thus we perceive that the mystery was narrowed down to a very small compass, and the clues and helps were abundant and excellent. Yet what is the result? Nothing. The "dog" has told no tales, the bloody tracks have led no whither, the murderer has not been found. Why, it is not even known whether there was one murderer, or twenty—or whether men or women did the deed—or how entrance was gained to the house or how exit was accomplished!

The reader perceives how illiterate detectives can blunder along, with whole volumes of clues to guide them, and yet achieve nothing. Now let me show him what "science" can do. Let me show what might have been done if New York had been intelligent enough to employ one deep paleontologist in the work instead of a dozen detectives.—Let me demonstrate that with no other clue than one small splinter off that "iron dog," or a gill of the water the bloody shirt was washed in, any cultivated paleontologist would have walked right off and fetched you that murderer with as unerring certainty as he would take a fragment of an unknown bone and build you the animal it used to belong to, and tell you which end his tail was on and what he preferred for dinner.

In this lesson I will treat only of one subject of paleontological "research"—PRIMEVAL MAN. Geology has revealed the fact that the crust of the earth is composed of five layers or strata. We exist on the surface of the fifth. Geology teaches, with scientific accuracy, that each of these layers was from ten thousand to two million years forming or cooling. [A disagreement as to a few hundred thousand years is a matter of little consequence to science.] The layer immediately under our layer, is the fourth or "quaternary"; under that is the third, or tertiary, etc. Each of these layers had its peculiar animal and vegetable life, and when each layer's mission was done, it and its animals and vegetables ceased from their labors and were forever buried under the new layer, with its new-shaped and new fangled animals and vegetables. So far, so good. Now the geologists Thompson, Johnson, Jones and Ferguson state that our own layer has been ten thousand years forming. The geologists Herkimer, Hildebrand, Boggs and Walker all claim that our layer has been four hundred thousand years forming. Other geologists just as reliable, maintain that our layer has been from one to two million years forming. Thus we have a concise and satisfactory idea of how long our layer has been growing and accumulating.

That is sufficient geology for our present purpose. The paleontologists Hooker, Baker, Slocum and Hughes claim that Primeval Man existed during the quaternary period—consequently he existed as much as ten thousand, and possibly two million, years ago. The paleontologists Howard, Perkins, de Warren and Von Hawkins assert that Primeval Man existed as far back as the *tertiary* period— and consequently he walked the earth at a time so remote that if you strung ciphers after a unit till there were enough to answer for a necklace for a mastodon you could not adequately represent the billions of centuries ago it happened. Now, you perceive, we begin to cramp this part of our subject into a corner where we can grasp it, as it were, and contemplate it intelligently. Let us—"for a flier," as the learned Von Humboldt phrases it—consider that this Primeval Man transpired eight or nine hundred thousand years ago, and not day before yesterday, like the Nathan murder.—What do we know of him, and how do we find it out? Listen, while I reduce the "revelations" of paleontology to a few paragraphs:

1. Primeval Man existed in the quaternary period—because his bones are found in caves along with bones of now extinct animals *of* that period—such as the "cave-hyena," the mammoth, etc.

2. The incredible antiquity of the Primeval Man's bones is further proven by their extreme "fragility."—No bones under a million years old "could be so fragile." [I quote strictly from the scientific authorities.] The reason royal skeletons in Westminster crumble to dust when exposed, although only a trifling eight hundred years old, is because they are shut up in leaden coffins, I suppose. Bones do not keep good in coffins. There is no sure way but to cord them up in caves. Paleontology reveals that they will then last you a million years without any inconvenience.

3. The Primeval Man possessed weapons—because along with his bones are found rude chips and flakes of flint that the paleontologist knows very well were regarded as knives by the Primeval Man; and also flints of a rude oval shape that in his pretty simplicity he regarded as "hatchets." These things have been found in vast quantities with his bones.

4. The Primeval Man "wore clothes"—because, along with his bones have been found skeletons of the reindeer, "*with marks still visible about the base of the horns, such as are made in our day when we cut there to loosen the hide in order to skin the animal.*" Could this paleontologist find the Nathan murderer?—Undoubtedly he could. The ignorant need not say that possibly the Primeval Man wore no clothes, but wanted the hide for a tent, or for bow-strings, or lassos, or beds, or to trade off for glass beads and whisky. The paleontologist knows what he wanted with the hide.

5. The Primeval Man had not only inventive powers and gropings toward civilization, as evidenced by his contriving and manufacturing flint hatchets and knives and wearing clothes, but he also had marked and unmistakable "art" inspirations—because, along with his bones have been found figures scratched on bone, vaguely suggestive of possible fishes; and a boar's tooth rudely carved into the shape of a bird's head, and "with a hole in it *to enable him to hang it around his neck.*" [I quote from authority.] I ask, could this person discover the Nathan murderer?

6. The Primeval Man "eat his wild game roasted"—because, "along with his bones are found the bones of wild animals which seem to have been scorched" some millions of years ago.

7. The Primeval Man was "passionately fond of marrow" [I still quote from the scientific authorities,]—because, along with his bones have been found animal bones *broken lengthwise,* "which shows that they had been thus broken *to extract the marrow,* of which our primitive forefathers *were inordinately fond,*" says the "Paleontological Investigations." Could *this* man read the secrets of an iron dog and a bloody shirt, or could he not?

8. The Primeval Man was—a—cannibal!—because, in Italy, and also in Scotland, along with his bones have been found children's bones which had "first been carefully cleansed and emptied to satisfy the inordinate taste for marrow, and then *gnawed.*"(!) This is horrible, but true. Let not the ignorant say that a dog might have done this gnawing, for paleontology has looked into that and decided that—

9. The Primeval Man had no dog—because *"there is no trace of dogs having been domesticated then."* Which settles that point.

10. The Primeval hyena gnawed bones, however—because paleontology proves that "the marks on some bones found in France were not made by dog, human, cat or mastodon teeth, but by the teeth of a hyena." And paleontology is aware that the hyena gnawed the bones *"after* the Primeval Man" was done with them—which was clever, but paleontology keeps the reasons for knowing this a scientific secret.

11. Primeval Man had graveyards—"because, along with great quantities of the roasted and gnawed bones of primeval animals, have been found quantities of human bones and flint weapons." And it is a precious privilege to live in an epoch of paleontologists, for the uneducated investigator would not be able to tell a primeval graveyard from a primeval restaurant.

12. The Primeval Man always had a banquet and a good time after a funeral—because, down the hill a little way from his graveyard (there is only one on record,) *"a bed of ashes was unearthed."* Von Rosenstein and some others say the banquet occurred *before* the funeral, but most paleontologists agree that it was nearly a week after the obsequies.

13. Primeval Man "made his flint knives and hatchets with a stone hammer"—and an English paleontologist has "proved" this, and overwhelmed all cavilers with confusion, and won thunders of applause and incalculable gratitude from his fellow-scientists by actually *making* a flint hatchet *with a stone hammer.* The fact that these weapons are so independent in form that if a man chipped a piece of flint with his eyes shut the result would infallibly be a primeval flint knife

or flint hatchet, one or the other, in spite of him, has got nothing to do with the matter. If cavilers say that the fact that we *could* carve our bread with an axe is no sign that we *do* carve it with an axe, I simply say that such an argument begs the question, inasmuch as it applies to the present time, whereas the science of paleontology only treats of matters of remote antiquity.

Now I come to the most marvellous "revelation" of all—the most unexpected, the most surprising, the most gratifying. It is this. Paleontology has discovered that—

14. "THE PRIMEVAL MAN BELIEVED IN IMMORTALITY!"—because, "else why did he bury those huge quantities of flint hatchets and other weapons with his dead, just as all savages do who desire to provide the loved and lost with means of amusement and subsistence in the happy hunting grounds of eternity?" Aha! What saith the caviler now? Poor purblind croaker, in this grand and awful evidence of the Primeval Man's belief in the immortality of his soul, *you* would find only evidence that the primeval cemetery, the primeval restaurant and the primeval arsenal were purposely compacted into the same premises to save rent. Idiot!

The lesson is ended. Do you see, now, how simple and easy "science" makes a thing? Do you see how—

Some animal bones, split, scratched and scorched; located in quaternary ground;

Some full sized human bones with them—and very "fragile";

Some small bones, marrowless and scratched;

Some flints of several uncertain shapes;

Some rude scratchings and carvings, done possibly by design;

Some deer horns, scratched at their bases;

An ash-pile;

The absence of dog-tracks;—

Do you see how these clues and "evidences" are all the materials the science of paleontology needs in order to give to the world the wonder of a—

Primeval Man;

And not only that but tell what was the particular period he lived in;

What weapons he carried;

What kind of clothes he wore;

What his art predilections and capacities were;

What he made his weapons with;

What his funeral customs were;

What part of a bear or a child he preferred for breakfast;

What animal got the remains of his feasts, and what animal didn't;

And finally, what the foundation and corner-stone of the religion of the lost and lamented old antediluvian commander-in-chief of all the fossils, was!

What a crying pity it is that the Nathan murder was not committed two million years ago—for I *do* so want to know all about it.

[Some of my own paleontological deductions differing in some respects from those of other paleontological authorities, I reserve them for expression in another chapter on "Science," which will appear next month.]

II. PALEONTOLOGY CONCLUDED—PRIMEVAL MAN

My brother paleontologists have "proved" by the finding of weapons (for use in the happy hunting grounds,) side by side with the Primeval Man's bones, that the Primeval Man was a believer in immortality. And I think they have done more than this. I think that in "proving" that he always broke the bones of animals "lengthwise" to get at the marrow, they have come near proving the Primeval Man an ass. For why should he break bones lengthwise to get at the marrow when anybody except a scientist knows that it is a deal easier to break a bone crosswise than lengthwise, and still more convenient to smash your stone down on it and let it break any way it pleases; and we all know that the marrow will taste just the same, no matter what plan of fracture you pursue. And yet nothing would suit this primeval "galoot" but the lengthwise style—it does *not* look reasonable. And I must call notice to the fact that neither the Primeval Man's elk-horn instruments, nor his flint knife, nor yet the awe-inspiring quoit which *he* thought was a flint "hatchet," could split a slippery, crooked, uneasy and vexatious bone lengthwise with facility —and I have always noticed that your Primeval Man looks to convenience *first*. That is his way, if I know whereof I speak—and if I do not, what am I a paleontologist for?

2. Somehow I cannot feel satisfied that those bears (whose bones are found mingled with those of the Primeval Man), were not the real parties that ate that marrow—and also the animals that used to own it. And without nibbling at heresy any further, I may as well come out and suggest that perhaps they ate the Primeval Man himself. Here is a pile of bones of primeval man and beast all mixed to-

gether, with no more damning evidence that the man ate the bears than that the bears ate the man—yet paleontology holds a coroner's inquest here in the fifth geologic period on an "unpleasantness" which transpired in the quaternary, and calmly lays it on the MAN, and then adds to it what purports to be evidence of CANNIBALISM. I ask the candid reader, Does not this look like taking advantage of a gentleman who has been dead two million years, and whose surviving friends and relatives——. But the subject is too painful. Are we to have another Byron-scandal case? Here are savage ways and atrocious appetites attributed to the dead and helpless Primeval Man —have we any assurance that the same hand will not fling mud at the Primeval Man's mother, next?

3. Again. Is there anything really so surprising about the absence of the marrow from bones a few hundred thousand years old as to make it worth while to sit up nights trying to figure out how it came to be absent? Now *is* there, considering that there are so many good chances that Age, Worms and Decay got the marrow?

4. If the student should ask why paleontologists call the Primeval Man a cannibal, I should answer that it was because they find toothmarks on primeval children's bones which they *"recognize as the marks of human teeth."* If the student should ask why paleontologists assert that primeval hyenas gnawed the bones of roasted animals after the Primeval Man had finished his meal, I should answer that they find teeth-marks upon said bones which they *"recognize as hyena teeth-marks."* If the student should ask me how the paleontologist tells the difference between hyena and human teeth-marks on a *bone*, and particularly a bone which has been rotting in a cave since the everlasting hills were builded, I should answer that I don't know.

A man could leave a sort of a tooth-mark (till decay set in,) in any fleshy substance that might remain sticking to a bone, but that he could make a tooth-mark on the bone itself I am obliged to question. Let the earnest student try to bite the handle of his tooth-brush and see if he can leave an autograph that will defy the ages. Aha! where are you *now!*

5. The frivolous are apt to take notice of a certain paleontological custom, which, not understanding, they take to be proper prey for their wit. I refer to the common paleontological custom of "proving" the vast age of primeval bones by their *"extreme fragility,"* and then accounting for their wonderful preservation by the fact that they were *"petrified and fossilized* by deposits of calcareous salts." If cavilers

had brains enough to comprehend this, they would not cavil so much about it.

6. In the celebrated paleontological "cave of Aurignac" were found bones of primeval men, woolly elephants, huge bears and elks and wolves of a singular pattern, and also bones of the august mastodon. What do my fellow paleontologists call that place? A "primeval *grave-yard.*" Why? Why graveyard? Reader, I have looked carefully into this matter and discovered the significant fact that they never found a single tomb-stone. Nor any sign of a grave. Then *why* call it a graveyard? Does a tangled mess of bones of men and beasts necessarily constitute a graveyard? I would not disturb any man's faith in the primeval cemetery, though, merely to hear myself talk. I have opened the subject for a nobler purpose—to give the paleontological student's faith a new direction and a worthier one. I have investigated the evidences and now feel tolerably satisfied that the contents of the cave of Aurignac are not the remains of a primeval grave-yard, but of a primeval menagerie. I ask the intelligent reader if it is likely that such rare creatures as a woolly elephant, a mastodon, and those huge and peculiar bears, wolves, etc., would simply *happen* together, along with a man or two, in a comfortable, roomy cave, with a small, low door, just suited to the admission of single files of country people, to say nothing of children and servants at half price? I simply ask the candid reader that question and let him sweat—as the historian Josephus used to say. If I should be asked for further suggestions in support of my hypothesis, I should hazard the thought that the treasurer of the menagerie was guilty of a hideous general massacre, while the proprietor and the beasts were asleep, and that his object was robbery. It is admitted by nearly one-sixth of all the paleontologists [observe the unusual unanimity] that the first part of the quaternary period must have been an uncommonly good season for public exhibitions—and in this one fact alone you have almost a confirmation of the criminal motive attributed to the treasurer. If I am asked for final and incontrovertible proof of my position, I point to the significant fact that *the bones of the treasurer have never been found, and* THE CASH BOX IS GONE. It is enough to make one's hair stand on end.

I desire nothing more than my dues. If I have thrown any light on the mystery of the cave of Aurignac, I desire that it shall be acknowledged—if I have not, I desire that it may be as though I had never spoken.

7. As concerns the proud paleontological trophy, the "flint hatchet"

and its companion the "flint knife," I am compelled again to differ with the other scientists. I cannot think that the so-called "flint knife" is a knife at all. I cannot disabuse my mind of the impression that it is a file. No knife ever had such a scandalous blade as that. If asked by scholars of the established faith what the Primeval Man could want with a file, I should, with customary paleontological diplomacy, ask what he could want with such a *knife?* Because he *might* file something with that thing, but I will hang if he could ever *cut* anything with it.

8. And as for the oval shaped flint which stands for the lauded primeval "hatchet," I cannot rid myself of the idea that it was only a paper-weight. If incensed brother-paleontologists storm at me and say the Primeval Man had no paper, I shall say calmly, "As long as it was nobody's business but his own, couldn't he carry his paper-weight around till he got some?"

But there is nothing intractable about me. If gentlemen wish to compromise and call it a petrified hoecake, or anything in *reason*, I am agreeable; for the Primeval Man had to have food, and might have had hoecakes, but he didn't have to have a flint "hatchet" like this thing, which he could not even cut his butter with without mashing it.

If any one should find fault with any arguments used by me in the course of the above chapter, and say that I jump to a conclusion over so much ground that the feat is in a manner ungraceful; and if he should say further, that in establishing one paleontological position of mine I generally demolish another, I would answer that these things are inseparable from scientific investigation. We all do it—all scientists. No one can regret it more than we do ourselves, but there really seems to be no remedy for it. First we had to recede from our assertion that a certain fossil was a primeval man, because afterward when we had found multitudes of saurians and had grown glib and facile in descanting upon them, we found that that other creature was of the same species. What could we do? It was too big a job to turn a thousand saurians into primeval men, and so we turned the solitary primeval man into a saurian. It was the cheapest way. And so it has always been with us. Every time we get a chance to assert something, we have to take back something. When we announced and established the great discovery of the "Glacial Period," how we did have to cart the dead animals around! Because, do not you see, the indiscriminate sort of distribution of fossil species which we had accommodated to the characteristic action of a general flood would not answer for a nicely discriminating "glacial period" which *ought* to transport only walruses, white bears, and other frigid creatures, from the North Pole down into Africa and not meddle with any other kind of animals. Well, we had only got the several species of fossil animals located to "back up" the "glacial period" when here comes some idiot down from Behring's Strait with a fossil elephant a hundred thousand years old! Of course we had to go to work and account for *him*. You see how it is. Science is as sorry as you are that this year's science is no more like last year's science than last year's was like the science of twenty years gone by. But science cannot help it. Science is full of change. Science is progressive and eternal. The scientists of twenty years ago laughed at the ignorant men who had groped in the intellectual darkness of twenty years before.

We derive pleasure from laughing at *them*. We have accounted for that elephant, at last, on the hypothesis that when he was alive Alaska was in the tropics. Twenty or thirty years from now the new crop of paleontologists will be just as likely as not to find an elephant and a petrified iceberg roosting in the same quaternary cave together up there in Alaska, and if they do, down *we* go, with our tropical theory, that is all.

1871

THE COMING MAN

GENERAL DEWLAP G. LOVEL, minister to Hong-Wo, has resigned and returned to this country. His successor will not be appointed at present. Some of General Lovel's friends are nominating him for the vacant English mission. [*Item in all the papers.*]

What a jar it gave me! For as I am a true man, I thought it meant my old fellow-soldier in the Nevada militia, General *Dun*lap G. Lovel. And so I read it again, and again, and once more, and repeatedly— and with ever augmenting astonishment. But at last I grew calmer and began to scrutinize the "internal evidences" of this item. They were equal—part for, and part against my Lovel. For instance, my Lovel, who always thought gunpowder tea was made from ordinary gunpowder boiled instead of burned (and will still think so until he sees this paragraph), is guileless enough to go on wearing a military title gained as Brigadier in a militia which never saw service even in a Fourth of July procession, and consider it a distinction far from ridiculous. Consequently this general is as likely to be as general as another's. But then the remaining point of evidence is against us— namely, that this Minister Lovel has resigned. So it is not my Lovel after all. For my Lovel would not have resigned.

No; my Lovel is a man who can always be relied upon—a man who would be faithful to the death. If intrusted with an office, he would cling to that office until it was abolished. I am acquainted with my Lovel.

The distinct evidence is against my Lovel, and yet that lifting of a serene, unblinking gaze aloft to the awful sublimity of St. James's, from the remote insignificance of the U.S. embassage to Hong-Wo, with its candle-box for an official desk, and boiled beans three times a day for subsistence, and peanuts on Sunday for grandeur, is so precisely like *my* Lovel!

But with sorrow I own that this General Lovel is *Dew*lap G., while mine is only *Dun*lap G. Consequently they are not the same— far from it. Yet it is possible that a kind word from me may attract attention and sympathy to my poor Lovel, and thus help a deserving man to fortune. So let me go on.

General P. Edward O'Connor has done the highest and faithfullest and best military service in Mormondom, that ever has been rendered there for our country. For about seven years or such a matter he has made both Brigham and the Indians reasonably civil and polite. Well——. However, I see by the papers that General O'Connor has *not* been appointed Governor of Utah, as the Pacific coast desired. I cannot think how I came to wander off to General O'Connor, for he has nothing whatever to do with my General Lovel. Therefore I will drop him and not digress again. I now resume.

When the nation rose, years ago, Dunlap G. Lovel of Virginia, Nevada (Territory), flew to arms and was created a Brigadier-General of the territorial militia; and with his hand on his heart he swore an oath that he never would budge from his post till the enemy came. Colonel O'Connor flew to arms and put down the Indians and the Mormons, and *kept* them down for years—and fought his gallant way up through bullets and blood to his brigadier-generalship. But this is not a biography of General O'Connor. Hang General O'Connor! It is General Lovel I desire to speak of.

General Lovel—how imposing he looked in his uniform! He was a very exceedingly microscopic operator in wild-cat silver-mining stocks, and so he could not wear it every day; but then he was always ready when a fireman was to be buried or a relative hung. And he did look really beautiful, any of the old citizens will say that. It was a fine sight when all the militia turned out at once. The territorial population was some 20,000 then, and the Territorial militia numbered 139 persons, including regimental officers, three major and eleven brigadier-generals. General Lovel was the eleventh.

I cannot now call to mind distinctly the several engagements General Lovel was in, but I remember the following, on account of their peculiar prominence:

When Thompson Billings the desperado was captured, Lovel's brigade guarded the front door of the jail that night. It was well for Billings that he left by the back door; for it was always thought that if he had come out the front way he would have been shot.

At the great Sanitary Ball in Carson City, General Lovel was present in his uniform.

When the Legislature met in 1863, General Lovel and brigade were promptly on duty, either to do honor to them or protect the public, I have forgotten which.

He was present in his uniform with his men, to guard the exit of the Legislature of 1862, and let the members retire in peace with the surplus steel pens and stationery. This was the Legislature that confirmed his appointment as Brigadier-General. It also elected as enrolling clerk of its House of Representatives a militia chieftain by the name of Captain G. Murphy, who could not write. This was a misunderstanding, however, rather than a blunder, for the Legislature of 1862 did not know it was necessary he should know how to write.

When the Governor delivered his farewell address, General Lovel and brigade were there, and never gave way an inch till it was done.

General Lovel was in several other engagements, but I cannot call them to mind now.

By-and-by the people began to feel that General Lovel's military services ought to be rewarded. So some one suggested that he run as an independent candidate for U. S. Senator (for Nevada was become a new-fledged State by this time). Modest as this old soldier was, backward as he was, naturally diffident as he was, he said he would do it, and he did. It was commonly reported and steadfastly believed by everybody that he spent the bulk of his fortune, which was fifteen or twenty thousand dollars, in "putting up" a legislative delegation from Virginia City which should fight under his Senatorial banner. AND YET THAT MAN WAS NOT ELECTED. I not only state it, but I swear to it. Why, unless my memory has gone entirely crazy, that polluted Legislature never even mentioned his name!

What was an old public servant to do after such treatment? Shake the dust from his sandals and leave the State to its self-invited decay and ruin. That was the course to pursue, and that was the one he did pursue. He knew a land where worth is always recognized, a city where the nation's faithful vassal cannot know the cold hand of neglect—WASHINGTON. He went there in Andrew Johnson's time. He probably got Captain John Nye to use his "influence" for him —ha! ha!

What do we behold a grateful nation instantly do? We see it send General O'Connor—no, I mean General Lovel—to represent us as resident minister at oriental Hong-Wo!

No, no, no—I have got it all wrong again. It is not my Dun-lap, but somebody's Dew-lap that was sent.

But might it not—no, it cannot be and *is* not my Lovel whose "friends" are pointing him towards august St. James's. The first syllable of the name is so different. But my Lovel would do very well indeed for that place. I am aware that he knows no French, and is not certain of his English. But then our foreign representatives seldom know the "language of diplomacy" anyhow. I do not know that he has any education to speak of—am confident he has not—but cannot a man learn? I am not even certain that he knows enough to come in when it rains, but I say it again, and repeat and reiterate it, cannot a man *learn?* We need a person at such a lordly court as the British who is well-bred and gentlemanly in his appearance and address, a man accustomed to the dignities and proprieties of the highest and best society. There is not a barkeeper, a desperado, an editor, or an Indian in Nevada but will speak in terms of respect of Dun-lap G. Lovel, and say that he always worthily bore himself among the very cream of society in that critical and exacting community. We want no mere unconsidered "Mr." at the Court of St. James's; we want a person with a title to his name—a General, nothing less. My General would answer. He could tell those old field-marshals from India and Abyssinia something about soldier-life which would be new to them, perhaps. But above all, we want a great-brained, profound diplomatic genius at the Court of St. James's—a man surcharged with experience likewise. Now if this deep, this bottomless Hong-Wooian diplomat were only *Dun*-lap G. Lovel—but no, it is Dew-lap. But my General would be a great card for us in England, and I wish we could have him. Contemplate him in Motley's place. Think of my dainty Lilliputian standing in Brobdingnag Motley's shoes, and peeping out smartly over the instep at the Great Powers. It would be a thing to bless and honor a heedful Providence for—this consummation.

Who are the "friends" who desire the appointment of that other Lovel, I wonder! If that Lovel were my Lovel, I should think the term "friends" referred to "Captain" John Nye, of the lobby, Washington, a man whom I love to call "the Wheels of Government," because if you could see him backing members up into corners by the button-hole, and "influencing" them in favor of this, that, and the other Lovel whom the back settlements have cast up undigested, you would believe as I do, that our Government could not proceed without him.

But sorrow to me, this Lovel is Dew-lap, and mine is totally another man—Dun-lap. Let it go. I care not. And yet my heart *knows* I would worship that President who should show my fading eyes and failing life the spectacle of "General" Dun-lap G. Lovel Envoy

Extraordinary and Minister Plenipotentiary to the Court of St. James's, and "Captain" John Nye, of the lobby, Washington, Secretary of Legation. I would be content to die then—entirely content. And so with loving zeal I add my name to the list of "General Lovel's friends" who are "nominating him for the vacant English mission."

1871

FRANCIS LIGHTFOOT LEE*

This man's life-work was so inconspicuous, that his name would
now be wholly forgotten, but for one thing—he signed the Declaration
of Independence. Yet his life was a most useful and worthy one. It
was a good and profitable voyage, though it left no phosphorescent
splendors in its wake.

A sketch of Francis Lightfoot Lee can be useful for but one
purpose, as showing what sort of material was used in the construction of congressmen in his day; since to sketch him is to sketch
the average congressman of his time.

He came of an old and excellent family; a family which had
borne an unsullied name, and held honorable place on both sides of
the water; a family with a reputation to preserve and traditions to
perpetuate; a family which could not afford to soil itself with political
trickery, or do base things for party or for hire; a family which was
able to shed as much honor upon official station as it received from it.

He dealt in no shams; he had no ostentations of dress or equipage;
for he was, as one may say, *inured* to wealth. He had always been
used to it. His own ample means were inherited. He was educated.
He was more than that—he was finely cultivated. He loved books; he
had a good library, and no place had so great a charm for him as
that. The old Virginian mansion which was his home was also the
home of that old-time Virginian hospitality which hoary men still
hold in mellow memory. Over their port and walnuts he and his
friends of the gentry discussed a literature which is dead and forgotten now, and political matters which were drowsy with the absence
of corruption and "investigations." Sundays he and they drove to
church in their lumbering coaches, with a due degree of grave and
seemly pomp. Week-days they inspected their domains, ordered their
affairs, attended to the needs of their dependents, consulted with

* NOTE.—The subject of this sketch was born on the fourteenth day of October, 1734,
and died in April, 1797.—Ed. Pa. Mag.

their overseers and tenants, busied themselves with active benevo-
lences. They were justices of the peace, and performed their unpaid
duties with arduous and honest diligence, and with serene, unhampered impartiality toward a society to which they were not be-
holden for their official stations. In short, Francis Lightfoot Lee
was a gentleman—a word which meant a great deal in his day,
though it means nothing whatever in ours.

Mr. Lee defiled himself with no juggling, or wire-pulling, or begging, to acquire a place in the provincial legislature, but went thither
when he was called, and went reluctantly. He wrought there in-
dustriously during four years, never seeking his own ends, but only
the public's. His course was purity itself, and he retired unblemished
when his work was done. He retired gladly, and sought his home
and its superior allurements. No one dreamed of such a thing as
"investigating" him.

Immediately the people called him again—this time to a seat in
the Continental Congress. He accepted this unsought office from a
sense of duty only, and during four of the darkest years of the
Revolution he labored with all his might for his country's best behests.
He did no brilliant things, he made no brilliant speeches; but the
enduring strength of his patriotism was manifest, his fearlessness in
confronting perilous duties and compassing them was patent to all,
the purity of his motives was unquestioned, his unpurchasable honor
and uprightness were unchallenged. His good work finished, he
hurried back to the priceless charms of his home once more, and
begged hard to be allowed to spend the rest of his days in the retirement and repose which his faithful labors had so fairly earned; but
this could not be, he was solicited to enter the State Legislature; he
was needed there; he was a good citizen, a citizen of the best and
highest type, and so he put self aside and answered to the call. He
served the State with his accustomed fidelity, and when at last his
public career was ended, he retired honored of all, applauded by all,
unaccused, unsmirched, utterly stainless.

This is a picture of the average, the usual Congressman of Francis
Lightfoot Lee's time, and it is vividly suggestive of what that people
must have been that preferred such men. Since then we have Progressed one hundred years. Let us gravely try to conceive how isolated,
how companionless, how lonesome, such a public servant as this
would be in Washington to-day.

1871

THE INDIGNITY PUT UPON THE REMAINS OF
GEORGE HOLLAND BY THE REV. MR. SABINE

What a ludicrous satire it was upon Christian charity!—even upon
the vague, theoretical idea of it which doubtless this small saint
mouths from his own pulpit every Sunday. Contemplate this freak of
Nature, and think what a Cardiff giant of self-righteousness is
crowded into his pigmy skin. If we probe, and dissect, and lay open
this diseased, this cancerous piety of his, we are forced to the conviction that it is the production of an impression on his part that
his guild do about all the good that is done in the earth, and hence
are better than common clay—hence are competent to say to such as
George Holland, "You are unworthy; you are a play-actor, and consequently a sinner; I cannot take the responsibility of recommending
you to the mercy of Heaven." It must have had its origin in that
impression, else he would have thought, "We are all instruments for
the carrying out of God's purposes; it is not for me to pass judgment
upon your appointed share of the work, or to praise or to revile it; I
have divine authority for it that we are *all* sinners, and therefore it is
not for me to discriminate and say we will supplicate for this sinner,
for he was a merchant prince or a banker, but we will beseech no
forgiveness for this other one, for he was a play-actor." It surely
requires the furthest possible reach of self-righteousness to enable
a man to lift his scornful nose in the air and turn his back upon so
poor and pitiable a thing as a dead stranger come to beg the last
kindness that humanity can do in its behalf. This creature has
violated the letter of the gospel and judged George Holland—not
George Holland either, but his *profession* through him. Then it is
in a measure fair that we judge this creature's guild through *him*.
In effect he has said, "We are the salt of the earth; we do all the good
work that is done; to learn how to be good and do good, men must

come to us; actors and such are obstacles to moral progress."* Pray
look at the thing reasonably for a moment, laying aside all biasses of
education and custom. If a common public impression is fair evidence
of a thing, then this minister's legitimate, recognized, and acceptable
business is to *tell* people calmly, coldly, and in stiff, written sentences,
from the pulpit, to go and do right, be just, be merciful, be charitable.
And his congregation forget it all between church and home. But
for fifty years it was George Holland's business, on the stage, to
make his audience go and do right, and be just, merciful, and charitable—because by his living, breathing, feeling pictures, he showed
them what it *was* to do these things, and *how* to do them, and how
instant and ample was the reward! Is it not a singular teacher of
men, this reverend gentleman who is so poorly informed himself as
to put the whole stage under ban, and say, "I do not think it teaches
moral lessons"?

Where was ever a sermon preached that could make filial ingratitude so hateful to men as the sinful play of "King Lear"? Or
where was there ever a sermon that could so convince men of the
wrong and the cruelty of harboring a pampered and unanalyzed
jealousy as the sinful play of "Othello"? And where are there ten
preachers who can stand in the pulpit teaching heroism, unselfish
devotion, and lofty patriotism, and hold their own against any one
of five hundred William Tells that can be raised up upon five hundred stages in the land at a day's notice? It is almost fair and just to
aver (although it is profanity) that nine-tenths of all the kindness
and forbearance and Christian charity and generosity in the hearts of
the American people to-day, got there by being filtered down from
their fountain-head, the gospel of Christ, *through dramas and
tragedies and comedies on the stage, and through the despised novel
and the Christmas story, and through the thousand and one lessons,
suggestions, and narratives of generous deeds that stir the pulses, and
exalt and augment the nobility of the nation day by day from the
teeming columns of ten thousand newspapers,* and NOT from the
drowsy pulpit!

*Reporter—What answer did you make, Mr. Sabine?
Mr. Sabine—I said that I had a distaste for officiating at such a funeral, and that I
did not care to be mixed up in it. I said to the gentleman that I was willing to bury
the deceased from his house, but that I objected to having the funeral solemnized at
a church.
Reporter—Is it one of the laws of the Protestant Episcopal Church that a deceased
theatrical performer shall not be buried from the church?
Mr. Sabine—It is not: but I have always warned the professing members of my
congregation to keep away from theatres and not to have anything to do with them.
I don't think that they teach moral lessons.—*New York Times.*

All that is great and good in our particular civilization came straight from the hand of Jesus Christ, and many creatures, and of divers sorts, were doubtless appointed to disseminate it; and let us believe that *this seed and the result* are the main thing, and not the cut of the sower's garment; and that whosoever, in his way and according to his opportunity, sows the one and produces the other, has done high service and worthy. And further, let us try with all our strength to believe that whenever old simple-hearted George Holland sowed this seed, and reared his crop of broader charities and better impulses in men's hearts, it was just as acceptable before the Throne as if the seed had been scattered in vapid platitudes from the pulpit of the ineffable Sabine himself.

Am I saying that the pulpit does not do its share toward disseminating the marrow, the *meat* of the gospel of Christ? (For we are not talking of ceremonies and wire-drawn creeds now, but the living heart and soul of what is pretty often only a spectre.)

No, I am not saying that. The pulpit teaches assemblages of people twice a week—nearly two hours, altogether—and does what it can in that time. The theatre teaches large audiences seven times a week—28 or 30 hours altogether; and the novels and newspapers plead, and argue, and illustrate, stir, move, thrill, thunder, urge, persuade, and supplicate, at the feet of millions and millions of people every single day, and all day long, and far into the night; and so these vast agencies till *nine-tenths* of the vineyard, and the pulpit tills the other tenth. Yet now and then some complacent blind idiot says, "You unanointed are coarse clay and useless; you are not as we, the regenerators of the world; go, bury yourselves elsewhere, for we cannot take the responsibility of recommending idlers and sinners to the yearning mercy of Heaven." How *does* a soul like that stay in a carcass without getting mixed with the secretions and sweated out through the pores? Think of this insect condemning the whole theatrical service as a disseminator of bad morals because it has Black Crooks in it; forgetting that if that were sufficient ground, people would condemn the pulpit because it had Cooks, and Kallochs, and Sabines in it.

No, I am not trying to rob the pulpit of any atom of its full share and credit in the work of disseminating the meat and marrow of the gospel of Christ; but I am trying to get a moment's hearing for worthy agencies in the same work, that with overwrought modesty seldom or never claim a recognition of their great services. I am aware that the pulpit does its excellent one-tenth (and credits itself with it now and then, though most of the time a press of business causes it to forget it); I am aware that in its honest and well-meaning way it bores the people with uninflammable truisms about doing good; bores them with correct compositions on charity; bores them, chloroforms them, stupefies them with argumentative mercy without a flaw in the grammar, or an emotion which the minister could put in in the right place if he turned his back and took his finger off the manuscript. And in doing these things the pulpit is doing its duty, and let us believe that it is likewise doing its best, and doing it in the most harmless and respectable way. And so I have said, and shall keep on saying, let us give the pulpit its full share of credit in elevating and ennobling the people; but when a pulpit takes to itself authority to pass judgment upon the work and the worth of just as legitimate an instrument of God as itself, who spent a long life preaching from the stage the self-same gospel without the alteration of a single sentiment or a single axiom of right, it is fair and just that somebody who believes that actors were made for a high and good purpose, and that they *accomplish the object of their creation* and accomplish it well, to protest. And having protested, it is also fair and just—being driven to it, as it were—to whisper to the Sabine pattern of clergyman, under the breath, a simple, instructive truth, and say, "Ministers are not the only servants of God upon earth, nor His most efficient ones either, by a very, very long distance!" Sensible ministers already know this, and it may do the other kind good to find it out.

But to cease teaching and go back to the beginning again, was it not pitiable, that spectacle? Honored and honorable old George Holland, whose theatrical ministry had for fifty years softened hard hearts, bred generosity in cold ones, kindled emotion in dead ones, uplifted base ones, broadened bigoted ones, and made many and many a stricken one glad and filled it brim full of gratitude, figuratively spit upon in his unoffending coffin by this crawling, slimy, sanctimonious, self-righteous reptile!

1871

ONE OF MANKIND'S BORES

I suppose that if there is one thing in the world more hateful than
another to all of us it is to have to write a letter. A private letter
especially. And business letters, to my thinking, are very little
pleasanter. Nearly all the enjoyment is taken out of every letter I get
by the reflection that it must be answered. And I do so dread the
affliction of writing those answers, that often my first and gladdest
impulse is to burn my mail before it is opened. For ten years I
never felt that sort of dread at all, because I was moving about
constantly, from city to city, from State to State, and from country
to country, and so I could leave all letters unanswered if I chose,
and the writers of them would naturally suppose that I had changed
my post-office and missed receiving my correspondence. But I am
"cornered" now. I cannot use that form of deception any more. I am
anchored, and letters of all kinds come straight to me with deadly
precision.

They are letters of all sorts and descriptions, and they treat of
everything. I generally read them at breakfast, and right often they
kill a day's work by diverting my thoughts and fancies into some new
channel, thus breaking up and making confusion of the programme
of scribbling I had arranged for my working hours. After breakfast I
clear for action, and for an hour try hard to write; but there is no
getting back into the old train of thought after such an interruption,
and so at last I give it up and put off further effort till next day. One
would suppose that I would now answer those letters and get them
out of the way; and I suppose one of those model young men we
read about, who enter New York barefoot and live to become insolent
millionaires, would be sure to do that; but I don't. I never shall be a
millionaire, and so I disdain to copy the ways of those men. I did not
start right. I made a fatal mistake to begin with, and entered New
York with boots on and above forty cents in my pocket. With such

an unpropitious beginning, any efforts of mine to acquire great wealth would be frowned upon as illegitimate, and I should be ruthlessly put down as an impostor. And so, as I said before, I decline to follow the lead of those chrysalis Croesuses and answer my correspondents with commercial promptness. I stop work for the day, and leave the new letters stacked up along with those that came the day before, and the day before that, and the day before that, and so on. And by-and-by the pile grows so large that it begins to distress me, and then I attack it and give full five and sometimes six hours to the assault. And how many of the letters do I answer in that time? Never more than nine; usually only five or six. The correspondence clerk in a great mercantile house would answer a hundred in that many hours. But a man who has spent years in writing for the press cannot reasonably be expected to have such facility with a pen. From old habit he gets to thinking and thinking, patiently puzzling for minutes together over the proper turning of a sentence in an answer to some unimportant private letter, and so the precious time slips away.

It comes natural to me in these latter years to do all manner of composition laboriously and ploddingly, private letters included. Consequently, I do fervently hate letter-writing, and so do all the newspaper and magazine men I am acquainted with.

The above remarks are by way of explanation and apology to parties who have written me about various matters, and whose letters I have neglected to answer. I tried in good faith to answer them—tried every now and then, and always succeeded in clearing off several, but always as surely left the majority of those received each week to lie over till the next. The result was always the same, to wit: the unanswered letters would shortly begin to have a reproachful look about them, next an upbraiding look, and by-and-by an aggressive and insolent aspect; and when it came to that, I always opened the stove door and made an example of them. The return of cheerfulness and the flight of every feeling of distress on account of neglected duty, was immediate and thorough.

I did not answer the letter of the Wisconsin gentleman, who inquired whether imported brads were better than domestic ones, because I did not know what brads were, and did not choose to "let on" to a stranger. I thought it would have looked much better in him, anyhow, to have asked somebody who he knew was in the habit of eating brads, or wearing them, whichever is the proper way of utilizing them.

I did manage to answer the little Kentucky boy who wished to send me his wildcat. I thanked him very kindly and cordially for his donation, and said I was very fond of cats of all descriptions, and told him to do like the little Indiana boy, and forward it to Rev. Mr. Beecher, and I would call and get it some time. I could not bear to check the warm young tide of his generosity, and yet I had no (immediate) use for the insect myself.

I did not answer the young man who wrote me from Tennessee, inquiring "how to become a good reporter and acceptable journalist," chiefly because if one marks out the nice easy method which he knows these kind of inquirers have in their mind's eye, they straightway begin to afflict him with semi-weekly specimens of what they can do, under the thin disguise of a friendly correspondence; and if he marks out the unromantic and unattractive method which he believes in his heart to be the absolutely necessary one, they always write back and call him a "nigger" or a "thief." These people are so illogical.

1871

THE TONE-IMPARTING COMMITTEE

When I get old and ponderously respectable, only one thing will be able to make me truly happy, and that will be to be put on the Venerable Tone-Imparting Committee of the city of New York, and have nothing to do but sit on the platform, solemn and imposing, along with Peter Cooper, Horace Greeley, etc., etc., and shed momentary fame at second hand on obscure lecturers, draw public attention to lectures which would otherwise clack eloquently to sounding emptiness, and subdue audiences into respectful hearing of all sorts of unpopular and outlandish dogmas and isms. That is what I desire for the cheer and gratification of my gray hairs. Let me but sit up there with those fine relics of the Old Red Sandstone Period and give Tone to an intellectual entertainment twice a week, and be so reported, and my happiness will be complete. Those men have been my envy for a long, long time. And no memories of my life are so pleasant as my reminiscence of their long and honorable career in the tone-imparting service. I can recollect the last time I ever saw them on the platforms just as well as I can remember the events of yesterday. Horace Greeley sat on the right, Peter Cooper on the left, and Thomas Jefferson, Red Jacket, Benjamin Franklin, and John Hancock sat between them. This was on the 22d of December, 1799, on the occasion of the state funeral of George Washington in New York. It was a great day, that—a great day, and a very, very sad one. I remember that Broadway was one mass of black crape from Castle Garden nearly up to where the City Hall now stands. The next time I saw these gentlemen officiate was at a ball given for the purpose of procuring money and medicines for the sick and wounded soldiers and sailors. Horace Greeley occupied one side of the platform on which the musicians were exalted, and Peter Cooper the other. There were other Tone-imparters attendant upon the two chiefs, but I have forgotten their names now. Horace

Greeley, gray-haired and beaming, was in sailor costume—white duck pants, blue shirt, open at the breast, large neckerchief, loose as an ox-bow, and tied with a jaunty sailor knot, broad turnover collar with star in the corner, shiny black little tarpaulin hat roosting daintily far back on head, and flying two gallant long ribbons. Slippers on ample feet, round spectacles on benignant nose, and pitchfork in hand, completed Mr. Greeley, and made him, in my boyish admiration, every inch a sailor, and worthy to be the honored great-grandfather of the Neptune he was so ingeniously representing. I shall never forget him. Mr. Cooper was dressed as a general of militia, and was dismally and oppressively warlike. I neglected to remark, in the proper place, that the soldiers and sailors in whose aid the ball was given had just been sent in from Boston—this was during the war of 1812. At the grand national reception of Lafayette, in 1824, Horace Greeley sat on the right and Peter Cooper on the left. The other Tone-imparters of that day are sleeping the sleep of the just now. I was in the audience when Horace Greeley, Peter Cooper, and other chief citizens imparted tone to the great meetings in favor of French liberty, in 1848. Then I never saw them any more until here lately; but now that I am living tolerably near the city, I run down every time I see it announced that "Horace Greeley, Peter Cooper, and several other distinguished citizens will occupy seats on the platform"; and next morning, when I read in the first paragraph of the phonographic report that "Horace Greeley, Peter Cooper, and several other distinguished citizens occupied seats on the platform," I say to myself, "Thank God, I was present." Thus I have been enabled to see these substantial old friends of mine sit on the platform and give tone to lectures on anatomy, and lectures on agriculture, and lectures on stirpiculture, and lectures on astronomy, on chemistry, on miscegenation, on "Is Man Descended from the Kangaroo?" on veterinary matters, on all kinds of religion, and several kinds of politics; and have seen them give tone and grandeur to the Four-legged Girl, the Siamese Twins, the Great Egyptian Sword Swallower, and the Old Original Jacobs. Whenever somebody is to lecture on a subject not of general interest, I know that my venerated Remains of the Old Red Sandstone Period will be on the platform; whenever a lecturer is to appear whom nobody has heard of before, nor will be likely to seek to see, I know that the real benevolence of my old friends will be taken advantage of, and that they will be on the platform (and in the bills) as an advertisement; and whenever any new and obnoxious deviltry in philosophy, morals, or politics is to be sprung upon the people, I know perfectly well that these intrepid old heroes will be on that platform too, in the interest of full and free discussion, and to crush down all narrower and less generous souls with the solid dead weight of their awful respectability. And let us all remember that while these inveterate and imperishable presiders (if you please) appear on the platform every night in the year as regularly as the volunteered piano from Steinway's or Chickering's, and have bolstered up and given tone to a deal of questionable merit and obscure emptiness in their time, they have also diversified this inconsequential service by occasional powerful uplifting and upholding of great progressive ideas which smaller men feared to meddle with or countenance.

1871

JOHN CAMDEN HOTTEN*

To the Editor of The Spectator:

SIR:—I only venture to intrude upon you because I come, in some sense, in the interest of public morality, and this makes my mission respectable. Mr. John Camden Hotten, of London, has, of his own individual motion, republished several of my books in England. I do not protest against this, for there is no law that could give effect to the protest; and, besides, publishers are not accountable to the laws of heaven and earth in any country, as I understand it. But my grievance is this: My books are bad enough just as they are written, then what must they be after Mr. John Camden Hotten has composed half-a-dozen chapters and added the same to them? I feel that all true hearts will bleed for an author whose volumes have fallen under such a dispensation as this. If a friend of yours, or even if you yourself, were to write a book and send it adrift among the people, with the gravest apprehensions that it was not up to what it ought to be intellectually, how would you like to have John Camden Hotten sit down and stimulate his powers, and drool two or three original chapters on to the end of that book? Would not the world seem cold and hollow to you? Would you not feel that you wanted to die and be at rest? Little the world knows of true suffering. And suppose he should entitle these chapters, "Holiday Literature," "True Stories of Chicago," "On Children," "Train Up a Child, and Away He Goes," and "Vengeance," and then, on the strength of having evolved these marvels from his own consciousness, go and "Copyright" the entire book, and put on the title-page a picture of a man with his hand in another man's pocket and the legend "All Rights Reserved," (I only suppose the picture; still it would be rather a neat thing). And, further, suppose that in the kindness of

* For a time Hotten regularly pirated Mark Twain's works in England. He was not alone in this activity. Clemens was also for awhile the victim of extensive piracy in Canada.

his heart and the exuberance of his untaught fancy, this thoroughly well-meaning innocent should expunge the modest title which you had given your book, and replace it with so foul an invention as this, "Screamers and Eye-Openers," and went and got *that* copyrighted, too. And suppose that on top of all this, he continually and persistently forgot to offer you a single penny or even send you a copy of your mutilated book to burn. Let us suppose all this. Let him suppose it with strength enough, and then he will know something about woe. Sometimes when I read one of those additional chapters constructed by John Camden Hotten, I feel as if I wanted to take a broom-straw and go and knock that man's brains out. Not in anger, for I feel none. Oh! not in anger; but only to see, that is all. Mere idle curiosity. And Mr. Hotten says that one *nom de plume* of mine is "Carl Byng." I hold that there is no affliction in this world that makes a man feel so downtrodden and abused as the giving him a name that does not belong to him. How would this sinful aborigine feel if I were to call him John Camden Hottentot, and come out in the papers and say he was entitled to it by divine right? I do honestly believe it would throw him into a brain fever, if there were not an insuperable obstacle in the way.

Yes—to come to the original subject, which is the sorrow that is slowly but surely undermining my health—Mr. Hotten prints unrevised, uncorrected, and in some respects, spurious books, with my name to them as author, and thus embitters his customers against one of the most innocent of men. Messrs. George Routledge and Sons are the only English publishers who pay me any copyright, and therefore if my books are to disseminate either suffering or crime among the readers of our language, I would ever so much rather they did it through that house, and then I could contemplate the spectacle calmly as the dividends came in.

I am sir, etc.,
SAMUEL L. CLEMENS

London, September 20, 1872.

BRITISH BENEVOLENCE

To the Editor of The Tribune.

SIR: Some people do not do generous things by halves, even in the old "effete" monarchies. I returned from England (where I had been spending a sort of business holiday) in November, in the Cunard steamer Batavia, Capt. John E. Mouland. In mid-ocean we encountered a fearful gale—a gale that is known to have destroyed a great many vessels, and is supposed to have made away with a great many more that have never been heard of to this day. The storm lasted two days with us; then subsided for a few brief hours; then burst forth again; and while this last effort was in full swing we came upon a dismasted vessel, the bark Charles Ward. She was nothing but a bursted and spouting hulk, surmounted with a chaos of broken spars and bits of fluttering rags—a sort of ruined flower-pot hung with last year's spider-webs, so to speak. The vast seas swept over her, burying her from sight, and then she would rise again and spew volumes of water through cracks in her sides and bows, and discharge white floods through the gateway that was left where her stern had been. Her captain and eight men were lashed in the remains of the main rigging. They were pretty well famished and frozen, for they had been there two nights and a part of two days of stormy wintry weather. Capt. Mouland brought up broadside to wind and sea, and called for volunteers to man the life-boat. D. Gillies, Third Officer: H. Kyle, Fourth Officer, and six seamen answered instantly. It was worth any money to see that life-boat climb those dizzy mountains of water, in a driving mist of spume-flakes, and fight its way inch by inch in the teeth of the gale. Just the mere memory of it stirs a body so, that I would swing my hat and disgorge a cheer now, if I could do it without waking the baby. But if you get a baby awake once you never can get it asleep again, and then you get into trouble with the whole family. Somehow I don't seem to have a chance to yell, now, the way I used to. Well, in just one hour's time that life-boat crew had rescued those shipwrecked men; and during 30 minutes of the time, their own lives were not worth purchase at a sixpence, their peril was so great.

The passengers showed their appreciation of this thing as far as they were able, and we were so proud of our captain and our life-boat crew that we ventured to join in a communication to the Royal Humane Society of London, detailing the circumstances and petitioning that they would take notice of our sailors' gallant achievement. I have just heard the result, and would like to communicate it to the passengers, and to all who take an interest in things nobler than the usual daily feast of Congress corruption and judicial rottenness.

The Humane Society promptly conferred the gold medal and a vote of thanks upon Capt. Mouland; they also gave silver medals to Officers Gillies and Kyle, and a money reward suited to their official grade, and thanked them; and they likewise thanked the six seamen and gave £7 gold ($35), to each of them—say somewhere about two months' wages. We are a nation of forty millions, and we have some little money. Cannot we have a society like that? Why, it is the next most noblest thing to sending moral tracts to Timbuctoo. And would cost less money, too. Not that I object to sending moral tracts to Timbuctoo; far from it; I write the most of them myself, and gain the larger part of my living in that way. I would grieve to see Timbuctoo redeemed, and have to lose its custom. But why not start a Humane Society besides? We have got one man worthy to conduct it, and that is Mr. Bergh. If God did not make Bergh, He certainly did not make the insects that try to thwart his purposes—and do not succeed.

We are the offspring of England; and so it is pleasant to reflect that the very first thing that astonishes a stranger when he arrives in that country is not its physical features, not the vastness of London, not the peculiarities of speech and dress of its people, but the curious lavishness with which that people pour money into the lap of any high and worthy object needing help. It is not done ostentatiously, but modestly. It comes from nobody knows where, about half the time, but it comes. Every few days you see a brief item like this in the papers: "The (such and such a charity) desire to acknowledge the receipt of £1000 from X.Y.Z. This is the fifth £1000 from the same source." X.Y.Z. don't give his name; he just gives his $25,000, and says no more about it. Some hospital will put up a contribution box by the door, and it will capture hundreds upon hundreds of pounds from unknown passers-by. The porter of the Charing-Cross hospital saw a gentleman stuff something into the contribution-box and pass on. He opened the box to see what it was; it was a roll of bank bills, amounting to $1250. One day an unknown lady entered Middlesex Hospital and asked leave to go round and talk with the patients; it was found, after she was gone, that she had been distributing half sovereigns among them; she had squandered $750 there. But why go on? I got so worked up about charity matters in London that I was near coming away from there ignorant of everything else. I could reel off instances of prodigal charity conferred by stealth in that city till even THE TRIBUNE's broad columns would cry for quarter. "Ginx's Baby" could not satirize the national disposition toward free-handed benevolence—it could only satirize instances of foolish and stupid methods in the application of the funds by some of the charitable organizations. But in most cases the great benevolent societies of England manage their affairs admirably.

It makes one dizzy to read the long list of enormous sums that individuals have given to the London hospitals. People die of want and starvation in that huge hive, just as they do in New York, merely because nine people in ten who beg help are imposters—the worthy and the sensitive shrink from making their condition known, and perish without making an appeal. In either city a thousand hands would be stretched forth to save such if the need could be known in time. I have forgotten many things I saw in London, but I remember yet what an outburst there was, and what a pang seemed to dart through the whole great heart of England when a poor, obscure, and penniless American girl threw herself from Waterloo bridge because she was hungry and homeless and had no friend to turn to. Everybody talked; everybody said "Shame, shame!" all the newspapers were troubled; one heard strong, honest regrets on every hand, and such expressions as, "What a pity, poor thing; she could have been smothered in money if a body could only have known of her case." You would have supposed an Emperor had fallen, and not a mere nameless waif from a far country. This mourning for the late Napoleon is lifeless and empty compared to it. That girl could have collected a whole fortune in London if she could have come alive again.

We know what the Royal Humane Society is; for it is always at work, and its fame is wide in the earth. Well, England is sown generously with just such institutions—not Government pets, but supported entirely by voluntary contributions of the people. And they make no pow-wow; one does not even see the names of their officers in print. Now there is the Royal National Life-Boat Institution, for instance. During the year 1869 it saved 28 vessels; its boats saved 1072 human lives; it paid, in cash rewards for saving life, $12,000 gold. It keeps its own boats and boat stations; has its men on guard night and day, under regular salaries, and pays them an extra reward for every life saved. Since it first began its work it has saved a fraction under 19,000 lives; it has conferred 90 gold medals and 807 silver ones; it has given away $158,000 in cash rewards for saving life, and has expended $1,183,330 on its life-boat stations and life-saving apparatus. And all that money was obtained by voluntary subscriptions.

To return to the life-boat crew of the "Batavia." The Cunard Steamship Company gave each of the six seamen £5 a piece, and promoted third officer Gillies and fourth officer Kyle to the rank and pay of *first* officers; the said rank and pay to commence, not upon the day we found the dismasted vessel, but upon the day our ship left Liverpool for America. Now how is that for "the clean white thing," as they say in the mountains? I have italicized the word "first," for I ask you to understand that that is a perfectly dazzling promotion to achieve with just sixty minutes' work—it would have taken those men ten or twelve years of slow hard work in the Company's service to accomplish that, as matters usually go in that methodical old private navy. Indeed those practical, hard-headed, unromantic Cunard people would not take Noah himself as first mate till they had worked him up through all the lower grades and tried him ten years or such a matter. They make every officer serve an apprenticeship under their eyes in their own ships before they advance him or trust him. Capt. Mouland had been at sea 16 years, and was in command of a big 1600-tun ship when they took him into their service; but they only made him fourth officer, and he had to work up tediously to earn his captaincy. He has been with them 18 years now. Officers Gillies and Kyle have suddenly jumped over a whole regiment of officers' heads and landed within one step of the captaincy, and all in good time they will be promoted that step, too. They hold the rank and receive the pay of first officers now, and will continue to do so, though there are no vacancies at present. But they will fill the first vacancies that occur.

It is a curious, self-possessed, old-fashioned Company, the Cunard.

(Scotchmen they are.) It was born before the days of steamships; it inaugurated ocean steamer lines; it never has lost more than one vessel; it has never lost a passenger's life at all; its ships are never insured; great mercantile firms do not insure their goods sent over in Cunard ships; it is rather safer to be in their vessels than on shore. Old-fashioned is the word. When a thing is established by the Cunarders, it is there for good and all, almost. Before adopting a new thing the chiefs cogitate and cogitate and cogitate; then they lay it before their head purveyor, their head merchant, their head builder, their head engineer, and all the captains in the service, and *they* go off and cogitate about a year; then if the new wrinkle is approved it is adopted, and put into the regulations. In the old days, near 40 years ago, when this was an ocean line of sailing vessels, corpses were not permitted by the company to take passage, or go as freight, either—sailor superstition, you know. Very well; to this day they won't carry corpses. Forty years ago they always had stewed prunes and rice for dinner on "duff" days; well, to this present time, whenever duff day comes around, you will always have your regular stewed prunes and rice in a Cunarder. If you don't get anything else, you can always depend on that—and depend on it with your money up, too, if you are that sort of a person.

It takes them about 10 or 15 years to manufacture a captain; but when they have got him manufactured to suit at last, they have full confidence in him. The only order they give a captain is this, brief and to the point: "Your ship is loaded, take her; speed is nothing; follow your own road, deliver her safe, bring her back safe—safety is all that is required."

The noted Cunard Company is composed simply of two or three grandchildren who have stepped into the shoes of two or three children who stepped into the shoes of a couple of old Scotch fathers; for Burns and MacIvor were the Cunard Company when it was born; it was Burns and MacIvor when the originators had passed away; it is Burns and MacIvor still in the third generation—never has been out of the two families. Burns was a Glasgow merchant, MacIvor was an old sea-dog who sailed a ship for him in early times. That vessel's earnings were cast into a sinking fund; with the money they built another ship, and then another, and thus the old original packet line from Glasgow to Halifax was established. At that time the mails were slowly and expensively carried in English Government vessels. Burns & MacIvor and Judge Haliburton ("Sam Slick") fell to considering a scheme of getting the job of carrying these mails in private bottoms. In order to manage the thing they needed to be quiet about it, and also they needed faster vessels. Haliburton had a relative who was not a shining success in practical life, but had an inventive head; name, Sam Cunard; he took his old jack-knife and a shingle and sat down and whittled out this enormous Royal Mail Line of vessels that we call the Cunarders—a great navy, it is—doing business in every ocean; owning forty-five steamships of vast cost; conducting its affairs with the rigid method and system of a national navy; promoting by merit, priority in routine, and for conspicuous service; using a company uniform; retiring superannuated and disabled men and officers on permanent pensions, and number-ing its servants by hundreds and thousands. In its own private establishment in Liverpool it keeps 4000 men under pay. That is what Sam Cunard whittled out. That is to say, he whittled out a little model for a fast vessel; it was satisfactory; he was instructed to go and get the mail contract, simply under his own name; he did it, and the company became commonly known as the Cunard Com-pany; then the Company tried steam and made it work; they pros-pered, and bought out Haliburton, and also Cunard's little interest; they removed Cunard to England and made him their London agent; he grew very rich and unspeakably respectable, and when he died he died not as a poor, dreaming provincial whittler of experimental models, but as the great Sir Samuel Cunard, K.C.B., or G.W.X., or something like that, for the sovereign had knighted him.

Well, the Cunard Company is a great institution, and has got more money than you and I both put together; and yet none of the family ever write editorials or deliver lectures. The Company have built school-houses and they educate the children of their employés; they are going to build dwellings for their shore men that shall be cheap and clean and comfortable; when one of their men dies, a subscription list goes about in his ship or in whatever arm of the service his name is booked, and whatever sum is raised the Cunard Company add just a similar sum, and it all goes to the man's heirs. Their system of pensions—

But I have never been offered a cent for all this; I am not even acquainted with a member of the Cunard Company. I think I will wait a while before I go on—it cramps my hand to write so much on a stretch. But it is all right, any way. So many thousands of Ameri-cans have traveled in those steamers that they will like to read about that Company.

Capt. Mouland has got the gold medal; but if I were to try to tell you how much fire and blood and peril a sailor will gladly go through to get that darling prize, I would have to write all night. I believe a captain would rather have that Royal Humane Society's gold medal for saving life at sea than be made a commodore and have a fleet of vessels under him.

The Cunard steamers always carry some casks of water and provisions where they can be hoisted out at a moment's warning for the relief of distressed vessels at sea, and they—

But, really, I can't advertise these parties for nothing. It isn't "business."

MARK TWAIN

Hartford, &c.

1873

FOSTER'S CASE*

To the Editor of the Tribune.

SIR: I have read the Foster petitions in Thursday's TRIBUNE. The lawyers' opinions do not disturb me, because I know that those same gentlemen could make as able an argument in favor of Judas Iscariot, which is a great deal for me to say, for I never can think of Judas Iscariot without losing my temper. To my mind Judas Iscariot was nothing but a low, mean, premature Congressman. The attitude of the jury does not unsettle a body, I must admit; and it seems plain that they would have modified their verdict to murder in the second degree if the Judge's charge had permitted it. But when I come to the petitions of Foster's friends and find out Foster's true character, the generous tears will flow—I cannot help it. How easy it is to get a wrong impression of a man. I perceive that from childhood up this one has been a sweet, docile thing, full of pretty ways and gentle impulses, the charm of the fireside, the admiration of society, the idol of the Sunday-school. I recognize in him the divinest nature that has ever glorified any mere human being. I perceive that the sentiment with which he regarded temperance was a thing that amounted to frantic adoration. I freely confess that it was the most natural thing in the world for such an organism as this to get drunk and insult a stranger, and then beat his brains out with a car-hook because he did not seem to admire it. Such is Foster. And to think that we came so near losing him! How do we know but that he is the Second Advent? And yet, after all, if the jury had not been hampered in their choice of a verdict I think I could consent to lose him.

---

* William Foster was sentenced to death for murder. His father, the murdered man's wife, members of the jury, and many prominent persons petitioned the governor of New York to commute the sentence to life imprisonment. The New York *Tribune* of March 6, 1873, had carried a full page of letters concerning the case. Mark Twain took the unconventional view.

The humorist who invented trial by jury played a colossal, practical joke upon the world, but since we have the system we ought to try to respect it. A thing which is not thoroughly easy to do, when we reflect that by command of the law a criminal juror must be an intellectual vacuum, attached to a melting heart and perfectly maca-ronian bowels of compassion.

I have had no experience in making laws or amending them, but still I cannot understand why, when it takes twelve men to inflict the death penalty upon a person, it should take any less than 12 more to undo their work. If I were a legislature, and had just been elected and had not had time to sell out, I would put the pardoning and commuting power into the hands of twelve able men instead of dumping so huge a burden upon the shoulders of one poor petition-persecuted individual.

Hartford, March 7, 1873.

MARK TWAIN

THE CURIOUS REPUBLIC OF GONDOUR*

As soon as I had learned to speak the language a little, I became greatly interested in the people and the system of government.

I found that the nation had at first tried universal suffrage pure and simple, but had thrown that form aside because the result was not satisfactory. It had seemed to deliver all power into the hands of the ignorant and non-taxpaying classes; and of a necessity the responsible offices were filled from these classes also.

A remedy was sought. The people believed they had found it; not in the destruction of universal suffrage, but in the enlargement of it. It was an odd idea, and ingenious. You must understand, the constitution gave every man a vote; therefore that vote was a vested right, and could not be taken away. But the constitution did not say that certain individuals might not be given two votes, or ten! So an amendatory clause was inserted in a quiet way; a clause which authorized the enlargement of the suffrage in certain cases to be specified by statute. To offer to "limit" the suffrage might have made instant trouble; the offer to "enlarge" it had a pleasant aspect. But of course the newspapers soon began to suspect; and then out they came! It was found, however, that for once—and for the first time in the history of the republic—property, character, and intellect were able to wield a political influence; for once, money, virtue, and intelligence took a vital and a united interest in a political question. For once these powers went to the "primaries" in strong force; for once the best men in the nation were put forward as candidates for that parliament whose business it should be to enlarge the suffrage. The weightiest half of the press quickly joined forces with the new movement, and left the other half to rail about the proposed "destruction of the liberties" of the bottom layer of society, the hitherto governing class of the community.

* Published anonymously in the *Atlantic Monthly* October 1875, an issue which contained an installment of *Roderick Hudson*, by Henry James.

The victory was complete. The new law was framed and passed. Under it every citizen, howsoever poor or ignorant, possessed one vote, so universal suffrage still reigned; but if a man possessed a good common-school education and no money, he had two votes; a high-school education gave him four; if he had property likewise, to the value of three thousand *sacos,* he wielded one more vote; for every fifty thousand sacos a man added to his property, he was entitled to another vote; a university education entitled a man to nine votes, even though he owned no property. Therefore, learning being more prevalent and more easily acquired than riches, educated men became a wholesome check upon wealthy men, since they could outvote them. Learning goes usually with uprightness, broad views, and humanity; so the learned voters, possessing the balance of power, became the vigilant and efficient protectors of the great lower rank of society.

And now a curious thing developed itself—a sort of emulation, whose object was voting-power! Whereas formerly a man was honored only according to the amount of money he possessed, his grandeur was measured now by the number of votes he wielded. A man with only one vote was conspicuously respectful to his neighbor who possessed three. And if he was a man above the commonplace, he was as conspicuously energetic in his determination to acquire three for himself. This spirit of emulation invaded all ranks. Votes based upon capital were commonly called "mortal" votes, because they could be lost; those based upon learning were called "immortal," because they were permanent, and because of their customarily imperishable character they were naturally more valued than the other sort. I say "customarily" for the reason that these votes were not absolutely imperishable, since insanity could suspend them.

Under this system, gambling and speculation almost ceased in the republic. A man honored as the possessor of great voting-power could not afford to risk the loss of it upon a doubtful chance.

It was curious to observe the manners and customs which the enlargement plan produced. Walking the street with a friend one day, he delivered a careless bow to a passer-by, and then remarked that that person possessed only one vote and would probably never earn another; he was more respectful to the next acquaintance he met; he explained that this salute was a four-vote bow. I tried to "average" the importance of the people he accosted after that, by the nature of his bows, but my success was only partial, because of the somewhat greater homage paid to the immortals than to the mortals. My friend explained. He said there was no law to regulate this thing, except that most powerful of all laws, custom. Custom had created these varying bows, and in time they had become easy and natural. At this moment he delivered himself of a very profound salute, and then said, "Now there's a man who began life as a shoemaker's apprentice, and without education; now he swings twenty-two mortal votes and two immortal ones; he expects to pass a high-school examination this year and climb a couple of votes higher among the immortals; mighty valuable citizen."

By and by my friend met a venerable personage, and not only made him a most elaborate bow, but also took off his hat. I took off mine, too, with a mysterious awe. I was beginning to be infected.

"What grandee is that?"

"That is our most illustrious astronomer. He hasn't any money, but is fearfully learned. Nine immortals is *his* political weight! He would swing a hundred and fifty votes if our system were perfect."

"Is there any altitude of mere moneyed grandeur that you take off your hat to?"

"No. Nine immortal votes is the only power we uncover for—that is, in civil life. Very great officials receive that mark of homage, of course."

It was common to hear people admiringly mention men who had begun life on the lower levels and in time achieved great voting-power. It was also common to hear youths planning a future of ever so many votes for themselves. I heard shrewd mammas speak of certain young men as good "catches" because they possessed such-and-such a number of votes. I knew of more than one case where an heiress was married to a youngster who had but one vote; the argument being that he was gifted with such excellent parts that in time he would acquire a good voting strength, and perhaps in the long run be able to outvote his wife, if he had luck.

Competitive examinations were the rule in all official grades. I remarked that the questions asked the candidates were wild, intricate, and often required a sort of knowledge not needed in the office sought.

"Can a fool or an ignoramus answer them?" asked the person I was talking with.

"Certainly not."

"Well, you will not find any fools or ignoramuses among our officials."

I felt rather cornered, but made shift to say—

"But these questions cover a good deal more ground than is necessary."

"No matter; if candidates can answer these it is tolerably fair evidence that they can answer nearly any other question you choose to ask them."

There were some things in Gondour which one could not shut his eyes to. One was, that ignorance and incompetence had no place in the government. Brains and property managed the state. A candidate for office must have marked ability, education, and high character, or he stood no sort of chance of election. If a hod-carrier possessed these, he could succeed; but the mere fact that he was a hod-carrier could not elect him, as in previous times.

It was now a very great honor to be in the parliament or in office; under the old system such distinction had only brought suspicion upon a man and made him a helpless mark for newspaper contempt and scurrility. Officials did not need to steal now, their salaries being vast in comparison with the pittances paid in the days when parliaments were created by hod-carriers, who viewed official salaries from a hod-carrying point of view and compelled that view to be respected by their obsequious servants. Justice was wisely and rigidly administered; for a judge, after once reaching his place through the specified line of promotions, was a permanency during good behavior. He was not obliged to modify his judgments according to the effect they might have upon the temper of a reigning political party.

The country was mainly governed by a ministry which went out with the administration that created it. This was also the case with the chiefs of the great departments. Minor officials ascended to their several positions through well-earned promotions, and not by a jump from gin-mills or the needy families and friends of members of parliament. Good behavior measured their terms of office.

The head of the government, the Grand Caliph, was elected for a term of twenty years. I questioned the wisdom of this. I was answered that he could do no harm, since the ministry and the parliament governed the land, and he was liable to impeachment for misconduct. This great office had twice been ably filled by women, women as aptly fitted for it as some of the sceptred queens of history. Members of the cabinet, under many administrations, had been women.

I found that the pardoning power was lodged in a court of pardons, consisting of several great judges. Under the old *régime*, this important power was vested in a single official, and he usually took care to have a general jail delivery in time for the next election.

I inquired about public schools. There were plenty of them, and of free colleges too. I inquired about compulsory education. This was received with a smile, and the remark—

"When a man's child is able to make himself powerful and honored according to the amount of education he acquires, don't you suppose that that parent will apply the compulsion himself? Our free schools and free colleges require no law to fill them."

There was a loving pride of country about this person's way of speaking which annoyed me. I had long been unused to the sound of it in my own. The Gondour national airs were forever dinning in my ears; therefore I was glad to leave that country and come back to my dear native land, where one never hears that sort of music.

1875

DUNCAN OF THE QUAKER CITY

To the Editor of The World.

SIR: I see by your report of a lecture delivered in your neighborhood very recently, that a bit of my private personal history has been revealed to the public. The lecturer was head-waiter of the Quaker City Excursion of ten years ago. I do not repeat his name for the reason that I think he wants a little notoriety as a basis for introduction to the lecture platform, and I don't wish to contribute. I harbor this suspicion because he calls himself "captain" of that expedition.

The truth is, that as soon as the ship was fairly at sea, he was degraded from his captaincy by Mr. Leary (owner of the vessel) and Mr. Bunsley (executive officer). As he was not a passenger, and had now ceased to be an officer, it was something of a puzzle to define his position. However, as he still had authority to discharge waiter-boys—an authority which the passengers did not possess—it was presently decided, privately, that he must naturally be the "head-waiter"; and thus was he dubbed. During the voyage he gave orders to none but his under-waiters; all the excursionists will testify to this. It may be humorous enough to call himself "captain," but then it is calculated to deceive the public

The "captain" says that when I came to engage passage in the Quaker City I "seemed to be full of whiskey, or something," and filled his office with the "fumes of bad whiskey." I hope this is true, but I cannot say, because it is so long ago; at the same time I am not depraved enough to deny that for a ceaseless, tireless, forty-year public advocate of total abstinence the "captain" is a mighty good judge of whiskey at second-hand.

He charges that I couldn't tell the Quaker City tea from coffee. Am I a god, that I can solve the impossible?

He charges that I uttered a libel when I said he made this speech at a Fourth of July dinner on shipboard: "Ladies and gentlemen, may you all live long and prosper; steward, pass up another basket of champagne."

Well, the truth is often a libel, and this may be one; yet it is the truth nevertheless. I did not publish it with malicious intent, but because it showed that even a total-abstinence gladiator can have gentle instincts when he is removed from hampering home influences.

The "captain" charges that when I came to his office to engage passage I represented myself to be a Baptist minister cruising after health. No; Mr. Edward H. House told him that, without giving me any warning, that he was going to do it. But no matter, I should have done it myself if I had thought of it. Therefore I lift this crime from Mr. House's shoulders and transfer it to mine. I was without conscience in those old days. It had been my purpose to represent that I was a son of the captain's whom he had never met, and consequently hadn't classified, and by this means I hoped to get a free passage; but I was saved from this great villainy by the happy accident of Mr. House's getting in his milder rascality ahead of me. I often shudder to think how near I came to saddling an old father on to myself forever whom I never could have made any use of after that excursion was finished. Still, if I had him now, I would make him lecture his head off at his customary 25 cents before I would support him in idleness. I consider idleness an immoral thing for the aged.

Certain of my friends in New York have been so distressed by the "captain's" charges against me that they have simply forced me to come out in print. But I find myself in a great difficulty by reason of the fact that I don't find anything in the charges that discomforts me. Why should I worry over the "bad whiskey?" I was poor—I couldn't afford good whiskey. How could I know that the "captain" was so particular about the quality of a man's liquor? I didn't know he was a purist in that matter, and that the difference between 5-cent and 40-cent toddy would remain a rankling memory with him for ten years.

The tea and champagne items do not trouble me—both being true and harmless. The Baptist minister fraud does not give me any anguish, since I did not invent it.

What I need, now that I am going into print, is a text. These little things do not furnish it. Why does the "captain" make no mention of the highway robbery which I committed on the road between Jerusalem and the Dead Sea? He must have heard of it—the land was full of it. Why does he make no mention of the fact that during the entire excursion I never drew a sober breath except by proxy? Why does he conceal the fact that I killed a cripple in Cairo because I thought he had an unpleasant gait? Why is he silent about my skinning a leper in Smyrna in order that I might have a little something to start a museum with when I got home? What is the use of making "charges" out of a man's few little virtuous actions when that man has committed real indiscretions by the dozen?

But where is the use in bothering about what a man's character was ten years ago, anyway? Perhaps the captain values his character of ten years ago? I never have heard of any reason why he should; but still he may possibly value it. No matter. I do not value my character of ten years ago. I can go out any time and buy a better one for half it cost me. In truth, my character was simply in course of construction then. I hadn't anything up but the scaffolding, so to speak. But I have finished the edifice now and taken down that worm-eaten scaffolding. I have finished my moral edifice, and frescoed it and furnished it, and I am obliged to admit that it is one of the neatest and sweetest things of the kind that I have ever encountered. I greatly value it, and I would feel like resenting any damage done to it. But that old scaffolding is no longer of any use to me; and inasmuch as the "captain" seems able to use it to advantage, I hereby make him a present of it. It is a little shaky, of course, but if he will patch it here and there he will find that it is still superior to anything of the kind he can scare up upon his own premises.

MARK TWAIN

February 14.

POSTSCRIPT—TWO DAYS LATER

The following paragraph, from the New York *Times*, has just reached my hands:

THE SHIP-OWNERS AND MR. DUNCAN.

The Ship-owners' Association have sent a long communication to the Senate Committee on Commerce, in support of the "Ward Amendments" bill. It recites that the old law gives no right of appeal from the Shipping Commissioner's decision except to the appointing power. It charges Commissioner Duncan with appropriating to his own use large amounts received as fees, in direct violation of the law, and says that it was decided that the law contains no provision to compel him to refund. It accuses him of paying salaries to his four sons and others, grossly in excess of the services rendered; of being arbitary and unjust in his decisions; of refusing to recognize exemptions specified in the law, and of renting his offices from the Seamen's Association, of which he is President, at a price four times greater than is just, the amount paid being exactly the sum required to pay the interest on the mortgage and unpaid taxes and assessments of the building owned by the Seamen's Association. It quotes a number of contradictory decisions given by courts in various localities as to the spirit of sections of the law, and mentions several points of the Amendatory bill, which give assurance that its passage will overcome all future troubles. —*New York Times.*

They do say that people who live in glass houses should not throw stones. Mr. Duncan has neglected his own character of to-day to hunt down mine of ten years ago. What my character was in that day can be a matter of importance to no one—not even me; but what the present character of the Shipping Commissioner of the great port of New York is, is a matter of serious importance to the whole public. What the character of the President of the Seamen's Association and master of the Sailors' Savings Bank connected with it is, is matter of similarly serious importance to the public. That character— Mr. Duncan's character—is vividly suggested by the charges recited in the above extract. I have known and observed Mr. Duncan for ten years, and I think I have good reason for believing him to be wholly without principle, without moral sense, without honor of any kind. I think I am justified in believing that he is cruel enough and heartless enough to rob any sailor or sailor's widow or orphan he can get his clutches upon; and I know him to be coward enough. I know him to be a canting hypocrite, filled to the chin with sham godliness, and forever oozing and dripping false piety and pharisaical prayers. I know his word to be worthless.

It is a shame and a disgrace to the civil service that such a man was permitted to worm himself into an office of trust and high responsibility. It is a greater shame and disgrace that he has been permitted to remain in it after he was found out and published, more than three years ago (for the present charges were made against him and printed as long ago as that).

If any one imagines that I am moved to speak in this way by Mr. Duncan's "charges" against me, I beg that he will dismiss that idea. A charge made by Mr. Duncan must naturally fall dead, for the source it emanates from is amply sufficient to sap it of effect.

SAMUEL L. CLEMENS
(Mark Twain).

Hartford, February 16.   1877

DUNCAN ONCE MORE

To the Editor of The World.

Sir: If you should glance over the letters which have come to me from New York and Brooklyn since last Sunday you would be surprised to perceive how general is the knowledge of Mr. Chas. C. Duncan's character in those cities, and how frank and outspoken the abhorrence of it. It seems that everybody has known for four or five years, that this Shipping Commissioner was diligently and constantly robbing the till of his office, with the exception of the brief intervals of time which he devoted to the Sunday-school of which he was (and is) Superintendent. And yet he has been allowed to keep his place. This ought to delight those sarcastic people who say we do not live under a "form of government" in America, but under a "system of organized imbecility."

I think that Mr. Duncan's strength has lain in the fact that he robs nobody but sailors and the United States Government. Nobody is personally interested in the protection of these, else the newspapers would have been flooded with the complaints of sufferers, and Mr. Duncan would have been driven from his office long ago.

Penning newspaper letters about this over-pious miscreant is not agreeable work, and I would much prefer to leave the present one unwritten; but one correspondent desires to know something about the law which made Mr. Duncan a Shipping Commissioner, and I am sure that there are others who would like to see a synopsis of its provisions. That law was devised by Mr. Duncan himself. It is plainly and simply a Black Flag, and the man who has sailed under it all these years is—but name him yourself.

That infamous law was most ably dissected and its purpose exposed four or five years ago, in a pamphlet published by Messres. Morris & Wilder, attorneys, of New York. That pamphlet will destroy Mr. Duncan and his law if the judiciary committees of Congress can be brought to read it.

The title of Mr. Duncan's law is a blistering sarcasm: "An Act for the Further Protection of Seamen." Further along the reader will see what "protection" means in a Shipping Commissioner's dictionary.

1. Under all previous laws the injured sailor could bring his case in a court of equity. His only recourse now is to a court of law; "his only remedy lies in the inflexible terms of a statute of which the court is compelled to be a strict and rigid interpreter." No more equity is permitted, no more "exercise of discretion in view of all the circumstances of a case."

2. Under the old laws a sailor's rights were clearly defined, and his remedy was simple and inexpensive. Under the new, the process is cumbered by all sorts of complications and obstructions, and the expenses increased to a prohibitory degree. "The maze of technicalities to which the seaman is now compelled to conform could not have been more cunningly devised by an organized band of conspirators intent upon perplexing and robbing him!"

3. This new law gives the sailor not a single right or privilege which he did not possess before; but it takes from him certain rights and privileges of inestimable value which he did possess before.

4. The new law creates a disease called a Shipping Commissioner, who is to "superintend" the shipping and discharge of sailors, and charge a fee for each man shipped or discharged. All these fees come eventually out of the sailor's pocket—and they have always gone into Mr. Duncan's.

5. The Shipping Commissioner "may refuse to proceed with any engagement or discharge unless the fees thereon are first paid." That is a quotation from the law! Jack may finish his voyage, but if he is unable to pay his fee he can remain the property of the ship-owner; for Mr. Duncan will not release him! This is "protection"—to the Shipping Commissioner.

6. The law gives the Shipping Commissioner $5000 a year for "superintending"; but he has charged the country more than $160,000 in four years for that needless service, by pocketing the fees.

7. "All acts done by a clerk or deputy shall be as valid and binding as if done by the Shipping Commissioner himself." Was ever a law more ingeniously devised for the coddling of a lazy pilferer? He was not even willing to take the trouble to do the pilfering himself.

8. A penalty is provided for the punishment of any one who shall

solicit a seaman's custom for a sailor boarding-house. That looks well, on its face, but—

9. "Every payment of wages to a seaman shall be valid in law, notwithstanding any previous sale or assignment of such wages; and no assignment or sale of such wages shall bind the party making the same." This is not a quotation from the rules and by-laws of a band of highwaymen, but is the exact wording of this most disgraceful statute. Its plain meaning is that the Government denies to the sailor the common human right to do as he pleases with his own! The effect is this: Formerly those dreadful boarding-house landlords fed and lodged the sailor on credit when his money was all gone, taking an assignment of his first advance-money (when he should next get a berth) as their security. The new law forbids the sailor to give such security now by making such security valueless; so the boarding-houses promptly turn him adrift when his money is gone, and—the Shipping Commissioner takes care of him? Suppose you apply at the Sunday-school in Brooklyn and ask Mr. Duncan that sarcastic question. No—Jack becomes a tramp. This law has filled the country with tramps. It ought to have been entitled "An act for the creation of a pirate and for the multiplication of tramps."

Everybody has heard of that horrible process of kidnapping sailors, called "shanghaeing"; everybody has loathed it, everybody has cursed it. Could anybody but a Duncan dream of so foul a crime as the creation of a law to legalize shanghaeing? Could anybody but a Duncan be heartless enough, cruel enough, shameless enough? I ask you to read this extract from the law framed by this bowelless Commissioner, and see if you can realize the fact that such a statute as this has blackened the code of America for five years (and almost unchallenged):

10. Whenever any seaman neglects or refuses to join, or deserts from or refuses to proceed to sea in any ship in which he is duly engaged to serve, or is found otherwise absenting himself therefrom without leave, the master, or any mate, or the owner, or consignee may in any place in the United States, with or without the assistance of the local public officers or constables (who are hereby directed to give their assistance, if required), apprehend him without first procuring a warrant, and may thereupon in any case, and shall, in case he so requires, and it is practicable, convey him before any court of justice, &c., and may, for the purpose of conveying him before such court of justice, detain him in custody for a period not exceeding twenty-four hours, or may, if he does not so require, or if there

is no such court at or near the place, at once convey him on board.

Let us suppose a case. A shanghaier has engaged to procure a crew for an outgoing vessel. He comes, with his little gang of assistants, to an isolated place and seizes a man he never saw before—Mr. Longfellow, for instance. An officer of the law interferes. Kidnapper—I have been formally constituted mate of the Osprey, and this man is one of my crew—a deserter. I propose to take him on board. Here is the law—read it for yourself.

Officer—He says he never shipped. You must convey him before a court of justice—he requires you to do it.

Kidnapper—I answer, according to the law, that "it is not practicable." There is no such court "near this place."

Officer—You have no warrant for his seizure.

Kidnapper—I require none—see the law.

Officer—You are right. Take him along.

Let me give an extract from the pamphlet I have before referred to:

Once on board, the mariner is secure. If the voyage be to the East Indies then the shanghaed sailor is left to shirk for himself at Bombay or Calcutta, lest if he returned home in the vessel he might seek to have the mate who kidnapped him punished. It is claimed that shanghaeing is prevented by section 53, which provides that if a sailor be carried to sea without entering into an agreement as prescribed by the act, that the ship shall be held liable, and for each offense shall incur a penalty not exceeding $200!!!

Without questioning here the soundness of so novel a doctrine as that a vessel is liable for the torts or crimes of a mate hired perhaps of a charterer, where is the protection against shanghaeing? Section 53 does not prohibit kidnapping, but says, in effect: "Kidnapping is permissible, provided you pay from $100 to $200 apiece for the kidnapped." And this money does not go to the sailor, but to the Government.

At this rate kidnapping is the cheapest way to get a crew for a long voyage, especially as the chances are that the vessel will not have to pay anything at all if the kidnapped sailors are forced to desert in a foreign port. The incentive to the master to force his crew to desert is not only to save the vessel from the penalty, but to hire cheaper crews abroad.

One further fact deserves to be considered in this connection. What becomes of the wages accrued and due to a crew at the time of their desertion? The answer is that, according to all maritime law, these, of course, are forfeited. Thus the horrible truth creeps over the mind that in the desertion of the seaman lies an actual source of revenue to the master's private pocket; then the still more horrible suspicion that that seaman's desertion has been, possibly, reckoned upon, calculated, forced upon him—that human ingenuity has been at work devising new methods of cruelty for the express purpose of driving this man, or this crew, to desertion. Should the port be favorable to the securing of cheap substitutes, the law offers every facility for "securing them on board." If not, then under section 53 it offers equal facilities for "securing" the runaways. But the wages of the latter are in either case forfeited. What a premium is thus placed upon cruelty! What deliberate perils are laid against the mariner's life! With what dignity does law now invest the brutal violence of his despot!

Please read a paragraph from the summing up of the same pamphlet:

The whole truth is that in not one line of this act can the intelligent reader find for the seaman "protection." Sixty sections are devoted to creating unnecessary officers, fixing their salaries, fees and perquisites, crushing all who might come in competition with their gains, and then binding the mariner, hand and foot, through their instrumentality, to the very class against whom he most needs protection. Of the eight remaining sections of the act, one alone, the sixty-first, bestows upon him, as we have seen above, the privilege of protecting himself by swindling all with whom he comes in contact. It is a noteworthy feature of this "benevolent" law that the only protection afforded by it to the sailor lies in a provision that he shall not suffer by his own fraudulent act. But the ship-owner is "protected" in the possession of his men, and protected also from paying them the high rates of wages hitherto paid them under the guidance of their landlords; the master is "protected" in his violence and brutality to them, as well as "protected" in the enjoyment of their wages when that violence has driven them from him; the mates are "protected" in the pursuit and recapture of them; both master and mates are "protected" in kidnapping sailors at all times, and "protected" always from the interference of local magistrates; and, above all and most of all, the Shipping Commissioner is "protected" in the exclusive enjoyment of the shipping business of his port and all the emoluments arising therefrom. But the sailor? As well call a lie the truth, or blasphemy pious, as to call this act, either in whole or in detail, "protection" to him. Such a prostitution of one of the noblest words of the English language to an act begotten in jobbery, chicanery and selfishness is absolutely without parallel.

Still further, this act is obnoxious not only in its centralizing tendencies, in its interference with the legitimate callings of citizens of the various seaports, in its multiplying Federal officers, and in its grinding effect upon the mariner, but, as a natural sequence of all this, it overreaches itself and infringes upon the constitutional and fundamental law. So far as the sailor is concerned, it is one continuous suspension of the habeas corpus! It deprives him of liberty without due process of law, "without first procuring a warrant." And it adds the infamous permission that this may be done by a mere private citizen.

This law is a curiosity in every possible way. It makes Mr. Duncan arbitrator between the sailor and his employer in cases of dispute. I judge that Mr. Duncan is a person whose decision is easily purchasable. This law makes this person's decision final and absolute! The sailor cannot appeal from it! Perhaps the reader now perceives the sarcasm which lurks in the title of the law—"for the further protection of seamen."

Perhaps no more infamous law than this has ever defiled the code of any Christian land in any age, and yet it is the work of a man whose stock in trade is sham temperance, sham benevolence, religious hypocrisy, and a ceaseless, unctuous drip of buttery prayers.

SAML. L. CLEMENS
(Mark Twain.)

Hartford, February 22.

1877

THE SANDWICH ISLANDS*

LADIES AND GENTLEMEN:—There doesn't appear to be anybody here to introduce me, and so we shall have to let that go by default. But I am the person who is to deliver the lecture, and I shall try to get along just the same as if I had been formally introduced. I suppose I ought to apologize for the weather [the night was very stormy], but I can't hold myself altogether responsible for it, so I will let it go as it is.

The only apology which I can offer for appearing before you to talk about the Sandwich Islands is the fact that the recent political changes there have rendered it rather necessary for us to post ourselves concerning that country; to know a little something about the people; what we have forgotten, to gather up again; and as I have spent several months in the Islands, several years ago, I feel competent to shed any amount of light upon the matter.

These islands are situated 2100 miles southwest from San Francisco, California, out in the middle of the Pacific Ocean. Why they were put away out there, so far away from any place and in such an out-of-the-way locality, is a thing which no one can explain. But it's no matter. They are twelve in number, and their entire area isn't greater than that of Rhode Island and Connecticut combined. They are all of volcanic origin and volcanic construction. There is nothing there but lava and pumice stone—except sand and coral. There isn't a spoonful of legitimate dirt in the entire group. Eighty or ninety years ago they had a native population of full 400,000 souls, and they were comfortable, prosperous, and happy. But then the white people came, and brought trade, and commerce, and education, and complicated diseases, and civilization, and other calamities, and as a

---

* Part of a lecture delivered at the Academy of Music in New York about 1877. According to Thomas B. Reed, the original editor of the piece, the text is reprinted from a newspaper report made at the time and is incomplete.

consequence the poor natives began to die off with wonderful rapidity, so that forty or fifty years ago the 400,000 had become reduced to 200,000. Then the white people doubled the educational facilities, and this doubled the death rate. The nation is doomed. It will be extinct within fifty years, without a doubt. Some people in this house may live to hear of the death of the last of the "Kanakas." In color the natives are a rich dark brown. The tropical sun and their easy-going ways have made them rather indolent. They are not a vicious, but a very gentle, kind-hearted, harmless race. In the rural districts the women wear a single long loose gown. But the men don't. The men wear—well, as a general thing, they wear—a smile, or a pair of spectacles—or any little thing like that. But they are not proud. They don't seem to care for display.

In the old times the King was the owner of all the lands, and supreme head of Church and State. His voice was superior to all law. If a common man passed by the King's house without prostrating himself, or came near the King with his head wet, or even allowed his shadow to fall upon the King's person, that man had to die. There was no hope for him. The King exercised absolute authority over the lives and property of his subjects. He could place a "taboo" (we get that word from the Hawaiian) upon land, or article, or person, and it was death for any man to walk on the ground or touch the article or speak to the person so "tabooed." And this King, Kamehameha, who died the other day, never had ceased to chafe at the restrictions imposed upon the power of his ancestors by the laws and constitution promulgated by the American missionaries.

Next after the King, at least in authority, came the priests of the old superstition. And they regulated "church affairs"—that is, they decreed the human sacrifices, they captured the victims and butchered them. After the priests came the chiefs, who held land by feudal tenure as they do in England to-day from the King—and did him service. But both the chiefs and priests were little better than slaves to the King. After them came the plebeians, the common men, who were slaves to priests and chiefs and King, a class who were cruelly treated and often killed upon any trifling provocation. After all this— at the bottom of this hideous pyramid of brutality, and superstition, and slavery—came the women, the abject slaves of the whole combination. They did all the work; they were degraded to the level of brutes, and were considered to be no better. They were cruelly maltreated, and they had absolutely no rights nor privileges. It was death for a woman to sit at table with her own husband, and even to eat from a dish from which he had eaten; and at all times it was death for a woman to eat of certain of the rarer fruits of the Islands, at any time, or in any place. Perhaps the men remembered the difficulty between another woman and some fruit some time back and didn't feel justified in taking any more chances.

But by and by the American missionaries came, and they struck off the shackles from the whole race, breaking the power of the kings and chiefs. They set the common man free, elevated his wife to a position of equality with him, and gave a piece of land to each to hold forever. They set up schools and churches, and imbued the people with the spirit of the Christian religion. If they had had the power to augment the capacities of the people, they could have made them perfect; and they would have done it, no doubt.

The missionaries taught the whole nation to read and write, with facility, in the native tongue. I don't suppose there is to-day a single uneducated person above eight years of age in the Sandwich Islands! It is the best educated country in the world, I believe. That has been all done by the American missionaries. And in a large degree it was paid for by the American Sunday-school children with their pennies. I know that I contributed. I have had nearly two dollars invested there for thirty years. But I don't mind it. I don't care for the money, if it has been doing good. I don't say this in order to show off. I only mention it as a gentle humanizing fact that may possibly have a beneficent effect upon some members of this audience.

These natives are very hospitable people indeed—very hospitable. If you want to stay a few days and nights in a native's cabin, you can stay and welcome. They will make you feel entirely at home. They will do everything they can to make you comfortable. They will feed you on baked dog, or poi, or raw fish, or raw salt pork, or fricasseed cats—all the luxuries of the season. Everything the human heart can desire they will set before you. Perhaps now, this isn't a captivating feast at first glance, but it is offered in all sincerity, and with the best motives in the world, and that makes any feast respectable whether it is palatable or not. But if you want to trade, that's quite another thing—that's business! And the Kanaka is ready for you. He is a born trader, and he will swindle you if he can. He will lie straight through from the first word to the last. Not such lies as you and I tell, but gigantic lies, lies that awe you with their grandeur, lies that stun you with their imperial impossibility. He will sell you a mole-hill at the market price of a mountain and will lie it up to an altitude that will make it cheap at the money. If he is caught he slips out of it with an easy indifference that has an unmistakable charm about it. Every one of these Kanakas has at least a dozen mothers—not his own mothers, of course, but adopted ones. They adhere to the ancient custom of calling any woman "mother," without regard to her color or politics, that they happen to take a particular liking to. It is possible for each of them to have one hundred and fifty mothers—and even that number will allow of a liberal stretch. This fact has caused some queer questions among people who didn't know anything about it.

They are an odd sort of people. They can die whenever they want to. They don't mind dying any more than a jilted Frenchman does. When they take a notion to die, they die, and it doesn't make any difference whether there is anything the matter with them or not, and they can't be persuaded out of it. When one of them makes up his mind to die, he just lies down and is as certain to die as though he had all the doctors in the world hold of him!

This people are peculiarly fond of dogs; not great, magnificent Newfoundlands, or stately mastiffs, or graceful greyhounds, but little mean curs that a white man would condemn to death on general principles. There is nothing about them to recommend them so far as personal appearance is concerned. These people love these puppies better than they love each other, and a puppy always has plenty to eat, even if the rest of the family must go hungry. When the woman rides, the puppy sits in front; when the man rides, the puppy stands behind—he learns to ride horseback with the greatest ease. They feed him with their own hands, and fondle and pet and caress him, till he is a full-grown dog, and then they eat him. Now, I couldn't do that. I'd rather go hungry two days than eat an old friend that way. There's something sad about that. But perhaps I ought to explain that these dogs are raised entirely for the table, and fed exclusively on a cleanly vegetable diet all their lives. Many a white citizen learns to throw aside his prejudices and eat of the dish. After all, it's only our own American sausage with the mystery removed. A regular native will eat anything—anything he can bite. It is a fact that he will eat a raw fish, fresh from the water; and he begins his meals too, before the fish has breathed his last. Of course, it's annoying to the fish, but the Kanaka enjoys it.

In olden times it used to be popular to call the Sandwich Islanders cannibals. But they never were cannibals. That is amply proven. There was one there once, but he was a foreign savage, who stopped there a while and did quite a business while he stayed. He was a useful citizen, but had strong political prejudices, and used to save up a good appetite for just before election, so that he could thin out the Democratic vote. But he got tired of that, and undertook to eat an old whaling captain for a change. That was too much for him. He had the crime on his conscience, and the whaler on his stomach, and the two things killed him. He died. I don't tell this on account of its value as an historical fact, but only on account of the moral which it conveys. I don't know that I know what moral it conveys, still I know there must be a moral in it somewhere. I have told it forty or fifty times and never got a moral out of it yet. But all things come to those who wait.

With all these excellent and hospitable ways, these Kanakas have some cruel instincts. They will put a live chicken in the fire just to see it hop about. In the olden times they used to be cruel to themselves. They used to tear their hair and burn their flesh, shave their heads, and knock out an eye or a couple of front teeth, when a great person or a king died—just to testify to their sorrow; and if their grief was so sore that they couldn't possibly bear it, they would go out and scalp a neighbor or burn his house down. And they used to bury some of their children alive when their families were too large. But the missionaries have broken all that up now.

These people do nearly everything wrong end first. They buckle the saddle on the right side, which is the wrong side; they mount a horse on the wrong side; they turn out on the wrong side to let you go by; they use the same word to say "good-by" and "good-morning"; they use "yes" when they mean "no"; the women smoke more than the men do; when they beckon to you to come, they always motion in the opposite direction; they dance at funerals, and drawl out a dismal sort of dirge when they are peculiarly happy. In their playing of the noble American game of "seven-up," the dealer deals to his right instead of to the left; and what is worse, the ten takes the ace! Now, such ignorance as that is reprehensible, and for one, I am glad the missionaries have gone there.

Now, you see what kind of voters you will have if you take these Islands away from these people, as we are pretty sure to do some day. They will do everything wrong end first. They will make a deal of trouble here, too. Instead of fostering and encouraging a judicious system of railway speculation, and all that sort of thing, they will elect the most incorruptible men to Congress. Yes, they will turn everything upside down.

There are about 3,000 white people on the Islands, and they will increase instead of diminishing. They control all the capital, and are at the head of all the enterprises in the Islands.

These white people get to be ministers—political ministers, I mean. There's a perfect raft of them there. Harris is one of them. Harris is minister of—well, he's minister of pretty much everything. He's a long-legged, light-weight, average lawyer from New Hampshire. Now, if Harris had brains in proportion to his legs, he would make Solomon seem a failure. If his modesty equaled his vanity, he would make a violet seem ostentatious. And if his learning equaled his ignorance, he would make Humboldt seem as unlettered as the back side of a tombstone. If his ideas were as large as his words, it would take a man three months to walk around one of them. Mr. Clemens then reviewed at some length the history of the late and present King of the Sandwich Islands; described the great volcanic eruption of 1840; told several funny stories, and closed his lecture as follows: The land that I have tried to tell you about lies out there in the midst of the watery wilderness, in the very heart of the limitless solitudes of the Pacific. It is a dreamy, beautiful, charming land. I wish I could make you comprehend how beautiful it is. It is a land that seems ever so vague and fairy-like when one reads about it in books. It is Sunday land, the land of indolence and dreams, where the air is drowsy and lulls the spirit to repose and peace, and to forgetfulness of the labor and turmoil and weariness and anxiety of life.

c. 1877

A BOSTON GIRL*

This note comes to me from the home of culture:—

DEAR MR ——: Your writings interest me very much; but I cannot help wishing you would not place adverbs between the particle and verb in the Infinitive. For example: "to *even* realize," "to *mysteriously* disappear" "to *wholly* do away." You should say, *even* to realize; to disappear mysteriously, etc. "rose up" is another mistake—tautology, you know. Yours truly

A BOSTON GIRL

I print the note just as it was written, for one or two reasons: (1.) It flatters a superstition of mine that a person may learn to excel in only such details of an art as take a particularly strong hold upon his native predilections or instincts. (2.) It flatters another superstition of mine that whilst all the details of that art may be of equal importance *he* cannot be made to feel that it is so. Possibly he may be made to *see* it, through argument and illustration; but that will be of small value to him except he *feel* it, also. Culture would be able to make him feel it by and by, no doubt, but never very sharply, I think. Now I have certain instincts, and I wholly lack certain others. (Is that "wholly" in the right place?) For instance, I am dead to adverbs; they cannot excite me. To misplace an adverb is a thing which I am able to do with frozen indifference; it can never give me a pang. But when my young lady puts no point after "Mr."; when she begins "adverb," "verb," and "particle" with the small letter, and aggrandizes "Infinitive" with a capital; and when

* This article was published anonymously in the June 1880 issue of the *Atlantic Monthly*, in a department known as the Contributors' Club. It was brought to my attention by Frederick Anderson, the assistant editor of the Mark Twain Papers at the University of California in Berkeley, who noted its stylistic resemblance to Mark Twain's manner. Proof of its authorship, I found, exists in the incident of the carriage and the circular driveway: Mark Twain related it again near the end of his life in his *Autobiography*, and identified the driver as his business agent, F. G. Whitmore.

she puts no comma after "to mysteriously disappear," etc., I am troubled; and when she begins a sentence with a small letter I even *suffer*. Or I suffer, *even*—I do not know which it is; but she will, because the adverb is in her line, whereas only those minor matters are in mine. Mark these prophetic words: though this young lady's grammar be as the drifted snow for purity, she will never, never, never learn to punctuate while she lives; this is her demon, the adverb is mine. I thank her, honestly and kindly, for her lesson, but I know thoroughly well that I shall never be able to get it into my head. Mind, I do not say I shall not be able to make it *stay* there; I say and mean that I am not capable of *getting it into* my head. There are subtleties which I cannot master at all—they confuse me, they mean absolutely nothing to me—and this adverb plague is one of them.

We all have our limitations in the matter of grammar, I suppose. I have never seen a book which had no grammatical defects in it. This leads me to believe that all people have my infirmity, and are afflicted with an inborn inability to feel or mind certain sorts of grammatical particularities. There are people who were not born to spell; these can never be taught to spell correctly. The enviable ones among them are those who do not take the trouble to care whether they spell well or not—though in truth these latter are absurdly scarce. I have been a correct speller, always; but it is a low accomplishment, and not a thing to be vain of. Why should one take pride in spelling a word rightly when he knows he is spelling it wrongly? *Though* is the right way to spell "though," but it is not *the* right way to spell it. Do I make myself understood?

Some people were not born to punctuate; these cannot learn the art. They can learn only a rude fashion of it; they cannot attain to its niceties, for these must be *felt*; they cannot be reasoned out. Cast-iron rules will not answer, here, any way; what is one man's comma is another man's colon. One man can't punctuate another man's manuscript any more than one person can make the gestures for another person's speech.

What is known as "dialect" writing looks simple and easy, but it is not. It is exceedingly difficult; it has rarely been done well. A man not born to write dialect cannot learn how to write it correctly. It is a gift. Mr. Harte can write a delightful story; he can *reproduce* Californian scenery so that you see it before you, and hear the sounds and smell the fragrances and feel the influences that go with it and belong to it; he can describe the miner and the gambler perfectly—as to gait and look and garb; but no human being, living or dead, ever had experience of the dialect which he puts into his people's mouths. Mr. Harte's originality is not questioned; but if it ever shall be, the caviler will have to keep his hands off that dialect, for that *is* original. Mind, I am not objecting to its use; I am not saying its inaccuracy is a fatal blemish. No, it is Mr. Harte's adverb; let him do as he pleases with it; he can no more mend it than I can mine; neither will any but Boston Girls ever be likely to find us out.

Yes, there are things which we cannot learn, and there is no use in fretting about it. I cannot learn adverbs; and what is more I won't. If I try to seat a person at my right hand, I have no trouble, provided I am facing north at the time; but if I am facing south, I get him on my left, sure. As this thing was born in me, and cannot be educated out of me, I do not worry over it or care about it. A gentleman picked me up, last week, and brought me home in his buggy; he drove past the door, and as he approached the circular turn I saw he meant to go around to the left; I was on his left—that is, I *think* I was, but I have got it all mixed up again in my head; at any rate, I halted him, and asked him to go round the circle the other way. He backed his horse a length or two, put his helm down and "slewed" him to the right, then "came ahead on him," and made the trip. As I got out at the door, he looked puzzled, and asked why I had particularly wanted to pass to the right around the circle. I said, "Because that would bring me next the door coming back, and I wouldn't have to crowd past your knees." He came near laughing his store teeth out, and said it was all the same whether we drove to the right or to the left in going around the circle; either would bring me back to the house on the side the door was on, since I was on the opposite side when I first approached the circle. I regarded this as false. He was willing to illustrate: so he drove me down to the gate and into the street, turned and drove back past the house, moved leftward around the circle, and brought me back to the door; and as sure as I am sitting here I *was* on the side next the door. I did not believe he could do it again, but he did. He did it eleven times hand running. Was I convinced? No. I was not *capable* of being convinced—*all through*. My sight and intellect (to call it by that name) were convinced, but not my *feeling*. It is simply another case of adverb. It is a piece of dead-corpsy knowledge, which is of no use to me, because I merely *know* it, but do not *understand* it.

The fact is, as the poet has said, we are all fools. The difference is simply in the degree. The mercury in some of the fool-thermometers stands at ten, fifteen, twenty, thirty, and so on; in some it gets up to seventy-five; in some it soars to ninety-nine. I never examine mine —take no interest in it.

Now as to "rose up." That strikes me as quite a good form; I will use it some more—that is, when I speak of a person, and wish to signify the full upright position. If I mean less, I will qualify, by saying he rose partly up. It is a form that will answer for the moon sometimes, too. I think it is Bingen on the Rhine who says—

> "The pale moon rose up slowly, and calmly she looked down,
>   On the red sands," etc.

But tautology cannot scare me, any way. Conversation would be intolerably stiff and formal without it; and a mild form of it can limber up even printed matter without doing it serious damage. Some folks are so afraid of a little repetition that they make their meaning vague, when they could just as well make it clear, if only their ogre were out of the way.

Talking of Unlearnable Things, would it be genteel, would it be polite, to ask members of this Club to confess what freightage of this sort they carry? Some of the revelations would be curious and instructive, I think. I am acquainted with one member of it who has never been able to learn nine times eight; he always says, "Nine times seven are sixty-three,"—then counts the rest on his fingers. He is at home in the balance of the multiplication-table. I am acquainted with another member, who, although he has known for many years that when Monday is the first of the month the following Monday will be the eighth, has never been able to *feel* the fact; so he cannot trust it, but always counts on his fingers, to make sure. I have known people who could spell all words correctly but one. They never could get the upper hand of that one; yet as a rule it was some simple, common affair, such as a cat could spell, if a cat could spell at all. I have a friend who has kept his razors in the top drawer and his strop in the bottom drawer for years; when he wants his razors, he always pulls out the bottom drawer—and swears. Change? Could one imagine he never thought of that? He did change; he has changed a dozen times. It didn't do any good; his afflicted mind was able to keep up with the changes and make the proper mistake every time. I knew a man—

THE OMITTED CHAPTER OF *THE PRINCE AND THE PAUPER**

"As I haven't a miscellaneous article at hand, nor a subject to make one of, nor time to write the article if I had a subject, I beg to offer the following as a substitute. I take it from the twenty-second chapter of a tale for boys which I have been engaged upon, at intervals during the past three years, and which I hope to finish, yet, before all the boys grow up. I will explain, for the reader's benefit, as follows: The lad who is talking is a slim, gentle, smileless creature, void of all sense of humor, and given over to melancholy from his birth. He is speaking to little Edward VI., King of England, in a room in the palace; the two are by themselves; the speaker was "whipping-boy" to the king when the latter was Prince of Wales. James I. and Charles II. had whipping boys when they were little fellows, to take their punishment for them when they fell short in their lessons, so I have ventured to furnish my small prince with one, for my own purposes. The time of this scene is early in the year 1548, consequently Edward VI. is about ten years of age; the other lad is fourteen or fifteen."—MARK TWAIN.

I will tell it, my liege, seeing thou hast so commanded (said the whipping-boy, with a sigh which was manifestly well freighted with painful recollections), though it will open the sore afresh, and I shall suffer again the miseries of that misbegotten day.

It was last midsummer—Sunday, in the afternoon—and drowsy, hot and breathless; all the green country-side gasped and panted with the heat. I was at home, alone; alone, and burdened with the solitude. But first it is best that I say somewhat of the old knight my father—Sir Humphrey. He was just turned of forty, in the time of the Field of the Cloth of Gold, and was a brave and gallant subject.

* "Beyond the publication of *The Prince and the Pauper* Clemens was sparingly represented in print in 1881. A chapter originally intended for the book, the 'Whipping Boy's Story,' he gave to the *Bazaar Budget*, a little special-edition sheet printed in Hartford. It was the story of the Bull and the Bees which he later adapted for use in *Joan of Arc*, the episode in which Joan's father rides a bull to a funeral."
—A. B. PAINE, *A Biography of Mark Twain*, p. 719.

He was rich, too, albeit he grew poor enough before he died. At the Field he was in the great cardinal's suite, and shone with the best. In a famous Masque, there, he clothed himself in a marvelous dress of most outlandish sort, imaginary raiment of some fabled prince of goblins, or spirits, or I know not what; but this I know, that it was a nine-days' wonder, even there, where the art of the broad world had been taxed in the invention of things gorgeous, strange and memorable. Even the king thy father said it was a triumph, and swore it with his great oath, "By the Splendor of God!" What a king hath praised is precious, though it were dirt before; so my father brought home this dress to England, and kept it always laid up in herbs to guard it from injurious insects and decay. When his wealth vanished, he clung to it still.

Age crept upon him, trouble wrought strangenesses in him, delusions ate into his mind. He was of so uncomfortable a piety, and so hot-spirited withal, that when he prayed, one wished he might give over, he so filled the heart with glooms of hell and the nose with the stink of brimstone; yet when he was done, his weather straightway changed, and he so raged and swore and laid about him, right and left, that one's thought was, "Would God he would pray again."

In time was he affected with a fancy that he could cast out devils —wo worth the day! This very Sunday, whereof I have spoken to your grace, he was gone, with the household, on this sort of godly mission, to Hengist's Wood, a mile and more away, where all the gaping fools in Bilton parish were gathered to hear him pray a most notorious and pestilent devil out of the carcase of Gammer Hooker, an evil-minded beldame that had been long and grievously oppressed with that devil's presence, and in truth a legion more, God pardon me if I wrong the poor old ash-cat in so charging her.

As I did advertise your grace in the beginning, the afternoon was come, and I was sore wearied with the loneliness. Being scarce out of my thirteenth year, I was ill stocked with love for solitude, or patience to endure it. I cast about me for a pastime, and in an evil hour my thought fell upon that old gala-suit my father had brought from the Field of the Cloth of Gold near thirty years bygone. It was sacred; one might not touch it and live, an my father found him in the act. But I said within myself, 'tis a stubborn devil that bides in Gammer Hooker, my father cannot harry him forth with one prayer, nor yet a hundred—there is time now—I will have a look, though I perish for the trespass.

I dragged the marvel out from its hiding, and fed my soul with the sight. O, thou shouldst have seen it flame and flash in the sun, my liege! It had all colors, and none were dull. The hose of shining green—lovely, silken things; the high buskins, red-heeled, and great golden spurs, jeweled, and armed with rowels a whole span long, and the strangest trunks, the strangest odd-fashioned doublet man ever saw, and so many-colored, so rich of fabric and so bespangled; and then the robe! it was crimson satin, banded and barred from top to hem with a webbed glory of precious gems, if haply they were not false—and mark ye, my lord, this robe was all of a piece, and covered the head, with holes to breath and spy through; and it had long, wide sleeves, of a most curious pattern; then there was a belt and a great sword, and a shining golden helmet, full three spans high, out of whose top sprung a mighty spray of plumes, dyed red as fire. A most gallant and barbaric dress—evil befall the day I saw it!

When I was sated with gazing at it, and would have hid it in its place again, the devil of misfortune prompted me to put it on. It was there that my sorrow and my shame began. I clothed myself in it, and girt on the sword, and fixed on the great spurs. Naught fitted —all was a world too large—yet was I content, and filled with windy vanity. The helmet sunk down and promised to smother me, like to a cat with its head fast in a flagon, but I stuffed it out with rags, and so mended the defect. The robe dragged the ground, wherefore was I forced to hold it up when I desired to walk with freedom. Marching hither and yonder before the mirror, the grand plumes gladdened my heart and the crimson splendors of the robe made my foolish soul to sing for joy, albeit, to speak plain truth, my first glimpse of mine array did well nigh fright the breath out of my lank body, so like a moving conflagration did I seem.

Now, forsooth, could I not be content with private and secluded happiness, but must go forth from the house, and see the full sun flash upon my majesty. I looked warily abroad on every side; no human creature was in sight; I passed down the stairs and stepped upon the greensward.

I beheld a something, then, that in one little fleeting instant whisked all thought of the finery out of my head, and brimmed it with a hot new interest. It was our bull—a brisk young creature that I had tried to mount a hundred times, and failed; now was he grazing, all peacefully and quiet, with his back to me. I crept toward him, stealthily and slow, and O, so eager and so anxiously, scarce breathing lest I should betray myself—then with one master bound I lit astride his back! Ah, dear my liege, it was but a woful triumph. He

ran, he bellowed, he plunged here and there and yonder, and flung his
heels aloft in so mad a fashion that I was sore put to it to stick
where I was, and fain to forget it was a jaunt of leasure, and busy
my mind with expedients to the saving of my neck. Wherefore, to
this end, I did take a so deadly grip upon his sides with those galling
spurs that the pain of it banished the slim remnant of his reason
that was left, and so forsook he all semblance of reserve, and set
himself the task of tearing the general world to rags, if so be, in the
good providence of God, his heels might last out the evil purpose of
his heart. Being thus resolved, he fell to raging in wide circles round
and round the place, bowing his head and tossing it, with bellow-
ings that froze my blood, lashing the air with his tail, and plunging
and prancing, and launching his accursed heels, full freighted with
destruction, at each perishable thing his fortune gave him for a prey,
till in the end he erred, to his own hurt no less than mine, delivering
a random kick that did stave a beehive to shreds and tatters, and
empty its embittered host upon us.

In good sooth, my liege, all that went before was but holiday pastime to that that followed after. In briefer time than a burdened man
might take to breath a sigh, the fierce insects did clothe us like a
garment, whilst their mates, a singing swarm, encompassed us as
with a cloud, and waited for any vacancy that might appear upon
our bodies. An I had been cast naked into a hedge of nettles, it had
been a blessed compromise, forasmuch as nettle-stings grew not so
near together as did these bee-stings compact themselves. Now, being
moved by the anguish of this new impulse, the bull did surpass himself. He raged thrice around the circuit in the time he had consumed
to do it once, before, and wrought final wreck and desolation upon
such scattering matters as he had aforetime overlooked and spared;
then, perceiving that the swarm still clouded the air about us, he was
minded to fly the place, and leave the creatures behind—wherefore,
uplifting his tail, and bowing his head, he went storming down the
road, praising God with a loud voice, and in a shorter space than a
wholesome pulse might take to beat a hundred was a mile upon his
way—but alack, so also were the bees. I noted not whither he tended,
I was dead to all things but the bees and the miserable torment;
the first admonishment I had that my true trouble was but now at
hand, was a wild, affrighted murmur that broke upon my ear, then
through those satin eye-holes I shot a glance, and beheld my father's
devout multitude of fools scrambling and skurrying to right and left
with the terrors of perdition in their souls; and one little instant

after, I, helmeted, sworded, plumed, and blazing in that strange un-
earthly panoply of red-hot satin, tore into the midst, on my roaring
bull—and my father and his ancient witch being in the way, we
struck them, full and fair, and all the four went down together, Sir
Humphrey crying out, in the joy of his heart, "See, 'tis the master
devil himself, and 'twas I that haled him forth!"

I marvel your majesty should laugh; I see naught in it of a merry
sort, but only bitterness. Lord, it was pitiful to see how the wrathful
bees did assault the holy congregation and harry them, turning their
meek and godly prayers into profane cursings and blasphemous execrations, whilst the whole multitude, even down to the aged mothers
in Israel and frosty-headed patriarchs did wildly skip and prance in
the buzzing air, and thrash their arms about, and tumble and sprawl
over one another in mad endeavor to flee the horrid place. And there,
in the grass, my good father rolled and tossed, hither and thither,
and everywhere—being sore beset with the bees—delivering a howl of
rage with every prod he got—ah, good my liege, thou shouldst have
heard him curse and pray!—and yet, amidst all his woes, still found
his immortal vanity room and opportunity to vent itself; and so, from
time to time shouted he with a glad voice, saying, "I wrought to
bring forth one devil, and lo, have I emptied the courts of hell!"

I was found out, my prince—ah, prithee spare me the telling
what happened to me then; I smart with the bare hint of it. My
tale is done, my lord. When thou didst ask me yesterday, what I
could mean by the strange reply I made to the lady Elizabeth, I
humbly begged thee to await another time, and privacy. The thing I
said to her grace was this—a maxim which I did build out of mine
own head: "All superfluity is not wealth; if bee-stings were farthings,
there was a day when Bilton parish had been rich."

1880

ON THE PHILOSOPHY OF SHAVING

It is safe to say that nine out of ten of the men one meets on the streets in our cities shave, or rather are shaved. Some shave the moustache, some the chin, some the cheeks. Indeed, one must go into mathematics to the tables of permutations and combinations to find how many varieties of shaving are possible. Woman is accused of being the party who devotes her time to appearances and frivolities of the mirror, but, after all, man does his share of it. The reason he escapes the charge is that he blandly sets down his decorative work as being a matter of necessity.

And it is true that shaving is a very old custom, nor have we anything to say against it, except that it is unnatural, and is, and should be acknowledged to be, a concession to the looking-glass and to vanity. But the point is that, old as is the art, it is a singular thing how few know how to shave. "Nearly all men shave in the passive voice." This may be taken as the grammatical phrase or as an acknowledgment of the voice of the barber which they have to endure. Each signification is true. And while nearly all men consent to refer their shaving to a few who make it a business, only a fraction of that few understand their art.

There is a financial blunder at the bottom of it that makes trouble all through. The dogma that a shave is a shave is a mistake. One man with a stiff beard and a full face will choose to have his whole expansive countenance clean shorn; another will shave on his upper lip. To each it is "a shave," and each is charged alike. One may require thirty minutes' attention, the other ten minutes. The first will dull a razor, the second not affect its edge. To each it is ten cents. Now, a barber's working day, we will assume, is ten hours long. If he is occupied three-quarters of the time, he must be busier usually than appears. This gives him seven hours' labor, and if he struck a day of half-hour faces his whole receipts would be $1.40. If his luck gave him ten-minute cases, he would take in $2.10. Even this would not pay were it not for the side issues—the hair-cuts and shampoos of the trade—that bring in more per hour than the fundamental industry.

Now, as the price and the circumstances of shaving go, it is a constant hurry to finish a man, as shaving scarcely pays at the best, and if he is one of the most absorbing subjects—full shave and a stiff beard—it is a loss to work upon him. To shave him carefully takes too much time and costs the edge of the razor. To skim over his face, cutting off sections of beard here and there, and leaving odd oases of hair along the deserts of the cheek, saves the razor and spoils the person who pays for the operation, and who should not be entirely forgotten. The scale of prices ought to be regulated by what one gets, and barbers ought to have the courage to charge for what they do.

This done, a revolution in the art would follow. Speed would not be the great aim. Attention could be given to the removal of the beard, which, in old times, it was as important to remove as the lather, and the man who went out of the barber's shop would leave satisfied, instead of hoping that the next time it would be better. We recommend these considerations to the trade without charge for the advice. Shaving is a custom of civilization; playing with soap bubbles is a game of childhood. It is now a matter of luck which of these operations falls to the barber's patron to-day.

1880

A TALE FOR STRUGGLING YOUNG POETS*

Well, sir, there was a young fellow who believed that he was a poet; but the main difficulty with him was to get anybody else to believe it. Many and many a poet has split on that rock—if it is a rock. Many and many a poet will split on it, thank God. The young fellow I speak of, used all the customary devices—and with the customary results—to wit: he competed for prizes, and didn't take any; he sent specimens of poetry to famous people, and asked for a "candid opinion," meaning a puff, and didn't get it; he took advantage of dead persons and obituaried them in ostensible poetry, but it made him no friends—certainly none among the dead. But at last he heard of another chance; there was going to be a fair in Buffalo, accompanied by the usual inoffensive paper, and the editor of that paper offered a prize of $10 for the best original poem on the usual topic of Spring, no poem to be considered unless it should possess positive value.

Well, sir, he shook up his muse, he introduced into her a rousing charge of information from his jug, and then sat down and dashed off the following madrigal just as easy as lying:

HAIL! BEAUTIOUS, GLADSOME SPRING
A POEM BY S. L. CLEMENS
No. 1163. Hartford, Conn, Nov. 17
GEO. P. BISSELL & CO.,
BANKERS,
Pay to Mrs. David Gray, or Order, for F
TEN.....................DOLLARS
Household Account

S. L. CLEMENS

Did he take the prize? Yes, he took the prize. The poem and its title didn't seem to go together very well; but, no matter, that sort

* Contributed to the *Bazaar Bulletin*, a small journal published during the course of a charity affair in Buffalo, N.Y. in November 1880.

of thing has happened before; it didn't rhyme, neither was it blank verse, for the blanks were all filled, yet it took the prize for this reason, no other poem offered was really worth more than $4.50, whereas there was no getting around the petrified fact that this one was worth $10. In truth there was not a banker in the whole town who was willing to invest a cent in those other poems, but every one of them said this one was good, sound, seaworthy poetry, and worth its face. Such is the way in which that struggling young poet achieved recognition at last, and got a start along the road that leads to lyric eminence—whatever that may mean. Therefore, let other struggling young poets be encouraged by this and go striving.

1880

SMOKING AS INSPIRATION

I have not had a large experience in the matter of alcoholic drinks. I find that about two glasses of champagne are an admirable stimulant to the tongue, and is, perhaps, the happiest inspiration for an after dinner speech which can be found; but, as far as my experience goes, wine is a clog to the pen, not an inspiration. I have never seen the time when I could write to my satisfaction after drinking even one glass of wine.

As regards smoking, my testimony is of the opposite character. I am forty-six years old, and I have smoked immoderately during thirty-eight years, with the exception of a few intervals, which I will speak of presently. During the first seven years of my life I had no health—I may almost say that I lived on allopathic medicine, but since that period I have hardly known what sickness is. My health has been excellent, and remains so. As I have already said, I began to smoke immoderately when I was eight years old; that is, I began with one hundred cigars a month, and by the time I was twenty I had increased my allowance to two hundred a month. Before I was thirty, I had increased it to three hundred a month. I think I do not smoke more than that now; I am quite sure I never smoke less. Once, when I was fifteen, I ceased from smoking for three months, but I do not remember whether the effect resulting was good or evil. I repeated this experiment when I was twenty-two; again I do not remember what the result was. I repeated the experiment once more, when I was thirty-four, and ceased from smoking during a year and a half. My health did not improve, because it was not possible to improve health which was already perfect. As I never permitted myself to regret this abstinence, I experienced no sort of inconvenience from it. I wrote nothing but occasional magazine articles during pastime, and as I never wrote one except under strong impulse, I observed no lapse of facility. But by and by I sat down with a contract behind me to write a book of five or six hundred pages—the book called "Roughing it"—and then I found myself most seriously obstructed. I was three weeks writing six chapters. Then I gave up the fight, resumed my three hundred cigars, burned the six chapters, and wrote the book in three months, without any bother or difficulty. I find cigar smoking to be the best of all inspirations for the pen, and, in my particular case, no sort of detriment to the health. During eight months of the year I am at home, and that period is my holiday. In it I do nothing but very occasional miscellaneous work; therefore, three hundred cigars a month is a sufficient amount to keep my constitution on a firm basis. During the family's summer vacation, which we spend elsewhere, I work five hours every day, and five days in every week, and allow no interruption under any pretext. I allow myself the fullest possible marvel of inspiration; consequently, I ordinarily smoke fifteen cigars during my five hours' labours, and if my interest reaches the enthusiastic point, I smoke more. I smoke with all my might, and allow no intervals.

1882

WOMAN, GOD BLESS HER!*

The toast includes the sex, universally; it is to Woman comprehensively, wheresoever she may be found. Let us consider her ways. First comes the matter of dress. This is a most important consideration, and must be disposed of before we can intelligently proceed to examine the profounder depths of the theme. For text let us take the dress of two antipodal types—the savage woman of Central Africa and the cultivated daughter of our high modern civilization. Among the Fans, a great negro tribe, a woman when dressed for home, or to go out shopping or calling, doesn't wear anything at all but just her complexion. That is all; it is her entire outfit. It is the lightest costume in the world, but is made of the darkest material. It has often been mistaken for mourning. It is the trimmest, and neatest, and gracefulest costume that is now in fashion; it wears well, is fast colors, doesn't show dirt, you don't have to send it down-town to wash, and have some of it come back scorched with the flat-iron, and some of it with the buttons ironed off, and some of it petrified with starch, and some of it chewed by the calf, and some of it rotted with acids, and some of it exchanged for other customers' things that haven't any virtue but holiness, and ten-twelfths of the pieces overcharged for and the rest of the dozen "mislaid." And it always fits; it is the perfection of a fit. And it is the handiest dress in the whole realm of fashion. It is always ready, always "done up." When you call on a Fan lady and send up your card, the hired girl never says, "Please take a seat, madame is dressing; she'll be down in three-quarters of an hour." No, madame is always dressed, always ready to receive; and before you can get the door-mat before your eyes she is in your midst. Then, again, the Fan ladies don't go to church to see what each other has got on; and they don't go back home and describe it and slander it.

* A speech delivered before the New England Society in the City of New York, December 22, 1882.

Such is the dark child of savagery, as to every-day toilet; and thus, curiously enough, she finds a point of contact with the fair daughter of civilization and high fashion—who often has "nothing to wear"; and thus these widely-separated types of the sex meet upon common ground. Yes, such is the Fan woman as she appears in her simple, unostentatious, every-day toilet; but on state occasions she is more dressy. At a banquet she wears bracelets; at a lecture she wears ear-rings and a belt; at a ball she wears stockings—and, with true feminine fondness for display, she wears them on her arms; at a funeral she wears a jacket of tar and ashes; at a wedding the bride who can afford it puts on pantaloons. Thus the dark child of savagery and the fair daughter of civilization meet once more upon common ground, and these two touches of nature make their whole world kin.

Now we will consider the dress of our other type. A large part of the daughter of civilization is her dress—as it should be. Some civilized women would lose half their charm without dress; and some would lose all of it. The daughter of modern civilization dressed at her utmost best, is a marvel of exquisite and beautiful art and expense. All the lands, all the climes, and all the arts are laid under tribute to furnish her forth. Her linen is from Belfast, her robe is from Paris, her lace is from Venice, or Spain, or France; her feathers are from the remote regions of Southern Africa, her furs from the remoter home of the iceberg and the aurora, her fan from Japan, her diamonds from Brazil, her bracelets from California, her pearls from Ceylon, her cameos from Rome; she has gems and trinkets from buried Pompeii, and others that graced comely Egyptian forms that have been dust and ashes now for forty centuries; her watch is from Geneva, her card-case is from China, her hair is from—from—I don't know where her hair is from; I never could find out. That is, her other hair—her public hair, her Sunday hair; I don't mean the hair she goes to bed with. Why, you ought to know the hair I mean; it's that thing which she calls a switch, and which resembles a switch as much as it resembles a brickbat or a shotgun, or any other thing which you correct people with. It's that thing which she twists and then coils round and round her head, beehive fashion, and then tucks the end in under the hive and harpoons it with a hairpin. And that reminds me of a trifle: any time you want to, you can glance around the carpet of a Pullman car, and go and pick up a hairpin; but not to save your life can you get any woman in that car to acknowledge that hairpin. Now, isn't that strange? But it's true. The woman who has never swerved from cast-iron veracity and fidelity in her whole life will, when confronted with this crucial test, deny her hairpin. She will deny that hairpin before a hundred witnesses. I have stupidly got into more trouble and more hot water trying to hunt up the owner of a hairpin in a Pullman car than by any other indiscretion of my life.

Well, you see what the daughter of civilization is when she is dressed, and you have seen what the daughter of savagery is when she isn't. Such is woman, as to costume. I come now to consider her in her higher and nobler aspects—as mother, wife, widow, grass-widow, mother-in-law, hired girl, telegraph operator, telephone hel-loer, queen, book-agent, wet-nurse, stepmother, boss, professional fat woman, professional double-headed woman, professional beauty, and so forth and so on.

We will simply discuss these few—let the rest of the sex tarry in Jericho till we come again. First in the list of right, and first in our gratitude, comes a woman who—why, dear me, I've been talking three-quarters of an hour! I beg a thousand pardons. But you see, yourselves, that I had a large contract. I have accomplished something, anyway. I have introduced my subject. And if I had till next Forefathers' Day, I am satisfied that I could discuss it as adequately and appreciatively as so gracious and noble a theme deserves. But as the matter stands now, let us finish as we began—and say, without jesting, but with all sincerity, "Woman—God bless her!"

1882

AH SIN, THE HEATHEN CHINEE*

This is a very remarkable play. I don't know as you noticed it as it went along, but it is. The construction of this play and the development of the story are the result of great research, and erudition, and genius, and invention—and plagiarism. When the authors wrote it they thought they would put in a lot of catastrophes and murders, and such things, because they always enliven an evening so; but we wanted to have some disaster that wasn't hackneyed, and after a good deal of thought we hit upon the breaking down of the stage-coach.

The worst of getting a good original idea like that is the temptation to overdo it; and, in fact, when the play was all done we found that we had got that stage-coach breaking down seven times in the first act. It was to come right along here every seven minutes or so, and spill all its passengers over on the musicians. Well, you see, that wouldn't do; it made it monotonous for the musicians, and it was too stagey; and we had to modify it; and there isn't anything left of the original plan now except one breakdown of the coach, and one carriage breakdown, and one pair of runaway horses. Maybe we might have spared even some of these; but you see we had the horses, and we didn't like to waste them. I wish to say, also, that this play is didactic rather than anything else. It is intended rather for instruction than amusement.

The Chinaman is getting to be a pretty frequent figure in the United States, and is going to be a great political problem; and we thought it well for you to see him on the stage before you had to deal with that problem. Then, for the instruction of the young, we have introduced a game of poker. There are few things that are so unpardonably neglected in our country as poker. The upper class

---

* A curtain speech by Mark Twain at the Fifth Avenue Theatre in New York on the occasion of the production of *Ah Sin, The Heathen Chinee,* a play by Twain and Bret Harte.

know very little about it. Now and then you find ambassadors who have a sort of general knowledge of the game, but the ignorance of the people is fearful. Why, I have known clergymen, good men, kind-hearted, liberal, sincere, and all that, who did not know the meaning of a "flush." It is enough to make one ashamed of one's species.

When our play was finished, we found it was so long, and so broad, and so deep—in places—that it would have taken a week to play it. I thought that was all right; we could put "To Be Continued" on the curtain, and run it straight along. But the manager said "No"; it would get us into trouble with the general public, and into trouble with the general Government, because the Constitution forbids the infliction of cruel or unusual punishment. So he cut out, and cut out, and the more he cut the better the play got. I never saw a play that was so improved by being cut down; and I believe it would have been one of the very best plays in the world if his strength had held out so that he could cut out the whole of it.

1884

ON TRAINING CHILDREN

Editor Christian Union:
I have just finished reading the admirably told tale entitled "What Ought He to have Done?" in your No. 24, and I wish to take a chance at that question myself before I cool off. What a happy literary gift that mother has!—and yet, with all her brains, she manifestly thinks there is a difficult conundrum concealed in that question of hers. It makes a body's blood boil to read her story!

I am a fortunate person, who has been for thirteen years accustomed, daily and hourly, to the charming companionship of thoroughly well-behaved, well-trained, well-governed children. Never mind about taking my word; ask Mrs. Harriet Beecher Stowe, or Charles Dudley Warner, or any other near neighbor of mine, if this is not the exact and unexaggerated truth. Very well, then, I am quite competent to answer that question of "What ought he to have done?" and I will proceed to do it by stating what he *would* have done, and what would have followed, if "John Senior" had been me, and his wife had been my wife, and the cub our mutual property. To wit:

When John Junior "entered the library, marched audaciously up to the desk, snatched an open letter from under his father's busy fingers, threw it upon the floor," and struck the ill-mannered attitude described in the succeeding paragraph, his mother would have been a good deal surprised, and also grieved: surprised that her patient training of her child to never insult any one—even a parent—should so suddenly and strangely have fallen to ruin; and grieved that she must witness the shameful thing.

At this point John Senior—meaning me—would not have said, either "judicially" or otherwise, "Junior is a naughty boy." No; he would have known more than this John Senior knew—for he would have known enough to keep still. He wouldn't have aggravated a case which was already bad enough, by making any such stupid remark—

stupid, unhelpful, undignified. He would have known and felt that there was one present who was quite able to deal with the case, in any stage it might assume, without any assistance from him. Yes, and there is another thing which he would have known, and does at this present writing know: that in an emergency of the sort which we are considering, he is always likely to be as thorough going and ludicrous an ass as this John Senior proved himself to be in the little tale.

No—he would have kept still. Then the mother would have led the little boy to a private place, and taken him on her lap, and reasoned with him, and loved him out of his wrong mood, and shown him that he had mistreated one of the best and most loving friends he had in the world; and in no very long time the child would be convinced, and be sorry, and would run with eager sincerity and ask the father's pardon. And that would be the end of the matter.

But, granting that it did not turn out in just this way, but that the child grew stubborn, and stood out against reasoning and affection. In that case, a whipping would be promised. That would have a prompt effect upon the child's state of mind; for it would know, with its mature two years' experience, that no promise of any kind was ever made to a child in our house and not rigidly kept. So this child would quiet down at this point, become repentant, loving, reasonable; in a word, its own charming self again; and would go and apologize to the father, receive his caresses, and bound away to its play, light-hearted and happy again, although well aware that at the proper time it was going to get that whipping, sure.

The "proper time" referred to is any time after both mother and child have got the sting of the original difficulty clear out of their minds and hearts, and are prepared to give and take a whipping on purely business principles—disciplinary principles—and with hearts wholly free from temper. For whippings are not given in our house for revenge; they are not given for spite, nor ever in anger; they are given partly for punishment, but mainly by way of impressive reminder, and protector against a repetition of the offense. The interval between the promise of a whipping and its infliction is usually an hour or two. By that time both parties are calm, and the one is judicial, the other receptive. The child never goes from the scene of punishment until it has been loved back into happy-heartedness and a joyful spirit. The spanking is never a cruel one, but it is always an honest one. It hurts. If it hurts the child, imagine how it must hurt the mother. Her spirit is serene, tranquil. She has not the support which is afforded by anger. Every blow she strikes the child bruises her own heart. The mother of my children adores them—there is no milder term for it; and they worship her; they even worship anything which the touch of her hand has made sacred. They know her for the best and truest friend they have ever had, or ever shall have; they know her for one who never did them a wrong, and cannot do them a wrong; who never told them a lie, nor the shadow of one; who never deceived them by even an ambiguous gesture; who never gave them an unreasonable command, nor ever contented herself with anything short of a perfect obedience; who has always treated them as politely and considerately as she would the best and oldest in the land, and has always required of them gentle speech and courteous conduct toward all, of whatsoever degree, with whom they chanced to come in contact; they know her for one whose promise, whether of reward or punishment, is gold, and always worth its face, to the uttermost farthing. In a word, they know her, and I know her, for the best and dearest mother that lives—and by a long, long way the wisest.

You perceive that I have never got *down* to where the mother in the tale really asks her question. For the reason that I cannot realize the situation. The spectacle of that treacherously-reared boy, and that wordy, namby-pamby father, and that weak, namby-pamby mother, is enough to make one ashamed of his species. And if I could cry, I would cry for the fate of that poor little boy—a fate which has cruelly placed him in the hands and at the mercy of a pair of grown up children, to have his disposition ruined, to come up ungoverned, and be a nuisance to himself and everybody about him, in the process, instead of being the solacer of care, the disseminator of happiness, the glory and honor and joy of the house, the welcomest face in all the world to them that gave him being—as he ought to be, was sent to be, and would be, but for the hard fortune that flung him into the clutches of these paltering incapables.

In all my life I have never made a single reference to my wife in print before, as far as I can remember, except once in the dedication of a book; and, so, after these fifteen years of silence, perhaps I may unseal my lips this one time without impropriety or indelicacy. I will institute one other novelty: I will send this manuscript to the press without her knowledge, and without asking her to edit it. This will save it from getting edited into the stove.

MARK TWAIN

1885

REMARKABLE GOLD MINES

I have just seen your dispatch from San Francisco in Saturday's *Evening Post* about gold in solution in Calistoga Springs, and about the proprietor having extracted $1600 in gold of the utmost fineness from ten barrels of water, during the past fortnight, by a process known only to himself.

This will surprise many of your readers, but it does not surprise me, for I once owned these springs myself. What does surprise me, however, is the falling off in richness of the water. In my time, the yield was a dollar a dipperful. I am not saying this to injure the property in case a sale is contemplated. I am saying it in the interest of history. It may be that this hotel proprietor's process may be an inferior one. Yes, that may be the fault. Mine was to take my uncle (I had an extra at that time, on account of his parents dying and leaving him on my hands) and fill him up and let him stand fifteen minutes, to give the water a chance to settle. Well, then I insert him in an exhausted receiver, which had the effect of sucking gold out through his pores. I have taken more than $11,000 out of that old man in a day and a half.

I should have held on to those springs but for the badness of the roads and the difficulty of getting the gold to market. I consider that the gold-yielding water is in many respects remarkable, and yet no more remarkable than the gold-bearing air of Catgut Canon, up there toward the head of the auriferous range. This air or this wind, for it is a kind of trade wind which blows steadily down through 600 miles of the richest quartz croppings during an hour and a quarter every day, except Sundays, is heavily charged with exquisitely fine, impalpable gold.

Nothing precipitates and solidifies this gold so readily as contact with human flesh heated by passion. The time that William Abrahams was disappointed in love he used to step out doors when that wind was blowing, and come in again and begin to sigh, and I would extract over a dollar and a half out of every sigh. He sighed right along, and the time that John Harbison and Aleck Norton quarreled about Harbison's dog they stood there swearing at each other; and they knew how, and what they did not know about swearing they couldn't learn from you and me, not by a good deal, and at the end of every three or four minutes they had to stop and make a dividend. If they didn't their jaws would clog up so that they couldn't get big nine-syllabled ones out at all, and when the wind was done blowing they cleared up just a little over $1600 apiece. I know these facts to be absolutely true, because I got them from a man whose mother I knew personally.

I did not suppose a person could buy the water-privilege at Calistoga now at any price, but several good locations along the course of the Catgut Canon gold-bearing trade-wind are for sale. They are going to be stocked for the New York market. They will sell, too; people will swarm for them as thick as Hancock veterans in the South.

1885

INTERNATIONAL COPYRIGHT

No one denies the foreign author's simple moral right to property in the product of his brain; so we may waive that feature and look at non-existent International Copyright from a combined business and statesmanship point of view, and consider whether the nation gains or loses by the present condition of the thing.

As for the business aspect, a great argument of politicians is that our people get foreign books at a cheap rate. Most unfortunately for the country, that is true: we do get cheap alien books—and not of one kind only. We get all kinds—and they are distributed and devoured by the nation strictly in these proportions: an ounce of wholesome literature to a hundred tons of noxious. The ounce represents the little editions of the foreign masters in science, art, history, and philosophy required and consumed by our people; the hundred tons represent the vast editions of foreign novels consumed here—including the welcome semiannual inundation from Zola's sewer.

Is this an advantage to us? It certainly is, if poison is an advantage to a person; or if to teach one thing at the hearthstone, the political hustings, and in a nation's press, and teach the opposite in the books the nation reads is profitable; or, in other words, if to hold up a national standard for admiration and emulation half of each day, and a foreign standard the other half, is profitable. The most effective way to train an impressible young mind and establish for all time its standards of fine and vulgar, right and wrong, and good and bad, is through the imagination; and the most insidious manipulator of the imagination is the felicitously written romance. The statistics of any public library will show that of every hundred books read by our people, about seventy are novels—and nine-tenths of them foreign ones. They fill the imagination with an unhealthy fascination for foreign life, with its dukes and earls and kings, its fuss and feathers, its graceful immoralities, its sugar-coated injustices and oppressions; and this fascination breeds a more or less pronounced dissatisfaction with our country and form of government, and contempt for our republican commonplaces and simplicities; it also breeds longings for something "better," which presently crop out in diseased shams and imitations of that ideal foreign life. Hence the "dude." Thus we have this curious spectacle: American statesmen glorifying American nationality, teaching it, preaching it, urging it, building it up— with their mouths; and undermining it and pulling it down with their acts. This is to employ an Indian nurse to suckle your child, and expect it not to drink in the Indian nature with the milk. It is to go Christian-missionarying with infidel tracts in your hands. Our average young person reads scarcely anything but novels; the citizenship and morals and predilections of the rising generation of America are largely under foreign training by foreign teachers. This condition of things is what the American statesman thinks it wise to protect and preserve—by refusing International Copyright, which would bring the national teacher to the front and push the foreign teacher to the rear. We do get cheap books through the absence of International Copyright; and any who will consider the matter thoughtfully will arrive at the conclusion that these cheap books are the costliest purchase that ever a nation made.

1886

AN AUTHOR'S SOLDIERING*

You Union veterans of Maryland have prepared your feast and offered
to me, a rebel veteran of Missouri, the wound-healing bread and salt
of a gracious hospitality. Do you realize all the vast significance of
the situation? Do you sense the whole magnitude of this conjunction,
and perceive with what opulence of blessing for this nation it is
freighted? What is it we are doing? Reflect! Upon this stage to-night
we play the closing scene of the mightiest drama of modern times,
and ring down, for good and all, the curtain raised at Sumter six-
and-twenty years ago. The two grand divisions of the nation, which
we name in general terms the North and the South, have shaken
hands long ago, and given and taken the kiss of peace. Was anything
lacking to make the reconciliation perfect, the fusion of feeling
complete? Yes. The great border States attached to those grand
divisions, but belonging to neither of them, and independent of
both, were silent; had made no forgiving sign to each other across
the chasm left by the convulsion of war, and the world grieved
that this was so. But tonight the Union veteran of Maryland clasps
hands with the rebel veteran of Missouri, and the gap is closed. In
this supreme moment the imperfect welding of the broken Union
is perfected at last, and from this hour the seam of the joining
shall no more be visible. The long tragedy is ended—ring down the
curtain!

When your secretary invited me to this reunion of the Union
Veterans of Maryland, he requested me to come prepared to clear
up a matter which he said had long been a subject of dispute and
bad blood in war circles in this country—to wit, the true dimensions
of my military service in the Civil War, and the effect which they
had upon the general result. I recognize the importance of this

---

* An address delivered at the banquet of the Union Veterans in Baltimore.

thing to history, and I have come prepared. Here are the details. *I was in the Civil War two weeks.*

In that brief time I rose from private to second lieutenant. The monumental feature of my campaign was the one battle which my command fought—it was in the summer of '61. If I do say it, it was the bloodiest battle ever fought in human history; there is nothing approaching it for destruction of human life in the field, if you take in consideration the forces engaged, and the proportion of death to survival. And yet you do not even know the name of that battle. Neither do I. It had a name, but I have forgotten it. It is no use to keep private information which you can't show off. Now look at the way history does. It takes the battle of Boonville, fought near by, about the date of our slaughter and shouts its teeth loose over it, and yet never even mentions ours; doesn't even call it an "affair"; doesn't call it anything at all; never even heard of it. Whereas, what are the facts? Why, these: In the battle of Boonville there were two thousand men engaged on the Union side, and about as many on the other—supposed to be. The casualties, all told, were two men killed; and not all of these were killed outright, but only half of them, for the other man died in hospital next day. I know that, because his great-uncle was second cousin to my grandfather, who spoke three languages, and was perfectly honorable and upright, though he had warts all over him, and used to—but never mind about that, the facts are just as I say, and I can prove it. Two men killed in that battle of Boonville, that's the whole result. All the others got away—on both sides. Now then, in our battle there were just fifteen men engaged, on our side—all brigadier generals but me, and I was a second lieutenant. On the other side there was one man. He was a stranger. We killed him. It was night, and we thought he was an army of observation; he looked like an army of observation —in fact, he looked bigger than an army of observation would in the daytime; and some of us believed he was trying to surround us, and some thought he was going to try to turn our position, and so we shot him. Poor fellow, he probably wasn't an army of observation, after all; but that wasn't our fault; as I say, he had all the look of it in that dim light. It was a sorrowful circumstance, but he took the chances of war, and he drew the wrong card; he overestimated his fighting strength, and he suffered the likely result; but he fell as the brave should fall—with his face to the foe and feet to the field—so we buried him with the honors of war, and took his things. So began and ended the only battle in the history of the world where the opposing force WAS UTTERLY EXTERMINATED, swept from the face of the earth—to the last man. And yet, you don't know the name of that battle; you don't even know the name of that man. Now, then, for the argument. Suppose I had continued in the war, and gone on as I began, and exterminated the opposing force every time—every two weeks—where would your war have been? Why, you see yourself, the conflict would have been too one-sided. There was but one honorable course for me to pursue, and I pursued it. I withdrew to private life, and gave the Union cause a chance. There, now, you have the whole thing in a nutshell; it was not my presence in the Civil War that determined that tremendous contest—it was my retirement from it that brought the crash. It left the Confederate side too weak. And yet, when I stop and think, I cannot regret my course. No, when I look abroad over this happy land, with its wounds healed and its enmities forgotten; this reunited sisterhood of majestic States; this freest of free commonwealths the sun in his course shines upon; this one sole country nameable in history or tradition where a man *is* a man and manhood the only royalty; this people ruled by the justest and wholesomest laws and government yet devised by the wisdom of men; this mightiest of the civilized empires of the earth, in numbers, in prosperity, in progress and in promise; and reflect that there is no North, no South any more, but that as in the old time, it is now and will remain forever, in the hearts and speech of Americans, our land, our country, our giant empire, and the flag floating in its firmament our flag, I would not wish it otherwise. No, when I look about me and contemplate these sublime results, I feel, deep down in my heart, that I acted for the best when I took my shoulder out from under the Confederacy and let it come down.

1887

AMERICAN AUTHORS AND BRITISH PIRATES

A PRIVATE LETTER AND A PUBLIC POSTSCRIPT

My Dear Matthews:*

Come, now, what your cause needs is, that some apparent sufferer shall say a fair word for the other side. That complaint which cannot hunt up a dissenting voice anywhere is out of luck. A thing which is all good or all bad is properly an object of suspicion in this world; we get a sort of impression that it is off its beat; that it belongs in the next world, above or below—climate not suited to it here.

English pirates have hurt me somewhat; how much, I do not know. But, on the other hand, English *law* has helped me vastly. Can any foreign author of books say that about American law? You know he can't.

Look at the matter calmly, reasonably. As I infer, from what you say about your article, your complaint is, that American authors are pirated in England. Well, whose fault is that? It is nobody's but the author's. England furnishes him a perfect remedy; if he does not choose to take advantage of it, let him have self-respect enough to retire to the privacy of his cradle, not sit out on the public curbstone and cry. To-day the American author can go to Canada, spend three days there, and come home with an English and Canadian copyright which is as strong as if it had been built out of railroad iron. If he does not make this trip and do this thing, it is a confession that he does not think his foreign market valuable enough to justify the expense of securing it by the above process. Now it may turn out that that book is presently pirated in London.

* Brander Matthews, who had published an article on the subject in the September 1887 *New Princeton Review*, and who published "An Open Letter to Close a Correspondence" immediately following Clemens's contribution in the *New Princeton Review* of the following January. There is no doubt that Clemens played wild with some of the facts, but the tone of his article, its sauciness and its rich style make the piece worth preserving.

What then? Why, simply this: the pirate has paid that man a compliment; he has thought more of the book than the man thought of it himself. And doubtless the man is not pecuniarily injured, since the pirate would probably not have offered anything for the book if it had been copyrighted, but would merely have left it in oblivion and unpublished.

I believe, and it stands to reason, that all the American books that are pirated in these latter days in England are of the complimentary sort, and that the piracies work no computable injury to the author's pocket; and I also believe that if this class of books should be copyrighted henceforth, their publication over there would cease, and then all the loss would fall upon the authors, since they wouldn't be any better off, as regards money, than they were before, and would lose their compliment besides.

I think we are not in a good position to throw bricks at the English pirate. We haven't any to spare. We need them to throw at the American Congress; and at the American author, who neglects his great privileges and then tries to hunt up some way to throw the blame upon the only nation in the world that is magnanimous enough to say to him: "While you are the guest of our laws and our flag, you shall not be robbed."

All the books which I have published in the last fifteen years are protected by English copyright. In that time I have suffered pretty heavily in temper and pocket from imperfect copyright laws; but they were American, not English. I have no quarrel over there.

Yours sincerely,
MARK TWAIN

P.S. (of the feminine sort). I wrote the above (but have concluded not to mail it directly to you) in answer to your letter asking me for facts and statistics concerning English piracies of my books. I had to guess at the probable nature of your NEW PRINCETON article from what you said of it. But I sent out for it this morning, and have read it through. Why, dear, dear distorted mind, I am amazed at you. You stand recorded in the directory, "Brander Matthews, lawyer, 71 Broadway." By your article I half suspected that you were a lawyer, and so I went to the directory to see. It seemed to me that only a lawyer—an old lawyer—a callous, leathery, tough old lawyer —could have the superb pluck to venture into court with such a ragged case as yours is. Why, dear soul, you haven't a leg to stand on, anywhere. I have known you long, and loved you always; but you must let me be frank and say, you haven't a fact that cannot be amply offset by the other side, you haven't an argument that cannot be promptly turned against you.

To start with, you wander a little off to one side of your real case, to tell the world that a couple of reverend British reprobates have been plagiarizing—stealing—from American books. That is a telling fact—if American preachers never steal. But, dear sir, they do. Take this case. E. H. House spends twelve or thirteen years in Japan; becomes exhaustively versed in Japanese affairs; coins these riches into an admirable article, and prints it in the *Atlantic* six years ago, under the title, "The Martyrdom of an Empire." This present year, Rev. James King Newton, A.M., "Professor of Modern Languages, Oberlin College," confers upon the literary museum of the *Bibliotheca Sacra* a crazy-quilt which he wordily names, "Obligations of the United States to Initiate a Revision of Treaties between the Western Powers and Japan." This queer work is made up of rags and scraps of sense and nonsense, sham and sincerity, theft and butter-mouthed piousness, modesty and egotism, facts and lies, knowledge and ignorance, first-rate English and fortieth-rate English, wind and substance, dignity and paltriness, and all through the air about it you seem to catch the soft clear note of flutes and birds, mingled with the wild weird whoopjamboreehoo of the embattled jackass. Now, part of that strange article is original. The rest of it was "smouched" from House's *Atlantic* paper. Will you have a sample?

Atlantic Monthly, May, 1881.	*Bibliotheca Sacra, January,* 1887.
The first effective commercial treaty with Japan was draughted by him in 1858, upon terms which, in general, were not disadvantageous to the unsophisticated people with whom he was dealing.	Mr. Harris made our first commercial treaty in 1858, upon terms which, in general, were reasonable, in an experimental treaty, and not disadvantageous to the unsophisticated people with whom he was dealing.
If he had taken the precaution to insure the absolute expiration of the treaty and its appendages at a proper date, all would have resulted as he desired.	If he had taken the precaution to insure the absolute expiration of the treaty and its appendages at some definite time, all would have resulted according to his honest intention.
The working of the treaty has proved flagrantly injurious to Japan and proportionately favorable to the foreign powers—exceptionally favor-	The working of the treaties has proved most disastrous to Japan, and proportionately favorable to the western powers; exceptionally so to England, as she has the largest trade connections.

able to England, that country having the most extensive trade connection.

Precisely what this country intended to accomplish by that imposing deed it would be difficult to say. What it did accomplish, etc.

Precisely what our government intended to accomplish by the imposing deed of opening Japan, it would be difficult to say. What it did acomplish, etc.

There you have four samples. I could give you twenty-four more, if they were needed, to show how exactly Mr. Newton can repeat slathers and slathers of another man's literature without ever missing a trick, when the police ain't around. You can get that thing if you would like to look at it. Brer Newton has issued it in pamphlet form, at a Boston admirer's expense; and has printed up in the corner of the cover, "With the Author's Compliments"—meaning House, per'aps.

But then, we are all thieves, and it wasn't worth your while to go out of your way to call particular attention to a couple of reverend British ones.

However, right away you come down to business, and open up your real case. You say: "In 1876, Longfellow" complained that he had been pirated by twenty-two publishers. Did he mean, *after* England had offered him and the rest of us protection, and was standing always ready to make her offer good?

Next, "in 1856, Hawthorne"—some more ancient history. You follow it with more and more and more examples—of ancient history; ancient history, and, properly and righteously, out of court. By no fairness can they be cited in this modern time; by no legitimate pretext can they be summoned to testify in this case of yours. What you are complaining about, what you are making all this trouble about, is a bitter grievance which passed out of this world and into its eternal grave more than fifteen years ago. When I say eternal, I mean, of course, if you will let it alone. Matthews, it is a dead issue—utterly dead, and legally forgotten—and I don't believe that even you can aggravate Parliament into resurrecting it, though you certainly do seem to be doing your level best in that direction.

Now, honestly, as between friend and friend, what could ever have put it into your head to hunt out such a grotesquely barren text for a magazine article? We are doing all the pirating in these days; the English used to be in the business, but they dropped out of it long ago. Just look at yourself and your fantastic complaint by the light of allegory. Suppose one of those big Mohammedan slave-dealers in the interior of Africa, lashing his yoked caravan of poor naked creatures through jungle and forest, should turn his grieved attention to us, and between his lashings and thrashings passionately upbraid us with the reminder that "in 1856," and other years and seasons of a hoary and odious antiquity, we used to own our brother human beings, and used to buy them and sell them, lash them, thrash them, break their piteous hearts—and we ought to be ashamed of ourselves, so we ought! What should we answer? What should we say to him? What would *you* say to him concerning so particularly dead an issue as that?—as a lawyer, that is, strictly as a lawyer. I do not know what you would say, but I know what you *could* say. You could say: "Let me take that obsolete case of yours into court; my hand is in, I have been handling one that is just like it—the twin to it, in fact."

In your dozen pages you mention a great many injured American authors, and a great many pirated American books. Now here is a thing which is the exact truth about all of those books and all of those authors: such of the books as were issued before England allowed us copyright, suffered piracy without help; and at the very same time, *five times as many* English books suffered piracy without help on our side of the water. The one fact offsets the other; and the honors are easy—the rascalities, I mean. But, such of those American books as were issued *after* England allowed us copyright, and yet suffered piracy, suffered it by their authors' own fault, not England's nor anybody else's. Their injuries are of their own creation, and they have no shadow of right to set up a single whimper. Why, I used to furnish a sick child in West Hartford with gratis milk; do you know, that cub's mother wasn't satisfied, but wanted me to come over there and warm it? I may be out in my calculations, but I don't believe England is going to warm the milk for this nursery over here.

Great Scott, what arguments you do set up! John Habberton writes *Helen's Babies*; could have English-copyrighted it; didn't; it was pirated, and he thinks he has something to complain about. What, for instance?—that they didn't warm the milk? He issued other books; took out no foreign copyrights, same as before; is pirated from Canada to Australia, and thinks he has something to complain about, once more. Oh, good land! However, "warned by his early experience, he"—does what? Attempts an evasion of the English law, and gets left. Pardon the slang, it does seem to fit in so handy there. With that attempted evasion in one's mind, the neat bit of sarcasm which Habberton fillips at the morals of "the average British publisher" loses some trifle of its bloom, don't you think?

Consider! Right in the midst of all your and Habberton's discontent and animadversion, you placidly give your cause a deadly stab under the fifth rib, and you don't seem to notice that you have done it at all; you meander right along, fretting the same as before. I refer to this remark of yours—and where you forgot to italicize, I have supplied the defect: "The English courts have held that under certain circumstances prior publication in Great Britain *will give an author copyright in England, whatever his nationality may be.*" How could you set down this great, big, generous fact, this fact which offers its fine and gracious hospitalities, without equivalent or even thank-you, to the swindled scribe of all the climes the sun in his course shines upon—even to you yourself—how could you set it down, and not uncover in its magnificent presence? How could you set it down, and not be smitten with a large and sudden realization of the contrast between its open broad palm and the stingy clinched fist of your own country? How could you look it in the face—that friendly, fresh, wholesome, hearty, welcoming, modern countenance —and go on throwing stale mud over its head at its predecessor, an old kiln-dried, moss-backed, bug-eaten, antediluvian mummy that wasn't doing anything to you, and couldn't if it had wanted to? How could you? You are the very wrong-headedest person in America. I tell it you for your own solace. Why, man, you—well, you are geometrically color-blind; you can't see the proportions of things. And you are injudicious. Don't you know that as long as you've got a goitre that you have to trundle around on a wheelbarrow you can't divert attention from it by throwing bricks at a man that's got a wart on the back of his ear? Those blacklegs in Congress keep us furnished with the prize goitre of the moral and intellectual world, and the thing for you to do is to let the wart-wearers strictly alone.

Well, next you cite another case like Habberton's. "Under certain circumstances," as you have said, the protection of the English law was free to both of these authors. You well know that it was their plain duty to find out what those "circumstances" were. They didn't do it, they exploited some smart ostensibilities instead, and their copyright failed. Those "circumstances" are quite simple and explicit, and quite easy to inform one's self about. It follows, and is a fact, that those sufferers had just themselves to blame, and nobody else.

I wonder what *would* satisfy some people. You are an American, I believe; in fact, I know you are. If you want to copyright a book, here at home, what must you do? This: you must get your title-page printed on a piece of paper; enclose it to the Librarian of Congress; apply to him, in writing, for a copyright; and send him a cash fee. That is what you, personally, have to do; the rest is with your publisher. What do you have to do in order to get the same book copyrighted in England? You are hampered by no bothers, no details of any kind whatever. When you send your manuscript to your English publisher, you tell him the date appointed for the book to issue here, and trust him to bring it out there a day ahead. Isn't that simple enough? No letter to any official; no title-page to any official; no fee to anybody; and yet that book has a copyright on it which the Charleston earthquake couldn't unsettle. "Previous publication" in Great Britain of an American book secures perfect copyright; to "previously publish" all but the tail-end of a book in America, and then "previously publish" that mere tail-end in Great Britain, has what effect? Why, it copyrights that tail-end, of course. Would any person in his right mind imagine that it would copyright any more than that? Mr. Habberton seems to have imagined that it would. Mr. Habberton knows better now.

Let the rest of your instances pass. They are but repetitions. There isn't an instance among your antiquities that has any bearing upon your case, or shadow of right to be cited in it—unless you propose to try a corpse, for crimes committed upon other corpses. Living issue you have none, nor even any spectral semblance of any. Your modern instances convict your clients of not knowing enough to come in when it rains. From your first page to your last one, you do not chance to get your hands on a single argument that isn't a boomerang. And finally, to make your curious work symmetrical and complete, you rest from your pitiless lathering of the bad English publisher, and fall to apologizing to him—and, apparently, to the good one, too, I don't know why: "At bottom, the publishers, good or bad, *are not to blame*." You are right, for once, perfectly right; they are not to blame—to-day; if they commit a piracy in these days, nine-tenths of the sin belongs with the American author. And since you perceive that they are not to blame, what did you blame them for? If you were going to take it all back, why didn't you take it back earlier, and not write it at all? Hang it, you are not logical. Do you think that to lather a man all through eleven pages and then tell him he isn't to blame after all, is treating yourself right? Why no, it puts you in such a rickety position. I read it to the cat—well, I never saw a cat carry on so before.

But, of course, somebody or something was to blame. You were in honor bound to make that fact clear, or you couldn't possibly excuse yourself for raising all this dust. Now, I will give any rational man 400,000 guesses, and go bail that he will run short before he has the luck to put his finger on the place where you locate that blame. Now listen—and try to rise to the size of this inspired verdict of yours: "*It is the condition of* THE LAW *which is at fault.*"(!) Upon my life, I have never heard anything to begin with the gigantic impudence of that. The cat—but never mind the cat; the cat is dead; a cat can't stand everything. "*The remedy is to* CHANGE THE LAW"—and then you go owling along, just as if there was never anything more serious in this world than the stupefying nonsense you are talking. Change the law? Change it? In what way, pray? A law which gives us absolutely unassailable and indestructible copyright at cost of not a single penny, not a moment of time, not an iota of trouble, not even the bother of *asking* for it! Change it? How are you going to change it? Matthews, I am your friend, and you know it; and that is what makes me say what I do say: you want a change of air, or you'll be in the asylum the first thing you know.

MARK TWAIN
1888

THE ART OF COMPOSITION

Your inquiry has set me thinking, but, so far, my thought fails to materialise. I mean that, upon consideration, I am not sure that I have methods in composition. I do suppose I have—I suppose I must have—but they somehow refuse to take shape in my mind; their details refuse to separate and submit to classification and description; they remain a jumble—visible, like the fragments of glass when you look in at the wrong end of a kaleidoscope, but still a jumble. If I could turn the whole thing around and look in at the other end, why then the figures would flash into form out of the chaos, and I shouldn't have any more trouble. But my head isn't right for that to-day, apparently. It might have been, maybe, if I had slept last night.

However, let us try guessing. Let us guess that whenever we read a sentence and like it, we unconsciously store it away in our model-chamber; and it goes with the myriad of its fellows to the building, brick by brick, of the eventual edifice which we call our style. And let us guess that whenever we run across other forms—bricks—whose colour, or some other defect, offends us, we unconsciously reject these, and so one never finds them in our edifice. If I have subjected myself to any training processes, and no doubt I have, it must have been in this unconscious or half-conscious fashion. I think it unlikely that deliberate and consciously methodical training is usual with the craft. I think it likely that the training most in use is of this un-conscious sort, and is guided and governed and made by-and-by unconsciously systematic, by an automatically-working taste—a taste which selects and rejects without asking you for any help, and patiently and steadily improves itself without troubling you to approve or applaud. Yes, and likely enough when the structure is at last pretty well up, and attracts attention, *you* feel complimented, whereas you didn't build it, and didn't even consciously superintend. Yes; one notices, for instance, that long, involved sentences confuse him, and that he is obliged to re-read them to get the sense. Unconsciously, then, he rejects that brick. Unconsciously he accustoms himself to writing short sentences as a rule. At times he may indulge himself with a long one, but he will make sure that there are no folds in it, no vaguenesses, no parenthetical interruptions of its view as a whole; when he is done with it, it won't be a sea-serpent, with half of its arches under the water, it will be a torchlight procession.

"Well, also he will notice in the course of time, as his reading goes on, that the difference between the *almost right* word and the *right* word is really a large matter—'tis the difference between the lightning-bug and the lightning. After that, of course, that exceedingly important brick, the *exact* word—however, this is running into an essay, and I beg pardon. So I seem to have arrived at this: doubtless I have methods, but they begot themselves, in which case I am only their proprietor, not their father.

1890

A KIND-HEARTED DRUGGIST*

About a thousand years ago, approximately, I was apprenticed as a printer's devil to learn the trade, in common with three other boys of about my own age. There came to the village a long-legged individual, of about nineteen, from one of the interior counties; fish-eyed, no expression, and without the suggestion of a smile—couldn't have smiled for a salary. We took him for a fool, and thought we would try to scare him to death. We went to the village druggist and borrowed a skeleton. The skeleton didn't belong to the druggist, but he had imported it for the village doctor, because the doctor thought he would send away for it, having some delicacy about using it. The price of a skeleton at that time was fifty dollars. I don't know how high they go now, but probably higher, on account of the tariff. We borrowed the skeleton about nine o'clock at night, and we got this man—Nicodemus Dodge was his name—we got him down-town, out of the way, and then we put the skeleton in his bed. He lived in a little, one-storied log-cabin in the middle of a vacant lot. We left him to get home by himself. We enjoyed the result in the light of anticipation; but, by-and-bye, we began to drop into silence; the possible consequences were preying upon us. Suppose that it frightens him into madness, overturns his reason, and sends him screeching through the streets! We shall spend sleepless nights the rest of our days. Everybody was afraid. By-and-bye, it was forced to the lips of one of us that we had better go at once and see what had happened. Loaded down with crime, we approached that hut and peeped through the window. That long-legged critter was sitting on his bed with a hunk of ginger-bread in his hand, and between the bites he played a tune on a jew's harp. There he sat perfectly happy, and all around him on the bed were toys and

* A speech delivered before the National Wholesale Druggists' Association at a meeting in Washington the latter part of 1890.

jimcracks and striped candy. The darned cuss, he had gone and sold that skeleton for five dollars. The druggist's fifty-dollar skeleton was gone. We went in tears to the druggist and explained the matter. We couldn't have raised that fifty dollars in two hundred and fifty years. We were getting board and clothing for the first year, clothing and board for the second year, and both of them for the third year. The druggist forgave us on the spot, but he said he would like us to let him have our skeletons when we were done with them. There couldn't be anything fairer than that; we spouted our skeletons and went away comfortable. But from that time the druggist's prosperity ceased. That was one of the most unfortunate speculations he ever went into. After some years one of the boys went and got drowned; that was one skeleton gone, and I tell you the druggist felt pretty badly about it. A few years after another of the boys went up in a balloon. He was to get five dollars an hour for it. When he gets back they will be owing him one million dollars. The druggist's property was decreasing right along. After a few more years, the third boy tried an experiment to see if a dynamite charge would go. It went all right. They found some of him, perhaps a vest-pocket-ful; still, it was enough to show that some more of that estate had gone. The druggist was getting along in years, and he commenced to correspond with me. I have been the best correspondent he has. He is the sweetest-natured man I ever saw—always mild and polite, and never wants to hurry me at all. I get a letter from him every now and then, and he never refers to my form as a skeleton; says: 'Well, how is it getting along—is it in good repair?' I got a night-rate message from him recently—said he was getting old and the property was depreciating in value, and if I could let him have a part of it now he would give time on the balance. Think of the graceful way in which he does everything—the generosity of it all. You can not find a finer character than that. It is the gracious characteristic of all druggists. So, out of my heart, I wish you all prosperity and every happiness.

1890

A LOVE SONG

[Inspired by a sojourn at a European Health Resort.]

I ask not "Is thy heart still sure,
Thy love still warm, thy faith secure?"
I ask not "Dream'st thou still of me?"
Long'st always to fly to me?"
    Ah, no—but as the sun includeth all
      The good gifts of the Giver,
    I sum all these in asking thee,
      "Oh, sweetheart, how's your liver"?

For if thy liver worketh right,
Thy faith stands sure, thy hope is bright,
Thy dreams are sweet, and I their God,
Doubt threats in vain—thou scorn'st his rod.
    Keeps only thy digestion clear,
    No other love my foe doth fear.

But indigestion hath the power
To mar the soul's serenest hour;
To crumble admantine trust,
And turn its certainties to dust;
To dim the eye with nameless grief,
To chill the heart with unbelief;
To banish hope, and faith, and love—
Place heaven below and hell above.
    Then list—details are naught to me,
      So thou'st the sum gift of the Giver,
    I ask thee all in asking thee,
      "Oh, darling, how's your liver?"

1895

TALK ABOUT TWINS

Year before last there was an Italian freak on exhibition in Philadelphia who was an exaggeration of the Siamese Twins. This freak
had one body, one pair of legs, two heads and four arms. I thought
he would be useful in a book, so I put him in.* And then the
trouble began. I called these consolidated twins Angelo and Luigi,
and I tried to make them nice and agreeable, but it was not possible.
They would not do anything my way, but only their own. They were
wholly unmanageable, and not a day went by that they didn't
develop some new kind of devilishness—particularly Luigi.

Angelo was of a religious turn of mind, and was monotonously
honest and honorable and upright, and tediously proper; whereas
Luigi had no principles, no morals, no religion—a perfect blather-
skite, and an inextricable tangle theologically—infidel, atheist, and
agnostic, all mixed together. He was of a malicious disposition, and
liked to eat things which disagreed with his brother. They were so
strangely organized that what one of them ate or drank had no
effect upon himself, but only nourished or damaged the other one.
Luigi was hearty and robust, because Angelo ate the best and most
wholesome food he could find for him; but Angelo was himself
delicate and sickly, because every day Luigi filled him up with
mince pies and salt junk, just because he knew he couldn't digest
them.

Luigi was very dissipated, but it didn't show on him, but only
on his brother. His brother was a strict and conscientious teetotaler,
but he was drunk most of the time on account of Luigi's habits.
Angelo was President of the Prohibition Society, but they had to turn
him out, because every time he appeared at the head of the procession
on parade he was a scandalous spectacle to look at. On the other
hand, Angelo was a trouble to Luigi, the infidel, because he was

* *Pudd'nhead Wilson* (1894), containing *Those Extraordinary Twins*.

always changing his religion, trying to find the best one, and he always preferred sects that believed in baptism by immersion, and this was a constant peril and discomfort to Luigi, who couldn't stand water outside or in; and so every time Angelo got baptized Luigi got drowned and had to be pumped out and resuscitated.

Luigi was irascible, yet was never willing to stand by the consequences of his acts. He was always kicking somebody and then laying it on Angelo. And when the kicked person kicked back, Luigi would say: "What are you kicking me for? I haven't done anything to you." Then the man would be sorry, and say: "Well, I didn't mean any harm. I thought it was you; but, you see, you people have only one body between you, and I can't tell which of you I'm kicking. I don't know how to discriminate. I do not wish to be unfair, and so there is no way for me to do but to kick one of you and apologize to the other."

They were a troublesome pair in every way. If they did any work for you, they charged for two; but at the boarding house they ate and slept for two and only paid for one. In the trains they wouldn't pay for two, because they only occupied one seat. The same at the theatre. Luigi bought one ticket and deadheaded Angelo in. They couldn't put Angelo out because they couldn't put the deadhead out without putting out the twin that had paid, and scooping in a suit for damages.

Luigi grew steadily more and more wicked, and I saw by and by that the way he was going on he was certain to land in the eternal tropics, and at bottom I was glad of it; but I knew he would necessarily take his righteous brother down there with him, and that would not be fair. I did not object to it, but I didn't want to be responsible for it. I was in such a hobble that there was only one way out. To save the righteous brother I had to pull the consolidated twins apart and make two separate and distinct twins of them. Well, as soon as I did that they lost all their energy and took no further interest in life. They were wholly futile and useless in the book; they became mere shadows, and so they remain.

1895

JAMES HAMMOND TRUMBULL

News has reached this shut-in corner of the world of the death of an illustrious neighbor and friend of mine, Dr. Trumbull of Hartford. He was probably the richest man in America in the matter of knowledge—knowledge of all values, from copper up to government bonds. It seems a great pity that this vast property is now lost to the world—that it could not have been left to some college, or distributed among deserving paupers, of whom we have so many. The increment of it was so distributed, and with a free hand, as long as the billionaire lived: one may say that of Dr. Trumbull. He spent his riches in a princely way upon any that needed and applied. That was a great and fine feature of his character, and I am moved to say this word about it lest it be forgotten or overlooked. He wrote myriads of letters to information-seekers all over the world—a service of self-sacrifice which made no show, and is all the more entitled to praise and remembrance for that reason.

I asked him a question once myself about twenty years ago. I remember it yet—vividly. His answer exhibited in a striking way his two specialties—the immensity of his learning, and the generous fashion in which he lavished that and his time and labor gratis upon the ignorant needy. I was summering somewhere away from home, and one day I had a new idea—a *motif* for a drama. I was enchanted with the felicity of the conception—I might say intoxicated with it. It seemed to me that no idea was ever so exquisite, so beautiful, so freighted with wonderful possibilities. I believed that when I should get it fittingly dressed out in the right dramatic clothes it would not only delight the world, but astonish it. Then came a stealthy, searching, disagreeable little chill: what if the idea was not new, after all? Trumbull would know. I wrote him some cold, calm, indifferent words out of a heart that was sweltering with anxiety, mentioning my idea, and asking him in a casual way if it had ever been used in a play. His answer covered six pages, written in his fine and graceful hand—six pages of titles of plays in which the idea had been used, the date of each piracy appended, also the country and language in which the felony had been committed. The theft of my idea had been consummated two hundred and sixty-eight times. The latest instance mentioned was English, and not yet three years old; the earliest had electrified China eight hundred years before Christ. Dr. Trumbull added in a foot-note that his list was not complete, since it furnished only the modern instances; but that if I wished it, he would go back to early times. I do not remember the exact words I said about the early times in my answer, but it is not material; they indicated the absence of lust in that direction. I did not write the play.

Years ago, as I have been told, a widowed descendant of the Audubon family, in desperate need, sold a perfect copy of Audubon's "Birds" to a commercially minded scholar in America for a hundred dollars. The book was worth a thousand in the market. The scholar complimented himself upon his shrewd stroke of business. That was not Hammond Trumbull's style. After the war a lady in the far South wrote him that among the wreckage of her better days she had a book which some one had told her was worth a hundred dollars, and had advised her to offer it to him; she added that she was very poor, and that if he would buy it at that price, it would be a great favor to her. It was Eliot's Indian Bible. Trumbull answered that if it was a perfect copy it had an established market value, like a gold coin, and was worth a thousand dollars; that if she would send it to him he would examine it, and if it proved to be perfect he would sell it to the British Museum and forward the money to her. It did prove to be perfect, and she got her thousand dollars without delay, and intact.

Weggis, Switzerland.

1897

THE PANAMA RAILROAD

That railroad down in Panama was a hard road to build. The tropical fevers slaughtered the laborers by the wholesale. It is a popular saying, that every railroad tie from Panama to Aspinwall rests upon a corpse. It ought to be a substantial road, being so well provided with sleepers—eternal ones and otherwise.

The Panama railroad was an American project, in the first place. Then the English got a commanding interest in it, and it became an English enterprise. They grew somewhat sick of it, and it began to swap back until it became American again. The Americans finished it. It proved a good investment. But the right of way granted by the Columbian States was limited to only a few years. The Americans tried to get the term extended. But they were not particularly popular with the Governments of the Isthmus, and could not suceed. Delegations of heavy guns were sent down, but they could not prevail. They offered a few million of dollars, and Government transportation free. President Mosquiera declined. The English saw an opportunity. They made an effort to secure to themselves the right of way whose term was so soon to expire. They were popular with the Isthmian chiefs. They made the Central Governments some valuable presents—gunboats and such things. They were progressing handsomely. Things looked gloomy for the Americans.

Very well; two American gentlemen, who were well acquainted with the Isthmus people and their ways, were commissioned by the Panama Railroad Company, about the time of the opposition English effort, to go down to the Isthmus and make a final trial for an extension of the right of way franchise. Did they take treasure boxes along? Did they take gun boats? Quite the contrary. They took down twelve hundred baskets of champagne and a shipload of whisky. In three days they had the entire population as drunk as lords, the President in jail, the National Congress crazy with delirium tremens, and a gorgeous revolution in full blast! In three more they were at sea again, with the documents for an extension of the railroad franchise to ninety-nine years in their pockets, procured for and in consideration of the sum of three million of dollars in coin, and transportation of Isthmian stores and soldiers over the road free of charge.

That is the legend. I don't know whether it is true, or not. I don't care, either. I only know that the American company had the franchise extended to ninety-nine years, and that all parties concerned were satisfied.

1897

THE PAINS OF LOWLY LIFE*

Sɪᴅɴᴇʏ G. Tʀɪsᴛ, Esǫ.,

Dear Sir—I believe I am not interested to know whether Vivisection produces results that are profitable to the human race or doesn't. To know that the results are profitable to the race would not remove my hostility to it. The pains which it inflicts upon unconsenting animals is the basis of my enmity towards it, and it is to me sufficient justification of the enmity without looking further. It is so distinctly a matter of feeling with me, and is so strong and so deeply-rooted in my make and constitution, that I am sure I could not even see a vivisector vivisected with anything more than a sort of qualified satisfaction. I do not say I should not go and look on; I only mean that I should almost surely fail to get out of it the degree of contentment which it ought, of course, to be expected to furnish.

I find some very impressive paragraphs in a paper which was read before the National Individualist Club (1898) by a medical man. I have read and re-read these paragraphs, with always augmenting astonishment, and have tried to understand why it should be considered a kind of credit and a handsome thing to belong to a human race that has vivisectors in it. And I have also tried to imagine what would become of the race if it had to be saved by my practising vivisection on the French plan. Let me quote:—

* Written as a letter to the secretary of the London Anti-Vivisection Society, and published by the Society. The piece is quite rare. It seems hardly worth reprinting, inasmuch as it contains so little of Mark Twain himself. But in its expression of anti-vivisectionist views it is related to two important stories, "A Dog's Tale" and "A Horse's Tale." "A Dog's Tale" appeared first in *Harper's Magazine* December 1903 and was reprinted as a pamphlet for the National Anti-Vivisection Society (of Great Britain). "A Horse's Tale" was published in 1907 and, according to Mark Twain's biographer, Paine, was written "to oblige Mrs. Minnie Maddern Fiske, to aid her in a crusade against bull-fighting in Spain. Mrs. Fiske wrote him that she had read his dog story, written against the cruelties of vivisection, and urged him to do something to save the horses that, after faithful service, were sacrificed in the bull-ring."

"Vivisectors possess a drug called curare, which, given to an animal, effectually prevents any struggle or cry. A horrible feature of curare is that it has no anaesthetic effect, but on the contrary it intensifies the sensibility to pain. The animal is perfectly conscious, suffers doubly, and is able to make no sign. Claude Bernard, the notorious French vivisector, thus describes the effect of curare: 'The apparent corpse before us hears and distinguishes all that is done. In this motionless body, behind that glazing eye, sensitiveness and intelligence persist in their entirety. The apparent insensibility it produces is accompanied by the most atrocious suffering the mind of man can conceive.' It has been freely admitted by vivisectors that they have used curare alone in the most horrible experiments, that these admissions are to be found multiplied to any extent in the report of the Royal Commission. And though it is illegal at the present day to dispense with anaesthetics, experiments are going on in which curare is the real means of keeping the animal quiet while a pretence is made of anaethetising them.

"I am not desirous of shocking you by reciting the atrocities of vivisection, but since the apologists try to deceive the public by vague statements that vivisectors would not, and do not perpetrate cruelty, I wish to say sufficient to disprove their assertions.

"There is unfortunately abundant evidence that innumerable experiments of the following character have been performed on sensitive animals. They have been boiled, baked, scalded, burnt with turpentine, frozen, cauterized; they have been partly drowned and brought back to consciousness to have the process repeated; they have been cut open and mangled in every part of the body and have been kept alive in a mutilated state for experiments lasting days or weeks. If I wished, I could pile up mountains of evidence, to be found in the publications of physiologists and in the report of the Royal Commission.

"Here are some by Dr. Drasch in 1889 (Du Bois Reymond's Archives): —'The frogs, curarised or not, are prepared in the following manner. The animal is placed on its back on a piece of cork fastened by a needle through the end of the nose, the lower jaw drawn back and also fastened with pins. Then the mucous membrane is cut away in a circular form, the right eyeball which protrudes into the back of the throat is seized, and the copiously bleeding vessels are tied. Next a tent hook is introduced into the cavity of the eye drawing out the muscles and optic nerves, which are also secured by a ligature. The eyeball is then split with a needle near the point where the optic nerve enters, a circular piece cut away from the sclerotic and the crystalline lens, etc., removed from the eyeball. I may remark that my experiments lasted a whole year, and I have therefore tried frogs at all seasons.' He calmly gives directions for keeping the animals still. If the frog is not curarised the sciatic and crural nerves are cut through. It is, however, sufficient to fasten the head completely to the cork to immobilise the animal. The dissection of the trigeminus nerve is difficult.

"Professor Brücke says ('Lectures of Physiology,' Vol. 2. p. 76). 'The first sign that the trigeminus is divided is a loud piercing shriek from the animal. Rabbits we know are not very sensitive, but in this operaton they invariably send forth a prolonged shriek.'

"In Pflüger's 'Archives,' Vol. 2. p. 234, are accounts of similar experiments on curarised cats, a large number of them having the nerves cut, dissected out, and stimulated, the spine opened, spinal marrow cut, etc."

I could quote still more shameful vivisection records from this paper but I lack the stomach for it.

Very truly yours,
(Signed) MARK TWAIN

Vienna, May 26th, 1899.

1900

A DEFENCE OF GENERAL FUNSTON

I

February 22. To-day is the great Birth-Day; and it was observed so widely in the earth that differences in longitudinal time made curious work with some of the cabled testimonies of respect paid to the sublime name which the date calls up in our minds; for, although they were all being offered at about the same hour, several of them were yesterday to us and several were to-morrow.

There was a reference in the papers to General Funston.

Neither Washington nor Funston was made in a day. It took a long time to accumulate the materials. In each case, the basis or moral skeleton of the man was inborn disposition—a thing which is as permanent as rock, and never undergoes any actual and genuine change between cradle and grave. In each case, the moral flesh-bulk (that is to say, *character*) was built and shaped around the skeleton by training, association and circumstances. Given a crooked-disposition skeleton, no power nor influence in the earth can mould a permanently shapely form around it. Training, association and circumstances can truss it, and brace it, and prop it, and strain it, and crowd it into an artificial shapeliness that can endure till the end, deceiving not only the spectator but the man himself. But there is nothing there but artificiality, and if at any time the props and trusses chance to be removed, the form will collapse into its proper and native crookedness.

Washington did not create the basic skeleton (disposition) that was in him; it was born there, and the merit of its perfection was not his. It—and only It—moved him to seek and prefer associations which were contenting to Its spirit; to welcome influences which pleased It and satisfied It; and to repel or be indifferent to influences which were not to Its taste. Moment by moment, day by day, year by year, It stood in the ceaseless sweep of minute influences, auto-matically arresting and retaining, like a magnet of mercury, all dust-particles of gold that came; and, with automatic scorn, repelling certain dust-particles of trash; and, with as automatic indifference, allowing the rest of that base kinship to go by unnoticed. It had a native affinity for all influences fine and great, and gave them hospitable welcome and permanent shelter; It had a native aversion for all influences mean and gross, and passed them on. It chose Its subject's associations for him; It chose his influences for him; It chose his ideals for him; and, out of Its patiently gathered materials, It built and shaped his golden character.

And we give *him* the credit!

We give God credit and praise for being all-wise and all-powerful; but that is quite another matter. No exterior contributor, no birth-commission, conferred these possessions upon Him; He did it *Himself*. But Washington's disposition was *born* in him, he did not create It; It was the architect of his character; his character was the architect of his achievements. If my disposition had been born in him and his in me, the map of history would have been changed. It is our privilege to admire the splendor of the sun, and the beauty of the rainbow, and the character of Washington; but there is no occasion to praise them for these qualities, since *they* did not create the source whence the qualities sprang—the sun's fires, the light upon the falling rain-drops, the sane and clean and benignant disposition born to the Father of his Country.

Is there a value, then, in having a Washington, since we may not concede to him *personal merit* for what he was and did? Necessarily, there is a value—a value so immense that it defies all estimate. Acceptable outside influences were the materials out of which Washington's native disposition built Washington's character and fitted him for his achievements. Suppose there hadn't *been* any. Suppose he had been born and reared in a pirate's cave; the acceptable materials would have been lacking, the Washington character would not have been built.

Fortunately for us and for the world and for future ages and peoples, he was born where the sort of influences and associations acceptable to his disposition were findable; where the building of his character at its best and highest was possible, and where the accident of favorable circumstances was present to furnish it a conspicuous field for the full exercise and exhibition of its commanding capabilities.

Did Washington's great value, then, lie in what he accomplished? No; that was only a minor value. His major value, his vast value, his immeasurable value to us and to the world and to future ages and peoples, lies in his permanent and sky-reaching conspicuousness as an *influence*.

We are *made*, brick by brick, of *influences*, patiently built up around the framework of our born dispositions. It is the sole process of construction; there is no other. Every man and woman and child is an influence; a daily and hourly influence which never ceases from work, and never ceases from affecting for good or evil the characters about it—some contributing gold-dust, some contributing trash-dust, but in either case helping on the building, and never stopping to rest. The shoemaker helps to build his two-dozen associates; the pickpocket helps to build his four dozen associates; the village clergyman helps to build his five hundred associates; the renowned bank-robber's name and fame help to build his hundred associates and three thousand persons whom he has never seen; the renowned philanthropist's labors and the benevolent millionaire's gifts move to kindly works and generous outlays of money a hundred thousand persons whom they have never met and never will meet; and to the building of the character of every individual thus moved these movers have added a brick. The unprincipled newspaper adds a baseness to a million decaying character-fabrics every day; the high-principled newspaper adds a daily betterment to the character-fabric of another million. The swiftly-enriched wrecker and robber of railway systems lowers the commercial morals of a whole nation for three generations. A Washington, standing upon the world's utmost summit, eternally visible, eternally clothed in light, a serene, inspiring, heartening example and admonition, is an influence which raises the level of character in all receptive men and peoples, alien and domestic; and the term of its gracious work is not measurable by fleeting generations, but only by the lingering march of the centuries.

Washington was more and greater than the father of a nation, he was the Father of its Patriotism—patriotism at its loftiest and best; and so powerful was the influence which he left behind him, that that golden patriotism remained undimmed and unsullied for a hundred years, lacking one; and so fundamentally right-hearted are our people by grace of that long and ennobling teaching, that to-day, already, they are facing back for home, they are laying aside their foreign-born and foreign-bred imported patriotism and resuming that which Washington gave to their fathers, which is American and the only American—which lasted ninety-nine years and is good for a million more. Doubt—doubt that we did right by the Filipinos—is rising steadily higher and higher in the nation's breast; conviction will follow doubt. The nation will speak; its will is law; there is no other sovereign on this soil; and in that day we shall right such unfairnesses as we have done. We shall let go our obsequious hold on the rear-skirts of the sceptred land-thieves of Europe, and be what we were before, a *real* World Power, and the chiefest of them all, by right of the only clean hands in Christendom, the only hands guiltless of the sordid plunder of any helpless people's stolen liberties, hands recleansed in the patriotism of Washington, and once more fit to touch the hem of the revered Shade's garment and stand in its presence unashamed. It was Washington's influence that made Lincoln and all other real patriots the Republic has known; it was Washington's influence that made the soldiers who saved the Union; and that influence will save us always, and bring us back to the fold when we stray.

And so, when a Washington is given us, or a Lincoln, or a Grant, what should we do? Knowing, as we do, that a *conspicuous* influence for good is worth more than a billion obscure ones, without doubt the logic of it is that we should highly value it, and make a vestal flame of it, and keep it briskly burning in every way we can—in the nursery, in the school, in the college, in the pulpit, in the newspaper—even in Congress, if such a thing were possible.

The proper inborn disposition was required to start a Washington; the acceptable influences and circumstances and a large field were required to develop and complete him. The same with Funston.

II

"The war was over"—end of 1900. A month later the mountain refuge of the defeated and hunted, and now powerless but not yet hopeless, Filipino chief was discovered. His army was gone, his Republic extinguished, his ablest statesman deported, his generals all in their graves or prisoners of war. The memory of his worthy dream had entered upon a historic life, to be an inspiration to less unfortunate patriots in other centuries; the dream itself was dead beyond resurrection, though he could not believe it.

Now came his capture. An admiring author* shall tell us about it. His account can be trusted, for it is correctly synopsized from General Funston's own voluntary confession made by him at the time. The italics are mine.

* *"Aguinaldo,"* By Edwin Wildman. Lothrop Publishing Co., Boston.

"It was not until February, 1901, that his actual hiding-place was discovered. The clew was in the shape of a letter from Aguinaldo commanding his cousin, Baldormero Aguinaldo, to send him four hundred armed men, the bearer to act as a guide to the same. The order was in cipher, but among other effects captured at various times a copy of the Insurgent cipher was found. The Insurgent courier was convinced of the error of his ways (though by exactly what means, history does not reveal), and offered to lead the way to Aguinaldo's place of hiding. Here was an opportunity that suggested an adventure equal to anything in penny-awful fiction. It was just the kind of a dare-devil exploit that appealed to the romantic Funston. It was something out of the ordinary for a brigadier-general to leave his command and turn into a scout, but Funston was irresistible. He formulated a scheme and asked General MacArthur's permission. It was impossible to refuse the daring adventurer, the hero of the Rio Grande, anything; so Funston set to work, imitating the peculiar handwriting of Lacuna, the Insurgent officer to whom Aguinaldo's communication referred. Some little time previous to the capture of the Tagalog courier, several of Lacuna's letters were found, together with Aguinaldo's cipher code. Having perfected Lacuna's signature, Funston wrote two letters on February 24 and 28, acknowledging Aguinaldo's communication, and informing him that he (Lacuna) was sending him a few of the best soldiers in his command. Added to this neat forgery General Funston dictated a letter which was written by an ex-Insurgent attached to his command, telling Aguinaldo that the relief force had surprised and captured a detachment of Americans, taking five prisoners whom they were bringing to him because of their importance. This ruse was employed to explain the presence of the five Americans: General Funston, Captain Hazzard, Captain Newton, Lieutenant Hazzard, and General Funston's aide, Lieutenant Kitchell, who were to accompany the expedition.

"Seventy-eight Macabebes, hereditary enemies of the Tagalogs, were chosen by Funston to form the body of the command. These fearless and hardy natives fell into the scheme with a vengeance. Three Tagalogs and one Spaniard were also invited. The Macabebes were fitted out in cast-off Insurgent uniforms, and the Americans donned field-worn uniforms of privates. Three days' rations were provided, and each man was given a rifle. The 'Vicksburg' was chosen to take the daring impostors to some spot on the east coast near Palanan, where Aguinaldo was in hiding. Arriving off the coast of Casignan, some distance from the Insurgent-hidden capital, the party was landed. Three Macabebes, who spoke Tagalog fluently, were sent into the town to notify the natives that they were bringing additional forces and important American prisoners to Aguinaldo, and request of the local authorities guides and assistance. The Insurgent president readily consented, and the little party, after refreshing themselves and exhibiting their prisoners, started over the ninety-mile trail to Palanan, a mountain retreat on the coast of the Isabella province. Over the stony declivities and through the thick jungle, across bridgeless streams and up narrow passes, the foot-sore and bone-racked adventurers tramped, until their food was exhausted, and they were *too weak to move*, though but eight miles from Aguinaldo's rendezvous.

"A messenger was sent forward to inform Aguinaldo of their position and to *beg for food*. The rebel chieftain promptly replied by despatching rice and a letter to the officer in command, instructing him to treat the American prisoners well, but to leave them outside the town. What better condition could the ingenious Funston have himself dictated? On the 23d of March the party reached Palanan. Aguinaldo sent out eleven men to take charge of the American prisoners, but Funston and his associates succeeded in dodging them and scattering themselves in the jungle until they passed on to meet the Americans whom the Insurgents were notified were left behind.

"Immediately joining his command, Funston ordered his little band of dare-devils to march boldly into the town and present themselves to Aguinaldo. At the Insurgent headquarters they were received by Aguinaldo's bodyguard, dressed in blue drill uniforms and white hats, drawn up in military form. The spokesman so completely hoodwinked Aguinaldo that he did not suspect the ruse. In the meantime the Macabebes manoeuvred around into advantageous positions, directed by the Spaniard, until all were in readiness. Then he shouted, 'Macabebes, now is your turn!' whereupon they emptied their rifles into Aguinaldo's bodyguard. . . .

"The Americans joined in the skirmish, and two of Aguinaldo's staff were wounded, but escaped, the treasurer of the revolutionary government surrendering. The rest of the Filipino officers got away. Aguinaldo accepted his capture with resignation, though greatly in fear of the vengeance of the Macabebes. But General Funston's assurance of his personal safety set his mind easy on that point, and he calmed down and discussed the situation. He was greatly cast down at his capture and asserted that *by no other means* would he have been taken alive—an admission which added all the more to Funston's achievement, for Aguinaldo's was a difficult and desperate case, and demanded extraordinary methods."

Some of the customs of war are not pleasant to the civilian; but ages upon ages of training have reconciled us to them as being justifiable, and we accept them and make no demur, even when they give us an extra twinge. Every detail of Funston's scheme—but one—has been employed in war in the past and stands acquitted of blame by history. By the custom of war, it is permissible, in the interest of an enterprise like the one under consideration, for a brigadier-general (if he be of the sort that can so choose) to persuade or bribe a courier to betray his trust; to remove the badges of his honorable rank and disguise himself; to lie, to practise treachery, to forge; to associate with himself persons properly fitted by training and instinct for the work; to accept of courteous welcome, and assassinate the welcomers while their hands are still warm from the friendly handshake.

By the custom of war, all these things are innocent, none of them is blameworthy, all of them are justifiable; none of them is new, all of them have been done before, although not by a Brigadier-General. But there is one detail which is new, absolutely new. It has never been resorted to before in any age of the world, in any country, among any people, savage or civilized. It was the one meant by Aguinaldo when he said that *"by no other means"* would he have been taken alive. When a man is exhausted by hunger to the point where he is "too weak to move," he has a right to make supplication to his enemy to save his failing life; but if he take so much as one taste of that food—which is holy, by the precept of all ages and all nations —*he is barred from lifting his hand against that enemy for that time.*

It was left to a Brigadier-General of Volunteers in the American Army to put shame upon a custom which even the degraded Spanish friars had respected. *We promoted him for it.*

Our unsuspecting President was in the act of taking his murderer by the hand when the man shot him down. The amazed world dwelt upon that damning fact, brooded over it, discussed it, blushed for it, said it put a blot and a shame upon our race. Yet, bad as he was, he had not—dying of starvation—begged food of the President to strengthen his failing forces for his treacherous work; he did not proceed against the life of a benefactor who had just saved his own.

April 14. I have been absent several weeks in the West Indies; I will now resume this Defence.

It seems to me that General Funston's appreciation of the Capture needs editing. It seems to me that, in his after-dinner speeches, he spreads out the heroisms of it—I say it with deference, and subject to correction—with an almost too generous hand. He is a brave man; his dearest enemy will cordially grant him that credit. For his sake it is a pity that somewhat of that quality was not needed in the episode under consideration; that he would have furnished it, no one doubts. But, by his own showing, he ran but one danger—that of starving. He and his party were well disguised, in dishonored uni-

forms, American and Insurgent; they greatly outnumbered Aguinaldo's guard;* by his forgeries and falsehoods he had lulled suspicion
to sleep; his coming was expected, his way was prepared; his course
was through a solitude, unfriendly interruption was unlikely; his party
were well armed; they would catch their prey with welcoming smiles
in their faces, and with hospitable hands extended for the friendly
shake—nothing would be necessary but to shoot these people down.
That is what they did. It was hospitality repaid in a brand-new, up-
to-date, Modern Civilization fashion, and would be admired by many.

"The spokesman so completely hoodwinked Aguinaldo that he did not
suspect the ruse. In the meantime, the Macabebes manoeuvred around
into advantageous positions, directed by the Spaniard, until all were in
readiness; then he shouted, 'Macabebes, now is your turn!' whereupon
they emptied their rifles into Aguinaldo's bodyguard."—*From Wildman's
book, already quoted.*

The utter completeness of the surprise, the total absence of suspicion which had been secured by the forgeries and falsehoods, is
best brought out in Funston's humorous account of the episode in
one of his rollicking speeches—the one he thought the President said
he wanted to see republished; though it turned out that this was only
a dream. Dream of a reporter, the General says:

"The Macabebes fired on those men and two fell dead; the others
retreated, firing as they ran, and I might say here that they retreated with
such great alacrity and enthusiasm that they dropped eighteen rifles and
a thousand rounds of ammunition.

"Sigismondo rushed back into the house, pulled his revolver, and told
the insurgent officers to surrender. They all threw up their hands except
Villia, Aguinaldo's chief of staff; he had on one of those newfangled Mauser revolvers and he wanted to try it. But before he had the Mauser out of
its scabbard he was shot twice; Sigismondo was a pretty fair marksman
himself.

"Alambra was shot in the face. He jumped out of the window; the
house, by-the-way, stood on the bank of the river. He went out of the
window and went clear down into the river, the water being twenty-five
feet below the bank. He escaped, swam across the river and got away, and
surrendered five months afterwards.

"Villia, shot in the shoulder, followed him out of the window and
into the river, but the Macabebes saw him and ran down to the river bank,

* Eighty-nine to forty-eight.—*Funston's Lotus Club Confession.*

and they waded in and fished him out, and kicked him all the way up the bank, and asked him how he liked it." (Laughter.)

While it is true that the Dare Devils were not in danger upon this occasion, they *were* in awful peril at one time; in peril of a death so awful that swift extinction by bullet, by the axe, by the sword, by the rope, by drowning, by fire, is a kindly mercy contrasted with it; a death so awful that it holds its place unchallenged as the supremest of human agonies—death by starvation. Aguinaldo saved them from that.

These being the facts, we come now to the question, Is Funston to blame? I think not. And for that reason I think too much is being made of this matter. He did not make his own disposition, It was born with him. It chose his ideals for him, he did not choose them. It chose the kind of society It liked, the kind of comrades It preferred, and imposed them upon him, rejecting the other kinds; he could not help this; It admired everything that Washington did not admire, and hospitably received and coddled everything that Washington would have turned out of doors—but It, and It only, was to blame, not Funston; his It took as naturally to moral slag as Washington's took to moral gold, but only It was to blame, not Funston. Its moral sense, if It had any, was color-blind, but this was no fault of Funston's, and he is not chargeable with the results; It had a native predilection for unsavory conduct, but it would be in the last degree unfair to hold Funston to blame for the outcome of his infirmity; as clearly unfair as it would be to blame him because his conscience leaked out through one of his pores when he was little —a thing which he could not help, and he couldn't have raised it, anyway; It was able to say to an enemy, "Have pity on me, I am starving; I am too weak to move, give me food; I am your friend. I am your fellow-patriot, your fellow-Filipino, and am fighting for our dear country's liberties, like you—have pity, give me food, save my life, there is no other help!" and It was able to refresh and restore Its marionette with the food, and then shoot down the giver of it while his hand was stretched out in welcome—like the President's. Yet if blame there was, and guilt, and treachery, and baseness, they are not Funston's, but only Its; It has the noble gift of humor, and can make a banquet almost die with laughter when it has a funny incident to tell about; this one will bear reading again—and over and over again, in fact:

"The Macabebes fired on those men and two fell dead; the others retreated, firing as they ran, and I might say here that they retreated with such alacrity and enthusiasm that they dropped eighteen rifles and a thousand rounds of ammunition.

"Sigismondo rushed back into the house, pulled his revolver, and told the insurgent officers to surrender. They all threw up their hands except Villia, Aguinaldo's chief of staff; he had on one of those newfangled Mauser revolvers and he wanted to try it. But before he had the Mauser out of its scabbard he was shot twice; Sigismondo was a pretty fair marksman himself.

"Alambra was shot in the face. He jumped out of the window; the house, by-the-way, stood on the bank of the river. He went out of the window and went clear down into the river, the water being twenty-five feet below the bank. He escaped, swam across the river and got away, and surrendered five months afterwards.

"Villia, shot in the shoulder, followed him out of the window and into the river, but the Macabebes saw him and ran down to the river bank, and they waded in and fished him out, and kicked him all the way up the bank, and asked him how he liked it." (Laughter.)

(This was a wounded man.) But it is only It that is speaking, not Funston. With youthful glee It can see sink down in death the simple creatures who had answered Its fainting prayer for food, and without remorse It can note the reproachful look in their dimming eyes; but in fairness we must remember that this is only It, not Funston; by proxy, in the person of Its born servant, It can do Its strange work, and practise Its ingratitudes and amazing treacheries, while wearing the uniform of the American soldier, and marching under the authority of the American flag. And It—not Funston— comes home now, to teach us children what Patriotism is! Surely It ought to know.

It is plain to me, and I think it ought to be plain to all, that Funston is not in any way to blame for the things he has done, does, thinks, and says.

Now, then, we have Funston; he has happened, and is on our hands. The question is, what are we going to do about it, how are we going to meet the emergency? We have seen what happened in Washington's case: he became a colossal example, an example to the whole world, and for all time—because his name and deeds went everywhere, and inspired, as they still inspire, and will always inspire, admiration, and compel emulation. Then the thing for the world to do in the present case is to turn the gilt front of Funston's evil notoriety to the rear, and expose the back aspect of it, the right and black aspect of it, to the youth of the land; otherwise *he* will become an example and a boy-admiration, and will most sorrowfully and grotesquely bring his breed of Patriotism into competition with Washington's. This competition has already begun, in fact. Some may not believe it, but it is nevertheless true, that there are now public-school teachers and superintendents who are holding up Funston as a model hero and Patriot in the schools.

If this Funstonian boom continues, Funstonism will presently affect the army. In fact, this has already happened. There are weak-headed and weak-principled officers in all armies, and these are always ready to imitate successful notoriety-breeding methods, let them be good or bad. The fact that Funston has achieved notoriety by paralyzing the universe with a fresh and hideous idea, is sufficient for this kind—they will call that hand if they can, and go it one better when the chance offers. Funston's example has bred many imitators, and many ghastly additions to our history: the torturing of Filipinos by the awful "water-cure," for instance, to make them confess—what? Truth? Or lies? How can one know which it is they are telling? For under unendurable pain a man confesses anything that is required of him, true or false, and his evidence is worthless. Yet upon such evidence American officers have actually—but you know about those atrocities which the War Office has been hiding a year or two; and about General Smith's now world-celebrated order of *massacre*—thus summarized by the press from Major Waller's testimony:

"Kill and burn—this is no time to take prisoners—the more you kill and burn, the better—Kill all above the age of ten—make Samar a howling wilderness!"

You see what Funston's example has produced, just in this little while—even before he produced the example. It has advanced our Civilization ever so far—fully as far as Europe advanced it in China. Also no doubt, it was Funston's example that made us (and England) copy Weyler's *reconcentrado* horror after the pair of us, with our Sunday-school smirk on, and our goody-goody noses upturned toward heaven, had been calling him a "fiend." And the fearful earthquake out there in Krakatoa, that destroyed the island and killed two million people— No, that could not have been Funston's example; I remember now, he was not born then.

However, for all these things I blame only his It, not him. In conclusion, I have defended him as well as I could, and indeed I have found it quite easy, and have removed prejudice from him and rehabilitated him in the public esteem and regard, I think. I was not able to do anything for his It, It being out of my jurisdiction, and out of Funston's and everybody's. As I have shown, Funston is not to blame for his fearful deed; and, if I tried, I might also show that he is not to blame for our still holding in bondage the man he captured by unlawful means, and who is not any more rightfully our prisoner and spoil than he would be if he were stolen money. He is entitled to his freedom. If he were a king of a Great Power, or an ex-president of our republic, instead of an ex-president of a destroyed and abolished little republic, Civilization (with a large C) would criticise and complain until he got it.

MARK TWAIN

P.S. *April 16*. The President is speaking up, this morning, just as this goes to the printer, and there is no uncertain sound about the note. It is the speech and spirit of a President of a people, not of a party, and we all like it, Traitors and all. I think I may speak for the other Traitors, for I am sure they feel as I do about it. I will explain that we get our title from the Funstonian Patriots—free of charge. They are always doing us little compliments like that; they are just born flatterers, those boys.

M.T.
1902

THE YACHT RACES*

"Aren't you charging rather high rates for this interview?"

"Not any higher than I always charge when I am present in person during the interview."

"Sometimes you are not present?"

"Yes; in those cases I do not know I have been interviewed until I see it in the papers."

"Do you enjoy that?"

"Well, no; I think it is not quite fair. It is my trade to talk and write; it is my bread and butter. A man cannot honorably take it from my family without consent. What is it we are to talk about now?"

"The yacht races. The HERALD would like you to explain the reasons of the results."

"Why—that is all right, but I doubt if I can earn the money."

"Why?"

"Well, because I can only state the facts. I can't intelligently philosophize them, analyze them, deduce results from them—and all that wise kind of thing, you know. Do you care for facts—just mere cold, unemotional facts?"

"Dear sir, we prefer them to anything else."

"Allow me. Give me your hand! We meet upon holy ground. I have no longer any tremblings at the heart, no longer any disturbing anxieties. Facts are my passion. I"——

"You have been called the slave of truth."

"Have you heard it? You make me proud, happy; you sing all my solicitudes to rest. Proceed."

"You have seen all of the races?"

"Yes, all of them."

* I have not placed this among the interviews because it only pretends to be an interview.

"On board the Kanawha?"

"Yes."

"She is the fastest steam yacht afloat, I believe."

"Yes, she has beaten all the flyers. When I am feeling good I can make thirty-seven knots an hour with her. * * * Why do you look at me like that?"

"I beg pardon. I assure you I didn't mean to. How"——

"Well, you mustn't look at me like that. I am very sensitive."

"It was an oversight, I give you my word. I would not wound you for anything. My hearing is not good, and I did not quite catch the number of knots, I think. How many did you say it was?"

"Forty-five. She's a bird—just a bird. She"——

"Do you take her gait yourself?"

"No, it is done by one of the men—Patrick Clancy. He is in the forecastle. She has made as high as forty-nine. He told me so himself."

"Is he—is he trustworthy?"

"Who—Clancy? I should think so! I wouldn't trust a statement of my own sooner."

"Neither would I."

"Let me take you by the hand. Is Clancy trustworthy? Why, it would make everybody in the ship smile to hear you say that. Patrick Clancy"——

"Is he experienced? Is he calm, unexcitable; does he know the boat well?"

"Knows her like a book! Knows every inch of her hundred and twenty-seven feet; knows every ton of her four hundred; can tell by the flutter of her screw when she's making her Sabbath-day 290 revolutions and when she's on the warpath and turning out four thousand a minute. Does Patrick Clancy know the Kanawha? Why, man, he's been in her ever since she was a little thing not thirty feet long and couldn't make ten miles an hour; he told me so himself."

"Do you own the Kanawha?"

"Well, no, I don't exactly own her. I only help to run her. Mr. Rogers owns her."

"Do you command her?"

"Well, no, not exactly that. I only superintend."

"By request?"

"Well, I wouldn't put it quite as strong as that; but I do a good deal of work, you know; in fact, the important part of it. Superintending is more important than commanding, and more worrying and fatiguing, you know, because you have to be everywhere and attend to everything. Superintending is much the most exacting function on board a ship, and requires more varied talent and alertness, and more patience and calmness under explosions of resentment and insubordination than any other in the service. There are but few really good superintendents."

"The salary must be very large?"

"No, there isn't any salary; all a person gets is neglect and ingratitude. If a superintendent conscientiously does his whole duty, there's never anything going on but mutiny and insurrection. If I have ever had an order obeyed without being requested to mind my own business, I have no recollection of it. It is just a dog's life, and that is the best you can say about it."

"Why don't you resign?"

"Resign? How can I resign when I haven't been appointed? If I could get appointed I would resign in a minute."

"Is there no way to"——

"To what? No, there isn't. When you are a superintendent, there you are, and you can't help yourself. Sometimes I wish I was dead."

"It does seem to be a sorrowful vocation."

"Funerals is hilarity compared to it. Daily and hourly your feelings are hurt. Hurt by disobedience; yes, and almost always accompanied by remarks which—why, let me give you an instance. You remember that first day when we were racing with those steamrockets, the Corsair and the Revolution and the Hauoli and Mr. Leeds' Clipper and hanging their scalps up there on the mizzenforetopgallant halyards to dry, one by one? I found the second mate off his base and ordered him into irons as a lesson, and he told me to go to—never mind where he told me to go, but how would you like to be treated like that, and you doing the best you could?"

"Ah, that gives me an idea. It would be just like such a man as that to keep crossing the Monmouth's bow the way the Kanawha did Saturday in the race home. It was scandalous. Was he steering?"

"It's getting late, let's talk about something else. I was at the wheel myself. Are you intemperate? Would you like something? So would I. Push the button. What were you saying about—about"——

"I wasn't saying anything about anything, but now that I think of it, what was the reason that the Shamrock performed so indifferently in the first race—that one that was a failure?"

"Well, I know the reason, for I got it from Clancy at the time. It is pretty technical, but, barring that, it is easy to understand. It was a case of British easy-going carelessness on the part of the Shamrock plant—good enough sailors, you know, but heedless, oh, beyond imagination! Not just one case of it, but two or three—Clancy explained the whole thing to me. In the first place, when they came to set the anchor watch it was a Waterbury, and they lost two minutes in the winding, and that took off the whole time allowance and three seconds besides—ought to have been wound up before, of course.

"And then, when they got it set, there they were again—an anchor watch, all right enough, but they found they hadn't any anchor. It had been left at the Waldorf, by some oversight, and they had to throw over ballast to make up for it. Also, they had to remeasure the boat, and that shortened her by an inch. I do not know why, but Clancy does. An inch is not much, but if you take it off the front end, that end does not arrive at the homestake as early as it would if it were an inch longer, and, of course, as you can see yourself, even that little could lose a race. It didn't in this case, because there was a lot more inches that did not arrive in time, but the principle is sound; you can see it yourself."

"Yes, it looks so. But they lost the second race, too—the first real race. How does Clancy account for that?"

"Difference in seamanship, he says. That and other things. Accidents and one thing and another."

"Did the Shamrock have accidents?"

"She had one that lost her the race. When she turned the stake she broke out her spinnaker. She might as well have broken her back, Clancy says. The spinnaker is a sail, you know. I don't know which one it is, but I think it is the tall one that bows out like a shirt front and gives the yacht such a dressy look. The other one is the balloon jib, which connects the garboard strake with the futtock shrouds and enables you to point high on a wind when you couldn't possibly do it any other way. Clancy told me these things."

"Does Clancy charge you anything for revealing these mysteries?"

"No, he doesn't really charge me, but I make it up to him in other ways. I let him charge me five dollars for telling me how to bet so as not to lose. He told me to bet a hundred on each boat. That was on the first race—the one that went to a finish. If I won either bet I was to give him another five and if I won both he was to get ten. So he got only ten altogether, because I only won on one of the boats. I lost on the other, so he didn't charge anything on that one."

"Have you always been as intelligent as you are now?"

"Yes, I think so, but sometimes Mr. Rogers thinks I am failing. He thinks it is on account of age and decrepitude; others think it is on account of mental disturbance; others think it is on account of the company I keep; but that cannot be, because I was never particular about the kind of people I went with, yet I was always just as intelligent as I am now, perhaps even more."

"You lose your way sometimes in a long sentence. Do you notice it? You remem"——

"Yes, I know what you mean; it's when I'm working up to wind'ard on a difficult proposition. Clancy says himself that I don't point as high as I used to. But it is no matter; as long as my teeth remain good I don't mind about my intellect; I don't eat with my intellect. But go on—I interrupted you."

"Granting that we now understand why the Reliance won in the first race, what specialty was it, in your judgment, that secured for her the second one?"

"Oh, reaching!"

"Reaching?"

"That is what did it. Reliance is sublime when it comes to reaching. Clancy says so himself. I remember his very words. He said, 'When it comes to that competition isn't possible; she's got a reach like a Christian mob with a nigger in sight.'"

"I am very much obliged to you for clarifying the races and making plain the reasons for the Shamrock's defeats. There was much confusion in the public mind before. Could you go on now, and"——

"Well, no, not now. It would take too much time, and you are pretty busy; so am I. We've done enough for a preliminary; I will finish in a magazine presently. How do you like my style?"

"I think it admirable. It is exceedingly simple and direct and lucid, and it has a special and unusual feature which is golden—that is the word, golden!"

"What is that?"

"You hardly ever use a long word."

"Ah, you've noticed it! Do you guess the secret of that?"

"No, but if you would tell me"——

"I'm paid by the word—do you get the idea?"

"Well, no, I believe I don't."

"I'll show you. In a newspaper you are paid by 'space'—that is your term for it. The longer the words the more space you occupy and the greater is your cash reward. Naturally you hunt the dictionary for long words—it's bread and butter. And naturally you get the habit of using lucrative, vast words—the sesquipedalian habit, so to speak. But when you are paid by the word you can't afford long ones, you understand—it's just simply impoverishing. The family would starve. Would you ever catch me saying 'unincomprehensibility?' Not at twenty cents a word, and don't you make any mistake about it! By my enforced habit of using only the shortest discoverable words I should break that nine jointed monster up into modest little, wee, single words and get as much as a dollar and a half out of him. Do you get the idea now?"

"By my halidom, yes—and it is just great, too!"

"I thought you would be able to see it. Do you know, in German literature the average word measures twenty-two syllables? You divine the reason?"

"I do; they pay by space there."

"That's it. It has ruined the language. They are starting a College of Journalism here. Let them look to that matter. Let them inculcate in the young student the principle of charging always by the word. It will result in a noble simplicity of style; it will be the salvation of our beautiful language. Even at twenty cents it will do it; even at that figure it will cramp the average word down to five letters. I would to God somebody would give me a chance to show what kind of a shrinkage I could put on our long words at a dollar a squeeze! Must you go? Don't go. Sit down and let me unshackle my tongue and give you an exhibition. I will undertake to financially embarrass your paper before I break out my spinnaker."

"I thank you most kindly, but I am afraid I must be going. Are you going to the banquet?"

"I wish I could, but I have to go home. I wish I could see Sir Thomas. He is the only Englishman I have never seen, except Lord Roberts. Gallant men, both."

"What are you going to Italy for?"

"By order of the doctors. It is to get back my wife's health."

"When do you sail?"

"October 24, in the Princess Irene—North German Lloyd."

"A good ship?"

"I designed her myself."

"That settles it. Goodby."

"Goodby."

1903

LETTER TO GOVERNOR FRANCIS*

Villa di Quarto, Firenze (Florence), Italy, May 26, 1904.—Dear Governor Francis: It has been a dear wish of mine to exhibit myself at the great Fair and get a prize, but circumstances beyond my control have interfered and I must remain in Florence. Although I have never taken prizes anywhere else, I used to take them at school in Missouri half a century ago, and I ought to be able to repeat now, if I could have a chance. I used to get the medal for good spelling every week, and I could have had the medal for good conduct if there hadn't been so much corruption in Missouri in those days; still, I got it several times by trading medals and giving boot. I am willing to give boot now, if—however, those days are forever gone by, in Missouri, and perhaps it is better so. Nothing ever stays the way it was in this changeable world.

Although I cannot be at the Fair, I am going to be represented there, anyway, by a portrait by Professor Gelli. You will find it excellent. Good judges here say it is better than the original. They say it has all the merits of the original, and keeps still, besides. It sounds like flattery, but it is just true.

I suppose you will get a prize, because you have created the most prodigious and in all ways most wonderful Fair the planet has ever seen. Very well you have, indeed, earned it; and with it the gratitude of the State and the nation. Sincerely yours,

MARK TWAIN
1904

* A reply to an invitation to attend the World's Fair in St. Louis. Mark Twain's wife was dying when he wrote the letter (she died June 5) but he allowed no hint of his mental state to enter his note.

CONCERNING COPYRIGHT*

AN OPEN LETTER TO THE REGISTER OF COPYRIGHTS

Thorwald Stolberg, Esq.,
    Register of Copyrights,
        Washington, D. C.

Dear Sir:

I have received your excellent summary of the innumerable statutes and substitutes and amendments which a century of Congresses has devised in trying to mete out even-handed justice to the public and the author in the vexed matter of copyright; and, in response to your invitation to the craftsmen of my guild to furnish suggestions for further legislation upon the subject, I beg to submit my share in the unconventional form of

Question and Answer

Question. How many new American books are copyrighted *annually* in the United States?

Answer. Five or six thousand.

Q. How many have been copyrighted in the last twenty-five years?

A. More than 100,000.

Q. How many altogether in the past 104 years?

A. Doubtless 250,000.

Q. How many of them have survived or will survive the 42-year limit?

A. An average of five per year. Make it ten, to be safe and certain.

Q. Only *ten* a year!

A. That is all. Ten.

Q. Do you actually believe that 249,000 of these books have had no sort of use for a 42-year limit?

---

* Mark Twain made a number of statements on the subject of copyright, but this one is by far the best, in my opinion.

A. I can swear to it. They would not have outlived a 20-year limit.

Q. Then where is the use of a 42-year limit?

A. I know of none.

Q. What does it accomplish?

A. Nothing useful, nothing worthy, nothing modest, nothing dignified, nothing honest, so far as I know. An Italian statesman has called it "the Countess Massiglia of legal burlesque." Each year ten venerable copyrights fall in, and the bread of ten persons is taken from them by the Government. This microscopic petty larceny is all that is accomplished.

Q. It does seem a small business.

A. For a big nation—yes. A distinct reversal of the law of the survival of the fittest. It is the assassination of the fittest.

Q. Of course, the lawmakers knew they were arranging a hardship for some persons—all laws do that. But they could not have known how few the number was, do you think?

A. Of course not. Otherwise, they would not have been worrying and suffering over copyright laws for a hundred years. It has cost you, sir, 41 pages of printed notes to merely *outline* the acres of amendments and substitutes they have ground out in a century—*to take the bread out of the mouths of ten authors per year*; usually the ten poorest and most distinguished literary servants of the nation! One book from each of them. It takes a hundred years to hook a thousand books, and by that time eight hundred of them have long ago fallen obsolete and died of inanition.

Q. Certainly there is something most grotesque about this! Is this principle followed elsewhere in our laws?

A. Yes, in the case of the inventors. But in that case it is worth the Government's while. There are a hundred thousand new inventions a year, and a thousand of them are worth seizing at the end of the 17-year limit. But the Government *can't* seize the really great and immensely valuable ones—like the telegraph, the telephone, the air-brake, the Pullman car, and some others, the Shakespeares of the inventor-tribe, so to speak—for the prodigious capital required to carry them on is their protection from competition; their proprietors are not disturbed when the patents perish. Tell me, who are of first importance in the modern nation?

Q. Shall we say the builders of its civilization and promoters of its glory?

A. Yes. Who are they?

Q. Its inventors; the creators of its literature; and the country's defenders on land and sea. Is that correct?

A. I think so. Well, when a soldier retires from the wars, the Government spends $150,000,000 a year upon him and his, and the pension is continued to his widow and orphans. But when it retires a distinguished author's book at the end of 42 years, it takes the book's subsequent profits away from the widow and orphans and gives them—to whom?

Q. To the public.

A. Nothing of the kind!

Q. But it does—the lawmaker will tell you so himself.

A. Who deceived the lawmaker with that limpid falsehood?

Q. Falsehood?

A. That is what it is. And the proof of it lies in this large, and eloquent, and sarcastic fact: that the Government does not give the book to the *public*, it gives it to the *publishers*.

Q. How do you make that out?

A. It is very simple: the publisher *goes on publishing*—there is no law against it—and he takes *all* the profit, both the author's and his own.

Q. Why, it looks like a crime!

A. It doesn't merely look like it, it *is* a crime. A crime perpetrated by a great country, a proud World Power, upon ten poor devils a year. *One book apiece.* The profits on "Uncle Tom's Cabin" continue to-day; nobody but the publishers get them—Mrs. Stowe's share ceased seven years before she died; her daughters receive nothing from the book. Years ago they found themselves no longer able to live in their modest home, and had to move out and find humbler quarters. Washington Irving's poor old adopted daughters fared likewise. Come, does that move you?

Q. Ah, dear me! Well, certainly, there is something wrong about this whole copyright business.

A. Something wrong? Yes, I think so! Something pitifully wrong, pathetically wrong! Consider the nation's attitude toward the Builder of its Material Greatness, toward the Defender of its Homes and its Flag, and (by contrast) toward its Teacher, who is also the Promoter of its Fame and Preserver of it—that Immortal Three! Behold, the spirit of prophecy is upon me, and a picture of a future incident rises upon my sight. You shall share the vision with me: The President sits in state in the White House, with his official family around him; before him stand three groups. In the first group, Edison,

Graham Bell, Westinghouse, and other living inventors, and, back of them, dim and vague, the shades of Fulton, Whitney, Morse, Hoe, Howe, Ericsson and others; in the second group stand Dewey, Schley, Miles, Howard, Sickles, Chaffee, together with a private soldier and sailor representing 200,000 fellow-survivors of the bloody field, the sutler's tents and the teamster's camp, and back of these the stately shades of Washington, Paul Jones, Jackson, Taylor, Scott, McClellan, Grant, Sherman, Sheridan, Farragut, Foote, Worden, Sampson and others; in the third group stand three or four living authors, and back of them, with averted faces and ashamed, loom the mighty shades of Emerson, Bancroft, Bryant, Whittier, and behind these, dim and spectral, the shades of Cooper, Judd, Irving, Poe, Hawthorne, Long-fellow, Holmes, Lowell, Harriet Beecher Stowe, Parkman and others.

The President Speaks

"By command of the Nation, whose servant I am, I have summoned you, O illustrious ones! I bring you the message of eighty grateful millions—a message of praise and reward for high service done your country and your flag: from my lips, hear the nation's word! To you, inventors, builders of the land's material greatness, past and present, the people offer homage, worship and imperishable gratitude, with enduring fame for your dead, and untold millions of minted gold for you that survive. To you, defenders of the flag, past and present, creators of the nation's far-shining military glory, the people offer homage, worship and imperishable gratitude, with enduring fame for your dead; and, for you that survive, a hundred and fifty coined millions a year to protect the highest and the humblest of you from want so long as you shall live. To you, historians, poets, creators of ennobling romance—Teachers—this: you have wrought into enduring form the splendid story of the Great Republic; you have preserved forever from neglect, decay and oblivion the great deeds of the long line of the nation's Builders, Defenders and Preservers; you have diligently and faithfully taught and trained the children of the Republic in lofty political and social ideals, and in that love of country and reverence for the flag which is Patriotism—and without you this would be a Russia to-day, with not an intelligent patriot in it; you have made the American home pure and fragrant and beautiful with your sweet songs and your noble romance-literature; you have carried the American name in honor and esteem to the ends of the earth; in spite of unequal laws which exalt your brother the soldier and inflict upon you an undeserved indignity, you have furnished to your country that great asset, that golden asset, that imperial asset, lacking which no modern State can hold up its head and stand unchallenged in the august company of the sisterhood of Nations—a fine and strong and worthy National Literature! For these inestimable services, the people, by my voice, grant these rewards: to your great dead, as also to you who still live, homage, worship, enduring fame, imper—no, I mean gratitude, just gratitude; gratitude with a 42-year limit, and the poor-house for your widows and children. God abide with you, O illustrious company of the Builders, Defenders and Patriot-Makers of the grateful Republic! Farewell, the incident is closed."

Q. (*After a long and reflective pause.*) Isn't there some right and fair way to remedy this strange and dishonorable condition of things?

A. I think there is.

Q. Suggest it, then.

A Suggestion

A. In making a 42-year limit, the Government's intention was, to be fair all around. It meant that the ten authors (it supposed the number was greater) should enjoy the profit of their labors a fair and reasonable time; then extinguish the copyright and thus *make the book cheap*—this for the benefit of the public. I repeat, to *insure cheap editions for the public*: now, wasn't that *the* intention? and wasn't it the whole and *only* intention?

Q. It certainly was.

A. Well, that intention has often been defeated. In many a case, the publisher has not lowered the price; in other cases, so many publishers issued editions of the unprotected book that they clogged the market and *killed* the book. And often it was a book that could have survived but for this misfortune. The remedy that I would suggest is this: *that, during the 42d year of the copyright limit, the owner of the copyright shall be obliged to issue an edition of the book at these following rates, to wit: twenty-five cents for each 100,000 words, or less, of its contents, and keep said edition on sale always thereafter, year after year, indefinitely. And if in any year he shall fail to keep such edition on sale during a space of three months, the copyright shall then perish.*

Q. That seems to cover the ground. It meets the Government's sole desire—to *secure a cheap edition for the public*.

A. Why, certainly. It *compels* it. No existing law in any country does that.

Q. You would not put a price upon the publisher's other editions?

A. No; he could make the others as high-priced as he chose.

Q. Would you except books of a certain class?

A. No book occurs to me that could not stand the reduction—I mean a book that promises to live 42 years and upwards. It could not apply to unabridged dictionaries, for they are revised and newly copyrighted every ten or twelve years. It is the one and only book in America whose copyright is *perpetual.*

Q. Your own proposition makes all copyrights perpetual, doesn't it?

A. It does not. It extends the limit indefinitely. But there is still a limit; for in any year after the forty-first that the cheap edition fails, during the space of three months, the copyright dies.

Q. The proposed rate seems excessively cheap. How would the thing work out? About how much of a reduction would it make? Give me an illustration or two.

A. Very well, let me cite my own books—I am on familiar ground there. "Huck Finn" contains 70,000 words; present price $1.50; an edition of it would have to be kept permanently on sale at 25 cents. "Tom Sawyer," 70,000 words, price $1.50; the imagined cheap edition would be 25 cents. Several two-volume books of mine contain a trifle more than 100,000 words per volume; present price $1.75 per volume; the cheap-edition price would be 75 cents per volume—or 75 cents for the complete book if compressed into one volume. My "works," taken together, number 23 volumes; cheapest present price of the set, $36.50. To meet the requirements of the copyright-preserving law, I would compress the aggregate contents into 10 volumes of something more than 200,000 words each, and sell the volumes at 75 cents each—or $7.50 for the lot, if a millionaire wanted the whole treasure.

Q. It is a reduction of *four-fifths,* or thereabouts! Would there be any profit?

A. The printer and the binder would get their usual percentage of profit, the middle-man would get his usual commission on sales. The publisher's profit would be very small, mine also would be very small.

Q. Then you are proposing commercial suicide for him and for yourself—is that it?

A. Far from it. I am proposing high commercial prosperity and advantage for him and for me.

Q. How?

A. First of all, the books would remain my children's possession and support, instead of being confiscated by various publishers and issued in cheap form or dear, as they chose, for the support of *their* children.

Q. And secondly?

A. Secondly—let us not overlook the importance of this detail —the cheap edition would advertise our higher-priced editions, and the publisher and my orphans would live on canvasback duck and Cape Cod oysters—not on ham-and-not-enough-of-it, the way certain Government-robbed orphans of my acquaintance are doing now.

Q. Why don't you and your publisher try that cheap edition now, without waiting?

A. Haven't I told you that almost all the profit would go to printer, binder and middle-man? And has this Government ever heard of a publisher who would get out a dirt-cheap edition without being *compelled* to do it? The Government has tried persuasion for many a year, in the interest of the public, and achieved no cheap edition by it: what I am after now is *compulsion.*

Q. Are you guessing at cheap-edition possibilities, or are you speaking from knowledge?

A. From knowledge. Knowledge and experience. I know what it costs to make a book and what it costs to sell it.

Q. If your figures on cheap editions should be challenged by the trade—how then?

A. I could prove my case, and would do it.

Very respectfully,
S. L. CLEMENS (Mark Twain)
1905

THE CZAR'S SOLILOQUY

After the Czar's morning bath it is his habit to meditate an hour before dressing himself.—*London Times Correspondence.*

[*Viewing himself in the pier-glass.*] Naked, what am I? A lank, skinny, spider-legged libel on the image of God! Look at the waxwork head—the face, with the expression of a melon—the projecting ears —the knotted elbows—the dished breast—the knife-edged shins—and then the feet, all beads and joints and bone-sprays, an imitation X-ray photograph! There is nothing imperial about this, nothing imposing, impressive, nothing to invoke awe and reverence. Is it this that a hundred and forty million Russians kiss the dust before and worship? Manifestly not! No one could worship this spectacle, which is Me. Then who is it, what is it, that they worship? Privately, none knows better than I: it is my clothes. Without my clothes I should be as destitute of authority as any other naked person. Nobody could tell me from a parson, a barber, a dude. Then who is the real Emperor of Russia? My clothes. There is no other.

As Teufelsdröckh suggested, what would man be—what would *any* man be—without his clothes? As soon as one stops and thinks over that proposition, one realizes that without his clothes a man would be nothing at all; that the clothes do not merely make the man, the clothes *are* the man; that without them he is a cipher, a vacancy, a nobody, a nothing.

Titles—another artificiality—are a part of his clothing. They and the dry-goods conceal the wearer's inferiority and make him seem great and a wonder, when at bottom there is nothing remarkable about him. They can move a nation to fall on its knees and sincerely worship an Emperor who, without the clothes and the title, would drop to the rank of the cobbler and be swallowed up and lost sight of in the massed multitude of the inconsequentials; an Emperor who, naked in a naked world, would get no notice, excite no remark, and be heedlessly shouldered and jostled like any other uncertified stranger, and perhaps offered a kopek to carry somebody's gripsack; yet an Emperor who, by the sheer might of those artificialities— clothes and a title—can get himself worshipped as a deity by his people, and at his pleasure and unrebuked can exile them, hunt them, harry them, destroy them, just as he would with so many rats if the accident of birth had furnished him a calling better suited to his capacities than empering. It is a stupendous force—that which resides in the all-concealing cloak of clothes and title; they fill the onlooker with awe; they make him tremble; yet he knows that every hereditary regal dignity commemorates a usurpation, a power illegitimately acquired, an authority conveyed and conferred by persons who did not own it. For monarchs have been chosen and elected by aristocracies only: a Nation has never elected one.

There is no power without clothes. It is the power that governs the human race. Strip its chiefs to the skin, and no State could be governed; naked officials could exercise no authority; they would look (and be) like everybody else—commonplace, inconsequential. A policeman in plain clothes is one man; in his uniform he is ten. Clothes and title are the most potent thing, the most formidable influence, in the earth. They move the human race to willing and spontaneous respect for the judge, the general, the admiral, the bishop, the ambassador, the frivolous earl, the idiot duke, the sultan, the king, the emperor. No great title is efficient without clothes to support it. In naked tribes of savages the kings wear some kind of rag or decoration which they make sacred to themselves and allow no one else to wear. The king of the great Fan tribe wears a bit of leopard-skin on his shoulder—it is sacred to royalty; the rest of him is perfectly naked. Without his bit of leopard-skin to awe and impress the people, he would not be able to keep his job.

[*After a silence.*] A curious invention, an unaccountable invention—the human race! The swarming Russian millions have for centuries meekly allowed our Family to rob them, insult them, trample them under foot, while they lived and suffered and died with no purpose and no function but to make that Family comfortable! These people are horses—just that—horses with clothes and a religion. A horse with the strength of a hundred men will let one man beat him, starve him, drive him; the Russian millions allow a mere handful of soldiers to hold them in slavery—and these very soldiers are their own sons and brothers!

A strange thing, when one considers it: to wit, the world applies to Czar and System the same moral axioms that have vogue and acceptance in civilized countries! Because, in civilized countries, it is wrong to remove oppressors otherwise than by process of law, it is held that the same rule applies in Russia, where there is no such thing as law—except for our Family. Laws are merely restraints —they have no other function. In civilized countries they restrain all persons, and restrain them all alike, which is fair and righteous; but in Russia such laws as exist make an exception—our Family. We do as we please; we have done as we pleased for centuries. Our common trade has been crime, our common pastime murder, our common beverage blood—the blood of the nation. Upon our heads lie millions of murders. Yet the pious moralist says it is a crime to assassinate us. We and our uncles are a family of cobras set over a hundred and forty million rabbits, whom we torture and murder and feed upon all our days; yet the moralist urges that to kill us is a crime, not a duty.

It is not for me to say it aloud, but to one on the inside—like me —this is naïvely funny; on its face, illogical. Our Family is above all law; there is no law that can reach us, restrain us, protect the people from us. Therefore, we are outlaws. Outlaws are a proper mark for any one's bullet. Ah! what could our Family do without the moralist? He has always been our stay, our support, our friend; to-day he is our *only* friend. Whenever there has been dark talk of assassination, he has come forward and saved us with his impressive maxim, "Forbear: nothing politically valuable was ever yet achieved by violence." He probably believes it. It is because he has by him no child's book of world-history to teach him that his maxim lacks the backing of statistics. All thrones have been established by violence; no regal tyranny has ever been overthrown except by violence; by violence my fathers set up our throne; by murder, treachery, perjury, torture, banishment and the prison they have held it for four centuries, and by these same arts I hold it to-day. There is no Romanoff of learning and experience but would reverse the maxim and say: "Nothing politically valuable was ever yet achieved *except* by violence." The moralist realizes that to-day, for the first time in our history, my throne is in real peril and the nation waking up from its immemorial slave-lethargy; but he does not perceive that four deeds of violence are the reason for it: the assassination of the Finland Constitution by my hand; the slaughter, by revolutionary assassins, of Bobrikoff and Plehve; and my massacre of the unoffending innocents the other day. But the blood that flows in my veins—blood informed, trained, educated by its grim heredities, blood alert by its traditions, blood which has been to school four hundred years in the veins of professional assassins, my predecessors—*it* perceives, *it* understands! Those four deeds have set up a commotion in the inert and muddy deeps of the national heart such as no moral suasion could have accomplished; they have aroused hatred and hope in that long-atrophied heart; and, little by little, slowly but surely, that feeling will steal into every breast and possess it. In time, into even the *soldier's* breast—fatal day, day of doom, that! . . . . By and by, there will be results! How little the academical moralist knows of the tremendous moral force of massacre and assassination! . . . . Indeed there are going to be results! The nation is in labor; and by and by there will be a mighty birth—PATRIOTISM! To put it in rude, plain, unpalatable words—*true* patriotism, real patriotism: loyalty, not to a Family and a Fiction, but loyalty to the Nation itself!

. . . . There are twenty-five million families in Russia. There is a man-child at every mother's knee. If these were twenty-five million patriotic mothers, they would teach these man-children daily, saying: "Remember this, take it to heart, live by it, die for it if necessary: that our patriotism is medieval, outworn, obsolete; that the modern patriotism, the true patriotism, the only rational patriotism, is *loyalty to the Nation* ALL *the time, loyalty to the Government when it deserves it.*" With twenty-five million taught and trained patriots in the land a generation from now, my successor would think twice before he would butcher a thousand helpless poor petitioners humbly begging for his kindness and justice, as I did the other day.

(*Reflective pause.*) Well, perhaps I have been affected by these depressing newspaper-clippings which I found under my pillow. I will read and ponder them again. [*Reads.*]

POLISH WOMEN KNOUTED

RESERVISTS' WIVES TREATED WITH AWFUL BRUTALITY—AT LEAST ONE KILLED.

Special Cable to THE NEW YORK TIMES.

BERLIN, Nov. 27.—Infuriated by the unwillingness of the Polish troops to leave their wives and children, the Russian authorities at Kutno, a town on the Polish frontier, have treated the people in a manner almost incredibly cruel.

It is known that *one woman has been knouted to death* and that a number of others have been injured. Fifty persons have been thrown into jail. Some of the prisoners were *tortured into unconsciousness.*

Details of the brutalities are lacking, but it seems that the Cossacks tore the reservists from the arms of their wives and children and then *knouted the women who followed their husbands into the streets.*

In cases where reservists could not be found *their wives were dragged by their hair into the streets and there beaten. The chief official of the district and the Colonel of a regiment are said to have looked on while this was being done.*

A girl who had assisted in distributing Socialist tracts was *treated in an atrocious manner.*

CZAR AS LORD'S ANOINTED

PEOPLE SPENT NIGHT IN PRAYER AND FASTING BEFORE HIS VISIT TO NOVGOROD

LONDON TIMES—NEW YORK TIMES. Special Cablegram.
Copyright, 1904, THE NEW YORK TIMES

LONDON, July 27.—The London Times's Russian correspondents say the following extract from the Petersburger Zeitung, describing the Czar's recent doings at Novgorod, affords a typical instance of the servile adulation which the subjects of the Czar deem it necessary to adopt:

"The blessing of the troops, *who knelt devoutly before his Majesty,* was a profoundly moving spectacle. His Majesty held the sacred ikon aloft and pronounced aloud a blessing in his own name and that of the Empress. "Thousands *wept with emotion and spiritual ecstasy.* Pupils of girls' schools scattered roses in the path of the monarch.

"People pressed up to the carriage in order to carry away an indelible memory of the *hallowed features of the Lord's Anointed.* Many old people had spent the night in prayer and fasting *in order to be worthy to gaze at his countenance with pure, undefiled souls.*

"The greatest enthusiasm prevails *at the happiness thus vouchsafed to the people.*"

[*Moved.*] How shameful! . . . . how pitiful! . . . . And how grotesque! . . . . To think—it was *I* that did those cruel things. . . . There is no escaping the personal responsibility—it was I that did them. And it was I that got that grovelling and awe-smitten worship! I—this thing in the mirror—this carrot! With one hand I flogged unoffending women to death and tortured prisoners to unconsciousness; and with the other I held up the fetish toward my fellow deity in heaven and called down His blessing upon my adoring animals whom, and whose forebears, with His holy approval, I and mine have been instructing in the pains of hell for four lagging centuries. It is a picture! To think that this thing in the mirror—this vegetable—is an accepted deity to a mighty nation, an innumerable host, and nobody laughs; and at the same time is a diligent and practical professional devil, and nobody marvels, nobody murmurs about incongruities and inconsistencies! Is the human race a joke? Was it devised and patched together in a dull time when there was nothing important to do? Has it no respect for itself? . . . . I think my respect for it is drooping, sinking—and my respect for myself along with it. . . . There is but one restorative—*Clothes!* respect-reviving, spirit-uplifting clothes! heaven's kindliest gift to man, his only protection against finding himself out: they deceive him, they confer dignity upon hm; without them he has none. How charitable are clothes, how beneficent, how puissant, how inestimably precious! Mine are able to expand a human cipher into a globe-shadowing portent; they can command the respect of the whole world—including my own, which is fading. I will put them on.

1905

JOHN HAY AND THE BALLADS

NEW YORK, *October 3, 1905.*

To the Editor of Harper's Weekly:

SIR—In his article in the *North American Review* Mr. Howells expresses uncertainty in a matter concerning the Ballads, in the following remark:

"It was contemporaneously supposed that the Pike County Ballads were inspired or provoked by the Pike County balladry of Bret Harte, and they were first accepted as imitations or parodies. I believe they were actually written earlier, but if they were written later," etc.

They were not written later, they were written (and printed in newspapers) earlier. Mr. Hay told me this himself—in 1870 or '71, I should say. I believe—indeed I am quite sure—that he added that the newspapers referred to were obscure Western backwoods journals, and that the Ballads were not widely copied. Also, he said this: That by and by, when Harte's ballads began to sweep the country the noise woke his (Hay's) buried waifs, and they rose and walked. I think that that detail is interesting, now. It compels one to realize to oneself the difficult fact that there was a time when another person could advertise John Hay into notice better than he could do it himself. Hay made mention of the current notion that he was an imitator; he did not enlarge upon it, but he was not better pleased by it than you or I would be.

He was aware that I had been a Mississippi pilot, and he asked me if he had made any technical errors in the "Prairie Belle" ballad, and said he wanted to correct them if any existed. There was one very slight one, but it could not have been corrected without dividing the heroism between two persons, and that would have spoiled the poem; so Hay left it as it was.

It is true that "in later life he wished people would forget the Ballads," for he said the equivalent of that to a friend of mine before 1880; but at the time of which I have been speaking they had not yet become an inconvenience to him by obstructing his road to a graver fame. It was another case of "Heathen Chinee." When Harte was editing the *Overland*, and moving gradually and confidently along toward a coveted place in high-grade literature, an accident happened, one day, which blocked his progress for a time: the office-boy brought an urgent call for "copy" to fill a vacancy on the eve of going to press, and Harte, for lack of anything more to his taste, fished his H.C. ballad out of the wastebasket where he had thrown it, and gave it to the boy. Harte's reputation had been local, before; in a single day the Heathen Chinee made it universal. Then the Eastern world called for more Chinee, and was frantic to get it. Harte tried to appease it with higher literature, and got only censure in return, and reminders that he was wasting his time upon a sort of work which was out of his line and above his ability. He told me these things long afterward, and still showed a bitter and hostile feeling against that ballad, because it had stopped his lofty march when he was making such good progress, and had remained stubbornly in his road so long that he had begun to fear that he would never get a start again. Then relief and rescue came at last, and the "Luck of Roaring Camp" blasted the Heathen Chinee out of the way and opened the road.

I always recall that talk with Hay with pleasure, not only for its own sake, but because it was incidentally the occasion of my getting acquainted with Horace Greeley, a man whom I greatly admired and longed to see, and whose memory I still revere. It was difficult to get an interview with him, for he was a busy man, he was irascible, and he had an aversion to strangers; but I not only had the good fortune to meet him, but also had the great privilege of hearing him talk. The *Tribune* was in its early home, at that time, and Hay was a leader-writer on its staff. I had an appointment with him, and went there to look him up. I did not know my way, and entered Mr. Greeley's room by mistake. I recognized his back, and stood mute and rejoicing. After a little, he swung slowly around in his chair, with his head slightly tilted backward and the great moons of his spectacles glaring with intercepted light; after about a year —though it may have been less, perhaps—he arranged his firm mouth with care and said with virile interest:

"Well? What the hell do *you* want?"

So I think it must have been in 1870 or '71 that I had the talk with Hay about the ballads, because both he and Mr. Greeley were doing editorial duty on the *Tribune* in those years.

MARK TWAIN
1905

KING LEOPOLD'S SOLILOQUY

A DEFENSE OF HIS CONGO RULE

[*Throws down pamphlets which he has been reading. Excitedly combs his flowing spread of whiskers with his fingers; pounds the table with his fists; lets off brisk volleys of unsanctified language at brief intervals, repentantly drooping his head, between volleys, and kissing the Louis XI crucifix hanging from his neck, accompanying the kisses with mumbled apologies; presently rises, flushed and perspiring, and walks the floor, gesticulating*]

—— ——!! —— ——!! If I had them by the throat! [*Hastily kisses the crucifix, and mumbles*] In these twenty years I have spent millions to keep the press of the two hemispheres quiet, and still these leaks keep on occurring. I have spent other millions on religion and art, and what do I get for it? Nothing. Not a compliment. These generosities are studiedly ignored, in print. In print I get nothing but slanders—and slanders again—and still slanders, and slanders on top of slanders! Grant them true, what of it? They are slanders all the same, when uttered against a king.

Miscreants—they are telling *everything!* Oh, everything: how I went pilgriming among the Powers in tears, with my mouth full of Bible and my pelt oozing piety at every pore, and implored them to place the vast and rich and populous Congo Free State in trust in my hands as their agent, so that I might root out slavery and stop the slave raids, and lift up those twenty-five millions of gentle and harmless blacks out of darkness into light, the light of our blessed Redeemer, the light that streams from his holy Word, the light that makes glorious our noble civilization—lift them up and dry their tears and fill their bruised hearts with joy and gratitude—lift them up and make them comprehend that they were no longer outcasts and forsaken, but our very brothers in Christ; how America and thirteen great European states wept in sympathy with me, and were persuaded; how their representatives met in convention in Berlin and

made me Head Foreman and Superintendent of the Congo State, and
drafted out my powers and limitations, carefully guarding the persons
and liberties and properties of the natives against hurt and harm;
forbidding whisky traffic and gun traffic; providing courts of justice;
making commerce free and fetterless to the merchants and traders
of all nations, and welcoming and safe-guarding all missionaries of
all creeds and denominations. They have told how I planned and
prepared my establishment and selected my horde of officials—"pals"
and "pimps" of mine, "unspeakable Belgians" every one—and hoisted
my flag, and "took in" a President of the United States, and got him
to be the first to recognize it and salute it. Oh, well, let them
blackguard me if they like; it is a deep satisfaction to me to remember that I was a shade too smart for that nation that thinks
itself so smart. Yes, I certainly did bunco a Yankee—as those people
phrase it. Pirate flag? Let them call it so—perhaps it is. All the same,
they were the first to salute it.

These meddlesome American missionaries! these frank British
consuls! these blabbing Belgian-born traitor officials!—those tiresome parrots are always talking, always telling. They have told how
for twenty years I have ruled the Congo State not as a trustee of the
Powers, an agent, a subordinate, a foreman, but as a sovereign—
sovereign over a fruitful domain four times as large as the German
Empire—sovereign absolute, irresponsible, above all law; trampling
the Berlin-made Congo charter under foot; barring out all foreign
traders but myself; restricting commerce to myself, through con-
cessionaires who are my creatures and confederates; seizing and holding the State as my personal property, the whole of its vast revenues
as my private "swag"—mine, solely mine—claiming and holding its
millions of people as my private property, my serfs, my slaves; their
labor mine, with or without wage; the food they raise not their
property but mine; the rubber, the ivory and all the other riches of
the land mine—mine solely—and gathered for me by the men, the
women and the little children under compulsion of lash and bullet,
fire, starvation, mutilation and the halter.

These pests!—it is as I say, they have kept back nothing! They
have revealed these and yet other details which shame should have
kept them silent about, since they were exposures of a king, a sacred
personage and immune from reproach, by right of his selection and
appointment to his great office by God himself; a king whose acts
cannot be criticized without blasphemy, since God has observed
them from the beginning and has manifested no dissatisfaction

with them, nor shown disapproval of them, nor hampered nor interrupted them in any way. By this sign I recognize his approval of
what I have done; his cordial and glad approval, I am sure I may say.
Blest, crowned, beatified with this great reward, this golden reward,
this unspeakably precious reward, why should I care for men's cursings and revilings of me? [*With a sudden outburst of feeling*] May
they roast a million aeons in—[*Catches his breath and effusively
kisses the crucifix; sorrowfully murmurs, "I shall get myself damned
yet, with these indiscretions of speech."*]

Yes, they go on telling everything, these chatterers! They tell how
I levy incredibly burdensome taxes upon the natives—taxes which
are a pure theft; taxes which they must satisfy by gathering rubber
under hard and constantly harder conditions, and by raising and
furnishing food supplies gratis—and it all comes out that, when they
fall short of their tasks through hunger, sickness, despair, and ceaseless and exhausting labor without rest, and forsake their homes and
flee to the woods to escape punishment, my black soldiers, drawn
from unfriendly tribes, and instigated and directed by my Belgians,
hunt them down and butcher them and burn their villages—reserving
some of the girls. They tell it all: how I am wiping a nation of
friendless creatures out of existence by every form of murder, for
my private pocket's sake. But they never say, although they know it,
that I have labored in the cause of religion at the same time and
all the time, and have sent missionaries there (of a "convenient
stripe," as they phrase it), to teach them the error of their ways and
bring them to Him who is all mercy and love, and who is the sleepless
guardian and friend of all who suffer. They tell only what is against
me, they will not tell what is in my favor.

They tell how England required of me a Commission of Inquiry
into Congo atrocities, and how, to quiet that meddling country,
with its disagreeable Congo Reform Association, made up of earls
and bishops and John Morleys and university grandees and other
dudes, more interested in other people's business than in their own,
I appointed it. Did it stop their mouths? No, they merely pointed
out that it was a commission composed wholly of my "Congo
butchers," "the very men whose acts were to be inquired into." They
said it was equivalent to appointing a commission of wolves to
inquire into depredations committed upon a sheepfold. *Nothing
can satisfy a cursed Englishman!**

---

* Recent information is to the effect that the resident missionaries found the commission as a whole apparently interested to promote reforms. One of its members was a

And are the fault-finders frank with my private character? They could not be more so if I were a plebeian, a peasant, a mechanic. They remind the world that from the earliest days my house has been chapel and brothel combined, and both industries working full time; that I practised cruelties upon my queen and my daughters, and supplemented them with daily shame and humiliations; that, when my queen lay in the happy refuge of her coffin, and a daughter implored me on her knees to let her look for the last time upon her mother's face, I refused; and that, three years ago, not being satisfied with the stolen spoils of a whole alien nation, I robbed my own child of her property and appeared by proxy in court, a spectacle to the civilized world, to defend the act and complete the crime. It is as I have said: they are unfair, unjust; they will resurrect and give new currency to such things as those, or to any other things that count against me, but they will not mention any act of mine that is in my favor. I have spent more money on art than any other monarch of my time, and they know it. Do they speak of it, do they tell about it? No, they do not. They prefer to work up what they call "ghastly statistics" into offensive kindergarten object lessons, whose purpose is to make sentimental people shudder, and prejudice them against me. They remark that "if the innocent blood shed in the Congo State by King Leopold were put in buckets and the buckets placed side by side, the line would stretch 2000 miles; if the skeletons of his ten millions of starved and butchered dead could rise up and march in single file, it would take them seven months and four days to pass a given point; if compacted together in a body, they would occupy more ground than St. Louis covers, World's Fair and all; if they should all clap their bony hands at once, the grisly crash would be heard at a distance of—" Damnation, it makes

---

leading Congo official, another an official of the government in Belgium, the third a Swiss jurist. The commission's report will reach the public only through the king, and will be whatever he consents to make it; it is not yet forthcoming, though six months have passed since the investigation was made. There is, however, abundant evidence that horrible abuses were found and conceded, the testimony of missionaries, which had been scouted by the king's defenders, being amply vindicated. One who was present at one hearing of the commission writes: "Men of stone would be moved by the stories that are being unfolded as the commission probes into the awful history of rubber collection." Certain reforms were ordered in the one section visited, but the latest word is that after the commission's departure, conditions soon became worse than before its coming. Very well, then, the king has investigated himself. One stage is achieved. The next one in order is the investigation of conditions in the Congo State *by the Powers responsible for the creation of the Congo State.* The United States is one of these. Such an investigation is advocated by Lyman Abbott, Henry Van Dyke, David Starr Jordan and other prominent citizens in petitions to the President and Congress.—M.T.

me tired! And they do similar miracles with the money I have distilled from that blood and put into my pocket. They pile it into Egyptian pyramids; they carpet Saharas with it; they spread it across the sky, and the shadow it casts makes twilight in the earth. And the tears I have caused, the hearts I have broken—oh, nothing can persuade them to let *them* alone!

[*Meditative pause*] Well . . . no matter, I *did* beat the Yankees, anyway! there's comfort in that. [*Reads with mocking smile, the President's Order of Recognition of April 22, 1884*]

". . . the government of the United States announces its sympathy with and approval of the humane and benevolent purposes of (my Congo scheme,) and will order the officers of the United States, both on land and sea, to recognize its flag as the flag of a friendly government."

Possibly the Yankees would like to take that back, now, but they will find that my agents are not over there in America for nothing. But there is no danger; neither nations nor governments can afford to confess a blunder. [*With a contented smile, begins to read from "Report by Rev. W. M. Morrison, American missionary in the Congo Free State"*]

"I furnish herewith some of the many atrocious incidents which have come under my own personal observation; they reveal the *organized system* of plunder and outrage which has been perpetrated and is now being carried on in that unfortunate country by King Leopold of Belgium. I say King Leopold, because he and he *alone* is now responsible, since he is the *absolute sovereign. He styles himself such.* When our government in 1884 laid the foundation of the Congo Free State, by recognizing its flag, little did it know that this concern, parading under the guise of philanthropy, was really King Leopold of Belgium, one of the shrewdest, most heartless and most conscienceless rulers that ever sat on a throne. This is apart from his known corrupt morals, which have made his name and his family a byword in two continents. Our government would most certainly not have recognized that flag had it known that it was really King Leopold individually who was asking for recognition; had it known that it was setting up in the heart of Africa an *absolute monarchy;* had it known that, having put down African slavery in our own country at great cost of blood and money, it was *establishing a worse form of slavery right in Africa."*

[*With evil joy*] Yes, I certainly was a shade too clever for the Yankees. It hurts; it gravels them. They can't get over it! Puts a shame upon them in another way, too, and a graver way; for they never can rid their records of the reproachful fact that their vain Republic, self-appointed Champion and Promoter of the Liberties of the World, is the only democracy in history that has lent its power and influence to the establishing of an *absolute monarchy!*

[*Contemplating, with an unfriendly eye, a stately pile of pamphlets*] Blister the meddlesome missionaries! They write tons of these things. They seem to be always around, always spying, always eye-witnessing the happenings; and everything they see they commit to paper. They are always prowling from place to place; the natives consider them their only friends; they go to them with their sorrows; they show them their scars and their wounds, inflicted by my soldier police; they hold up the stumps of their arms and lament because their hands have been chopped off, as punishment for not bringing in enough rubber, and as proof to be laid before my officers that the required punishment was well and truly carried out. One of these missionaries saw eighty-one of these hands drying over a fire for transmission to my officials—and of course he must go and set it down and print it. They travel and travel, they spy and spy! And nothing is too trivial for them to print. [*Takes up a pamphlet. Reads a passage from Report of a "Journey made in July, August and September, 1903, by Rev. A. E. Scrivener, a British missionary"*]

". . . . Soon we began talking, and without any encouragement on my part the natives began the tales I had become so accustomed to. They were living in peace and quietness when the white men came in from the lake with all sorts of requests to do this and that, and they thought it meant slavery. So they attempted to keep the white men out of their country but without avail. The rifles were too much for them. So they submitted and made up their minds to do the best they could under the altered circumstances. First came the command to build houses for the soldiers, and this was done without a murmur. Then they had to feed the soldiers and all the men and women—hangers on—who accompanied them. Then they were told to bring in rubber. This was quite a new thing for them to do. There was rubber in the forest several days away from their home, but that it was worth anything was news to them. A small reward was offered and a rush was made for the rubber. 'What strange white men, to give us cloth and beads for the sap of a wild vine.' They rejoiced in what they thought their good fortune. But soon the reward was reduced until at last they were told to bring in the rubber for nothing. To this they tried to demur; but to their great surprise several were shot by the soldiers, and the rest were told, with many curses and blows, to go at once or more would be killed. Terrified, they began to prepare their food for the fortnight's absence from the village which the collection of rubber entailed. The soldiers discovered them sitting about. 'What, not gone yet?' Bang! bang! bang! and down fell one and another, dead, in the midst of wives and companions. There is a terrible wail and an attempt made to prepare the dead for burial, but this is not allowed. All must go at once to the forest. Without food? Yes, without food. And off the poor wretches had to go without even their tinder boxes to make fires. Many died in the forests of hunger and exposure, and still more from the rifles of the ferocious soldiers in charge of the post. In spite of all their efforts the amount fell off and more and more were killed. I was shown around the place, and the sites of former big chiefs' settlements were pointed out. A careful estimate made the population of, say, seven years ago, to be 2,000 people in and about the post, within a radius of, say, a quarter of a mile. All told, they would not muster 200 now, and there is so much sadness and gloom about them that they are fast decreasing."

"We stayed there all day on Monday and had many talks with the people. On the Sunday some of the boys had told me of some bones which they had seen, so on the Monday I asked to be shown these bones. Lying about on the grass, within a few yards of the house I was occupying, were numbers of human skulls, bones, in some cases complete skeletons. I counted thirty-six skulls, and saw many sets of bones from which the skulls were missing. I called one of the men and asked the meaning of it. 'When the rubber palaver began,' said he, 'the soldiers shot so many we grew tired of burying, and very often we were not allowed to bury; and so just dragged the bodies out into the grass and left them. There are hundreds all around if you would like to see them.' But I had seen more than enough, and was sickened by the stories that came from men and women alike of the awful time they had passed through. The Bulgarian atrocities might be considered as mildness itself when compared with what was done here. How the people submitted I don't know, and even now I wonder as I think of their patience. That some of them managed to run away is some cause for thankfulness. I stayed there two days and the one thing that impressed itself upon me was the collection of rubber. I saw long files of men come in, as at Bongo, with their little baskets under their arms; saw them paid their milk tin full of salt, and the two yards of calico flung to the headmen; saw their trembling timidity, and in fact a great deal that all went to prove the state of terrorism that exists and the virtual slavery in which the people are held."

That is their way; they spy and spy, and run into print with every foolish trifle. And that British consul, Mr. Casement, is just like them. He gets hold of a *diary which had been kept by one of my government officers,* and, although it is a private diary and intended for no eye but its owner's, Mr. Casement is so lacking in delicacy and refinement as to print passages from it. [*Reads a passage from the diary*]

"Each time the corporal goes out to get rubber, cartridges are given him. He must bring back all not used, and for every one used he must bring back a right hand. M.P. told me that sometimes they shot a cartridge at an animal in hunting; they then cut off a hand from a living man. As to the extent to which this is carried on, he informed me that in six months the State on the Mambogo River had used 6,000 cartridges, which means that 6,000 people are killed or mutilated. It means more than 6,000, for the people have told me repeatedly that the soldiers kill the children with the butt of their guns."

When the subtle consul thinks silence will be more effective than words, he employs it. Here he leaves it to be recognized that a thousand killings and mutilations a month is a large output for so small a region as the Mambogo River concession, silently indicating the dimensions of it by accompanying his report with a map of the prodigious Congo State, in which there is not room for so small an object as that river. That silence is intended to say, "If it is a thousand a month in this little corner, imagine the output of the whole vast State!" A gentleman would not descend to these furtivenesses.

Now as to the mutilations. You can't head off a Congo critic and make him stay headed-off; he dodges, and straightway comes back at you from another direction. They are full of slippery arts. When the mutilations (severing hands, unsexing men, etc.) began to stir Europe, we hit upon the idea of excusing them with a retort which we judged would knock them dizzy on that subject for good and all, and leave them nothing more to say; to wit, we boldly laid the custom on the natives, and said we did not invent it, but only followed it. Did it knock them dizzy? did it shut their mouths? Not for an hour. They dodged, and came straight back at us with the remark that "if a Christian king can perceive a saving moral difference between inventing bloody barbarities, and *imitating them from savages*, for charity's sake let him get what comfort he can out of his confession!"

It is most amazing, the way that that consul acts—that spy, that busy-body. [*Takes up pamphlet "Treatment of Women and Children in the Congo State; what Mr. Casement Saw in 1903"*] *Hardly two years ago! Intruding* that date upon the public was a piece of cold malice. It was intended to weaken the force of my press syndicate's assurances to the public that my severities in the Congo *ceased*, and ceased utterly, *years and years ago*. This man is fond of trifles—revels in them, gloats over them, pets them, fondles them, sets them all down. One doesn't need to drowse through his monotonous report to see that; the mere sub-headings of its chapters prove it. [*Reads*]

"Two hundred and forty persons, *men, women and children*, compelled to supply government with *one ton* of carefully prepared foodstuffs *per week*, receiving in remuneration, all told, the princely sum of 15s. 10d!"

Very well, it was liberal. It was not much short of a penny a week for each nigger. It suits this consul to belittle it, yet he knows very well that I could have had both the food and the labor for nothing. I can prove it by a thousand instances. [*Reads*]

"Expedition against a village behindhand in its (compulsory) supplies; result, slaughter of sixteen persons; among them three women and a boy of five years. Ten carried off, to be prisoners till ransomed; among them a child, who died during the march."

But he is careful not to explain that we are *obliged* to resort to ransom to collect debts, where the people have nothing to pay with. Families that escape to the woods sell some of their members into slavery and thus provide the ransom. He knows that I would stop this if I could find a less objectionable way to collect their debts. . . . Mm—here is some more of the consul's delicacy! He reports a conversation he had with some natives:

Q. "How do you know it was the *white* men themselves who ordered these cruel things to be done to you? These things must have been done without the white man's knowledge by the black soldiers."
A. "The white men told their soldiers: 'You only kill *women*; you cannot kill men. You must prove that you kill men.' So then the soldiers when they killed us" (here he stopped and hesitated and then pointing to . . . he said:) "then they . . . and took them to the white men, who said: 'It is true, you have killed *men.*'"
Q. "You say this is true? Were many of you so treated after being shot?"
All [*shouting out*]: "Nkoto! Nkoto!" ("Very many! Very many!")
There was no doubt that these people were not inventing. Their vehemence, their flashing eyes, their excitement, were not simulated."

Of course the critic had to divulge that; he has no self-respect. All his kind reproach me, although they know quite well that I took no pleasure in punishing the men in that particular way, but only did it as a warning to other delinquents. Ordinary punishments are no good with ignorant savages; they make no impression. [*Reads more sub-heads*]

"Devasted region; population reduced from 40,000 to 8,000."

He does not take the trouble to say how it happened. He is fertile in concealments. He hopes his readers and his Congo reformers, of the Lord-Aberdeen-Norbury-John-Morley-Sir Gilbert-Parker stripe, will think they were all killed. They were not. The great majority of them escaped. They fled to the bush with their families because of the rubber raids, and it was there they died of hunger. Could we help that?

One of my sorrowing critics observes: "Other Christian rulers tax their people, but furnish schools, courts of law, roads, light, water and protection to life and limb in return; King Leopold taxes his stolen nation, but provides *nothing in return but hunger, terror, grief, shame, captivity, mutilation and massacre.*" That is their style! I furnish "nothing!" I send the gospel to the survivors; these censure-mongers know it, but they would rather have their tongues cut out than mention it. I have several times required my raiders to give the dying an opportunity to kiss the sacred emblem; and if they obeyed me I have without doubt been the humble means of saving many souls. None of my traducers have had the fairness to mention this; but let it pass; there is One who has not overlooked it, and that is my solace, that is my consolation.

[*Puts down the Report, takes up a pamphlet, glances along the middle of it*]

This is where the "death-trap" comes in. Meddlesome missionary spying around—Rev. W. H. Sheppard. Talks with a black raider of mine after a raid; cozens him into giving away some particulars. The raider remarks:

"I demanded 30 slaves from this side of the stream and 30 from the other side; 2 points of ivory, 2,500 balls of rubber, 13 goats, 10 fowls and 6 dogs, some corn chumy, etc.

'How did the fight come up?' I asked.

'I sent for all their chiefs, sub-chiefs, men and women, to come on a certain day, saying that I was going to finish all the palaver. When they entered these small gates(the walls being made of fences brought from other villages, the high native ones) I demanded all my pay or I would kill them; so they refused to pay me, and I ordered the fence to be closed so they couldn't run away; then we killed them here inside the fence. The panels of the fence fell down and some escaped.'

'How many did you kill?' I asked.

'We killed plenty, will you see some of them?'

That was just what I wanted.

He said: 'I think we have killed between eighty and ninety, and those in the other villages I don't know, I did not go out but sent my people.'

He and I walked out on the plain just near the camp. There were three dead bodies with the flesh carved off from the waist down.

'Why are they carved so, only leaving the bones?' I asked.

'My people ate them,' he answered promptly. He then explained, 'The men who have young children do not eat people, but all the rest ate them.' On the left was a big man, shot in the back and without a head. (All these corpses were nude.)

'Where is the man's head?' I asked.

'Oh, they made a bowl of the forehead to rub up tobacco and diamba in.'

We continued to walk and examine until late in the afternoon, and counted forty-one bodies. The rest had been eaten up by the people.

On returning to the camp, we crossed a young woman, shot in the back of the head, one hand was cut away. I asked why, and Mulunba N'Cusa explained that they always cut off the right hand to give to the State on their return.

'Can you not show me some of the hands?' I asked.

So he conducted us to a framework of sticks, under which was burning a slow fire, and there they were, the right hands—I counted them, eighty-one in all.

There were not less than sixty women (Bena Pianga) prisoners. I saw them.

We all say that we have as fully as possible investigated the whole outrage, and find it was a plan previously made to get all the stuff possible and to catch and kill the poor people in the 'death-trap.' "

Another detail, as we see!—cannibalism. They report cases of it with a most offensive frequency. My traducers do not forget to remark that, inasmuch as I am absolute and with a word can prevent in the Congo anything I choose to prevent, then whatsoever is done there by my permission is my act, my *personal* act; that I do it; that the hand of my agent is as truly *my* hand as if it were attached to my own arm; and so they picture me in my robes of state, with my crown on my head, munching human flesh, saying grace, mumbling thanks to Him from whom all good things come. Dear, dear, when the soft-hearts get hold of a thing like that missionary's contribution they quite lose their tranquility over it. They speak out profanely and reproach Heaven for allowing such a fiend to live. Meaning me. They think it irregular. They go shuddering around, brooding over the reduction of that Congo population from 25,000,000 to 15,000,000 in the twenty years of my administration; then they burst out and call me "the King with Ten Million Murders on his Soul." They call me a "record." The most of them do not stop with charging merely the 10,000,000 against me. No, they reflect that but for me the population, by natural increase, would now be 30,000,000, so they charge another 5,000,000 against me and make my total death-harvest 15,000,000. They remark that the man who killed the goose that laid the golden egg was responsible for the eggs she would subsequently have laid if she had been let alone. Oh, yes, they call me a "record." They remark that twice in a generation, in India, the Great Famine destroys 2,000,000 out of a population of 320,000,000, and the whole world holds up its hands in pity and horror; then they fall to wondering where the world would find room for its emotions if I had a chance to trade places with the Great Famine for twenty years! The idea fires their fancy, and they go on and imagine the Famine coming in state at the end of the twenty years and prostrating itself before me, saying: "Teach me, Lord, I perceive that I am but an apprentice." And next they imagine Death coming, with his scythe and hour-glass, and begging me to marry his daughter and reorganize his plant and run the business. For the whole world, you see! By this time their diseased minds are under full steam, and they get down their books and expand their labors, with me for text. They hunt through all biography for my match, working Attila, Torquemada, Ghengis Khan, Ivan the Terrible, and the rest of that crowd for all they are worth, and evilly exulting when they cannot find it. Then they examine the historical earthquakes and cyclones and blizzards and cataclysms and volcanic eruptions: verdict, none of them "in it" with me. At last they do really hit it (as they think), and they close their labors with conceding—reluctantly—that I have *one* match in history, but only one —the *Flood*. This is intemperate.

But they are always that, when they think of me. They can no more keep quiet when my name is mentioned than can a glass of water control its feelings with a seidlitz powder in its bowels. The bizarre things they can imagine, with me for an inspiration! One Englishman offers to give me the odds of three to one and bet me anything I like, up to 20,000 guineas, that for 2,000,000 years I am going to be the most conspicuous foreigner in hell. The man is so beside himself with anger that he does not perceive that the idea is foolish. Foolish and unbusinesslike: you see, there could be no winner; both of us would be losers, on account of the loss of interest on the stakes; at four or five per cent, compounded, this would amount to— I do not know how much, exactly, but, by the time the term was up and the bet payable, a person could buy hell itself with the accumulation.

Another madman wants to construct a memorial for the perpetuation of my name, out of my 15,000,000 skulls and skeletons, and is full of vindictive enthusiasm over his strange project. He has it all ciphered out and drawn to scale. Out of the skulls he will build a combined monument and mausoleum to me which shall exactly duplicate the Great Pyramid of Cheops, whose base covers thirteen acres, and whose apex is 451 feet above ground. He desires to stuff me and stand me up in the sky on that apex, robed and crowned, with my "pirate flag" in one hand and a butcher-knife and pendant handcuffs in the other. He will build the pyramid in the centre of a depopulated tract, a brooding solitude covered with weeds and the mouldering ruins of burned villages, where the spirits of the starved and murdered dead will voice their laments forever in the whispers of the wandering winds. Radiating from the pyramid, like the spokes of a wheel, there are to be forty grand avenues of approach, each thirty-five miles long, and each fenced on both sides by skulless skeletons standing a yard and a half apart and festooned together in line by short chains stretching from wrist to wrist and attached to tried and true old handcuffs stamped with my private trade-mark, a crucifix and butcher-knife crossed, with motto, "By this sign we prosper"; each osseous fence to consist of 200,000 skeletons on a side, which is 400,000 to each avenue. It is remarked with satisfaction that it aggregates three or four thousand miles (single-ranked) of skeletons —15,000,000 all told—and would stretch across America from New York to San Francisco. It is remarked further, in the hopeful tone of a railroad company forecasting showy extensions of its mileage, that my output is 500,000 corpses a year when my plant is running full time, and that therefore if I am spared ten years longer there will be fresh skulls enough to add 175 feet to the pyramid, making it by a long way the loftiest architectural construction on the earth, and fresh skeletons enough to continue the transcontinental file (on piles) a thousand miles into the Pacific. The cost of gathering the materials from my "widely scattered and innumerable private grave-yards," and transporting them, and building the monument and the radiating grand avenues, is duly ciphered out, running into an aggre-gate of millions of guineas, and then—why then, (— —!!— —!!) this idiot asks me *to furnish the money!* [*Sudden and effusive application of the crucifix*] He reminds me that my yearly income from the Congo is millions of guineas, and that "*only*" 5,000,000 would be required for his enterprise. Every day wild attempts are made upon my purse; they do not affect me, they cost me not a thought. But *this one*—this one troubles me, makes me nervous; for there is no telling what an unhinged creature like this may think of next. . . . *If he should think of Carnegie*—but I must banish that thought out of my mind! it worries my days; it troubles my sleep. That way lies madness. [*After a pause*] There is no other way—I have got to buy Carnegie.

[*Harassed and muttering, walks the floor a while, then takes to the Consul's chapter-headings again. Reads*]

"Government starved a woman's children to death and killed her sons."
"Butchery of women and children."
"*The native has been converted into a being without ambition because without hope.*"
"Women chained by the neck by rubber sentries."
"Women refuse to bear children because, with a baby to carry, they can-not well run away and hide from the soldiers."
"Statement of a child. 'I, my mother, my grandmother and my sister, we ran away into the bush. A great number of our people were killed by the soldiers. . . . After that they saw a little bit of my mother's head, and the soldiers ran quickly to where we were and caught my grandmother, my mother, my sister and another little one younger than us. Each wanted my mother for a wife, and argued about it, so they finally decided to kill her. They shot her through the stomach with a gun and she fell, and when I saw that I cried very much, because they killed my grandmother and mother and I was left alone. I saw it all done!'"

It has a sort of pitiful sound, although they are only blacks. It carries me back and back into the past, to when my children were little, and would fly—to the bush, so to speak—when they saw me coming. . . . [*Resumes the reading of chapter-headings of the Consul's report*]

"They put a knife through a child's stomach."

"They cut off the hands and brought them to C.D. (white officer) and spread them out in a row for him to see."

"Captured children left in the bush to die, by the soldiers."

"Friends came to ransom a captured girl; but sentry refused, saying the white man wanted her because she was young."

"Extract from a native girl's testimony. 'On our way the soldiers saw a little child, and when they went to kill it the child laughed, so the soldier took the butt of his gun and struck the child with it and then cut off its head. One day they killed my half-sister and cut off her head, hands and feet, because she had bangles on. Then they caught another sister, and sold her to the W.W. people, and now she is a slave there.'"

The little child laughed! [*A long pause. Musing*] That innocent creature. Somehow—I wish it had not laughed. [*Reads*]

"Mutilated children."

"Government encouragement of inter-tribal slave-traffic. The monstrous fines levied upon villages tardy in their supplies of foodstuffs compel the native to sell their fellows—and children—to other tribes in order to meet the fine."

"A father and mother forced to sell their little boy."

"Widow forced to sell her little girl."

[*Irritated*] Hang the monotonous grumbler, what would he have me do! Let a widow off merely because she is a widow? He knows quite well that there is nothing much left, now, *but* widows. I have nothing against widows, as a class, but business is business, and I've got to live, haven't I, even if it does cause inconvenience to somebody here and there? [*Reads*]

"Men intimidated by the torture of their wives and daughters. (To make the men furnish rubber and supplies and so get their captured women released from chains and detention.) The sentry explained to me that he caught the women and brought them in (chained together neck to neck) by direction of his employer."

"An agent explained that he was forced to catch women in preference to men, as then the men brought in supplies quicker; but he did not explain how the children deprived of their parents obtained their own food supplies."

"A file of 15 (captured) women."

"Allowing women and children to die of starvation in prison."

[*Musing*] Death from *hunger*. A lingering, long misery that must be. Days and days, and still days and days, the forces of the body failing, dribbling away, little by little—yes, it must be the hardest death of all. And to see food carried by, every day, and you can have none of it! Of course the little children cry for it, and that wrings the mother's heart. . . . [*A sigh*] Ah, well, it cannot be helped; circumstances make this discipline necessary. [*Reads*]

"The crucifying of sixty women!"

How stupid, how tactless! Christendom's goose flesh will rise with horror at the news. "Profanation of the sacred emblem!" That is what Christendom will shout. Yes, Christendom will buzz. It can hear me charged with half a million murders a year for twenty years and keep its composure, but to profane the Symbol is quite another matter. It will regard this as serious. It will wake up and want to look into my record. Buzz? Indeed it will; I seem to hear the distant hum already. . . . It was wrong to crucify the women, clearly wrong, manifestly wrong, I can see it now, myself, and am sorry it happened, sincerely sorry. I believe it would have answered just as well to skin them. . . . [*With a sigh*] But none of us thought of that; one cannot think of everything; and after all it is but human to err.

It will make a stir, it surely will, these crucifixions. Persons will begin to ask again, as now and then in times past, how I can hope to win and keep the respect of the human race if I continue to give up my life to murder and pillage. [*Scornfully*] When have they heard me say I wanted the respect of the human race? Do they confuse me with the common herd? do they forget that I am a king? What king has valued the respect of the human race? I mean deep down in his private heart. If they would reflect, they would know that it is impossible that a king should value the respect of the human race. He stands upon an eminence and looks out over the world and sees multitudes of meek human things worshipping the persons, and submitting to the oppressions and exactions, of a dozen human things who are in no way better or finer than themselves—made on just their own pattern, in fact, and out of the same quality of mud. When it *talks*, it is a race of whales; but a king knows it for a race of tadpoles. Its history gives it away. If men were really *men*, how could a Czar be possible? and how could I be possible? But we *are* possible; we are quite safe; and with God's help we shall continue the business at the old stand. It will be found that the race will put up with us, in its docile immemorial way. It may pull a wry face now and then, and make large talk, but it will stay on its knees all the same.

Making large talk is one of its specialties. It works itself up, and froths at the mouth, and just when you think it is going to throw a brick—it heaves a poem! Lord, what a race it is! [Reads]

A CZAR—1905

"A pasteboard autocrat; a despot out of date;
  A fading planet in the glare of day;
  A flickering candle in the bright sun's ray,
Burnt to the socket; fruit left too late,
  High on a blighted bough, ripe till it's rotten.

By God forsaken and by time forgotten,
Watching the crumbling edges of his lands,
  A spineless god to whom dumb millions pray,
  From Finland in the West to far Cathay,
Lord of a frost-bound continent he stands,
  Her seeming ruin his dim mind appalls,
And in the frozen stupor of his sleep
  He hears dull thunders, pealing as she falls,
And mighty fragments dropping in the deep."*

It is fine, one is obliged to concede it; it is a great picture, and impressive. The mongrel handles his pen well. Still, with opportunity, I would cruci—flay him. . . . "A spineless god." It is the Czar to a dot—a god, and spineless; a royal invertebrate, poor lad; soft-hearted and out of place. "A spineless god to *whom dumb millions pray.*" Remorselessly correct; concise, too, and compact—the soul and spirit of the human race compressed into half a sentence. On their knees —140,000,000. On their knees to a little tin deity. Massed together, they would stretch away, and away, and away, across the plains, fading and dimming and failing in a measureless perspective—why, even the telescope's vision could not reach to the final frontier of that continental spread of human servility. Now *why* should a king value the respect of the human race? It is quite unreasonable to expect it. A curious race, certainly! It finds fault with me and with my occupations, and forgets that neither of us could exist an hour without its sanction. It is our confederate and all-powerful protector. It is our bulwark, our friend, our fortress. For this it has our gratitude, our

* B. H. Nadal, in *New York Times.*

deep and honest gratitude—but not our respect. Let it snivel and fret and grumble if it likes; that is all right; we do not mind that.

[*Turns over leaves of a scrapbook, pausing now and then to read a clipping and make a comment*] The poets—how they do hunt that poor Czar! French, Germans, English, Americans—they all have a bark at him. The finest and capablest of the pack, and the fiercest, are Swinburne (English, I think), and a pair of Americans, Thomas Bailey Eldridge and Colonel Richard Waterson Gilder, of the sentimental periodical called *Century Magazine and Louisville Courier-Journal.* They certainly have uttered some very strong yelps. I can't seem to find them—I must have mislaid them. . . . If a poet's bite were as terrible as his bark, why dear me—but it isn't. A wise king minds neither of them; but the poet doesn't know it. It's a case of little dog and lightning express. When the Czar goes thundering by, the poet skips out and rages alongside for a little distance, then returns to his kennel wagging his head with satisfaction, and thinks he has inflicted a memorable scare, whereas nothing has really happened—the Czar didn't know he was around. They never bark at me; I wonder why that is. I suppose my Corruption-Department buys them. That must be it, for certainly I ought to inspire a bark or two; I'm rather choice material, I should say. Why—here *is* a yelp at me. [*Mumbling a poem*]

> ". . . What gives thee holy right to murder hope
> And water ignorance with human blood?
>   *   *   *   *
> From what high universe-dividing power
> Draws't thou thy wondrous, ripe brutality?
>   *   *   *   *
> O horrible . . . Thou God who seest these things
> Help us to blot this terror from the earth."

. . . No, I see it is "To the Czar,"* after all. But there are those who would say it fits me—and rather snugly, too. "Ripe brutality." They would say the Czar's isn't ripe yet, but that mine is; and not merely *ripe* but rotten. Nothing could keep them from saying that; they would think it smart. "This terror." Let the Czar keep that name; I am supplied. This long time I have been "the monster"; that was their favorite—the monster of crime. But now I have a new one. They have found a fossil Dinosaur fifty-seven feet long and

* Louise Morgan Sill, in *Harper's Weekly.*

sixteen feet high, and set it up in the museum in New York and labeled it "Leopold II." But it is no matter, one does not look for manners in a republic. Um . . . that reminds me; I have never been caricatured. Could it be that the corsairs of the pencil could not find an offensive symbol that was big enough and ugly enough to do my reputation justice? [*After reflection*] There is no other way—I will buy the Dinosaur. And suppress it. [*Rests himself with some more chapter-headings. Reads*]

"More mutilation of children." (Hands cut off.)
"Testimony of American Missionaries."
"Evidence of British Missionaries."

It is all the same old thing—tedious repetitions and duplications of shop-worn episodes; mutilations, murders, massacres, and so on, and so on, till one gets drowsy over it. Mr. Morel intrudes at this point, and contributes a comment which he could just as well have kept to himself—and throws in some italics, of course; these people can never get along without italics:

"It is one heartrending story of human misery from beginning to end, and *it is all recent.*"

Meaning 1904 and 1905. I do not see how a person can act so. This Morel is a king's subject, and reverence for monarchy should have restrained him from reflecting upon me with that exposure. This Morel is a reformer; a Congo reformer. That sizes *him* up. He publishes a sheet in Liverpool called "The West African Mail," which is supported by the voluntary contributions of the sap-headed and the soft-hearted; and every week it steams and reeks and festers with up-to-date "Congo atrocities" of the sort detailed in this pile of pamphlets here. I will suppress it. I suppressed a Congo atrocity book there, after it was actually in print; it should not be difficult for me to suppress a newspaper.

[*Studies some photographs of mutilated negroes—throws them down. Sighs*] The kodak has been a sore calamity to us. The most powerful enemy that has confronted us, indeed. In the early years we had no trouble in getting the press to "expose" the tales of the mutilations as slanders, lies, inventions of busy-body American missionaries and exasperated foreigners who had found the "open door" of the Berlin-Congo charter closed against them when they innocently went out there to trade; and by the press's help we got the Christian nations everywhere to turn an irritated and unbelieving ear to those tales and say hard things about the tellers of them. Yes, all things went harmoniously and pleasantly in those good days, and I was looked up to as the benefactor of a down-trodden and friendless people. Then all of a sudden came the crash! That is to say, the incorruptible *kodak*—and all the harmony went to hell! The only witness I have encountered in my long experience that I couldn't bribe. Every Yankee missionary and every interrupted trader sent home and got one; and now—oh, well, the pictures get sneaked around everywhere, in spite of all we can do to ferret them out and suppress them. Ten thousand pulpits and ten thousand presses are saying the good word for me all the time and placidly and convincingly denying the mutilations. Then that trivial little kodak, that a child can carry in its pocket, gets up, uttering never a word, and knocks them dumb!

. . . . What is this fragment? [*Reads*]

"But enough of trying to tally off his crimes! His list is interminable, we should never get to the end of it. His awful shadow lies across his Congo Free State, and under it an unoffending nation of 15,000,000 is withering away and swiftly succumbing to their miseries. It is a land of graves; it is *The* Land of Graves; it is the Congo Free Graveyard. It is a majestic thought: that is, this ghastliest episode in all human history is the work of *one man alone*; one solitary man; just a single individual—Leopold, King of the Belgians. He is personally and solely responsible for all the myriad crimes that have blackened the history of the Congo State. He is *sole* master there; he is absolute. He could have prevented the crimes by his mere command; he could stop them today with a word. He withholds the word. For his pocket's sake.

It seems strange to see a king destroying a nation and laying waste a country for mere sordid money's sake, and solely and only for that. Lust of conquest is royal; kings have always exercised that stately vice; we are used to it, by old habit we condone it, perceiving a certain dignity in it; but *lust of money—lust of shillings—lust of nickels—lust of dirty coin*, not for the nation's enrichment but for *the king's alone*—this is new. It distinctly revolts us, we cannot seem to reconcile ourselves to it, we resent it, we despise it, we say it is shabby, unkingly, out of character. Being democrats we ought to jeer and jest, we ought to rejoice to see the purple dragged in the dirt, but—well, account for it as we may, we don't. We see this awful king, this pitiless and blood-drenched king, this money-crazy king towering toward the sky in a world-solitude of sordid crime, unfellowed and apart from the human race, sole butcher for personal gain findable in all his caste, ancient or modern, pagan or Christian, proper and legitimate target for the scorn of the lowest and the highest, and the execrations of all who hold in cold esteem the oppressor and the coward; and—well, it is a mystery, but *we do not wish to look*; for he is a king, and it hurts us, it troubles us, by ancient and inherited instinct it shames us to see a king degraded to this aspect, and we shrink from hearing the particulars of how it happened. *We shudder* and *turn away* when we come upon them in print."

Why, certainly—*that* is my protection. And you will continue to do it. I know the human race.

1905

A VISIT TO THE SAVAGE CLUB

About thirty-five years ago (1872) I took a sudden notion to go to England and get materials for a book about that not-sufficiently known country. It was my purpose to spy out the land in a very private way, and complete my visit without making any acquaintances. I had never been in England, I was eager to see it, and I promised myself an interesting time. The interesting time began at once, in the London train from Liverpool. It lasted an hour—an hour of delight, rapture, ecstasy. These are the best words I can find, but they are not adequate, they are not strong enough to convey the feeling which this first vision of rural England brought to me. Then the interest changed and took another form: I began to wonder why the Englishman in the other end of the compartment never looked up from his book. It seemed to me that I had not before seen a man who could read a whole hour in a train and never once take his eyes off his book. I wondered what kind of a book it might be that could so absorb a person. Little by little my curiosity grew, until at last it divided my interest in the scenery; and then went on growing until it abolished it. I felt that I must satisfy this curiosity before I could get back to my scenery, so I loitered over to that man's end of the carriage and stole a furtive glance at the book; it was the English edition of my *Innocents Abroad!* Then I loitered back to my end of the compartment, nervous, uncomfortable, and sorry I had found out: for I remembered that up to this time I had never seen that absorbed reader smile. I could not look out at the scenery any more, I could not take my eyes from the reader and his book. I tried to get a sort of comfort out of the fact that he was evidently deeply interested in the book and manifestly never skipped a line, but the comfort was only moderate and was quite unsatisfying. I hoped he would smile once—only just once—and I kept on hoping and hoping, but it never happened. By and by I perceived that he was getting close to the end; then I was glad, for my misery would soon be over. The train made only one stop in its journey of five hours and twenty minutes; the stop was at Crewe. The gentleman finished the book just as we were slowing down for the stop. When the train came to a standstill he put the book in the rack and jumped out. I shall always remember what a wave of gratitude and happiness swept through me when he turned the last page of that book. I felt as a condemned man must feel who is pardoned upon the scaffold with the noose hanging over him. I said to myself that I would now resume the scenery and be twice as happy in it as I had been before. But this was premature, for as soon as the gentleman returned he reached into his hand-bag and got out the second volume! He and that volume constituted the only scenery that fell under my eyes during the rest of the journey. From Crewe to London he read in that same old absorbed way, but he never smiled. Neither did I.

It was a bad beginning, and affected me dismally. It gave me a longing for friendly companionship and sympathy. Next morning this feeling was still upon me. It was a dreary morning, dim, vague, shadowy, with not a cheery ray of sunshine visible anywhere. By half-past nine the desire to see somebody, know somebody, shake hands with somebody, and see somebody smile had conquered my purpose to remain a stranger in London, and I drove to my publisher's place and introduced myself. The Routledges were about to sit down at a meal in a private room upstairs in the publishing house, for they had not had a bite to eat since breakfast. I helped them eat the meal; at eleven I helped them eat another one; at one o'clock I superintended while they took luncheon; durng the afternoon I assisted inactively at some more meals. These exercises had a strong and most pleasant interest for me, but they were not a novelty because, only five years before, I was present in the Sandwich Islands when fifteen men of the shipwrecked *Hornet's* crew arrived, a pathetic little group who hadn't had anything to eat for forty-five days.

In the evening Edmund Routledge took me to the Savage Club, and there we had something to eat again; also something to drink; also lively speeches, lively anecdotes, late hours, and a very hospitable and friendly and contenting and delightful good time. It is a vivid and pleasant memory with me yet. About midnight the company left the table and presently crystallised itself into little groups of three or four persons, and the anecdoting was resumed. The last group I sat with that night was composed of Tom Hood, Harry Leigh, and another good man—Frank Buckland, I think. We broke up at two in the morning; then I missed my money—five five-pound notes, new and white and crisp, after the cleanly fashion that prevails there. Everybody hunted for the money, but failed to find it. How it could have gotten out of my trousers-pocket was a mystery. I called it a mystery; they called it a mystery; by unanimous consent it was a mystery, but that was as far as we got. We dropped the matter there, and found things of higher interest to talk about. After I had gone to bed at the Langham Hotel I found that a single pair of candles did not furnish enough light to read by in comfort, and so I rang, in order that I might order thirty-five more, for I was in a prodigal frame of mind on account of the evening's felicities. The servant filled my order, then he proposed to carry away my clothes and polish them with his brush. He emptied all the pockets, and among other things he fetched out those five five-pound notes. Here was another mystery! and I inquired of this magician how he had accomplished that trick—the very thing a hundred of us, equipped with the finest intelligence, had tried to accomplish during half an hour and had failed. He said it was very simple; he got them out of the tail-coat pocket of my dress suit! I must have put them there myself and forgotten it. Yet I do not see how that could be, for as far as I could remember we had had nothing wet at the Savage Club but water. As far as I could remember.

In those days—and perhaps still—membership in the Lotus Club in New York carried with it the privileges of membership in the Savage, and the Savages enjoyed Lotus privileges when in New York. I was a member of the Lotus. Ten or eleven years ago I was made an honorary member of the Lotus, and released from dues; and seven or eight years ago I was made an honorary member of the Savage. At that time the honorary list included the Prince of Wales—now his Majesty the King—and Nansen the explorer, and another—Stanley, I think.

1907

THE SUPPRESSED CHAPTER OF *LIFE ON*
*THE MISSISSIPPI**

I missed one thing in the South—African slavery. That horror is gone, and permanently. Therefore, half the South is at last emancipated, half the South is free. But the white half is apparently as far from emancipation as ever.

The South is "solid" for a single political party. It is difficult to account for this; that is, in a region which purports to be free. Human beings are so constituted, that, given an intelligent, thinking, hundred of them, or thousand, or million, and convince them that they are free from personal danger or social excommunication for opinion's sake, it is absolutely impossible that they shall tie themselves in a body to any one sect, religious or political. Every thinking person in the South and elsewhere knows this: it is a truism.

Given a "solid" country, anywhere, and the ready conclusion is that it is a community of savages. But here are the facts—not conjectures, but facts—and I think they spoil that conclusion. The great mass of Southerners, both in town and country, are neighborly, friendly, hospitable, peaceable, and have an aversion for disagreements and embroilments; they belong to the church, and they frequent it; they are Sabbath-observers; they are promise-keepers; they are honorable and upright in their dealings; where their prejudices are not at the front, they are just, and they like to see justice done; they are able to reason, and they reason.

These characteristics do not describe a community of savages, they describe the reverse, an excellent community. How such a community should all vote one way, is a perplexing problem. That such a people should all be democrats or all republicans seems against nature.

It may be that a minor fact or two may help toward a solution. It

* This was Chapter 48 in the manuscript. It was set up in type and cancelled in the proofs, probably because it was thought it would offend many southern readers.

is imagined in the North that the South is one vast and gory murder-field, and that every man goes armed, and has at one time or another taken a neighbor's life. On the contrary, the great mass of Southerners carry no arms, and do not quarrel. In the city of New York, where killing seems so frightfully common, the mighty majority, the over-whelming majority of the citizens, have never seen a weapon drawn in their lives. This is the case in the South; murders are much commoner there than in the North; but these killings are scattered over a vast domain; in small places, long intervals of time intervene between events of this kind; and in both small and large places it is the chance half dozen who witness the killing—the vast majority of that community are not present, and may live long lives and die without ever having seen an occurrence of the sort.

As I have said, the great mass of Southerners are not personally familiar with murder. And being peaceably disposed, and also ac-customed to living in peace, they have a horror of murder and violence.

There is a superstition, current everywhere, that the Southern temper is peculiarly hot; whereas, in truth the temper of the average Southerner is not hotter than that of the average Northerner. The temper of the Northerner, through training, heredity, and fear of the law, is kept under the better command, that is all. In a wild country where born instincts may venture to the surface, this fact shows up. In California, Nevada and Montana, the most of the desperadoes and the deadliest of them, were not from the South, but from the North.

Now, in every community, North and South, there is one hot-head, or a dozen, or a hundred, according to distribution of popu-lation; the rest of the community are quiet folk. What do these hot-heads amount to, in the North? Nothing. Who fears them? Nobody. Their heads never get so hot but that they retain cold sense enough to remind them that they are among a people who will not allow themselves to be walked over by their sort; a people who, although they will not insanely hang them upon suspicion and with-out trial, nor try them, convict them, and then let them go, but will give them a fair and honest chance in the courts, and if conviction follow will punish them with imprisonment or the halter.

In the South the case is very different. The one hot-head defies the hamlet; the half dozen or dozen defy the village and the town. In the South the expression is common, that such-and-such a ruffian is the "terror of the town." Could he come North and be the terror of a town? Such a thing is impossible. Northern resolution, backing Northern law, was too much for even the "Mollie Maguires," powerful, numerous, and desperate as was that devilish secret organization. But it could have lived a long life in the South; for there it is not the rule for courts to hang murderers.

Why?—seeing that the bulk of the community are murder-hating people. It is hard to tell. Are they torpid, merely?—indifferent?—wanting in public spirit?

Their juries fail to convict, even in the clearest cases. That this is not agreeable to the public, is shown by the fact that very frequently such a miscarriage of justice so rouses the people that they rise, in a passion, and break into the jail, drag out their man and lynch him. This is quite sufficient proof that they do not approve of murder and murderers. But this hundred or two hundred men usually do this act of public justice with masks on. They go to their grim work with clear consciences, but with their faces disguised. They know that the law will not meddle with them—otherwise, at least, than by empty form—and they know that the community will applaud their act. Still, they disguise themselves.

The other day, in Kentucky, a witness testified against a young man in court, and got him fined for a violation of a law. The young man went home and got his shot gun and made short work of that witness. He did not invent that method of correcting witnesses; it had been used before, in the South. Perhaps this detail accounts for the reluctance of witnesses, there, to testify; and also the reluctance of juries to convict; and perhaps, also, for the disposition of lynchers to go to their grewsome labors disguised.

Personal courage is a rare quality. Everywhere in the Christian world—except, possibly, down South—the average citizen is not brave, he is timid. Perhaps he is timid down South, too. According to *The Times-Democrat*, "the favorite diversion of New Orleans' hoodlums is crowding upon the late street cars, hustling the men passengers and insulting the ladies." They smoke, they use gross language, they successfully defy the conductor when he tries to collect their fare. All this happens, and they do not get hurt. Apparently the average Southern citizen is like the average Northern citizen—does not like to embroil himself with a ruffian.

The other day, in Kentucky, a single highwayman, revolver in hand, stopped a stagecoach and robbed the passengers, some of whom were armed—and he got away unharmed. The unaverage Kentuckian, being plucky, is not afraid to attack half a dozen average

Kentuckians; and his bold enterprise succeeds—probably because the average Kentuckian is like the average of the human race, not plucky, but timid.

In one thing the average Northerner seems to be a step in advance of the average Southerner, in that he bands himself with his timid fellows to support the law, (at least in the matter of murder), protect judges, juries, and witnesses, and also to secure all citizens from personal danger and from obloquy or social ostracism on account of opinion, political or religious; whereas the average Southerners do not band themselves together in these high interests, but leave them to look out for themselves unsupported; the results being unpunished murder, against the popular approval, and the decay and destruction of independent thought and action in politics.

I take the following paragraph from a recent article in *The Evening Post*, published at Louisville, Ky. The italics are mine:

"There is no use in mincing matters. The condition of the State is worse than we have ever known it. Murders are more frequent, punishment is lighter, pardons more numerous, and abuses more flagrant than at any period within our recollection, running back fifteen years. Matters are getting worse day by day. The most alarming feature of all is the *indifference of the public.* No one seems to see the carnival of crime and social chaos to which we are rapidly drifting. No one seems to realize the actual danger which hangs over the lives of all. *Appeals to the order-loving and law-abiding element appear vain and idle. It is difficult to stir them.* Shocking tragedies at their very doors do not startle them to a realization of the evils that are cursing Kentucky, imperilling the lives of her citizens, barring us against the current of immigration and commerce, and presenting us to the eyes of the world as a reckless God-defying, reeking band of law-breakers and murderers."

That editor does not feel indifferent. He feels the opposite of indifferent. Does he think he is alone? He cannot be. I think that without question he is expressing the general feeling of the South. But it is not *organized,* therefore it is ineffective. Once organized it would be abundantly strong for the occasion; the condition of things complained of by the editor would cease. But it is not going to organize itself; somebody has got to take upon himself the disagreeable office of making the first move. In the Knoxville region of Tennessee that office has been assumed, and a movement is now on foot there to organize and band together the best people for the protection of Courts, juries and witnesses. There is no reason why the experiment should not succeed; and if it succeeds, there is no reason why the reform should not spread.

As to white political liberty in New Orleans. I take four pages, at random, from the city directory for the present year—1882. It "samples" the book, and affords one a sort of bird's eye view of the nationalities of New Orleans.

(Insert the 4 pages, 772 A B & C—reduce them in fac-simile and crowd them onto a single page of my book, to be read by a magnifier.)

"Many men, many minds," says the proverb, what a lovely thing it is to see all these variegated nationalities exhibiting a miracle which makes all other miracles cheap in comparison—that is, voting and feeling all one way, in spite of an eternal law of nature which pronounces such a thing impossible. And how pretty it is to see all these Germans and Frenchmen, who bitterly differ in all things else, meet sweetly together on the platform of a single party in the free and unembarrassed political atmosphere of New Orleans. How odd it is to see the mixed nationalities of New York voting all sorts of tickets, and the very same mixed nationalities of New Orleans voting all one way—and letting on that that is just the thing they wish to do, and are entirely unhampered in the matter, and wouldn't vote otherwise, oh, not for anything. As the German phrases it, "it is not thick enough."

c. 1910

PART II

Selected Interviews

POLITICAL VIEWS OF A HUMORIST

[New York *Herald*, August 28, 1876]

INTERVIEW WITH MARK TWAIN IN HIS MOUNTAIN STUDIO IN CHEMUNG—
REMARKABLE DECLARATIONS

ELMIRA, N.Y., August 26, 1876.

After a rather dusty ride of five miles up hill from Elmira the HERALD representative met Samuel L. Clemens (Mark Twain), temporarily residing at Quarry Hill farm, the property of one of the Langdon family, into which Mark happily married. He took me to his studio, an octagonal structure, still further up hill, and commanding a romantic view of Elmira and its surroundings for miles.

Mark was attired in a summer dress of snowy white, not dissimilar to that worn by Abraham Lincoln when the same correspondent interviewed the great lamented at his house in Springfield, Ill., in the memorable campaign of 1860, when Lincoln was first elected President of the United States.

A Remarkable Statement for a Literary Man.

HERALD CORRESPONDENT—Well, Mark, now we are in your cosey and breezy studio, suppose I interview you in regard to your opinions respecting the present political situation?

MARK TWAIN—Politics are rather out of my line, yet not outside of my interest. I am not much of a party man, but I have opinions. I should never have pushed them before the public, but if you want to catechise me I will answer, but I want easy questions—questions which a plain answer will meet.

"You shall have them. First, which platform do you prefer?"

"That is easily answered. Platforms are of such secondary importance that I have not thought it necessary to build up a preference. In most essentials the creeds of both parties are good enough for me.

But there is something back of the written creeds which is important. For instance, inflation and repudiation may be glossed over in a creed, but there are a good many erring people who want these things and would vote for them."

"What do you think is more important than platforms?"

"I think the men are. There used to be a party cry, 'Measures, not men.' That was in an honester day. We need to reverse that now. When you get below the politician scum—or above it, perhaps one ought to say—you will find that the solid men in both parties are equally good and equally well meaning. Both will furnish platforms which the country can survive and progress under. But of what use are these excellent platforms if the men elected upon them shamelessly ignore them and make them a dead letter? A sound and good democratic platform was powerless to save New York from the ravages of the Tweed gang; an excellent republican platform has no more been able to save the country from the ravages of the present administration's highwaymen than the pasting the four gospels on a bad man's back would be to save him from the tropical end of eternity. Platforms are not the essential things now—men are."

"Then how do you judge of your men?"

"Only by common report and their letters of acceptance."

"Which candidate do you prefer upon these grounds?"

"Hayes. He talks right out upon the important issues. You cannot mistake what he means concerning civil service, second term and the honest payment of the national debt. If you can understand what Mr. Tilden means it is only because you have got more brains than I have, but you don't look it. Mr. Tilden is a very able man; therefore I hold that he could have made himself understood. Why didn't he? Because one-half of his party believe in one thing and the other half in another, I suppose, and it was necessary to be a little vague. But Mr. Hendricks is not vague. He is in no hurry to have the national debt paid."

"Is there a democrat whom you would have preferred to Hayes?"

"Yes, Charles Francis Adams—a pure man, a proved statesman. I would vote for him in a minute. I wouldn't need to know what his platform was; the fact that he stood upon it would be sufficient proof to me that it was a righteous one. I want to see an honest government established once more. I mean to vote for Hayes because I believe, from his own manner of talking and from all I can hear of his character and his history, that he will appoint none but honest and capable men to office. I don't care two cents what party they belong to. I never tried to get a political office for but one man and I forgot to ask him what his politics were, but he was a clean man and mighty capable. Mr. Tilden is an old politician, dyed in the wool. History has tried hard to teach us that we can't have good government under politicians. Now, to go and stick one at the very head of the government couldn't be wise. You know that yourself."

"People speak well of both candidates, don't they?"

"I will tell you how it looks to me. I read a lot of newspapers of both creeds every day. The republicans tell me a great many things which Hayes has done; the democratic papers explain why Tilden didn't do a great many things. They keep on apologizing and apologizing all the time. I think that the woman or the candidate that has to be apologized for is a suspicious person. So do you. Now, let me urge you as an old friend to vote for Hayes—a man you don't have to apologize for."

"Well, but what do you think——"

"No, excuse me. You can't get any political elaborations out of me. I simply want to see the right man at the helm. I don't care what his party creed is. I want a man who isn't near sighted. I want a man who will not go on seeing angels from heaven in such buzzards as Delano, Belknap, Babcock and the rest of that lot, long after 40,000,000 of ordinary people have detected and come to loathe them. I want to see a man in the chief chair who can not only tell a buzzard when he sees it but will promptly wring its neck. I feel satisfied that Mr. Hayes is such a man; I am not satisfied that Mr. Tilden is. There, now, let us take a smoke. My opinions are important only to me. If they were important to others we would spread them all over the HERALD. Here is your pipe. Now we will talk of things less harrowing."

RUDYARD KIPLING ON MARK TWAIN

[New York *Herald*, August 17, 1890]

HOW THE ENGLISH STORY TELLER MET AND INTERVIEWED THE AMERICAN HUMORIST—SUGGESTIONS FOR NOVEL WRITING— CHAT ABOUT FICTION, CONSCIENCE, THE PROPOSED COPYRIGHT BILL AND HONESTY—MARK TWAIN UNBOSOMS HIMSELF— HIS OPINION OF AUTOBIOGRAPHIES—A SUGGESTION FOR FUTURE INTERVIEWERS—CRITICISM OF CLEMENS' LATEST WORK—IM-POSED UPON BY A CALLER

You are a contemptible lot out there, over yonder. Some of you are Commissioners and some Lieutenant Governors and some have the V.C., and a few are privileged to walk about the Mall arm in arm with the Viceroy; but I have seen Mark Twain this golden morning, have shaken his hand and smoked a cigar—no, two cigars—with him, and talked with him for more than two hours! Understand clearly that I do not despise you, indeed I don't. I am only very sorry for you all, from the Viceroy downward. To soothe your envy and to prove that I still regard you as my equals I will tell you all about it.

They said in Toronto that he was in Hartford, Conn., and again they said perchance he is gone upon a journey to Portland, Me.; and a big fat drummer vowed that he knew the great man intimately and that Mark was spending the summer in Europe, which information so upset me that I embarked upon the wrong train at Niagara and was incontinently turned out by the conductor three-quarters of a mile from the station, amid the wilderness of railway tracks. Have you ever, encumbered with great coat and valise, tried to dodge diversely minded locomotives when the sun was shining in your eyes? But I forgot that you have not seen Mark Twain, you people of no account!

On the Right Track

Saved from the jaws of the cowcatcher I, wandering devious, a stranger met.

"Elmira is the place. Elmira in the State of New York—this State, not two hundred miles away," and he added, perfectly unnecessarily, "Slide, Kelly, slide."

I slid on the West Shore line, I slid till midnight, and they dumped me down at the door of a frowzy hotel in Elmira. Yes, they knew all about "that man Clemens," but reckoned he was not in town; had gone East somewhere. I had better possess my soul in patience till the morrow and then dig up the "man Clemens'" brother-in-law, who was interested in coal.

The idea of chasing half a dozen relatives in addition to Mark Twain up and down a city of thirty thousand inhabitants kept me awake. Morning revealed Elmira, whose streets were desolated by railway tracks, and whose suburbs were given up to the manufacture of door sashes and window frames. It was surrounded by pleasant, fat little hills trimmed with timber and topped with cultivation. The Chemung River flowed generally up and down the town and had just finished flooding a few of the main streets.

Close on the Trail

The hotel man and the telephone man assured me that the much desired brother-in-law was out of town and no one seemed to know where "the man Clemens" abode. Later on I discovered that he had not summered in that place for more than nineteen seasons and so was comparatively a new arrival.

A friendly policeman volunteered the news that he had seen Twain or some one very like him driving a buggy on the previous day. This gave me a delightful sense of nearness to the great author. Fancy living in a town where you could see the author of "Tom Sawyer" or "some one very like him" jolting over the pavements in a buggy!

"He lives way out yonder at East Hill," said the policeman, "three miles away from here."

Then the chase began—in a hired hack, up an awful hill, where sunflowers blossomed by the roadside and crops waved and *Harper's Magazine* cows stood in eligible and commanding attitudes knee deep in clover, all ready to be transferred to photogravure. The great man must have been persecuted by outsiders aforetime and fled up the hill for refuge.

Presently the driver stopped at a miserable little white wood shanty and demanded "Mister Clemens."

"I know he's a big bug and all that," he explained, "but you can never tell what sort of notions those sort of men take it into their heads to live in, anyways."

There rose up a young lady who was sketching thistle tops and golden rod, amid a plentiful supply of both, and set the pilgrimage on the right path.

"It's a pretty Gothic house on the left hand side a little way further on."

"Gothic h—," said the driver, "very few of the city hacks take this drive, specially if they knew they are coming out here," and he glared at me savagely.

A New Scent

It was a very pretty house, anything but Gothic, clothed with ivy, standing in a very big compound and fronted by a veranda full of all sorts of chairs and hammocks for lying in all sorts of positions. The roof of the veranda was a trellis work of creepers and the sun peeped through and moved on the shining boards below.

Decidedly this remote place was an ideal one for working in if a man could work among these soft airs and the murmur of the long-eared crops just across the stone wall.

Appeared suddenly a lady used to dealing with rampageous outsiders. "Mr. Clemens has just walked down town. He is at his brother-in-law's house."

Then he was within shouting distance after all and the chase had not been in vain. With speed I fled, and the driver, skidding the wheel and swearing audibly, arrived at the bottom of that hill without accidents.

It was in the pause that followed between ringing the brother-in-law's bell and getting an answer that it occurred to me for the first time Mark Twain might possibly have other engagements than the entertainment of escaped lunatics from India, be they ever so full of admiration. And in another man's house—anyhow what had I come to do or say? Suppose the drawing room should be full of people, a levee of crowned heads; suppose a baby were sick anywhere, how was I to explain I only wanted to shake hands with him?

Face to Face

Then things happened somewhat in this order. A big, darkened drawing room, a huge chair, a man with eyes, a mane of grizzled hair, a brown mustache covering a mouth as delicate as a woman's, a strong, square hand shaking mine, and the slowest, calmest, levellest voice in all the world saying:—

"Well, you think you owe me something and you've come to tell me so. That's what I call squaring a debt handsomely."

"Piff!" from a cob pipe (I always said a Missouri meerschaum was the best smoking in the world) and behold Mark Twain had curled himself up in the big arm chair and I was smoking reverently, as befits one in the presence of his superior.

The thing that struck me first was that he was an elderly man, yet, after a minute's thought, I perceived that it was otherwise, and in five minutes, the eyes looking at me, I saw that the gray hair was an accident of the most trivial kind. He was quite young. I had shaken his hand. I was smoking his cigar, and I was hearing him talk—this man I had learned to love and admire fourteen thousand miles away.

Reading his books I had striven to get an idea of his personality and all my preconceived notions were wrong and beneath the reality. Blessed is the man who finds no disillusion when he is brought face to face with a revered writer. That was a moment to be remembered, the land of a twelve pound salmon was nothing to it. I had hooked Mark Twain and he was treating me as though under certain circumstances I might be an equal.

A One Sided Talk

About this time I became aware that he was discussing the copyright question. Here, as far as I remember, is what he said. Attend to the words of the oracle through this unworthy medium transmitted. You will never be able to imagine the long, slow surge of the drawl, and the deadly gravity of the countenance, any more than the quaint pucker of the body, one foot thrown over the arm of the chair, the yellow pipe clinched in one corner of the mouth and the right hand casually caressing the square chin:—

"Copyright. Some men have morals and some men have—other things. I presume a publisher is a man. He is not born. He is created —by circumstances. Some publishers have morals. Mine have. They pay me for the English productions of my books. When you hear men talking of Bret Harte's works and other works and my books being pirated ask them to be sure of their facts. I think they'll find the books are paid for. It was ever thus.

"I remember an unprincipled and formidable publisher. Perhaps he's dead now. He used to take my short stories—I can't call it steal or pirate them. It was beyond these things altogether. He took my stories one at a time and made a book of it. If I wrote an essay on dentistry or theology or any little thing of that kind—just an essay that long (he indicated half an inch on his finger), any sort of essay—that publisher would amend and improve my essay.

"He would get another man to write some more to it or cut it about exactly as his needs required. Then he would publish a book called 'Dentistry by Mark Twain,' that little essay and some other things not mine added. Theology would make another book and so on. I do not consider that fair. It's an insult. But he's dead now, I think. I didn't kill him.

Truth About Copyright

"There is a great deal of nonsense talked about international copyright. Are you interested in it? So am I." I don't think that he meant to be crushingly ironical, but I would cheerfully have wrapped myself up in the carpet and burrowed into the cellar when those eyes turned on me.

"The proper way to treat a copyright is to make it exactly like real estate in every way.

"It will settle itself under these conditions. If Congress were to bring in a law that a man's life were not to extend over a hundred and sixty years somebody would laugh. It wouldn't concern anybody. The men would be out of the jurisdiction of the court. A term of years in copyright comes to exactly the same thing. No law can make a book live or cause it to die before the appointed time.

"Tottletown, Cal., was a new town, with a population of 3000—banks, fire brigades, brick buildings and all modern improvements. It lived, it flourished and it disappeared. To-day no man can put his foot on any remnant of Tottletown, Cal. It's dead. London continues to exist.

"Bill Smith, author of a book read for the next year or so, is real estate in Tottletown. William Shakespeare, whose works are extensively read, is real estate in London. Let Bill Smith, equally with Mr. Shakespeare now deceased, have as complete a control over his copyright as he would over real estate. Let him gamble it away, drink it away or—give it to the church. Let his heirs and assigns treat it in the same manner.

Congressional Arguments

"Every now and again I go up to Washington, sitting on a board, to drive that sort of view into Congress. Congress takes its arguments against international copyright delivered ready made and—Congress isn't very strong. I put the real estate view of the case before one of the Senators.

"He said, 'Suppose a man has written a book that will live forever?'

"I said, 'Neither you nor I will ever live to see that man, but we'll assume it.' What then?

"He said, 'I want to protect the world against that man's heirs and assigns working under your theory.'

"I said, 'You think all the world are as big fools as ——, that all the world has no commercial sense. The book that will live forever can't be artificially kept up at inflated prices. There will always be very expensive editions of it and cheap ones issuing side by side.'

"Take the case of Sir Walter Scott's novels, he continued, turning to me. When the copyright notes protected them I bought editions as expensive as I could afford, because I liked them. At the same time the same firm were selling editions that a cat might buy. They had their real estate, and not being fools recognized that one portion of the plot could be worked as a gold mine, another as a vegetable garden and another as a marble quarry. Do you see?"

Changing the Subject

What I saw with the greatest clearness was Mark Twain being forced to fight for the simple proposition that a man has as much right in the work of his brains (think of the heresy of it!) as in the labor of his hands. When the old lion roars the young whelps growl. I growled assentingly, and the talk ran on from books in general to his own in particular.

Growing bold, and feeling that I had a few hundred thousand folk at my back, I demanded whether Tom Sawyer married Judge Thatcher's daughter and whether we were ever going to hear of Tom Sawyer as a man.

As to Tom Sawyer's Future

"I haven't decided," quoth Mark Twain, getting up, filling his pipe and walking up and down the room in his slippers. "I have had a notion of writing the sequel to Tom Sawyer in two ways. In one I would make him rise to great honor and go to Congress, and in the other I should hang him. Then the friends and enemies of the book could take their choice."

Here I lost my reverence completely and protested against any theory of the sort, because, to me at least, Tom Sawyer was real.

"Oh, he is real," said Mark Twain. "He's all the boy that I have known or recollect; but that would be a good way of ending the book"; then, turning round, "because, when you come to think of it, neither religion, training nor education avails anything against the force of circumstances that drive a man. Suppose we took the next four-and-twenty years of Tom Sawyer's life and gave a little joggle to the circumstances that controlled him. He would logically and according to the joggle turn out a rip or an angel."

"Do you believe that, then?"

"I think so. Isn't it what you call kismet?"

"Yes, but don't give him two joggles and show the result, because he isn't your property any more. He belongs to us."

Concerning Truthful Autobiographies

Thereat he laughed—a large, wholesome laugh—and this began a dissertation on the rights of a man to do what he liked with his own creations, which being a matter of purely professional interest, I will mercifully omit.

Returning to the big chair he, speaking of truth and the like in literature, said that an autobiography was the one work in which a man against his own will and in spite of his utmost striving to the contrary, revealed himself in his true light to the world.

"A good deal of your life on the Mississippi is autobiographical, isn't it?" I asked.

"As near as it can be—when a man is writing a book, and about himself. But in genuine autobiography, I believe it is impossible for a man to tell the truth about himself or to avoid impressing the reader with the truth about himself.

"I made an experiment once. I got a friend of mine—a man painfully given to speaking the truth on all occasions—a man who wouldn't dream of telling a lie—and I made him write his autobiography for his own amusement and mine. He did it. The manuscript would have made an octavo volume, but, good honest man though he was, in every single detail of his life that I knew about he turned out, on paper, a formidable liar. He could not help himself.

"It is not in human nature to write the truth about itself. None the less the reader gets a general impression from an autobiography whether the man is a fraud or a good man. The reader can't give his reasons any more than a man can explain why a woman struck him as being lovely when he doesn't remember her hair, eyes, teeth or figure. And the impression that the reader gets is a correct one."

"Do you ever intend writing an autobiography?"

"If I do, it will be as other men have done—with the most earnest desire to make myself out to be the better man in every little business that has been to my discredit, and I shall fail, like the others, to make the readers believe anything except the truth."

Mark Twain's Conscience

This naturally led to a discussion on conscience. Then said Mark Twain, and his words are mighty and to be remembered:—

"Your conscience is a nuisance. A conscience is like a child. If you pet it and play with it and let it have everything it wants, it becomes spoiled and intrudes on all your amusements and most of your griefs. Treat your conscience as you would treat anything else. When it is rebellious spank it—be severe with it, argue with it, prevent it from coming to play with you at all hours and you will secure a good conscience. That is to say, a properly trained one. A spoiled conscience simply destroys all the pleasure in life. I think I have reduced mine to order. At least I haven't heard from it for some time. Perhaps I've killed it through over severity. It's wrong to kill a child, but in spite of all I have said a conscience differs from a child in many ways. Perhaps it is best when it's dead."

How the Humorist Talks

Here he told me a little—such things as a man may tell a stranger —of his early life and upbringing, and in what manner he had been influenced for good by the example of his parents. He spoke always through his eyes, a light under the heavy eyebrows; anon crossing the room with a step as light as a girl's to show me some book or other; then resuming his walk up and down the room puffing at the cob pipe. I would have given much for nerve enough to demand the gift of that pipe, value five cents when new. I understood why certain savage tribes ardently desire the liver of brave men slain in combat. That pipe would have given me, perhaps, a hint of his keen insight into the souls of men. But he never laid it aside within stealing reach of my arms.

Once indeed he put his hand on my shoulder. It was an investiture of the Star of India, blue silk, trumpets and diamond studded jewel, all complete. If hereafter among the changes and chances of this mortal life I fall to cureless ruin I will tell the superintendent of the workhouse that Mark Twain once put his hand on my shoulder, and he shall give me a room to myself and a double allowance of paupers' tobacco.

Opinions of Current Literature

"I never read novels myself," said he, "except when the popular persecution forces me to—when people plague me to know what I think of the last book that every one is reading."

"And how did the latest persecution affect you?"

"Robert?" said he interrogatively.

I nodded.

"I read it, of course, for the workmanship. That made me think I had neglected novels too long—that there might be a good many books as graceful in style somewhere on the shelves; so I began a course of novel reading. I have dropped it now. It did not amuse me. But as regards Robert the effect on me was exactly as though a singer of street ballads were to hear excellent music from a church organ. I didn't stop to ask whether the music was legitimate or necessary. I listened and I liked what I heard. I am speaking of the grace and beauty of the style."

How is one to behave when one differs altogether with a great man? My business was to be still and to listen. Yet Mark—Mark Twain, a man who knew men—"big Injun, heap big Injun, dam mighty heap big Injun"—master of tears and mirth, skilled in wisdom of the true inwardness of things, was bowing his head to the labored truck of the schools where men act in obedience to the books they read and keep their consciences in spirits of homemade wine. He said the style was graceful, therefore it must be graceful. But perhaps he was making fun of me. In either case I would lay my hand upon my mouth.

"You see," he went on, "every man has his private opinion about a book. But that is my private opinion. If I had lived in the beginning of things I should have looked around the township to see what popular opinion thought of the murder of Abel before I openly condemned Cain. I should have had my private opinion, of course, but I shouldn't have expressed it until I had felt the way. You have my private opinion about that book. I don't know what my public ones are exactly. They won't upset the earth."

He recurled himself into the chair and talked of other things.

Working Under Difficulties

"I spend nine months of the year at Hartford. I have long ago satisfied myself that there is no hope of doing much work during those nine months. People come in and call. They call at all hours, about everything in the world. One day I thought I would keep a list of interruptions. It began this way:—

"A man came and would see no one but Mister Clemens. He was an agent for photogravure reproductions of Salon pictures. I very seldom use Salon pictures in my books.

"After that man another man, who refused to see any one but Mister Clemens, came to make me write to Washington about something. I saw him. I saw a third man, then a fourth. By this time it was noon. I had grown tired of keeping the list. I wished to rest.

"But the fifth man was the only one of the crowd with a card of his own. He sent it up—this card of his own. 'Ben Koontz, Hannibal, Mo.' I was raised in Hannibal. Ben was an old schoolmate of mine. Consequently I threw the house wide open and rushed with both hands out at a big, fat, heavy man, who was not the Ben I had ever known—nor anything of him.

"'But is it you, Ben,' I said. 'You've altered in the last thousand years.'

"The fat man said:—'Well, I'm not Koontz exactly, but I met him down in Missouri and he told me to be sure and call on you, and he gave me his card and—here he acted the little scene for my benefit—'if you'll wait a minute till I can get out the circulars—I'm not Koontz exactly, but I'm travelling with the fullest line of rods you ever saw.'"

"And what happened?" I asked breathlessly.

"I shut the door. He was not Ben Koontz—exactly—not my old schoolfellow, but I had shaken him by both hands in love and * * * I had been bearded by a lightning rod man in my own house. As I was saying, I do very little work in Hartford. I come here for three months every year, and I work four or five hours a day in a study down the garden of that little house on the hill. Of course I do not object to two or three interruptions. When a man is in the full swing of his work these little things do not affect him. Eight or ten or twenty interruptions retard composition."

Facts and Fiction

I was burning to ask him all manner of impertinent questions as to which of his works he himself preferred, and so forth, but standing in awe of his eyes I dared not. He spoke on and I listened grovelling.

It was a question of mental equipment that was on the carpet, and I am still wondering whether he meant what he said.

"Personally I never care for fiction or story books. What I like to read about are facts and statistics of any kind. If they are only facts about the raising of radishes they interest me. Just now, for instance, before you came in"—he pointed to an encyclopaedia on the shelves— "I was reading an article about 'Mathematics.' Perfectly pure mathematics.

"My own knowledge of mathematics stops at 'twelve times twelve,' but I enjoyed that article immensely. I didn't understand a word of it, but facts, or what a man believes to be facts, are always delightful. That mathematical fellow believed in his facts. So do I. Get your facts first, and," the voice died away to an almost inaudible drone, "then you can distort 'em as much as you please."

The Parting

Bearing this precious advice in my bosom I left, the great man assuring me with gentle kindness that I had not interrupted him in the least. Once outside the door I yearned to go back and ask some questions—it was easy enough to think of them now—but his time was his own, though his books belonged to me.

I should have ample time to look back to that meeting across the graves of the days. But it was sad to think of the things he had not spoken about.

In San Francisco the men of the *Call* told me many legends of Mark's apprenticeship in their paper five and twenty years ago; how he was a reporter delightfully incapable of reporting according to the needs of the day. He preferred, so they said, to coil himself into a heap and meditate till the last minute. Then he would produce copy bearing no sort of relationship to his legitimate work—copy that made the editor swear horribly and the readers of the *Call* ask for more.

I should like to have heard Mark's version of that and some stories of his joyous and variegated past. He has been journeyman printer (in those days he wandered from the banks of the Missouri even to Philadelphia), pilot cub and full blown pilot, soldier of the South (that was for three weeks only), private secretary to a Lieutenant Governor of Nevada (that displeased him), miner, editor, special correspondent in the Sandwich Islands, and the Lord only knows what else. If so experienced a man could by any means be made drunk it would be a glorious thing to fill him up with composite liquors, and, in the language of his own country, "let him retrospect." But these eyes will never see that orgie fit for the gods.

*   *   *   *   *

LATER.—Oh shame! Oh shock! O fie! I have been reading the new book which you also will have read by this time—the book about the yankee animal in the court yard. It's * * * but I don't believe he ever wrote it; or, if he did, I am certain that if you held it up to a looking glass or picked out every third word or spelled it backward you would find that it hid some crystal clean tale as desirable as Huck Finn.

RUDYARD KIPLING

"OF COURSE I AM DYING"

[New York *Herald*, June 6, 1897*]

"Of course I am dying," Mark Twain smiled grimly. "But I do not know that I am doing it any faster than anybody else. As for dying in poverty, I had just as soon die in poverty here in London as anywhere. But it would be a little more difficult, because I have got quite a number of friends, any one of whom would be good for a month's provisions, and that would drag out the agony a fairly long time.

"No, I assure you I am as well as ever I was. You see you must not attach too much importance to my wife's remark that I was not in a condition to receive visitors. That simply means that I was in bed. Now most women think that if a man does not get up before twelve o'clock there must be something wrong with him, and as I never get up before then, my wife thinks that I am not in good health. As a matter of fact when you were announced I told her to have you shown up to my room, but you can never persuade a tidy woman to show a stranger into an untidy bedroom, and so that did not work.

"I said to her, 'Show him up, send some cigars up. I am comfortable enough!'

"'Yes,' she said, 'But what about him?'

"'Oh,' I said, 'if you want him to be as comfortable as I am make him up a bed in the other corner of the room.' That did not work, either, so I thought the best thing to do was to get up and come to see you.

"Poverty is relative. I have been in poverty so often that it does not worry me much. A more serious matter is the money owing to other people, not by any fault of mine, and yet owing to them by me.

---

* This is the source given by Merle Johnson in A *Bibliography of Mark Twain*, 1935, p. 146. There is no interview with Mark Twain in the *Herald* of this date, nor in any of the days immediately preceding or following it. This is by no means a unique error in Johnson. Johnson reprinted the interview pp. 146–50 and I am reprinting it from him.

But I do not trouble about the rumors that go about in regard to me. Why should I? The rumor will die itself if you will only give it three days. Start any rumor, and if the public can go with its curiosity unsatisfied for three days something else will spring up which will make the public forget all about the first one. Therefore when people talk about my dying, or as really happened a few days ago, about my being dead, I do not take the slightest notice. I know perfectly well that the public will forget all about it if I let it alone. I keep on ploughing away and working and working and hoping and hoping, but the idea of being in poverty does not either trouble me or frighten me."

(What are you working about, just now?)

"Oh, my journey about the world. Everybody has done his little circumnavigation act, and I thought it about time I did mine, so I have been getting it ready for the press since I have been here, and therefore, for the matter of that, the book is just my impressions of the world at large. I go into no details. I never do for that matter. Details are not my strong point, unless I choose for my own pleasure to go into them seriously. Besides, I am under no contract to supply details to the reader. All that I undertake to do is to interest him. If I instruct him that is his fate. He is that much ahead."

(What is to be its name?)

"I had thought of calling it 'Another Innocent Abroad' but following advice, as the lawyers say, I have decided to call it 'The Surviving Innocent Abroad.'

"Now, my wife said, 'But that is not true, because there's so-and-so in Cleveland, and that and the other in Philadelphia,' but I said to her, 'I will fix that': so I am going to put a little explanatory note to that title pointing out that although there are still in existence some eight or ten of the pilgrims who went on the 'Quaker City' expedition some twenty-eight years ago, I am the only surviving one that has remained innocent.

"In fact that title 'The Innocents Abroad,' could only be strictly applied to two even at the time it was written, and the other is dead."

(When do you expect the survivor to appear?)

"Oh, about Christmas. Christmas is a good time to bring out a book. Everybody is thinking about Christmas presents, and the pious are praying that Divine Providence may give them some clue as to what to give for a present, and the book if it comes just at the right time, is about as good a thing as one could desire. It must come just at the right time though. In other words the opportunity to secure the present must happen just at the moment when the impulse to give one is felt.

*   *   *   *   *

"Similarly, we make a lawyer study Blackstone and statute law and common law, and we try him before a jury and see what his skill as an orator is, but we never ask him the crucial question—Have you ever committed a crime? Have you ever undergone a term of imprisonment? Because that has been done, a man is not fit to sit in judgment upon his fellow creatures. It is such a little thing that stands between all of us and crime at one time or another of our lives.

"As I said about charity, if the impulse to kill and the opportunity to kill always came at the same instant, how many of us would escape hanging. We have all of us at one time or another felt like killing something, and we have all of us at one time or another had the opportunity to kill something, but luckily for us, impulse and opportunity did not coincide. If a man is rich and he does want to kill something he can take his gun and go out and shoot. He lets off steam in that way, and the sore place gives over hurting. I used to have a rage and let it expand in the letter box.

"If anyone had done something to me that annoyed me or put me out, I would sit down and write a letter to him, and I would pour out all my thoughts and all the bitterness and anger and contempt and indignation and invective in my heart, and when I had cleaned myself out thoroughly I would put that letter in the box and my wife would see that it did not go.

"She used to say when she saw me sitting down: 'What are you going to do?"

"'I am going to answer this letter. I would——'

"'But you know you won't send it.'

"'I know that, but, by George, I am going to write it.'

"I have been very sorry many a time that those letters were not kept, because when a man is in a thoroughgoing temper, he finds things to say worth preserving."

MARK TWAIN SAYS HE'S DISCOURAGED

[New York *World*, June 17, 1900]

EVERY SORT OF CRANK EXCEPT HIMSELF HAS A PRESIDENTIAL FOLLOWING—IS ADVISED TO WITHDRAW—BUT HE THINKS IT UNNECESSARY, AS HIS CANDIDACY "WILL WITHDRAW ITSELF AT THE PROPER MOMENT"

(Special Cable Despatch to The World.)

LONDON, June 16.—"I have postponed sailing for home until October," said Mark Twain to The World's correspondent yesterday.

"Then you have abandoned your Presidential candidacy?"

"Well, you see, it's so discouraging. I had a letter from a friend in America the other day saying there were all kinds of candidates for the Presidency in the field, and every sort of crank except myself seemed to have some following; but he could not discover any one who followed me. He suggested that I should withdraw, but my candidacy will withdraw itself at the proper moment."

"What plans have you formed as to your future movements?"

"I am going home for good this time. I don't anticipate leaving America again. I should have gone back this month, but my younger daughter's health has been benefited so much by our stay here that we have postponed our departure on that account. But unless some such reason should arrive I won't leave home any more."

The world-famous humorist is himself in excellent health. He has been steadily working on his new book during his stay in London, living very quietly and keeping away from society so as not to be interrupted in his writing. Seeing the reverence and affection in which Mark Twain is held in this country, this self-denying ordinance is typical of his quiet determination.

MARK TWAIN, THE GREATEST AMERICAN HU-MORIST, RETURNING HOME, TALKS AT LENGTH TO THE *WORLD*

[New York *World*, October 14, 1900]

IN HIS LAZY, DRAWLING WAY HE MAKES BREEZY COMMENT ON CURRENT TOPICS—HE LIKES TO DINE OUT—FOR THAT REASON LONDON HAS PROVED A DELIGHTFUL PLACE OF RESIDENCE—WE'VE NO BUSINESS IN CHINA—NOR CAN HE UNDERSTAND ON JUST WHAT PRINCIPLES WE ARE PROCEEDING IN PHILIPPINES

Mark Twain, aboard the Minnehaha, is due at this port now. He is returning after many years' absence abroad to dwell permanently in his native land. He talked with The World correspondent in London, who gives this interesting account of what he said:

LONDON, Oct. 6—If it were the good fortune of the journalist to have only Mark Twains to interview his lot would indeed be cast in pleasant places.

When The World correspondent called upon him to-day at his London hotel he was received with that charming courtesy and dignified geniality which are the outward stamp of the noble personal character of the greatest living humorist. The inevitable Brobding-nagian pipe was produced and lit, and throwing himself back on the smoke-room couch at Brown's Hotel in Albemarle street, Mark Twain began in that dreamy New England accent of his with its delightful musical cadences: "Why, of course I am very glad to speak for The World. Whenever I arrive in a new place or whenever I leave it I always make it a point to answer as well as I can any questions that may be put to me by the boys. But between seasons I never talk. The same rule guides me in connection with public appearances. I have to work, and I like to do it as systematically as I can."

He Loves to Dine

"Have you been busy with your pen amid the distractions of London?"

"Well, London, you see, doesn't distract me. I find it about the best possible place to work in. I like it too as a place of residence better than any I know outside Hartford, where I am always happiest and feel best. Here I meet men of my own tongue and I have many friends. For although seemingly I live a retired life here, I am constantly going out to dinners. You can understand that at the close of a day's work it is a big luxury, a great relaxation, to dine in pleasant company, in absolute privacy, where you can say what you like with the knowledge that it will not get into print. These dinners I enjoy; it's the luncheons that break in upon your time and upset your working arrangements. But dinners! Why I can do with millions of dinners!"

He Never Makes Pledges

"Is it true that you have resolved never to leave the United States again?"

"Not a word of truth in it. Perhaps we may spend the rest of our days at home. I don't know and no consideration on earth could induce me to give a pledge about that or anything else. That is another of my rules of life. I never give pledges or promises about things of that sort. If I felt myself under the constraint of a pledge the situation would become so irksome to me that only on that account alone, I should be irresistibly compelled to come away again. No—as far as I am able to speak about a subject on which other people have the controlling voice more or less—I propose to stay the winter in New York, and then go back to Hartford in the spring."

"But do you really think it possible that such an indefatigable traveller as you have been can settle down at home? Won't you feel restless?"

"An indefatigable traveller! That's where I am misunderstood. Now I have made thirty-four long journeys in my life, and thirty-two of them were made under the spur of absolute compulsion. I mean it—under nothing but sheer compulsion. There always was an imperative reason. I had to gather material for books or sketches, I had to stump around lecturing to make money, or I had to go abroad for the health or the education of my family. For love of travel—never any of these thirty-two journeys. There is no man living who cares less about seeing new places and peoples than I. You are surprised—but it's the gospel truth. I had a surfeit of it.

"Innocents Abroad" a Nightmare

"When I started out, in 1867, for a six months' tour in the Quaker City I was a voracious sightseer. With nearly all the rest of that gang I said to myself: 'This is the opportunity of my life— never again shall I have the chance, the time or the money to see the Old World.' We lived up to that idea. We went in for seeing everything that was to be seen. In a city of inexhaustible treasures like Rome we got up at 6 in the morning and throughout the whole day, in rain or shine, we made a perpetual procession through picture galleries, churches, museums, palaces—looking at things which for the most part did not interest us one cent but which we thought we had to see. And we saw them. If our meals interfered with our seeing any old thing our meals were put aside. At 9 or 10 at night we returned to our hotel, our brains and our bodies reeling with fatigue and utter exhaustion. My head used to ache, my eyes to swim, but I would not succumb to the terrible temptation to throw myself on the bed, as if I did so I could not rise from it again before morning. I had to resist because we had to see something else by moonlight or because there was no moon or some other foolish reason. The only rest we had was when we went a short voyage from one port to another in the Mediterranean, and then I slept all the time. What was the result of this insensate sightseeing? Why, that I was so fagged that I lost the capacity to appreciate most of what I saw or to carry away any coherent idea of it. Since then only hard necessity has ever driven me travelling. When I went around the world, five years ago, it was because I wanted money to pay off debts that were a nuisance to me—they burdened my conscience. People say that it was to relieve my creditors. Not at all. It was far more to relieve Clemens than creditors. I could not be happy until I got rid of that debt. I have never recovered from the Quaker City surfeit of sightseeing, and don't think there is any reasonable prospect of my doing so now."

Surfeited with Theatres

"Don't you find theatres as much of a relaxation as dinners?"
"No: that is another mistake. I had a surfeit of theatres, too. My

family are fond of the play and go very often, but they don't enjoy themselves as much as they otherwise would when they persuade me to go with them. You see, when I was a reporter on the San Francisco Call I always had a full day's work. I had to do all the police reports, together with any other odd assignments that might turn up, always finishing up by going to seven theatres every evening. I had to write something about each of them, and as a reporter yourself you can understand that with the fag end of my day's work to finish and seven critical notices of high-class performances of the most varied kind to write up, I could not devote that leisure to each play that as a conscientious dramatic critic I should like. Ten minutes here, a quarter of an hour there—that was all I could afford, because there might be a couple more night assignments waiting me at the office. I was very hurried all the time. The result is that when I go to a playhouse now and I have been there about fifteen minutes or half an hour, I begin to fidget around, thinking, 'I shall get all behind if I stay here any longer; I must be off to the other three or four houses, and I have still that murder story to write.' So that the family don't care much about my company at the theatre. That is another example of how bad a surfeit is."

"How long did you continue to keep the San Francisco Call going?"

"Let me see—just about twelve months. At the end of that time I was reduced to such a pitiable condition of mental destitution, was so completely worn out and impoverished in mind and body by the responsibilities of my position, that the editor invited me to resign. I didn't want to be ungrateful to a man who had allowed me to learn so much of different kinds of newspaper work in so short a time, so I resigned. And, mind you, there was very little chance of another job, either—in fact it was three or four months before I got one."

His Autobiography—100 Years Hence!

"Have you been doing much lately with that autobiography that is to be published a hundred years after your death?"

"Oh, yes, I have added a good deal to it from time to time. I only write it when the spirit moves me and don't lay myself out to keep it regularly going. I find it one of the most interesting works I have ever undertaken. There is something very pleasant in thinking that what you are writing won't be published until the person you are writing about and every one who can have any personal affection for him or her is dead. I find I can take such large, calm views of people, so free from flattery on the one hand and from any taint of malice on the other, when I am writing my own unvarnished, unbiased opinions and impressions. There has never been an autobiography or biography or diary or whatever you like to call it that has been written with quite the detachment from all anxiety about what the readers may think of it or its writer as this one of mine. Pepys, you might be disposed to think, was a miracle of candor even at his own expense, but even Pepys wrote with the consciousness that his contemporaries were looking over his shoulder, and despite all he could do he was fettered by a sense of restraint that consciousness produced. I am free from all that and I think that any work undertaken in that spirit and with that intention of quietly and frankly giving a faithful picture of the men of this or any time will be of interest to posterity. It should be a human document of value provided it is reasonably intelligent and above all wholly true to life as the writer sees life and judges it."

"Is it your method to describe events or only men?"

"You can't do one without touching upon the other. When I meet a man or a woman who interests me, and I feel I can write something about them that would be of interest or value to people a hundred years hence, I jot down my impressions. It is just as the fit takes me."

Home and Foreign Elections

"Have you been watching the elections here with any interest?"

"Not very much. I have not had time to read the papers. But from what I can judge the system of appealing to the country here is preferable to ours—I mean it is less of a strain on the country. The dissolution is proclaimed here one day, and the next the arrangements for the elections are in full swing, while by the end of the week a good many members of the new House are elected. We have the elections on one day, but our candidates are nominated way back in June and are not elected until November. I think the strain and dislocation of business here is less. When one district elects its member there is an end of the turmoil as far as that one is concerned, and its constituents just go about their business as usual, looking on at the fight as it proceeds elsewhere. But what I don't understand is why this dissolution has been proclaimed just now. The Government had a big majority, the Opposition had nothing particular to say against the settlement in South Africa that the Government intended, and now after it all it seems that they will get about the same majority that they had before."

"And what do you think about the American campaign?"

"Well, you see, I have only read scraps and snatches of news in the papers here, not sufficient to stir my prejudices or partialities. I am going back to vote—I mean, I shall vote, as I shall happen to be there when the election comes on. I have been paying taxes all the time I have been away, so I suppose I am entitled to exercise the franchise.

Not an Imperialist

"You ask me about what is called imperialism. Well, I have formed views about that question. I am at the disadvantage of not knowing whether our people are for or against spreading themselves over the face of the globe. I should be sorry if they are, for I don't think that it is wise or a necessary development. As to China, I quite approve of our Government's action in getting free of that complication. They are withdrawing, I understand, having done what they wanted. That is quite right. We have no more business in China than in any other country that is not ours. There is the case of the Philippines. I have tried hard, and yet I cannot for the life of me comprehend how we got into that mess. Perhaps we could not have avoided it—perhaps it was inevitable that we should come to be fighting the natives of those islands—but I cannot understand it, and have never been able to get at the bottom of the origin of our antagonism to the natives. I thought we should act as their protector —not try to get them under our heel. We were to relieve them from Spanish tyranny to enable them to set up a government of their own, and we were to stand by and see that it got a fair trial. It was not to be a government according to our ideas, but a government that represented the feeling of the majority of the Filipinos, a government according to Filipino ideas. That would have been a worthy mission for the United States But now—why, we have got into a mess, a quagmire from which each fresh step renders the difficulty of extrication immensely greater. I'm sure I wish I could see what we were getting out of it, and all it means to us as a nation."

"Have you any literary plans for the future?"

"No, but I have some work on hand which I'm getting along with now and then. I have a book half finished, but when the other half will be done the Lord only knows."

His Lumbago Jag

"I need scarcely ask how you are—you look the picture of health?"

"I have been to the doctor lately—nothing more serious than lumbago. I have invested all the capital possible to produce a good, prosperous lumbago. It is not my fault that it didn't succeed."

"What are your plans on returning to America?"

"Our original plan was to stay in New York, as I said, for the winter, and go to Hartford in the spring. I heard to-day, however, that there is a chance of this being altered. I do not complain. I only ask that I shall be told in time to arrange. This is my last day here—we sail in the morning from Tilbury on the American Transport liner Minnehaha. I could not get on one of the fast steamers—they are engaged over and over again. But I don't mind. I like the long voyage, although it is not so agreeable to the family. I am never seasick. Now I must be off to see my friend Poultney Bigelow in Chelsea. I hope the rain has not made it impossible to go on the top of a 'bus. That is the mode of conveyance I prefer in London."

And so, with a hearty handshake and good wishes, Mark Twain departed.

MARK TWAIN HOME, AN ANTI-IMPERIALIST

[New York *Herald*, October 16, 1900]

VIEWS OF THE AUTHOR CHANGED DURING HIS LONG TRAVELS IN FOREIGN
LANDS, BUT HE WILL NOT SUPPORT BRYAN—NOTES OF THE
AUTHOR'S TRIP AROUND THE GLOBE

"Mark Twain," sometime known as Samuel Clemens, returned home last night after an absence in the outside world of five years, and landed on his native shores with a smile of good-natured fun on his lips that even the terrible experiences he has passed through could not dim. The great humorist has triumphed over his own misfortunes, as well as those of others, a thing which is said to be impossible even for philosophers.

"I have had lots of fun," remarked Mr. Clemens, as he came down the gangplank. "I have enjoyed myself, except for a twinge of dyspepsia now and then, in every country and under every sky. Fun has no nationality. It has the freedom of the world. But I think I had most fun in Vienna, with the poor old Reichsrath. I was there for a year and a half, and had plenty of time to take it in. It was one of the biggest jokes I have ever seen, and I enjoyed it immensely.

"Fate has its revenge on the humorist," said Mr. Clemens, after he had got well ashore and felt his legs more secure under him, and could risk a more serious tone. "Now, I have lied so much, in a genial, good-natured way, of course, that people won't believe me when I speak the truth. I may add that I have stopped speaking the truth. It is no longer appreciated—in me.

Do Not Believe the Truth

"I have found that when I speak the truth, I am not believed, and that I have never told a lie so big but that some one had sublime confidence in my veracity. I have, therefore, been forced by fate to adopt fiction as a medium of truth. Most liars lie for the love of the lie; I lie for the love of truth. I disseminate my true views by means of a series of apparently humorous and mendacious stories.

"If any man can do that, and finds that he can disseminate facts through the medium of falsehood, he should never speak the truth— and I don't.

"The English, you know, take everything that is very serious as an immense joke, and everything that is really side splitting as terribly dull. They even pretended to think me jesting when I spoke about writing a history to be read one hundred years after it was written.

"If ever I spoke truth—and at that time I had not given up the habit of resorting to it occasionally—I spoke it then. I was in dead earnest, but of course the English set it down as a great joke.

"Am I really going to write that history? I have never said that I would, and if I said so now no one would believe me. I merely suggested that it would be an ideal sort of narrative that could slash away at sores without fear of hurting any one—not even the author."

"Mr. Clemens, have you had time to give any thought to the grave question of imperialism?" I asked.

Now an Anti-Imperialist

"It is most too grave a question for one of any temperament, but I have taken a try at it. I have thought of it, and it has got the best of me.

"I left these shores, at Vancouver, a red-hot imperialist. I wanted the American eagle to go screaming into the Pacific. It seemed tiresome and tame for it to content itself with the Rockies. Why not spread its wings over the Philippines, I asked myself? And I thought it would be a real good thing to do.

"I said to myself. Here are a people who have suffered for three centuries. We can make them as free as ourselves, give them a government and country of their own, put a miniature of the American constitution afloat in the Pacific, start a brand new republic to take its place among the free nations of the world. It seemed to me a great task to which we had addressed ourselves.

"But I have thought some more, since then, and I have read carefully the treaty of Paris, and I have seen that we do not intend to free, but to subjugate the people of the Philippines. We have gone there to conquer, not to redeem.

"We have also pledged the power of this country to maintain and protect the abominable system established in the Philippines by the Friars.

"It should, it seems to me, be our pleasure and duty to make those people free, and let them deal with their own domestic questions in their own way. And so I am an anti-imperialist. I am opposed to having the eagle put its talons on any other land.

Not for Bryan, However

"But I want to say that I cannot conscientiously support Mr. Bryan. I am not so much of an anti-imperialist as that. I have been told that I cannot vote in this election, but if I could I should not vote for Mr. Bryan. As to what I would do I cannot say, as I am a mugwump, and a mugwump won't vote until he has had plenty of time to look the thing over.

"And then, I don't want to commit myself too far, as, if I find that I cannot vote, I shall run for President. A patriotic American must do something around election time, and that's about the only thing political that is left for me."

"Have you any books about ready for publication?"

"No; but I have several on the way. I wrote myself out in the line of anecdotes and humorous sketches in my last book. I ran short even in that and could barely find enough material to fill it.

"I am now falling back upon fiction; but, as I have said, my fiction is different from the fiction of others. No matter what I write in that line people will think that I am hiding some truth behind the stalking horse of a story."

"Will you have an American story?"

"You see, I write the story and then fill in the place, like blanks in a railway form. The places don't count so much. The story is the thing."

"But you will give your people some of their own types, with characteristic dialect, will you not? And won't that require you to select your scenes first?"

"No, not entirely. Even that can be filled in. It is astonishing how much can be filled in. I rewrote one of my books three times, and each time it was a different book. I had filled in, and filled in, until the original book wasn't there. It had evaporated through the blanks, and I had an entirely new book. I shall write my story, and then lay the scene where I want it, and, if necessary, change other things to suit the places.

Story with Scene in America

"I shall very probably write a story with the scene laid in this country, or I shall place the scene of one of my present uncompleted stories here. This can be done rather handily, after the whole story is written.

"But I am not going to publish another book for at least a year. I have just published a small one, and a book every two or three years is enough."

"Will you have any more like 'Huckleberry Finn' and 'Tom Sawyer?'"

"Perhaps," and Mr. Clemens smiled as he thought of these creations. "Yes, I shall have to do something of that kind, I suppose. But one can't talk about an unwritten book. It may grow into quite a different thing from what one thinks it may be."

When I asked Mr. Clemens to tell some of his experiences of travel, he replied:—

"That is another old story, and almost everything I saw or thought or imagined during my trip around the world has been told in my books.

"I had a very unusual and pleasant experience in Australasia. I was travelling through Australasia and lecturing in the larger cities during the time of the excitement over the Venezuelan boundary dispute.

"When Mr. Cleveland's sizzling message came I thought that the people of the British colonies would feel a little chilly toward me. But I was mistaken. They didn't let it interfere with our relations, and laughed at my jokes just as much as ever.

"I even think they strained a point to laugh, or they laughed sometimes where I didn't intend that they should. I found that they had learned to like me a little through reading my books, and that friendship was warm enough to carry me smilingly through President Cleveland's crisis.

Some Fun in Pretoria

"In Pretoria, also, I had some little fun. It was with the Jameson raiders, who were in jail when I reached there. They were very disconsolate, expecting to be shot, or something of the sort, every morning. I went down to cheer them up a bit.

"I talked to them. I told them that they didn't seem to appreciate the privilege of being confined in a jail. Bunyan, I told them, would not have written the "Pilgrim's Progress" if some one had not shut him up in a cell, and that we should not have had the pleasure of reading "Don Quixote" if Cervantes had not spent several years in prison. Some of the fellows smiled sadly. They didn't appreciate the point of view. I told them that some men went through life without having the privilege they were enjoying."

Mr. Clemens said that five years ago, when he sailed from Vancouver, he was in bad health and spirits, and that there was but one thing that cheered him up—his debts.

"They were so many, that I could afford to be cheerful after I got used to them," he said. "I was determined to pay them off, to the last cent, and I have done it. I finished paying the last debt that I owed to any man about two years and a half ago, or in a little more than two years after I set myself the task of meeting my obligations.

"I had estimated that it would take at least five years, but with good luck and with a far greater appreciation of my efforts to please than I had any right to expect, I was able to pay off every cent in far less time.

"They are gone now, and when they fell from around my neck, I felt like the Ancient Mariner when the dead albatross fell into the sea. I became a new man. I think the hope of paying them made me funnier than usual, for the English people laughed at all my stories."

"I ought not to overlook Mr. Kruger, especially at this time, when he has become almost as interesting a personage as Napoleon at St. Helena. I saw the heroic old man at his capital, Pretoria, at the time of the Jameson raid.

"I had heard so much about him everywhere, read so much about him in every newspaper and magazine of the world, had painted his picture in my brain so often, that I knew him before I saw him. He did not astonish me. He was exactly as I had fancied him.

"He treated me very graciously, and I had a long talk with him. He is just the stalwart old fellow one would imagine, who has read his life story—a great rugged character, that will live."

To Spend Winter in This City

Mr. Clemens says that he has made his plans for at least a year.

"I shall spend the winter in New York, making my home at the Earlington Hotel. I shall spend the time very quietly, doing nothing but reading and writing a little on my books, and doing some little work for the magazines."

"I do not expect to see much of the bright side of the city; that is, I shall not go out much to the theatres and other places of amusement. I expect to keep close and devote my time to reading, smoking and as little work as possible.

"In the spring I shall return to Hartford, Conn., where Mrs. Clemens, my daughters and myself will settle down for some home life, after nine years of wandering up and down on the earth.

"No, I shall not lecture. I have abandoned the lecture tour that I had almost arranged. I did want very much, at one time, to go through the Southern States, where I have not done much travelling, and lecture in the big cities. But I withdrew from the engagement, although $50,000 was offered to me for a hundred lectures.

"I don't want to lecture again, and will not unless forced to do so. I am tired of it and want to rest."

Mr. Clemens is looking as young as he did nine years ago, when he left this country on his first extended tour abroad. His face has as few wrinkles, and there does not seem to be one in that kindly countenance that has not been traced and graven by good nature, fun and laughter. His hair and mustache are a shade whiter, and his form is a little more bowed, but he seems to be in better health than he was in 1891.

He has acquired or accentuated some tricks that accompany the humorist. His drawl is a trifle longer and more pronounced, and he has a trick of bending his knees and throwing back his head as if in preparation for a good story. It is equivalent to one of President Lincoln's "That reminds me."

He left America in 1891 and went to the baths of Aix les Bains; then, in a few months, to Berlin, where he lectured. In 1892 he lived on the Riviera, then retreated again to the German baths, and in 1893 went to Florence, Italy, where he lived for several months, and while there completed "Joan of Arc" and "Pudd'nhead Wilson."

After this he spent two years in France, where he says he wrestled, like Jacob, day and night, but in vain, with the intricacies of the French grammar. He gave it up.

In 1895 he returned for a short time to this country. Then he started on another tour, which embraced Asia, Africa and Australasia.

When the Minnehaha, of the Atlantic Transport Company, reached her pier last night at nine o'clock, there were only a handful of persons on the deck. Most of those had come down to see "Mark

Twain," but they did not make up a good sized reception committee.

When Mr. Clemens came down the gangplank there was some applause and some cries of "Welcome," and nearly every one on the pier came around him and pressed his hands, and hung about in the hope of catching a ray of fun.

They were not disappointed, for the genial humorist, who left his country under clouds of disappointment, came back with sunny smiles, and in a humor that was good natured enough and broad enough to make the whole world sharers in his mood.

"MY IMPRESSIONS OF AMERICA"
MARK TWAIN

[New York *World*, October 21, 1900]

AND KATE CAREW'S IMPRESSIONS OF THE GREAT HUMORIST—AN
INTERVIEW IN WHICH HE REFUSES TO BE INTERVIEWED—
ELUDING THE SUBJECT PROPOSED, HE TALKS ABOUT ALMOST
EVERYTHING ELSE, INCLUDING TRUTH, WAITERS, EARLY BREAK-
FAST, WISDOM AND NOISE—

*The World's clever caricaturist, Kate Carew, was sent the other day
to get Mark Twain's impressions of America.*

*"As he has been away from the United States for some years,"
said the editor, "you might get him to express himself just as if he
were a foreigner coming here for the first time.*

*"Have him tell what he thinks about the bay, the Statue of Liberty,
the policemen, the manners of the people, the hotels, the cabs,
bootblacks, fashions, the theatres and everything else that has interested him in New York."*

*Here is the interview which Miss Carew obtained, in which he
talks about nearly everything else.*

BY MISS KATE CAREW

"The trouble with us in America," said Mark Twain, "is that we
haven't learned to speak the truth."

He was sitting at breakfast opposite an exceedingly embarrassed
young woman who was taking pains to keep her pencil and sketch-
book below the level of the table, because she did not wish to excite
the curiosity of the waiter—though he would be a bold waiter that
betrayed curiosity in the presence of Samuel L. Clemens.

What led up to the remark about truth was that others were
clamoring to see Mark Twain, and the embarrassed young woman
had ventured to say:

"Don't you find that one's time is more respected on the other side?"

"Well, yes," he replied, after a pause occupied in carefully breaking the end off a roll—and I wish I could convey the solemnity of utterance and the long, oft-broken drawl. "Well, yes. I guess—perhaps —it is. Now—in London I always had—a—regular time set for myself. But there—I'd—go—'way down into the—city—and people— would know where to find me, and wouldn't—know—my other— address.

A FIRST IMPRESSION OF MARK TWAIN

He had just come downstairs, and, after trying vainly to get a London paper at the newsstand and contenting himself with a local one, meandered breakfastward. A fresh, spotless little old man, good to look upon and suggesting spring water and much soap, with the more metropolitan advantages of shoe blacking and starched linen. On closer acquaintance he proved not such a very little man, not so very shrunken and not so very old as he seemed at that first glimpse. Great, unaffected dignity he has, great poise, great simplicity and strength. White hairs are not always admirable, I have heard, but Mark Twain's are. They are also beautiful.

"Except friends, of course—but then—no one would think of calling —at ten in the morning—there; and if—they did—one wouldn't hesitate—to—say—'I'm at—breakfast'—or—'I'm—about—to breakfast.'

"But here—well, of course—our—friends—are anxious to see—us, and they—come—whenever—they think they can—find us. And— the—trouble with us in America is we haven't learned how to—speak the—truth—yet.

"If we had it would be—a—pleasure—for me to—tell—my friend— that he was intruding, and he would be—benefited—and not injured.

"Now, it is an—art—high art—to speak the—truth—so that the object does not object—does not become offended. The trouble—is— with our social laws. The only—way to get reform is to—educate— both sides—one to—give, the other to—receive; one to tell the truth, the—other to—listen to it without—getting—mad."

A pause. A longer pause than usual. An abominably protracted pause. A pause hovering on the abyss of irretrievable silence. Heavens! Would he say no more? He whom it had been so much trouble to coax into speaking at all? It was a desperate chance. I broke in, hardly knowing what I was saying:

"But I always thought that the art was in telling lies, and—and telling the truth seems so easy!"

The waiter flitted forward, and then vanished, like a wraith, with an empty dish. Mark Twain took a mouthful of coffee and carefully dabbed his mustache with his napkin. I was admiring his hands— delicate, pinky-white hands matching the pinky-white cheeks of a wholesome old man.

"Don't believe it," he said, dropping his napkin to his knee. "Lying—is not an art—not that I have ever been able to—discover— and I have—tried—hard all my life. It is a—device—of primitive intelligences. The best—liars—are savages and—children. The most cultured—people—speak the truth as often as they—think about it, and enjoy—hearing it spoken by—others. In heaven I shouldn't won- der but they—use—the truth—most of the time."

I had been listening too hard to do much work, though there was never a more tempting head for pencil or brush than this silver-crowned one. He observed my inertia, and inquired, with a touch of fatherly reproof:

"Are you getting—what—you wanted?"

"Not much," I replied, all confusion. "Only a few notes."

"Notes!" He half rose from his chair. "Notes!" There was a sudden drawing down of his shaggy eyebrows.

"An artist's notes, you know," I hastened to explain. "Just scratches on the paper—an eyebrow, a wrinkle, a coat collar."

He sank back, much relieved.

"Make all the notes—that kind of notes—you want to," he said. "So long as—you—don't interview me, I—don't care. I won't be interviewed. I don't—approve—of interviews; don't like them—on—principle."

This was not a very good omen for further conversation. I tried him on Vienna, having caught a glimpse of him there two years ago. This recollection of mine did not excite him perceptibly. I remarked that it was a beautiful little city. Yes, beautiful, he confessed into his mustache. I told him how my travelling companion and I had felt tempted to speak to him, but had found ourselves incapable of taking such a liberty.

"You might—just—as well," he said, with a vague look in the eyes which suggested memories of other travelling Americans who had been less diffident. "That would have—been—all right." He waved a reminiscently hospitable hand. "I would not have hurt—you."

Of his experiences in Vienna and his friendships there—not a word. Paris, London—the same.

New York? If I could only get this most taciturn of humorists and philosophers to tell his impressions of America—not a whole budget of impressions, just one or two tiny ones that might escape his determination not to be interviewed!

Ah, what a master of the art of silence is Mark Twain! The skyscrapers? Not a word. The torn-up streets? Not a word. Rapid transit? Not a word. Politics? Not a word. Noise? Let me see.

"Don't you find New York very noisy after the quiet of European cities?" I ventured.

"No; it doesn't annoy me," he said. "I don't—hear it. You don't have to hear—noise—unless you want to. The only time I hear the elevated—is—when it—stops."

The waiter flitted back with a note. Another caller.

"They don't do this—sort of—thing—in London," he remarked. "There one can—breakfast—between 10 and 12 in beautiful—safety. I don't know why I breakfast at—the same hour—here. It's just habit, I guess. The early breakfast habit is one of—the American institutions —I admire most—when I am abroad.

"But these early morning—calls—are meant in a kindly spirit. They touch my heart, even when—the coffee gets—cold."

It would be impossible to exaggerate the composure and gravity with which Mark Twain utters his quaintnesses—and I'm sure he wasn't in much of a mood for quaintnesses that morning. There is no after-gleam of self-appreciation, no swift glance to see how his point has "taken." I am sure he does not try to say funny things, only he sees life through a glass that distorts every fact into a paradox. Or perhaps it is the serious people that have a distorted view of life. I wish Mark Twain would say what he thinks about it.

You can't imagine anything more solemn than the atmosphere he carries with him. I, in my innocence, had pictured to myself one who would be surrounded with faces wreathed in smiles. In fancy

I had heard waiters giggling behind their napkins and seen the hotel clerk with a broad smile repeating "Mr. Clemens's latest" to an admiring circle.

But, bless your heart! they all walk on tiptoe and speak in awed whispers when Mr. Clemens appears. His long residence abroad has taught him to expect the ministration of servants whose parents were servants, who will be servants all their lives, and whose children will be servants. Europe spoils many good Americans for the free and easy "help" of their own dear land, and I fancy that Mark Twain finds it so.

He had occasion to send for the head waiter and ask him why something hadn't been done, or why it hadn't been done sooner. He didn't scold, he just said:

"You understand, it's better—for me to—know—about these things, so I'll know what to do about it next time."

The tremulous head waiter explained that there had been something the matter with the speaking-tube by which the original order had been transmitted.

"Oh, that was it, was it?" said Mr. Clemens. "I just wanted to—know." And then, turning to me, he added: "I don't suppose we—have a right—to know as much as cooks and—waiters, anyway."

They know him now, after having him with them for a week, and it's safe to say that there isn't a person in New York better waited on than Samuel L. Clemens, who has made more people laugh than any other living man.

MARK TWAIN BEARDED IN HIS NEW YORK DEN BY A CAMERA FIEND

[New York *Herald*, January 20, 1901]

WON'T BE INTERVIEWED IN ANY CITY AFTER THE FIRST TWENTY-FOUR HOURS THERE, BUT CONSENTED TO CARRY HIS STUDY ATMOSPHERE ALONG WITH HIS TRAVELLING BAG ON A BOSTON TRAIN, WHEREON HE DISCUSSES SOME DEPRAVITIES OF HUMAN NATURE

Mark Twain in his study, a brown study, can be a very serious man. There is about him a calm, benevolent dignity, a practical belligerence toward those misguided human beings who have everything to get, as it were. He feels a parental sympathy tempered with a judicial tendency for the depravities of human nature.

He approaches each phase of human weakness with an earnest, kindly care that explains the world wide affection his books have gained for him.

When I talked with him the local atmosphere of New York city was dark with depraved conditions. The shadow that had threatened the decencies of life for so many years in this city had but just been illumined by indignant men and women.

The night before Mark Twain had stood up with Bishop Potter in defence of clean politics.

It was quite understood that he was not to be interviewed in New York. Mark Twain is a disciplinarian; he subdues all difficulties with fixed ironbound rules.

For the first twenty-four hours that he arrives in a new city he receives everybody, and will talk to every one who asks for an opinion; after that, as he himself puts it, "Never again, in that city, forever and ever."

This fact was emphatically impressed upon me by the author, in the hushed atmosphere of his study.

Mark Twain's study has never been presented to the public eye before, nor has it ever been possible to secure so faithful a record of this author actually at work, until now. The special interest in these pictures is their faithful record of Mark Twain in a serious mood—Mark Twain, as he sits at his desk, conspiring against the evils of human nature.

Realizing that I was not supposed to obtain any opinions, I took a seat beside the desk, looked into the pleasant, cheerful countenance of a wood fire, and silently resigned my curiosity to the camera.

There it stood, on its three long legs, staring greedily at the great man, who silently ignored it with patient tolerance.

So we three sat in silence some five minutes, Mark Twain, Mark Camera and myself. The room was very quiet, particularly suited to studious reverie. Somewhere beyond the door we heard the occasional rustle of a feather duster, a whispering voice, and far off, as far away as possible without going into the street, some one was practising vocal music.

Slowly the author opened his letters with a paper knife and turned his correspondence inside out.

In the Forbidden City

At last, moved by a sense of companionship, or a desire to share the literary musings of a quiet half hour, he leaned back in his chair, and, turning a closely written four page letter over and over, that no pen stroke of it should escape investigation, he spoke.

But, alas! it was in the forbidden city of New York, one of the cities where he would not be interviewed, "Never again, forever and ever."

While the artist has faithfully recorded a reminiscent study of Mark Twain as I saw him in his den in New York, the actual spoken thoughts of the man himself had been given me under bond of secrecy, as it were, the social seal of privacy stamped upon them.

"Is there no place where we can revive the memories of this half hour in vivid type?" I asked, as I was leaving.

He told me he was going to Boston on the 14th of the month, discovering that this would be his first trip there since his return from Europe.

I determined to make a geographical compromise, rather than lose a pen and ink sketch of Mark Twain in a serious mood.

So it was agreed that we should meet on the train at Worcester, and there resume the inspiration I had gathered from the author in his study. It so happened when I boarded the train that the author was looking over his mail and enjoying his latest pipe, patented in Ireland.

I turned my back upon the landscape as we sped by, watched the author attentively, and felt as if we were together in his study in New York, as we had been a few days ago.

"There's a strange thing," he said slowly, and read aloud portions of a letter. It was from the daughter of an old friend. She recalled having seen the celebrated author at her father's house when she was a little girl. She had been married since then and lost her father. Also, she had been unfortunate, and was in destitute circumstances. She possessed a painting by the animal painter, Beard, which her father had purchased for $500.

Would Mark Twain buy it for $150?

Slowly and deliberately the author answered this communication aloud, addressing his correspondent with practical kindliness, as if she were there before him.

Values, Present and Posthumous

"Well! If I could buy a painting by a famous artist that was worth $500 when he was alive, I should certainly not pay a cent less for it after he was dead. It seems to me it ought to be worth more, since he has passed away. I remember seeing a picture of his of some bears. They were wonderful; the creatures were human beings in everything but their shapes."

Up went the value of Beard's picture, and a momentary resentment of reducing the value of this particular one showed itself in the author's countenance.

"Women are impractical in the face of trouble sometimes!" I suggested.

"Yes, they run to extremes both ways. They either ask you four times as much as a thing is worth, or not half enough. Of course I can't buy the picture, but I should think the Museum of Art ought to have it."

A reflective pause followed, in which the commercial instinct which is no small factor in Mark Twain's success crystallized.

"Of course, if the Museum of Art in New York can get this painting for $150 they won't pay any more for it. As a corporation, it would be their duty to pay no more for it," argued the author, then, tempering his worldly reason with sympathy for the writer of this letter, he laid it aside, saying, "I will not send it to the Museum of Art. I'll see if I can't find some one who will pay full price because he knows it is worth it."

It was evident that if Mark Twain had not been gifted as a writer he would have been a successful business agent.

Two more letters were opened and laid aside with the faintest suspicion of a sigh.

"I can't do it. There isn't money enough in New York or Boston to go round."

He hadn't spoken to me, but had answered a condition of depravity in human nature that his letters had revealed.

"I suppose they can't help it; it's a dreadful habit, though."

"More requests for money?" I asked.

"Yes. I don't mind helping people I know; friends should depend on each other when the world doesn't treat them well, but no wonder the figures of Charity are made to look so haughty and stuck up in statues."

Mechanically he took a puff or two at his big pipe, and looking out of the window, surveyed human nature comfortably.

All the World a Beggar

"We're all beggars, more or less, the whole lot of us. It is a depraved condition in all of us. One man, in good clothes, asks a favor, another asks for a quarter because he's hungry. I asked a man to give me the address of another man. He mailed it to me. I might just as well have found it out myself, but by begging I saved myself exertion and trouble.

"I remember a certain day in San Francisco, when, if I hadn't picked up a dime that I found lying in the street, I should have asked some one for a quarter. Only a matter of a few hours and I'd have been a beggar. That dime saved me, and I have never begged—never!"

He was distinctly proud of this fact, not for his own strength of achievement, but for a fortunate escape from violation of his principle. A good deal of fun has been made of Mark Twain's endeavors to arouse New Yorkers to a sense of their rights of citizenship. His recent resentment of a cabman's attempted extortion was only a shade of the principle and uprightness that make the ideal American citizen.

There is no one living in New York to-day who is more sanely equipped with an insight of the depravities in human nature than Mark Twain. His nature is so strong in its original simplicity that he bristles at the mere suggestion of an abuse as a cat will at the sight of a dog.

The Postmaster of New York city loomed up in the unpleasant guise of an autocrat to the author's vision.

"Why do we have to go down to the Post Office and present an official with a carefully revised edition of our family tree before we can get a registered letter?" asked Mark Twain, glancing at me, as if I were the Postmaster.

"Abominable!" I said, soothingly.

"I didn't do it. I refused to do it. I received a notice that a registered letter had got into the United States for me, from Europe, and a request to go down town and confide the secrets of my family history to prove that I was not attempting to defraud the authorities. I sent my colored boy down with a note and got the letter."

"You were favored," I suggested.

"Why should I be? Why should the Postmaster break a rule that he considers necessary for the proper transaction of his official business for one man, and enforce it for others? Something wrong about the rule."

"Local tyranny," I suggested.

The European Plan

"No such trouble in Europe. A registered letter means important letter to the authorities over there, and they can't get it into your hands too quickly. Not only that, but you're not obliged to receive it if you don't want it. Nearly all begging letters abroad are sent by registered mail, so that you can't say you didn't receive them. I never accepted a registered letter unless the handwriting was familiar to me after awhile."

"Do they write begging letters in Europe?"

"Oceans of them. They have a habit of enclosing soiled and time-worn letters and documents of recommendation, signed by famous people who are not on earth to deny them. I used to leave them with the hall porter of the hotel, with a note thanking them for the opportunity afforded me of reading their testimonials, and stating that they could receive them intact from the hands of the porter."

I suggested that these letter writers made a mark of celebrated men, who had been poor themselves, relying on fellow sympathy and so on.

"All the professional beggars, or rather the men and women afflicted with the complaint, need are a name and address. They scan the newspapers for arrivals at the hotels, and labor diligently in this way to make a living."

He handed me a letter on which was printed the statement that the sender, having a "nice collection of autographs," would be quite willing to add Mark Twain's to the collection. A stamped envelope, addressed to Bloomington, Ill., completed the bargain so far as he was concerned.

Too Rich for the Twain Blood

"What gorgeous type," mused the author, grimly.

"There's another phase of human depravity, the organized autograph hunter. Now, I don't object to answering a letter if the writer will show me the common courtesy of using pen, ink and notepaper to address me, but when he goes to a printing machine, and seems to begrudge the time he must spend to write me personally, I don't feel compelled to answer him. I can't afford a printing press in my establishment to turn out my correspondence in colored inks, bound and folded automatically. I still have to use the primitive methods of correspondence. He's too rich for my blood," and he laid the letter aside.

"How often have you been photographed?" I asked, as I showed him the pictures taken in his den in New York.

"Twenty-three times in twenty-three minutes the day before yesterday," was the answer.

"Harpers wanted to be sure to get something lifelike," explained Mark Twain. "I felt as a moving picture must feel going at full speed. It's wonderful how ugly we are sometimes, too, when we get a real, good, faithful likeness. No one would have believed a horse was such a homely acting animal till we got a picture of him in action. It won't do for us to be too self-conscious in these snapshot days of inquiry. Now, I said a thing last night in a speech that I didn't mean to say. It just slipped out because I had been writing an article on the subject. I didn't intend to say it there."

It was in reference to the Presidential policy in the Philippines. I showed him the paragraph as reported in the daily papers.

"There it is, sure enough. Now, I don't believe in saying a thing that is an opinion but once, in one way, at one time and in one place, and I did not intend to say it last night, though I have substantially written about it, fully."

"You do not approve of the policy of the administration in the Philippines?" I asked indifferently.

"If we desire to become members of the international family let us enter it respectably, and not on the basis at present proposed in Manila. We find a whole heap of fault with the war in South Africa, and feel moved to hysterics for the sufferings of the Boers, yet we don't seem to feel so very sorry for the natives in the Philippines."

"Another phase of depravity," I suggested.

"That's it. Human nature is selfish, and it's only real noble for profit."

"Have you been to the opera?" I asked.

"Once; the other night." He spoke with the slow utterance of re-served thought and a little sadly, I thought.

"You don't like it?"

The Disappointment of Too Much

"Yes—and—no. I think opera is spoiled by attempting to combine instrumental and vocal effects. I love instrumental music and I love a good voice, but I don't like them together. It's too generous. I can't fully take it in. Either the instruments spoil the voice or the voice spoils the instruments."

He got up, restlessly shaking off discordant operatic memories, and picked up a book.

"Here's an illustration of what I mean. This is a Scotch story, sent to me by a lady who is the authoress, and when I began to read it, I found that she had got a man to tell the story for her. I expected to hear a simple Scotch tale from the lips of a charming woman and I get a duet, as it were, with a man. The surprise of finding so much more than I expected was a disappointment. And yet I approve of her idea in one way. You see, the story is all about an old lord, and as it required a very constant and intimate companionship with him to tell the story at all, it was absolutely necessary that a man should be employed by her to figure in her stead. She had a truly Scottish sense of the proprieties. It would have been quite improper for an authoress to tell so much about an old lord, except through another's lips."

I showed him one of the photographs taken at his desk.

"Now, if Mrs. Clemens had come in and seen that desk being photographed in this shape she would have been aghast at its apparent disorder. But that is not disorder. I know exactly where everything is, top and bottom, from a telegraph blank in its hiding place to a manuscript or a letter. What looks like disorder to some people is the best of order to others.

"My mother had the same disordered sense of order that I have. I might buy her reams and reams of the most magnificent note paper, blue, green, red, pale peacock, anything you like; it was no use. She never would write on anything but odd scraps. Many's the letter I've received from her written on uneven scraps of paper, different colors and qualities all bunched together in an envelope and unpaged. My mother's letters were as hard to understand as any problem book I ever read."

For the first time since we had been talking Mark Twain laughed at his loving reminiscence of her tender frailties.

Mark Twain is great because of his simplicity, his honesty and his intelligent antagonism to even the minor "depravities of human nature"—and his objection to being interviewed.

PENDENNIS

MARK TWAIN WOULD CONVERT TAMMANY POLICE

[New York *Herald,* October 14, 1901]

HUMORIST INSISTS HIS PROSELYTING IN THIS FIELD IS NO JOKE—SEED IN FRUITFUL SOIL—FIRST CONVERT ISN'T PARTICULARLY ENTHUSIASTIC, BUT HE'LL VOTE RIGHT ON ELECTION DAY

Mark Twain has declined regretfully to take the stump for Seth Low, because, he says, he cannot persuade folks to take him seriously, even in his most lofty flights of spellbinding eloquence.

Among his new neighbors up in the pastoral suburb of Riverdale it is whispered, however, that Mr. Clemens is conducting a subtle still hunt in the interest of the fusion ticket. He has set himself the herculean task, they say, of converting the rank and file of the Tammany police force to reform principles between now and election day, and in his mildly insinuating manner has made already astonishing headway.

For the purpose of persuading Mr. Clemens to report progress a reporter for the HERALD called upon him in his charming new home in the Appleton Mansion, overlooking the Hudson River. It is a spacious stone house, with a roomy hall in the centre, in which appear many of the humorist's cherished trophies, gathered from all parts of the world. Standing back from the road, the house is shaded by fine old trees, on whose limbs countless squirrels were romping in the autumn rainfall. Mr. Clemens and his family moved into the Appleton Mansion on October 2, and since then have been enjoying the enchanting atmosphere of their rural home.

"Sh-h-h! Not so loud," said the author of "Tom Sawyer," with a warning finger at his lips. "Yes, it is too true, but if I am discovered I am lost.

"You see, I have undertaken this proselyting effort wholly on my own responsibility, and with only the tacit support of the fusion Campaign Committee. I understand that 'Billy' Leary was not even consulted about it. The fact is, my advisers thought it would be better so. In this way the Campaign Committee does not have to pay heavy sums for my services, and in the event of my imperfect success the disgrace of failure falls upon my own head alone and does not dishonor the cause. The report that the enemy has tried to buy me off by offering a life interest in the profits of the Police Department is a base canard.

No Bribes from Opposition

"I violate no confidence when I say that I have not yet been approached either by Mr. Croker or Senator Sullivan. I have entered upon this crusade without promise of reward or emolument, either by Mr. Low or Mr. Shepard. It is a labor of love.

"I will tell you in confidence that I am much encouraged. I began my campaign on a Tammany policeman whom I met the other day at my gate. Personal suasion is my long suit. I am more successful at that than I am on the stump, though I used much good cart-tail eloquence on this particular policeman, and I could see that he was impressed. I convinced him that there was no authentic record of any Tammany man ever having gone to heaven. But, while he seemed measurably pleased by my attentions, I noticed that he appeared to restrain his enthusiasm. I soon saw that this was a very judicious policeman, the kind who does not blurt right out all the things that may be in his mind and so does not get transferred oftener than twice a week.

"Well, now, I'm willing to bet you a squirrel's nest that if this policeman were watched on election day he would be found voting for Seth Low. If I were a policeman I should do just what I think this policeman intends to do. I should let Tammany think I was with them right up to the time I marked my ballot, and then I should vote according to my conscience, but I should be careful not to make any improper exposure of my conscience to the public view beforehand.

"I don't know just when I will be able to approach the other men on the force, but I regard this particular policeman as a rather promising convert. At least, I have impressed him with a sense of my interest in his personal salvation, and I am pleased to think that he may keep a special eye on these premises, for you know there has been a band of burglars operating around here rather actively of late, and I have no means of knowing with which party they are affiliated.

Neighbors Scoff at Him

"I am really fearful that Tammany may have heard something of my political activity up here. Certain of my new neighbors who are democrats are throwing out dark hints that they will challenge my vote if I attempt to poll it on election day. They even insinuate that I am no better than any other vulgar thirty day colonizer, and have just come up here to electioneer and then get in my vote. Of course it is a fact that I have not been thirty days in this district, and this may subject me to suspicion in the eyes of a partisan. I have tried to assure my neighbors that I am above such sordid motives, and that I will have lived here a full month before election day, but still they look at me askance and talk about watching the house to see if cheap cots are being carried into it.

"In one of the daily papers I saw a notice—not in agate, nonpareil or minion type, which is soft and soothing—but in the heavy, black-face characters which jar one, to the effect that I dare not register nor vote, because the last registration day is October 19, and unless I perjure myself I could not swear on that date that I had lived thirty days in Riverdale. Now, I do not wish to perjure myself unless there be strong provocation, and, being a good republican, I feel great respect for Mr. McCullagh's deputies. So I think of asking Mr. Croker to grant me a special dispensation and permit me to register all by myself on October 31."

When Mr. Clemens' attention was called to the rumor that Mr. Croker thought of taking a house in Riverdale for the winter, and so might become one of his neighbors, the author smiled delightfully, and said, with a twinkle of the eye:—

"Wouldn't that be charming? I should then certainly ask the Tammany chief to take my family as lodgers and boarders. I should feel so much more secure from burglars, sneak thieves and second story men if I could only feel that Mr. Croker's protecting aegis were spread over us and our household gods. Think what such an arrangement would save me in the cost of burglar alarms, special watchmen, firearms and patent electric doormats!"

His Real Campaign Work

Becoming more serious, Mr. Clemens said that while he did not intend to make any speeches for Mr. Low during the campaign, he had written an article on Tammany and Croker for the November issue of the North American Review.

"Apart from the suspicion that I may be a thirty-day colonizer," added the humorist, "I have been 'pleasantly welcomed by every inhabitant' of Riverdale, except the little squirrels in the trees about my house. These little chaps seem to resent my invasion of their playground. They chatter and scold at me incessantly, as though they would say, 'We don't like the way you are acting around here, Mr. Clemens. We were here long before you, anyhow, Mr. Clemens, and don't you think you are just a bit of an interloper?'

"Lord bless you," the genial merrymaker concluded, with a toss of his long, gray shock of hair and a parting handclasp, "these little squirrels have a heap of sense.

"Now, don't betray my police still hunt to the public," was his final injunction. "Shepard and Croker and Devery might bring such pressure to bear upon the structure of my moral integrity as to cause some of its girders to buckle under the strain."

"MY FIRST VACATION AND MY LAST"— MARK TWAIN

[New York *World*, September 7, 1902]

AN INTERVIEW AT HIS MAINE RETREAT WITH THE GREAT HUMORIST, WHO DECLARES THAT HE IS NEVER INTERVIEWED EXCEPT IN FOREIGN COUNTRIES, BUT WHO FINALLY CONCEDES, WITH DOOLEY, THAT MAINE IS OUTSIDE THE BORDER, AND SO TALKS FREELY BETWEEN SMOKES—ABOUT THE NEW NOVEL ON WHICH HE IS AT WORK—ABOUT MARY MACLANE, FUNSTON AND WALTER SCOTT—ABOUT THE ASSESSMENT OF HIS TARREYTOWN PROPERTY—AND ABOUT HIS FIRST VACATION, SIXTY YEARS AGO, WHEN HE STOLE HIS FIRST RIDE ON A MISSISSIPPI RIVER STEAMBOAT

Mark Twain, the great humorist, is spending his vacation at York Harbor, Me. The place, if Mr. Funston or any of the Denver Library people care to know, is in that exact spot frequently referred to as the southeastern part of the State.

The genial philosopher has been enjoying the summer working there since early in July, and he says that he is going to do his best to hold out at his cottage until the eleventh day of October. As to the reason for the "eleventh" he absolutely refuses to commit himself.

In about a year the reading public, however, will be very thankful to York Harbor. For the novel upon which Mark Twain is now engaged will be issued then and he says that the bracing sea air that comes to him in his retreat is helping him to do fine work.

He hasn't wholly succeeded, though, in keeping care off his porch and the forty acres that surround his cottage, perched high above the waters of York River, for in the early part of August Mrs. Clemens fell sick with heart failure, and since then her famous husband has been nursing her back to health.

The writer for The World's Sunday Magazine discovered the author of "Tom Sawyer" the other day walking slowly to and fro on the lawn. Now, Mark Twain has made it a rule to be interviewed only when in a foreign country or when coming from or going to a strange land. But here it was proved beyond all doubt or peradventure that "Huckleberry Finn's" creator is a humorist, for he laughed at and agreed to the logic of another man's joke.

"I—am—only—interviewed," began the sage, with the deliberate, premeditated and immortal Mark Twain drawl, "in—foreign—countries."

He Surrenders—Humorously

A most decided and dramatic period after "countries."

"But you know, Mr. Clemens; Misther Dooley speaks in thim furrin' countries, such as Harrlem an' Hoboken an' Maine."

"He does," he said, with his hearty smile, "he does. I guess"—a pause which would easily give him an opportunity to change his mind twenty times—"I guess I'll have to give in."

Then he led the way into the house, excusing himself for a moment "just to see how Mrs. Clemens was getting along." He returned presently.

"So you want me to tell you about my first vacation," he said. "My first vacation?"

Very deliberately he took from his vest pocket a long black deadly looking cigar. Then, after groping for an interminable time in his coat pocket, he pulled out three matches and placed them side by side on the table. He was very particular about those matches, for he rearranged them six times.

"That was long ago."

A pause.

"That"—the matches again engage his attention—"was sixty years ago."

He lit the cigar—not placing it in his mouth, but assuring himself that he had a good light before the match was wholly consumed.

A pause certainly of three minutes.

He puffed at his cigar three or four times, but only mechanically.

It became very clear indeed that he was away back in his boyhood days again with Tom Sawyer and Huckleberry Finn, wading in the Mississippi or playing leap-frog in the dusty streets of Florida, Mo.

Recalls His First Vacation

"Ah, I shall never forget that first vacation," he said. "It wasn't as long as this one, nor in some respects as pleasant, but"—very slowly—"what it lacked in length it made up in excitement.

"Do you know what it means to be a boy on the banks of the Mississippi, to see the steamboats go up and down the river, and never to have had a ride on one? Can you form any conception of what that really means? I think not.

"Well, I was seven years old and my dream by night and my longing by day had never been realized. But—I—guess—it—came—to—pass. That—was—my—first—vacation."

A pause.

"One day when the big packet that used to stop at Hannibal swung up to the mooring at my native town, a small chunk of a lad might have been seen kiting on to the deck and in a jiffy disappearing from view beneath a yawl that was placed bottom up.

"I was the small chunk of a lad.

"They called it a life-boat," said Mr. Clemens, "but it was one of that kind of life-boats that wouldn't save anybody.

After That It Rained

"Well, the packet started along all right, and it gave me great thrills of joy to be on a real sure-enough steamboat. But just then it commenced to rain. Now, when it rains in the Mississippi country it rains. After the packet had started I had crawled from beneath it and was enjoying the motion of the swift-moving craft. But the rain drove me to cover and that was beneath the yawl. No. It was not a life-boat, for the manner in which that rain came pouring down upon me from the bottom of that yawl made me wonder if I was ever to return home again.

"To add to the fun the red-hot cinders from the big stacks came drifting down and stung my legs and feet with a remorseless vigor, and if it hadn't been a steamboat that I was on I would have wanted to be safe at home in time for supper.

"Well, it kept on raining and storming generally until toward evening, when, seventeen miles below Hannibal, I was discovered by one of the crew."

A very deliberate pause.

"They put me ashore at Louisiana."

Another pause.

"I was sent home by some friends of my father's.

"My father met me on my return."

A twinkle in the steel-blue eyes. "I remember that quite distinctly."

Then as an afterthought: "My mother had generally attended to that part of the duties of the household, but on that occasion my father assumed the entire responsibility."

Reminiscently: "That was my first vacation and its ending"—he bit his cigar—"and I remember both.

"So now, sixty years after that event," emphasis on "event," "I'm enjoying another vacation at the age, I believe, of sixty-seven.

Stronger Mentally Than Ever

"Fact of it is," he drawled, "the best part of a man's life is after he is sixty. I feel stronger, mentally, now, than ever before."

He lit another of those ominous looking cigars. Their mere appearance compels comment. You express surprise that the first one was not guilty of murder.

"No. Smoking doesn't seem to affect my health at all. Perhaps though, that's because I only take one smoke a day." A brief pause and with a flash of humor from his eyes—"That commences in the morning and ends just before I go to bed. But, Lord bless me! I like to smoke and have since I was seven years old. That first smoke was a fine one, but it made me very sick. I rolled a cigar from green tobacco and when my father found out about it he did the rest.

"I find," he added seriously, "that smoking aids me while I am engaged in writing."

He looked far out to sea.

"This bracing salt air makes me do good work," he said. "I work harder in the summer than in any other season of the year. Just at present, because of Mrs. Clemens's illness, I am not doing much writing, but up to the 11th of August I was busily engaged upon the novel that isn't finished yet, though I've been at it for four years. It's to be a fantastic book," he added, "not so serious as Joan d'Arc—it took me twelve years to write that—but up to the present I can't tell how the book is going to end. Confidentially, I won't know until it's finished.

"In fact," said the humorist, "that's the purpose of the book."

He placed his hands on the table as he spoke. They are the hands of a strong man, of a worker, prehensile yet artistic and with nails which are kept in beautiful condition. In shaking hands with him you note that while his hands are as soft as a woman's, there is a manly vigor in the grip he gives you that carries with it instantly the mark of good-fellowship and kindliness.

He spoke of his recent trip to the scenes of his boyhood days, and told how he met his chum and playmate, John Briggs.

"Together," said the Mark Twain of "Huckleberry Finn," in serious tones, "we visited some of the scenes of our former crimes and misdemeanors."

Meditatively—"Stealing apples, though, isn't a crime or a misdemeanor. The elements of danger and self-hero worship are too largely involved in the deed.

"What I consider a crime was the act of John Briggs and myself when we got hold of a boat along the Mississippi at Hannibal and painted it red over its coat of white. Just as we had finished our job the owner of the boat appeared and 'lowed that if that boat had been white he would have sworn that it was his own."

Who Finally Got the Boat?

As to whether or not the boat ever got back into the hands of the original owner Mr. Clemens refused to say.

He did talk freely, however, about his now famous letter written from his vacation retreat on Aug. 14 to a Denver friend anent the attempt to exclude "Huckleberry Finn" from the Denver Public Library. "Now, that was a very funny thing about that letter getting into print," he said. "You see I sent it to my man marked 'Private,' and that was a sure sign that it was going to be published. That is the reason I don't care to be interviewed, too. You see, it puts it up to the other man."

He lights his fourth cigar. "If I write a letter and then it is published through the carelessness or base intent of the man to whom it is sent, I am not being directly interviewed for the benefit of the readers of a paper, but am only expressing a private opinion, which, however much I might mean it, was only intended for the man to whom the letter was written.

"But as to Denver," he drawled, "it isn't so far removed from Butte, Montana. I subscribe for a weekly paper which gets here every two weeks, and I learn from that that Mary MacLane is exploring the East for The World.

"Is the young woman a genie," he asked, "or is her book a composite of thoughts that had been written before?"

Can't Take Her Word for It

It was suggested to the genial philosopher that he take the lady's word for it.

"But I can't," he said, "in view of her frank declarations about her own mendacity."

He sat there smoking his fourth cigar. In the advertising papers of a monthly on the table before him was a picture of Sir Walter Scott. Looking at the picture with evident affection, he said:

"There never was a man in the history of all literature who was confronted by so gigantic a task as that undertaken by Scott in his magnificent effort to rid himself of a mountain of debts for which he was not responsible."

Yet, but a few years before, the man who had paid this tribute to Sir Walter Scott had himself won the admiration of the world for a transaction similar in almost every detail.

He went upstairs again "to see about Mrs. Clemens," saying as he left, "Now, make yourself as comfortable as you can."

The room in which much of his writing is done is large and cheery, with everywhere the evidence of woman's taste—and an author's carelessness. An edition of Saintine's "Picciola" lay on a table in the centre of the room. One of the villainous-looking cigars had been left on it, presumably to frighten burglars.

Upon the mantelpiece was a huge bouquet of golden rod, Mrs. Clemens's favorite flower, and on either side of it were pipes and bric-a-brac. In one corner of the room was a tobacco cabinet and on top of it lay the brother of the "Missouri meerschaum" corn-cob pipe that Rudyard Kipling once hungered for.

Wears a Real Panama

In another corner was a roomy window-seat, and upon it had been thrown the Panama which, on the lawn, the lord of the demesne had earlier referred to "not as a nearly but a real one." The morning mail—some twenty or thirty letters—had been dumped into it.

"We'll take a look 'round," he said, as he stepped to the veranda, "and then you can take the pictures you've hinted at"—a pause—"I believe."

The blue sea stretched away to the eastward, while between it and the delightful spot where Mark Twain is spending the summer the deep and silent waters of York River glided by.

His Funny Assessment

"This is almost as good as my Tarrytown place," he said, with a chuckle. Evidently he was thinking of the famous over-assessment.

"When a friend of mine," he continued, "heard that I had been assessed $70,000 for the property there that I had paid $45,000 for, he asked me why I didn't sell the property to Tarrytown. That wouldn't be bad, now, would it?"

"This is as good a place as any," he remarked, with the kodak prospect still in mind. Then, with the greatest good nature, the King of Humor posed in the pine woods for several characteristic photographs.

Very evidently Mark Twain's sojourn at York Harbor is doing him a world of good.

Bronzed and ruddy, with clear eye and alert step, he is the picture of perfect health. Yet walking is his only exercise. The pleasures of boating, bathing, golfing or driving do not appeal to him.

MARK TWAIN'S DOOR OPEN TO BURGLARS

[New York *Herald*, June 15, 1903]

HUMORIST DEPLORES FACT THAT HE HAS BEEN OVERLOOKED IN RE-
CENT RAIDS—FULL LARDER FOR THEM—FEELING OF KINSHIP
PROMPTS HIM TO INVITE THEM IF THEY "HUSTLE"

Undisturbed by the recent activity of thieves in the Bronx, Mark
Twain, at his home at Riverdale, in the extreme northern end of the
borough, expressed himself yesterday as not averse to the powers
that prey on his neighbors.

"I just wish I knew the fellows on my route," said the humorist,
his eyes twinkling with merriment. "I have been expecting them about
here, and from feelings of brotherhood, if for no more noble reason,
I have been intending to give them a warm reception. My larder
is open to them, and if they smoke they can have the best in the
box. You know all we literary people and second story men have a
good deal akin. We all travel in groups. We work one neighborhood
until we feel that we have sapped the lemon dry and then we move
on to more fruitful soil. I don't know, but I am ready to believe
that the gentlemen who visited Riverdale and stolen everything they
could lay their hands on are now laying away treasure down in Ohio
and some other rich preserve of the Union. These grafters are pretty
wise fellows. They know when they have been long enough in one
neighborhood and when their victims seem to have become tired of
them.

"There is such a thing as despoiling even the fatted calf, and these
fellows understand that as well as we do. I'd like to meet the
gentlemen who have this route now. I would treat them well. In fact,
I fear I might succumb to the temptation to treat them too well.
Perhaps that is why they have passed my door without giving me
a call, but that's one of the fashionable habits they have—they never

come around when you want to see them. I am going to leave here in a little while, and they will have to hustle if they expect to see me.

"Burglary, like many other things, has got to be a science, and the man who is a success at it ought to be respected. He has a family to support, maybe—little babies and a wife, who need nice clothes and things—and it is only fair that he should be given a chance to ply his chosen trade. It is cruel to put him in jail with forgers and common swindlers."

Since the last visit of burglars to Riverdale all of the houses have been provided with burglar alarm systems, and in some of the larger houses watchmen are employed.

On their last sortie they broke into the Appleton mansion, in which the novelist lives, and stole oil paintings and other articles, valued at about $500.

MARK TWAIN WOULD KILL BOSSES BY THIRD PARTY

[New York *Herald*, November 12, 1905]

AUTHOR ADVISES ORGANIZATION OF PERMANENT THIRD PARTY TO HOLD BALANCE OF POWER AND COMPEL NOMINATION OF BEST POSSIBLE MEN BY GIVING ITS VOTE TO THE FITTEST—WOULD MAKE IMPOSSIBLE DICTATION BY IGNORANT POLITICAL TYRANTS —TYPE OF MAN TO LEAD THIS GREAT THIRD PARTY OF "MUG-WUMPS" HE FINDS IN JOHN WANAMAKER—ORGANIZATION'S STRENGTH WOULD KILL CHANCE OF IMPROPER NOMINATIONS

"Mark Twain" has suggested a remedy for bossism, a way to over-throw the Murphys, the McCarren's, the Coxes and make them stay overthrown. He believes his treatment will not entail the abandon-ment of that habit, so dear to most citizens of this great Republic, of voting for their party candidates. Under the new order of things a man who cast his first ballot for the democratic nominee, and has done so every election since, because his father and his grandfather were partisan democrats, may continue to vote the democratic ticket and advise his son to vote the same way, with the comforting assurance that he will be honestly following the dictates of his conscience and that the election of his nominee will mean political purity, no bosses and the best administration possible.

Mr. Clemens believes it is simple to bring about this state of political perfection. All that is required is the organization of a permanent third party, call it "mugwump," if you choose, which shall continually hold the balance of power in municipal, State and national elections. It must be a party with no candidates and no political or personal interests to further, and its members may not even suggest the appointment of any of their friends to office.

* Reprinted by permission of the New York *Sun*, Inc.

Mr. Clemens, as he lay propped up in bed in his city home, at No. 21 Fifth avenue, explained his theory yesterday to a Herald reporter. He was not ill. In fact, he said he hadn't enjoyed such good health for years. He was only resting in preparation for a trip to Washington next Saturday.

Liberty Responsible for Boss

"It is a peculiar condition, but none the less true," said Mr. Clemens, "that the political liberty of which we are so proud is mainly responsible for the existence of the political boss. At any election the people, if they choose, may turn out the whole crowd. This is shown by the re-election of Mr. Jerome by citizens who believe in his honesty of purpose and that his qualifications fit him for the office of District Attorney.

"But this very power which rests with the people is accountable for the laxity which permits the Murphys and the McCurdys and the McCalls and Hegemans to flourish. We know that whenever we get tired of the domination of the bosses or those in office who represent them we have an unfailing remedy. We may apply it at any time, and for that reason we don't until some flagrant act causes an upheaval such as we have just seen in this city and in Philadelphia and in some other places.

"There is a way to escape from the thralldom of bossism, and that is by the organization of a third party, an independent party, made up of those who are generally called 'mugwumps.' I'm a 'mugwump.' I have never tied myself to any party, but have voted for the nominee who appealed to me as being the best man."

Mr. Clemens lighted his favorite pipe and blew a great cloud of smoke into which he gazed thoughtfully.

What Is Party, Any Way?

"What is party, anyway? That fog labelled 'democrat' or 'republican,' which means nothing to the average mind when it is analyzed. The democratic party shouts for free trade while the republican party shrieks for high tariff. Which is right? Why, there is no possible way of deciding which is right. If in the great party politic one-half believe high tariff is right and the other is certain free trade is the proper thing, who is there to settle the question?

"If you ask me what I suggest as a remedy for present conditions, I'll tell you that some one, a man of great executive ability, John

Wanamaker, for instance, will have to enlist all his energies in the formation of a permanent third party. It must be composed of men who are willing to give up all affiliations with either of the great parties. No man in it can have any political aspirations. He must not have any friends whom he wishes to push forward for political preferment. The sole reason for the existence of this new third party must be to elect the candidate of either the democratic or the republican party who is believed to be the best fitted for the office for which he is nominated.

"It is not the idea that this independent party is to consist of another fog of non-individualities to be swung in a mass for any candidate at any one's dictation. There would be nobody who could deliver that vote in a mass.

Vote for Best Men

"It is a party made up of separate individualities, each holding and prizing the privilege of voting as he chooses, the rest to vote as they choose. And therefore you have this result, that if the candidate of one of the great parties is conspicuously a better man than the candidate of the other great party it is believable that the independent party would vote as a mass for that man.

"But if both are equally conspicuous for merit it is believable that this would split the independent vote in two with this final result, that, both of these candidates being excellent men, no one would care which was elected.

"If an independent party can obtain the nomination of excellent men on both sides this would certainly justify the organization of a third party."

"What if both the nominee are bad men?" Mr. Clemens was asked.

He turned upon the questioner a look of pity which there was no mistaking.

"Can't you see that if this third party has power to elect whomever it pleases, neither will select for its nominees any but the very best men? Don't you realize with what pains the names of the candidate would be considered before they were chosen for a place on the tickets? There could never be any question about their eligibility. All the 'mugwumps' would have to do would be to decide which man they liked best and vote for him. I admit it would be a mixed government, but that wouldn't matter.

"I have often wondered at the condition of things which set aside morality in politics and make possible the election of men whose unfitness is apparent. A mother will teach her boy at her knee to tell the truth, to be kind, to avoid all that is immoral. She will painstakingly guide his thoughts and actions so that he may grow up possessed of all the manly virtues, and the father of that boy will, when it comes time for his son to cast his first vote, take him aside and advise him to vote for a bad man who is on the democratic ticket because he has always adhered to democratic principles. Could anything be more absurd?

Turn Outs "Too Previous"

"I see by the newspapers that there has been a switching of affairs in Ohio, and that Boss Cox has thrown up his job. By the way, that was the first time I ever heard of a boss being, as the slang phrase has it, 'too previous.' Then I read of an overturning of things in Philadelphia. Why, I don't believe the new conditions will last the year out. How can they? There is no organized party to hold matters as they are. It has been the history of such political upheavals that as soon as the thing is accomplished those who brought it about settle back and let everything drift until the old conditions return.

"Mr. Hearst's fight for the Mayoralty was evidence of what the people can do if they choose. Just think what it would mean if, instead of a spontaneous uprising of voters who are tired of the conditions existing at present, these same voters were members of an organized third party held together by a leader so that it could be counted on as the deciding factor in our municipal elections. It is probable that these same voters will soon forget all about it and then the boss will pick up his lines again and drive as before.

"Personally I would trust Mr. McClellan as Mayor of the city. I believe he is capable and honest, and gives the best administration possible under the prevailing state of affairs. Free from any possible domination of a boss he would make a good chief magistrate. But we need some one to come forward and offer to lead this army of mugwumps who can set all straight.

"As a matter of fact, we hear of a good deal that isn't so. Recently we were told in the cable despatches that the Tsar had proclaimed liberty in his country, with freedom of the press and political representation, very large matters in themselves. By the time we had got used to believing that such things could happen it was discovered that the people of Russia hadn't got so much after all, because the half dozen concessions mentioned don't amount to so much when we know the revenues of the country and the control of the army and navy are still in the Tsar's hands."

Mr. Clemens punched his pillows into more comfortable shape and lit another pipe.

Wanamaker Type of Man Needed

"When I mentioned Mr. Wanamaker as the man to do this I only used him as an example of the type of man who must stand at the head of such a movement. There are many others who would serve as well, men who have devoted their energies to accomplishing great effects by the employment of remarkable executive ability. He must be a builder up who would prove an acceptable leader of this 'mugwump' party.

"I cannot understand the philosophy of the man who, looked up to as a model citizen, loses sight of the morality of politics when it comes to casting his ballot. Why, it's nothing but a question of morality. And I know lots of men who will throw aside all considerations of morality when they go to the polls, and will vote for the man nominated by his party irrespective of his personal fitness for the place. Prejudice influences him. He won't heed the dictates of his conscience.

"This question of prejudice is very important. There are lots of people who don't believe that a slice of ripe watermelon will cure dysentery. It cures my personal friends every time, but I'll bet if I tried to teach the gospel of ripe watermelon to a hospital full of dysentery patients and would sell watermelons for three cents a dozen they'd put me out of the institution."

Mr. Clemens became quite animated as he turned to the subject of cures. There is no gainsaying the fact that the author has improved greatly in bodily strength during the last year. His eyes are bright and his cheeks bear the glow of health. All his motions were vigorous as he emphasized the points of his argument.

"You see," he said, "I am in bed so as to beat a threatened attack of bronchitis. When it gets hold of me it means six weeks in bed for me, two of them without my pipe. I don't intend to take any chances. I am going to Washington on the eighteenth and want to be in trim. I think this is a good time to see things there. It's been a long time since I was in Washington and now that I haven't any gout or any indigestion I hope to enjoy it.

"Speaking of indigestion, I've adopted a new method of treatment that has done the business for me. For thirty years I have suffered from that most annoying of ailments. Six months ago I began to try Mr. Fletcher's cure, which is to thoroughly masticate one's food and saturate it with saliva. Within the last two weeks I have begun to realize the full benefits of this simple preventive.

"I have learned that when you have an attack of dyspepsia and you get those awful grinding pains in your stomach it's a sign you're all right. The stomach craves food and wants something to work on.

"Now I keep a glass of milk and some crackers beside my bed and I wait for the signal my stomach gives me. When it comes I eat and feel all right."

MARK TWAIN'S SEVENTY YEARS

[New York *American and Journal*, November 26, 1905]

WITH A FEW REMARKS ON HOME LIFE, BY THE WORLD'S MOST FAMOUS HUMORIST

November 30 is Mark Twain's birthday—that date marks the end of his seventieth year of genial beneficence. It has been a long and undisputed reign for the prince of humorists, and long may it continue! That it began seventy years ago need not be disputed, for, though in his various recollections he has given the public as yet none of his babyhood observations, who will doubt that he could do so if he would? A man who is so miraculously acquainted with the childhood of the race as to be able to reproduce the diaries of Adam and Eve would find anecdotes of his own infancy a mere bagatelle. That such recollections would prove him to have been a humorist from the day of his birth is not to be questioned.

The observant reporter finds that Mr. Clemens's seventy years have been only mellowing in their effect. The wonderful shock of hair has been gray these several decades, and any lines in his grave countenance are only the marks of quizzical observation or perhaps of inward laughter. The year finds him, after as widely varied a life as man could have, a citizen of New York, and this is probably a permanent abiding place. He is domiciled in one of those dignified old mansions of lower Fifth avenue, in sight of the Washington Arch, which hold their own against the encroachments of office buildings and the noise of business streets with a grim determination that earns for them added respect.

Mr. Clemens will tell you, however, that dignified old mansions have their drawbacks at times in the matter of heat. He has surmounted various difficulties in his lifetime, in ways all his own, and

* Reprinted by permission of the New York *Journal-American*.

callers in the cold days of last Spring cherish the memory of being received at his bedside, where the distinguished author carried on his end of the conversation warm and comfortable beneath bed-clothes drawn to his chin.

A "Mark Twain" Dwelling

It is a pity that Mr. Clemens has not been moved to give a full record of his householding experiences, Summer and Winter. His first experience in householding, as a man of family, was in Buffalo, where he began his married life. This was about 1870. He had bought a third interest in the Buffalo Express, and the house was a wedding gift from his father-in-law. For a time he was a member of the staff of this paper, but his days of working in harness were past. The demand for his work had so increased that he could choose his own time and place for writing. The inevitable move was made within a year. Samuel E. Moffett, in his biographical sketch, describes the event in interesting fashion.

"There was at that time," Mr. Moffett says, "a tempting literary colony at Hartford; the place was steeped in an atmosphere of antique peace and beauty, and the Clemens family were captivated by its charm. They moved there in October 1871, and soon built a house which was one of the earliest fruits of the artistic revolt against the mid-century philistinism of domestic architecture in America. For years it was an object of wonder to the simple-minded tourist. The fact that its rooms were arranged for the convenience of those who were to occupy them, and that its windows, gables and porches were distributed with an eye to the beauty, comfort and picturesque-ness of that particular house, instead of following the traditional lines laid down by the carpenters and contractors who designed most of the dwellings of the period, distracted the critics and gave rise to grave discussions in the newspapers throughout the country of 'Mark Twain's practical joke.'"

Hartford was for many years his home, though in the Summer intervals various mountain or seaside cottages got in some of their dread work, while so recently as a Summer or two ago an Italian villa added strange new items to the sum total of his domiciliary experience.

His latest solution of the Summer question is Dublin, New Hampshire. There he was last Summer, and there he hopes to be again. His own account of how he reached so satisfactory a solution is entertaining, and may be instructive.

His Own Account of His Experiences

"Yes," he said, when asked about the matter. "I have tried a number of Summer homes, here and in Europe together.

"Each of these homes and charms of its own; charms and delights of its own, and some of them—even in Europe—had comforts. Several of them had conveniences, too. They all had a 'view.'

"It is my conviction that there should always be some water in a view—a lake or a river, but not the ocean, if you are down on its level. I think that when you are down on its level it seldom inflames you with an ecstacy which you could not get out of a sand-flat. It is like being on board ship, over again; indeed, it is worse than that, for there's three months of it. On board ship one tires of the aspects in a couple of days and quits looking. The same vast circle of heaving humps is spread around you all the time, with you in the centre of it and never gaining an inch on the horizon, so far as you can see; for variety, a flight of flying fish, mornings; a flock of porpoises throwing somersaults, afternoons; a remote whale spouting Sundays; occasional phosphorescent effects, nights; every other day a streak of black smoke trailing along under the horizon; on the one single red-letter day the illustrious iceberg. I have seen that iceberg thirty-four times in thirty-seven voyages; it is always the same shape, it is always the same size, it always throws up the same old flash when the sun strikes it; you may set it on any New York doorstep of a June morning and light it up with a mirror-flash and I will engage to recognize it. It is artificial and is provided and anchored out by the steamer companies. I used to like the sea, but I was young then, and could easily get excited over any kind of monotony, and keep it up till the monotonies ran out, if it was a fortnight.

Handy for the "Outliars"

"Last January, when we were beginning to inquire about a home for this Summer, I remembered that Abbott Thayer had said, three years before, that the New Hampshire highlands was a good place. He was right—it is a good place. Any place that is good for an artist in paint is good for an artist in morals and ink. Brush is here, too: so is Colonel T. W. Higginson; so is Raphael Pumpelly; so is Mr. Secretary Hitchcock; so is Henderson; so is Learned; so is Sumner; so is Franklin MacVeagh; so is Joseph L. Smith; so is Henry Copley Greene, when I am not occupying his house, which I am doing this season. Paint, literature, science, statesmanship, history, professorship, law, morals—these are all represented here, yet crime is substantially unknown.

"The Summer homes of these refugees are sprinkled, a mile apart, among the forest-clad hills, with access to each other by firm and smooth country roads which are so embowered in dense foliage that it is always twilight in there, and comfortable. The forests are spider-webbed with these good roads—they go everywhere; but for the help of the guideboards, the stranger would not arrive anywhere.

"These Summer homes are commodious, well built and well furnished—facts which sufficiently indicate that the owners built them to live in themselves. They have furnaces and wood-fire places, and the rest of the comforts and conveniences of a city home, and can be comfortably occupied all the year round.

"We cannot have this house next season, but I have secured Mrs. Upton's house, which is over in the law and science quarter, two or three miles from here, and about the same distance from the art, literary and scholastic groups. The science and law quarter has needed improving this good while.

New Hampshire Air Good for Work

"The nearest railway station is distant something like an hour's drive; it is three hours from there to Boston, over a branch line. You can go to New York in six hours per branch lines if you change cars every time you think of it, but it is better to go to Boston and stop over and take the trunk line next day; then you do not get lost.

"It is claimed that the atmosphere of the New Hampshire highlands is exceptionally bracing and stimulating, and a fine aid to hard and continuous work. It is a just claim, I think. I came in May, and wrought thirty-five successive days without a break. It is possible that I could not have done that elsewhere. I do not know; I have not had any disposition to try it before. I think I got the disposition out of the atmosphere this time. I feel quite sure, in fact, that that is where it came from.

"I am ashamed to confess what an intolerable pile of manuscript I ground out in the thirty-five days, therefore I will keep the number of words to myself. I wrote the first half of a long tale—'The Adventures of a Microbe'—and put it away for a finish next summer, and started another long tale—'The Mysterious Stranger.' I wrote the first half of it and put it with the other for a finish next summer. I stopped then. I was not tired but I had no books on hand that needed finishing this year except one that was seven years old. After a little I took that one up and finished it. Not for publication, but to have it ready for revision next summer."

Surely no man has reached his seventieth birthday with a more perfect title to Winter comfort and Summer rest than Mark Twain. His life has been as full of wandering and varied adventure as an egg is full of meat. In 1835 he was born in Florida, Mo., and while he was a child the home was moved to Hannibal, in the same State.

His father, a local judge, died when he was twelve years old, and at thirteen he was at work in his elder brother's printing office. But to the care-free boyhood preceding that date we are indebted for those classic histories of small-boydom written very many years later, "Tom Sawyer" and "Huckleberry Finn." By 1853 he had become a wanderer, working in chance printing offices in New York, St. Louis, Muscatine and Keokuk. Some memories of those days, softened by the intervening years, are gathered together in the little volume "Editorial Wild Oats," or scattered through his various collections of shorter sketches.

In such varied ways has his life been cast, each year broadening and deepening his experience; and it was long ago that the mere humorist was merged in the philosopher. The effect of such a career on the kindly heart and keen, observant nature of the man has been to build greater things than the present generation has as yet appreciated, generous as its judgment may have been. It will remain for later critics to view his work with a surer vision, knowing nothing, perhaps, of that great part of his contemporary public who asked only that he be "funny," and write him down in his rightful place, between Dickens and Thackeray—America's greatest student of human nature and common life.

TWAIN CALLS LEOPOLD SLAYER OF 15,000,000

[New York *World*, December 3, 1905]

SEEKS THROUGH THE WORLD TO AROUSE AMERICANS AGAINST KING
WHO BUTCHERS CONGO NATIVES—HAS EVIDENCE TO PROVE
HIS AWFUL CHARGES—NERO AN AMATEUR IN KILLING COM-
PARED WITH LEOPOLD, HE DECLARES

*. . . Mr. Clemens dictated the following remarkable statement to
the* World *reporter on the eve of his seventieth birthday:*

"Beside Leopold, Nero, Caligula, Attilo, Torquemada, Genghis
Khan and such killers of men are mere amateurs."

My interest in the Congo and the Belgian King's connection with
that State is not personal further than that I am a citizen of the
United States and am pledged, like every other citizen of the United
States to superintend that King as foreman and superintendent of that
property. Thirteen Christian nations stand pledged like our own. The
thirteen are responsible for that King's good conduct, for his humane
conduct; we are all officially committed to see that King Leopold
does his righteous duty in the Congo State, or, if he falls short of his
duty, to call him to strict account.

By the arrangement in 1884 at Berlin the Christian powers gave
the well-being of the Congo State into the hands of the International
Association and charged that association with a couple of very important responsibilities. The association was required to protect the
natives from harm and to advance their well-being in various ways;
also it was charged with the duty of seeing that the several Christian
states have freedom of trade in the Congo State.

The King of the Belgians has taken over the whole property; he is

* Reprinted by permission of the Press Publishing Company.

acting as an absolute sovereign in that State. He has over-ridden all the restrictions put upon at Berlin in 1884, and by the conference of Brussels in 1890. He has thus, in taking over this vast State, which is twice as large as the German Empire, very rich and very populous before he began his devastation, robberies and massacres of the natives, taken upon himself all the responsibilities which were placed upon the International Association. By the terms of the two conventions it is not only the privilege of those Christian powers to call him to account, but it is their duty to do this—a duty which they solemnly assumed, and which they are neglecting.

The responsibility of the United States may be said to take first place, because we were the first of the nations to recognize the Congo flag, which was done by a Presidential order in 1884. We occupied the office of midwife to the Congo State and brought it into the world.

But we are not any more responsible than are the other powers. There should be a concert of action between them. That concert will be brought about in due time; the movement is on foot on the other side of the water and is making progress, particularly in England, where the Government is becoming more and more interested in the matter, and where the people are strongly stirred and are giving voice to their outraged feelings.

The outlook is that England will presently invite the other powers to join her in demanding a searching inquiry into Leopold's performance, this inquiry to be conducted by a commission, not appointed by him as was the late one, but by themselves. We shall need to take a hand in this righteous proceeding, and it is not likely that we shall be backward about it.

The packed commission appointed by Leopold finished its work and prepared its report many months ago. It was made as mild as possible, but it was nevertheless not the sort of report which the King wanted to spread before the civilized nations. He kept it back several months and issued it lately, and with very proper reluctance.

There is a matter connected with that report history which had a good deal of significance at the time. I speak of the suicide of the chief Congo official, a governor-general or something like that. That man had been representing the King a good many years; his treatment of the natives had been merciless; he harried them with the torch and the sword; he robbed and burned right and left; he was bitterly hated, not by the natives only but by the whites. He read the report of the commission in its original shape there on the Congo before Leopold had had an opportunity to blue-pencil it.

Late that night two white men, one of whom was an Englishman of high character and position, occupied a room next to the Governor-General's. They heard a peculiar noise, and one of them said to the other: "Something is happening in that room."

They went in there and found the Governor-General gasping out his life with his throat cut. The noise they had heard was the streaming of his blood upon the floor. His last act had been the writing of a note of a rather impressive character. I cannot quote its language, but in substance it was to this effect:

"I cannot stand up against that report, yet I can only say in all sincerity that everything I have done was by command of the King himself."

That note was brought away, and is now in the possession of that Englishman. I have these facts from an American missionary who was on the spot at the time, and who vouches for their authenticity.

The King has not mended the condition of things in the Congo since he blue-penciled that report and issued it. The atrocities go on just as before, and the world must expect them to continue until the Christian powers shall exercise the right which they have reserved to themselves at Berlin and Brussels to put an end to them.

The pamphlet which I lately issued contains a small part of the twenty-year accumulation of evidence against King Leopold, and this evidence is of an authority which cannot be disputed. It comes from English officials, Belgian officials, and from American missionaries of unimpeachable character. I intend that the pamphlet shall go into the hands of every clergyman in America, and this purpose will be carried out. We have eighty millions of people who will speak, and speak audibly, when they find out the infamies that are being perpetrated in the Congo, and that our whole nation has a personal interest in the matter and is under written engagement to look after it.

In the pamphlet to which Mr. Clemens refers in his signed interview he epitomizes the evidence against King Leopold in the form of a soliloquy by the King. The pamphlet is entitled "King Leopold's Soliloquy," and is published at Mr. Clemens's expense. . . .

MARK TWAIN TOO LAZY FOR A UNITED STATES SENATOR

[New York *Herald*, March 11, 1906]

"CONGRESS NEEDS INDUSTRY," SAYS THE VETERAN MIRTH INVENTOR, WHO THEN PROCEEDS TO ARGUE WHY NO VACANT TOGA WOULD BECOME HIM

Suggestions having come from various sources that in the event of the retirement from Congress of either of the New York Senators Samuel L. Clemens (Mark Twain) would be named as successor, a reporter for the HERALD called upon the humorist yesterday at his home, in Fifth avenue, to get his expressions on the subject.

Mr. Clemens, who was clothed in his pajamas and busily engaged in shaving when he was asked if he would accept a Senatorial seat, instantly stopped wielding the razor and, turning to his questioner with an expansive smile on his lathered face, said:—

"If such an offer as that were made to me it would be the most gigantic compliment I ever received. I would not consider myself, however, a worthy successor to Dr. Depew or Mr. Platt, as I am in no way qualified for the post. A Senator needs to know the political history of the country, past and present, as well as its commercial, industrial and financial affairs. Of these things I am blissfully ignorant.

Too Lazy for a Senator

"Even if I were qualified, the duties of a Senator would be distasteful to me. My own particular work is the greatest source of pleasure I have, and for that reason I do not consider it as work at all. I regard myself as the most lazy human being on earth. I have absolutely no industry in me whatever, and to 'make good' as a Senator one must

* Reprinted by permission of the New York *Sun*, Inc.

be in love with the job and be industrious. If a man is to succeed in any occupation the work to him must be a labor of love. It has always been so with me and my work, and I think I can justly say, without vanity, that my career has been, to a fair degree, a success.

"For five days every week I am busy writing or dictating, and I'm in a modified paradise the while. Saturdays and Sundays I take off, and during these two holidays, as I call them, I'm in a modified hades."

When reminded that the Senate, as a body, is sadly lacking in humor and needs livening up, Mr. Twain said, smilingly:—

"Well, as 'Falstaff to the Senate' I guess I could fill the bill and earn my salary. But as a representative of the people I would be certain to prove dead timber."

"But can't humorists be serious as well as other mortals, Mr. Twain?"

"Most assuredly. There is no man alive—not even excepting a Scotch Presbyterian minister—who can be more serious than I. But as a Senator the people would refuse to take me any more seriously than they do in my natural capacity as a humorist, and I would score a failure if I attempted to convince them that I was in earnest. I don't care to make an unattractive exhibition of myself. It's a humorist's business to laugh at other folks, not inspire other folks to laugh at him."

Mr. Twain is now writing his autobiography. He started on the book on January 9, he said, and has now one hundred thousand words of it completed. He devotes one hour and three-quarters to the work every morning, dictating it while in bed.

MIGHTY MARK TWAIN OVERAWES MARINES

[New York *Times*, May 12, 1907]

HE TELLS HOW THE MINIONS OF GOVERNMENT QUAIL AS THEY PLAN HIS ARREST—POTTER A GREAT MAN, TOO—PHILOSOPHER HAS MOTORMAN'S AUTHORITY—GOOD GROWS OUT OF THE "WITHDRAWAL" OF A WATERMELON

Special to The New York Times

ANNAPOLIS, May 11.—"Yes," said Mark Twain, with an air of conscious importance, "I have been arrested. I was arrested twice, so that there could be no doubt about it. I have lived many years in the sight of my country an apparently uncaught and blameless life, a model for the young, an inspiring example for the hoary-headed. But at last the law has laid its hand upon me.

"Mine was no ordinary offense. When I affront the law I choose to do so in no obscure, insignificant, trivial manner. Mine was a crime against nothing less than the Federal Government. The officers who arrested me were no common, or garden, policemen; they were clothed with the authority of the Federal Constitution. I was charged with smoking a cigar within a Government reservation. In fact, I was caught red-handed. I came near setting a stone pile on fire.

"It is true that the arrest was not made effective. One of the party whispered to the marines what Gov. Warfield was going to say, and did say, in introducing me to the audience at my lecture—that I was one of the greatest men in the world. I don't know who proposed to tell that to the marines, but it worked like a charm. The minions of the law faltered, hesitated, quailed, and to-day I am a free man. Twice they laid hands upon me; twice were overcome by my deserved reputation.

"Perhaps I ought not to say myself that it is deserved. But who am

* Reprinted by permission of The New York *Times*.

I, to contradict the Governor of Maryland? Worm that I am, by what right should I traverse the declared opinion of that man of wisdom and judgment whom I have learned to admire and trust?

"I never admired him more than I did when he told my audience that they had with them the greatest man in the world. I believe that was his expression. I don't wish to undertake his sentiments, but I will go no further than that—at present. Why, it fairly warmed my heart. It almost made me glad to be there myself. I like good company.

Potter's Claim to Greatness

"Speaking of greatness, it is curious how many grounds there are for great reputations—how many different phases, that is to say, greatness may take on. There was Bishop Potter. He was arrested a few months ago for a crime similar to mine, though he lacked the imagination to select United States Government property as the scene of his guilty deed. Now, Bishop Potter is a great man. I am sure he is, because a street car motorman told me so. A motorman is not a Governor of Maryland, but then Bishop Potter is not a humorist. He could hardly expect a certificate like mine.

"I rode with the motorman one day on the front seat of his car. There was a blockade before we got very far, and the motorman, having nothing to do, became talkative. 'Oh, yes,' he said, 'I have a good many distinguished men on this trip. Bishop Potter often rides with me. He likes the front seat. Now there's a great man for you— Bishop Potter.'

" 'It is true,' I responded. 'Dr. Potter is indeed a mighty man of God, an erudite theologian, a wide administrator of his great diocese, an exegete of—'

" 'Yes,' broke in the motorman, his face beaming with pleasure as he recognized the justice of my tribute and hastened to add one of his own. 'Yes, and he's the only man who rides with me who can spit in the slot every time.'

"That's a good story, isn't it? I like a good story well told. That is the reason I am sometimes forced to tell them myself. Here is one, of which I was reminded yesterday as I was investigating the Naval Academy. I was much impressed with the Naval Academy. I was all over it, and now it is all over me. I am full of the navy. I wanted to march with them on parole, but they didn't think to ask me; curious inattention on their part, and I just ashore after a celebrated cruise.

"While I was observing the navy on land," said Mr. Clemens, "I thought of the navy at sea and of this story, so pathetic, so sweet, so really touching. This is one of my pet stories. Something in its delicacy, refinement, and the elusiveness of its humor fits my own quiet tastes.

"The time is 2 A.M., after a lively night at the club. The scene is in front of his house. The house is swaying and lurching to and fro. He has succeeded in navigating from the club, but how is he going to get aboard this rolling, tossing thing? He watches the steps go back and forth, up and down. Then he makes a desperate resolve, braces himself, and as the steps come around he jumps, clutches the hand-rail, gets aboard, and pulls himself safely up on the piazza. With a like manoeuvre he gets through the door. Watching his chance, he gains the lowest step of the inside staircase, and painfully makes his way up the swaying and uncertain structure. He has almost reached the top when in a sudden lurch he catches his toe and falls back, rolling to the bottom. At this moment his wife, rushing out into the upper hall, hears coming up from the darkness below, from the discomfited figure sprawled on the floor with his arms around the newel post, this fervent, appropriate, and pious ejaculation, 'God help the poor sailors out at sea.'

"I trust this matter of my arrest will not cause my friends to turn from me. It is true that, no matter what may be said of American public morals, the private morals of Americans as a whole are exceptionally good. I do not mean to say that in their private lives all Americans are faultless. I hardly like to go that far, being a man of carefully weighed words and under a peculiarly vivid sense of the necessity of moderation in statement. I should like to say that we are a faultless people, but I am restrained by recollection. I know several persons who have erred and transgressed—to put it plainly, they have done wrong. I have heard of still others—of a number of persons, in fact, who are not perfect. I am not perfect myself. I confess it. I would have confessed it before the lamentable event of yesterday. For that was not the first time I ever did wrong. No; I have done several things which fill my soul now with regret and contrition.

Withdrawing a Watermelon

"I remember, I remember, it so well. I remember it as if it were yesterday, the first time I ever stole a watermelon. Yes, the first time.

At least I think it was the first time, or along about there. It was, it was, must have been, about 1848, when I was 13 or 14 years old. I remember that watermelon well. I can almost taste it now.

"Yes, I stole it. Yet why use so harsh a word? It was the biggest of the load on a farmer's wagon standing in the gutter in the old town of Hannibal, Missouri. While the farmer was busy with another —another—customer, I withdrew this melon. Yes, 'I stole' is too strong. I extracted it. I retired it from circulation. And I myself retired with it.

"The place to which the watermelon and I retired was a lumber yard. I knew a nice, quiet alley between the sweet-smelling planks and to that sequestered spot I carried the melon. Indulging a few moments' contemplation of its freckled rind, I broke it open with a stone, a rock, a dornick, in boy's language.

"It was green—impossibly, hopelessly green. I do not know why this circumstance should have affected me, but it did. It affected me deeply. It altered for me the moral values of the universe. It wrought in me a moral revolution. I began to reflect. Now, reflection is the beginning of reform. There can be no reform without reflection—

"I asked myself what course of conduct I should pursue. What would conscience dictate? What should a high-minded young man do after retiring a green watermelon? What would George Washington do? Now was the time for all the lessons inculcated at Sunday School to act.

"And they did act. The word that came to me was 'restitution.' Obviously, there lay the path of duty. I reasoned with myself. I labored. At last I was fully resolved. 'I'll do it,' said I. 'I'll take him back his old melon.' Not many boys would have been heroic, would so clearly have seen the right and so sternly have resolved to do it. The moment I reached that resolution I felt a strange uplift. One always feels an uplift when he turns from wrong to righteousness. I arose, spiritually strengthened, renewed and refreshed, and in the strength of that refreshment carried back the watermelon—that is, I carried back what was left of it—and made him give me a ripe one.

"But I had a duty toward that farmer, as well as to myself. I was as severe on him as the circumstances deserved. I did not spare him. I told him he ought to be ashamed of himself giving his—his customers green melons. And he was ashamed. He said he was. He said he felt as badly about it as I did. In this he was mistaken. He hadn't eaten any of the melon. I told him that the one instance was bad enough, but asked him to consider what would become of him if this should become a habit with him. I pictured his future. And I saved him. He thanked me and promised to do better.

Farmer's First False Step

"We should always labor thus with those who have taken the wrong road. Very likely this was the farmer's first false step. He had not gone far, but he had put his foot on the downward incline. Happily, at this moment a friend appeared—a friend who stretched out a helping hand and held him back. Others might have hesitated, have shrunk from speaking to him of his error. I did not hesitate nor shrink. And it is one of the gratifications of my life that I can look back on what I did for that man in his hour of need.

"The blessing came. He went home with a bright face to his rejoicing wife and I—I got a ripe melon. I trust it was with him as it was with me. Reform with me was no transient emotion, no passing episode, no Philadelphia uprising. It was permanent. Since that day I have never stolen a water—never stolen a green watermelon."

MARK TWAIN TELLS THE SECRETS OF NOVELISTS

[New York *American*, May 26, 1907]

Throwing one knee carelessly across the top of the desk, the other dangling until the foot nearly touched the floor, the twinkle in Mark Twain's eyes ceased for a moment and the furrows in his forehead became somewhat more pronounced. In a most serious way he said,

"Authors rarely write books. They conceive them, but the books write themselves. This is practically true of all characteristics intended to be portrayed. A sketch is begun in one locality. It may be with one view in sight. Soon, however, the dialogue surrounds the individual and he or she is carried away beyond the point at first intended.

"Who can tell what is to become of a character once created? It goes hither and thither as fancy dictates, much as an individual would do in the daily course of the lives of many. The start may be made with the view of meeting only certain classes or assumed conditions. These change rapidly and the first thought may evolve into something entirely different from the first conception.

"This is what I mean to imply when I say the book writes itself.

"I never deliberately sat down and 'created' a character in my life. I begin to write incidents out of real life. One of the persons I write about begins to talk this way and one another, and pretty soon I find that these creatures of the imagination have developed into characters, and have for me a distinct personality. These are not 'made,' they just grow naturally out of the subject. That was the way Tom Sawyer, Huck Finn and other characters came to exist. I couldn't to save my life deliberately sit down and plan out a character according to diagram. In fact, every book I ever wrote just wrote itself. I am really too lazy to sit down and plan and fret to 'create' a 'character.' If anybody wants any character 'creating,' he will have to go somewhere else for it. I'm not in the market for that. It's too much like industry."

* Reprinted by permission of the New York *Journal-American*.

MARK TWAIN SAILS; SHIEST MAN ABOARD

[New York *American,* June 9, 1907]

HUMORIST TAKES HIS LAST TRIP TO LONDON "FROM THIS SPHERE"
—HOPES TO GO AFTER DEATH—WILL RETURN WITH OXFORD
DEGREE THIS MONTH, IF "LET BOYS" WILL LET HIM

Mark Twain sailed on the Atlantic Transport Liner Minneapolis yesterday for what he said was probably the last trip he would make to London from this sphere. He felt certain that, having led so exemplary a life, he would be permitted to go to London when he died. Just at present, though, he was in excellent health.

The humorist did not wear his white suit, but he did appear in the lightest of gray suits with an overcoat to match and a white tie. The white dress suit was in his trunk.

As soon as Mr. Clemens went on deck he took a cigar from his overcoat pocket and carefully peeled off its several wrappers. There was a smile of anticipation on his face, until he found the crowd had broken it.

"There," he said. "Just for that I will not smoke a cigar on the whole voyage."

Two minutes later he slipped away from his friends and searched out the deck steward.

"Get me the blackest cigar you have," he said.

As the ship slipped from the dock he was seen lighting it and his smile returned and expanded with each puff.

"I am going to Oxford University to receive the degree of Doctor of Literature on June 26, and shall spend two days in London before I return," he said. "I am booked to come back on this same ship on June 29, that is, I expect to return then. But you never can tell. I lived eight years in London and the boys there may tempt me to stay longer. I do not know what they will do with me.

"However, I shall do my part. I am always ready to take my

proper share of dissipation to teach other people how to be better than I am myself.

"I have given up all work, you know. I did so on my seventieth birthday and that was so long ago I have almost forgotten it. Now my idleness consists in dictating two hours a day for five days a week. I am writing my autobiography, and it is not to be published until I am well and thoroughly dead.

"It has in it all the caustic and fiendish and devilish things I want to say. It will be many volumes, I cannot say how many, because that depends on how long I live.

"It is not to appear until the people in it are dead and their children and their grandchildren also. I would hate so to hurt anybody's feelings. In fact, it will not appear in print until I am canonized."

Mr. Clemens was asked who the people were who had come to see him off.

"Oh, I do not know," he answered. "The fact is, I am the shyest person you ever saw. Most people are shy, but mine is of a peculiar sort. I never look people in the face, because they may know me and I not know them. And that is so embarrassing.

"I never observe anybody or anything. I gave that up years ago. I do not know what goes on around me until it happens and then I get away as soon as I can. If you do not use an ability it will atrophy. That is what has happened to me. All my powers of observation are dried up and withered."

MARK TWAIN TELLS SEA TALES

[New York *Sun*, June 19, 1907]

GREAT DINNER EXPERIENCE AHEAD OF HIM IN LONDON—BERNARD
SHAW INTRODUCES HIMSELF AT RAILWAY STATION—NOTES
FROM LOG OF A FAIR WEATHER VOYAGE—BIG SLEEP PROBLEM
—WON'T COME BACK UNTIL JULY 7

Special Cable Despatch to THE SUN.

LONDON, June 18.—A newspaper reporter awaiting the arrival of Mark
Twain to-day caught sight of George Bernard Shaw and said "You've
come to meet Mark Twain?"

"No," replied Mr. Shaw with surprise, "I've come to meet Prof.
Henderson of the University of North Carolina. He is writing my
biography and has come over here to find out something about me."

Mr. Shaw proceeded at once to give his views at great length until
Mr. Clemens turned up, when Mr. Shaw introduced himself. They
had a few pleasant words, then Mr. Shaw went off.

Mark Twain was left at the mercy of the interviewers, who discovered that the humorist is greatly interested in the pageants now
so popular here and that he intends to go to the Oxford pageant.

He will dine at the Pilgrims' Club and also at the Mansion House
as a member of the Savage Club, at a banquet the Lord Mayor is
giving. He will be at the American Society's dinner on July 4, and also
at one to be given by the Mayor of Liverpool.

He spent the afternoon in paying calls on Lord Curzon and Ambassador and Mrs. Reid and in receiving a host of callers himself.
He has postponed his return to the United States until July 7, owing
to his numerous engagements.

Mr. Clemens said to THE SUN's correspondent: "With all these

* Reprinted by permission of Thomas W. Dewart.

affairs, how am I to get my usual quota of sleep, which is about twenty-two hours daily, is something that's puzzling me. I usually spend most of the time in bed, rise about 12 o'clock and very seldom have lunch, so that I can go back to bed again by 2 o'clock. If I have no engagements on, why I can then remain in bed until noon the next day.

"I am very glad that the stories are being circulated that I spend twenty-six hours daily on my autobiography. It is well to have such a reputation for work, but somehow I feel for once obliged to tell the truth and admit that three hours a week, at most, constitutes my period of labor.

"My trip over was delightful. The captain was most courteous, but firm. As I felt that he needed my assistance in running the boat I used to go up on the bridge in a nice neighborly fashion when he wasn't there and tell the other officers what to do. This lasted just three days. At the end of that time Capt. Gates came to me and said very courteously:

"'Twain, this is the third time I have found that while I was lunching you have gone to the bridge and altered the course of the ship and haven't told me about it. As it's up to me to get the Minneapolis to Tilbury would you mind quitting and allowing me to earn my money well?'

"Of course, after the man had shown a spirit like that it rather discouraged me giving him my invaluable assistance, so I let him manage the ship himself. And somehow the Minneapolis managed to arrive safely at Tilbury."

Mr. Clemens was delighted with the passengers he met on board the Minneapolis and entered into the spirit of all the ship's games and played with the children. At the ship's concert he let the passengers into a few secrets of his autobiography, dealing principally with the expurgations of his early works by Mrs. Clemens and her constant thwarting of his efforts to introduce real, human cuss words into the stories.

At the end of the voyage the passengers overwhelmed him with attentions. Their attitude was expressed in the sentiments of one who said: "Mr. Clemens, we knew of you and respected you, but now we just love you."

Mark Twain also had his first experience with wireless telegraphy. One day messages were received from America and England. His astonishment did not diminish when he found they did not come direct, but had been passed on from ship to ship.

His meeting with Mr. Shaw gave him great pleasure.

"I like his face," he said. "I want to see more of him."

Some one suggested that it would be nice to have Mr. Shaw answer questions on Mark Twain's views and vice versa. Another with more acquaintance with Mr. Shaw said the latter would want to do both, wherupon Twain spoke up, saying:

"That's even better still. It makes me more anxious to meet him again. It would save me a lot of trouble if some one would give my opinions for me."

MARK TWAIN HOME IN GOOD HUMOR

[New York *Times*, July 23, 1907]

HAD DINNER WITH THE KING AND IS SURE THAT THE KING EN-
JOYED IT—HE'S DR. CLEMENS, PLEASE—THOUGH THE DIG-
NITY OF HIS OXFORD TITLE DOESN'T SEEM TO WEIGH HEAVILY
—72, BUT DOESN'T FEEL GUILTY

Mark Twain came home yesterday after his six weeks' stay in England. The dignity of his Oxford degree of Doctor of Literature, for
which he went to the English seat of learning, does not appear to
weigh heavily on him, although, with a merry twinkle in his eye, he
said he wished that his American friends would understand that from
now on he is Dr. Clemens, with the accent very strongly on the
"Doctor."

"Just how my old friends are going to get away from calling me
'Mark' is something they will have to work out for themselves," he
said, "and when they see me in my new cap and gown they will be
bound to fall."

Mark Twain was, as usual, the centre of an admiring group of
women when the reporters greeted him aboard the Atlantic Transport
Company steamship Minnetonka at Quarantine upon her arrival yesterday afternoon. He came over in Cabin 23, but said it had no
significance, and was a poor joke.

"How do you like America?" the reporters all asked at once.

"I was afraid I would be asked that question," began Dr. Clemens,
but before he got any further another was fired at him.

"Have you seen the Statue of Liberty?"

"I decline to commit myself, young men; you cannot trap me into
any damaging admissions."

* Reprinted by permission of the New York *Times*.

Getting down to his stay in England, he was asked about his dinner with King Edward.

"Did you enjoy the dinner very much?"

"The King did."

"What did you think of the King? When Tim Sullivan returned a short time ago he said 'Ed's all right; I like him. He is the goods.'"

"I am not competing with Mr. Sullivan."

Dr. Clemens was asked about the handsome Ascot gold cup which had disappeared shortly after his arrival in England, and which the English reporters had humorously connected with his arrival.

"Oh, yes; I have the cup on board, and I hope some of you reporters are slick enough to help me smuggle it through the Custom House. It would be too bad to give it up after getting so close to home with it.

"But I didn't get the Dublin jewels. With the character they gave me over on the other side I should certainly not have left the case. I would have taken both," he added.

Dr. Clemens said that it was all a mistake that the English could not understand a joke.

"I had not the slightest trouble in getting mine through their heads," he said.

"What was the best joke you told them?"

"That will cost you 30 cents a word, and I am having no bargain days now."

"Did they laugh?"

"Why, surely; but if you want to hear it you must be prepared to pay heavily for it. At this time of life one must get all one can for one's wits.

"I have been interviewed a great deal while away, but many of the interviews, when they appeared in print, were grossly exaggerated."

Asked about his appearance in the lobby of Brown's Hotel, in London, in his pajamas and bath robe prior to walking across the street to the Bath Club, he said:

"When a man reaches my age he has certain privileges that younger men cannot have. I did that, and there was absolutely nothing improper in it."

"Are the Englishwomen as attractive as those in America?" was another question.

"That is too leading, and I refuse to commit myself," was the diplomatic reply.

Dr. Clemens said that he had enjoyed his trip abroad immensely, and that the people had treated him royally.

Shortly after the Minnetonka left the other side the ship was in collision with a bark. Several of the plates of the big ship were dented and the bowsprit knocked off the sailing vessel. Dr. Clemens said that he was not awake at the time, but that he was soon aroused, grabbed his bath robe, and rushed to the deck to see what the trouble was. Some of the passengers say that he thought he had grabbed his bath robe, but that in reality he had put on his Oxford gown in the darkness.

Mark Twain spoke at the concert last Saturday night. He chose to talk about the improvement of the condition of the adult blind, and repeated the story told in "A Tramp Abroad" of his having been caught with a companion in Berlin in the dark for an hour or more and of his great horror at not being able to see for even so short a time. He said that he would devote much of the rest of his life to the subject of aiding the blind, and the passengers promised their aid in anything he undertakes.

Coming over he was always the centre of a group of passengers listening to his stories with great interest. He made a particular pet of little Dorothy Quick, daughter of Mrs. E. G. Quick of Brooklyn, and during the time he was on deck would not let her out of his sight. When he landed he was dressed in white flannels and wore a black derby hat.

As the reporters were leaving one of them asked Dr. Clemens if he objected to telling his age.

"Not in the least. I shall be 72 in November. I do not mind it. Every year that I gain furnishes a new privilege, and all I want to dodge is second childhood.

"At 2 o'clock in the morning I feel as old as any man. At that time you must know that life in every person is at its lowest. At that hour I feel as sinful, too, as possible. But the rest of the time I feel as though I were not over 25 years old. You know one gets back both youth and courage by 6 o'clock in the morning."

Dr. Clemens spent the night at his Fifth Avenue home, and will go to Tuxedo this morning to spend the Summer. He has leased a cottage there.

SOURCES

Essays, Sketches and Tales

LIFE AS I FIND IT. *Agricultural Almanac for the Year 1874*, Lancaster, Pa.

THE FACTS IN THE CASE OF THE SENATE DOORKEEPER. N.Y. *Citizen*, Dec. 21, 1867.

FEMALE SUFFRAGE. *Missouri Democrat* (St. Louis), March 12, 13, and 15, 1867.

PRIVATE HABITS OF HORACE GREELEY. *The Spirit of the Times*, Nov. 7, 1868. Reprinted in *Sins of America as "Exposed" by the* Police Gazette, by Edward Van Every, 1931.

YE CUBAN PATRIOT: A CALM INSPECTION OF HIM. Buffalo *Express*, Dec. 25, 1869. Reprinted in *A Bibliography of Mark Twain*, by Merle Johnson, N.Y., 1935.

LAST WORDS OF GREAT MEN. Buffalo *Express*, Sept. 11, 1869.

THE LATE RELIABLE CONTRABAND. *Packard's Monthly*, July 1869.

A MYSTERY CLEARED UP. *Wood's Household Magazine*, Oct. 1869.

OPEN LETTER TO COMMODORE VANDERBILT. *Packard's Monthly*, Mar. 1869.

TO THE CALIFORNIA PIONEERS. Buffalo *Express*, Oct. 19, 1869. Reprinted in *Mark Twain's Letter to the California Pioneers*, Oakland, Calif., 1911.

THE WILD MAN INTERVIEWED. Buffalo *Express*, Sept. 18, 1869.

ABOUT SMELLS. *The Galaxy*, May 1870.

THE APPROACHING EPIDEMIC. *The Galaxy*, Sept. 1870.

BREAKING IT GENTLY. *The Galaxy*, June 1870.

A COUPLE OF SAD EXPERIENCES. *The Galaxy*, June 1870.

CURIOUS RELIC FOR SALE. *The Galaxy*, Oct. 1870.

A DARING ATTEMPT AT A SOLUTION OF IT. *The Galaxy*, July 1870.

THE EUROPEAN WAR. Buffalo *Express*, July 25, 1870.

FAVORS FROM CORRESPONDENTS. *The Galaxy*, Sept. 1870.

A GENERAL REPLY. *The Galaxy*, Nov. 1870.

GOLDSMITH'S FRIEND ABROAD AGAIN. *The Galaxy*, Oct. and Nov. 1870 and Jan. 1871.

"HOGWASH." *The Galaxy*, June 1870.

INTRODUCTORY TO *Memoranda*. *The Galaxy*, May 1870.

A LITERARY "OLD OFFENDER." *The Galaxy*, June 1870.

MAP OF PARIS. *The Galaxy*, Nov. 1870.

A MEMORY. *The Galaxy*, Aug. 1870.

THE NOBLE RED MAN. *The Galaxy*, Sept. 1870.

OUR PRECIOUS LUNATIC. Buffalo *Express*, May 14, 1870.

THE "PRESENT" NUISANCE. *The Galaxy*, Dec. 1870.

THE RECEPTION AT THE PRESIDENT'S. *The Galaxy*, Oct. 1870.

A ROYAL COMPLIMENT. *The Galaxy*, Sept. 1870.

THE "TOURNAMENT" IN A.D. 1870. *The Galaxy*, July 1870.

UNBURLESQUABLE THINGS. *The Galaxy*, July 1870.

A BRACE OF BRIEF LECTURES ON SCIENCE. *The American Publisher*, Sept. and Oct. 1871.

THE COMING MAN. *The Galaxy*, Feb. 1871.

FRANCIS LIGHTFOOT LEE. *The Pennsylvania Magazine*, 1877, v. 1.

THE INDIGNITY PUT UPON THE REMAINS . . . *The Galaxy*, Feb. 1871.

ONE OF MANKIND'S BORES. *The Galaxy*, Feb. 1871.

THE TONE-IMPARTING COMMITTEE. *The Galaxy*, Feb. 1871.

JOHN CAMDEN HOTTEN. A letter to *The Spectator*, reprinted in *The Lectures of Bret Harte*, edited by C. M. Kozlay, 1909. Also reprinted in *A Bibliography of Mark Twain*, by Merle Johnson, 1935.

BRITISH BENEVOLENCE. N.Y. *Tribune*, Jan. 27, 1873.

FOSTER'S CASE. N.Y. *Tribune*, Mar. 10, 1873.

THE CURIOUS REPUBLIC OF GONDOUR. *Atlantic Monthly*, Oct. 1875.

DUNCAN OF THE *Quaker City*. N.Y. *World*, Feb. 18, 1877.

DUNCAN ONCE MORE. N.Y. *World*, Feb. 25, 1877.

THE SANDWICH ISLANDS. *Modern Eloquence*, edited by Thomas B. Reed, N.Y., 1901, v. 4.

A BOSTON GIRL. *Atlantic Monthly*, June 1880.

THE OMITTED CHAPTER OF *The Prince and the Pauper*. *Bazaar Budget*, Hartford, June 4, 1880. Privately printed as a four-page pamphlet entitled *A Boy's Adventure*, 1929 (?).

ON THE PHILOSOPHY OF SHAVING. N.Y. *Sun*, Sept. 19, 1880.

A TALE FOR STRUGGLING YOUNG POETS. *Mark Twain, His Life and Work*, by W. M. Clemens, 1892.

SMOKING AS INSPIRATION. *Study and Stimulants*, edited by A. Arthur Reade, Manchester, 1883.

WOMAN, GOD BLESS HER! *Modern Eloquence*, edited by Thomas B. Reed, 1901, v. 1.

AH SIN, THE HEATHEN CHINEE. *Tid-Bits*, Dec. 20, 1884. Reprinted in *A Bibliography of Mark Twain*, by Merle Johnson, 1935.

ON TRAINING CHILDREN. *The Christian Union*, July 16, 1885.

REMARKABLE GOLD MINES. *Phunny Phellows*, Chicago, 1885.

INTERNATIONAL COPYRIGHT. *The Century Magazine*, Feb. 1886.

An Author's Soldiering. *Masterpieces of American Eloquence*, 1900.

American Authors and British Pirates. *The New Princeton Review*, Jan. 1888.

The Art of Composition. *The Art of Authorship*, edited by George Bainton, N.Y., 1890.

A Kind-Hearted Druggist. *The Argonaut*, Jan. 5, 1891. Reprinted from the *Pharmaceutical Era*.

A Love Song. *The Medical Muse Grave and Gay*, edited by John F. B. Lillard, N.Y., 1895.

Talk about Twins. *Frank Leslie Christmas Book*, N.Y., 1895.

James Hammond Trumbull. *The Century Magazine*, Nov. 1897.

The Panama Railroad. *Sixty and Six Chips from Literary Workshops*, edited by W. M. Clemens, N.Y., 1897.

The Pains of Lowly Life. *The Pains of Lowly Life*, London, 1900.

A Defence of General Funston. *North American Review*, May 1902.

The Yacht Races. *N.Y. Herald*, Aug. 30, 1903.

Letter to Governor Francis. St. Louis *Republic*, June 14, 1904.

Concerning Copyright. *North American Review*, Jan. 1905.

The Czar's Soliloquy. *North American Review*, March 1905.

John Hay and the Ballads. *Harper's Weekly*, Oct. 21, 1905.

King Leopold's Soliloquy. This was issued as a small, paper-covered book in Boston, Sept. 1905.

A Visit to the Savage Club. *The Savage Club*, by Aaron Watson, London, 1907, Chapter 12.

The Suppressed Chapter of *Life on the Mississippi*. Privately printed as a four-page pamphlet (1910?). Also printed in *The Bookman*, May 1914.

INDEX OF TITLES

INDEX

OTHER COOPER SQUARE PRESS TITLES OF INTEREST

THE SELECTED LETTERS OF MARK TWAIN
Edited by Charles Neider
352 pp., 1 b/w photo
0-8154-1011-5
$16.95

TOLSTOY
Tales of Courage and Conflict
Leo Tolstoy
Edited by Charles Neider
576 pp.
0-8154-1010-7
$19.95

ANTARCTICA
Firsthand Accounts of Exploration and Endurance
Edited by Charles Neider
468 pp.
0-8154-1023-9
$17.95

THE LANTERN-BEARERS AND OTHER ESSAYS
Robert Louis Stevenson
Edited by Jeremy Treglown
320 pp.
0-8154-1012-3
$16.95

Available at bookstores; or call 1-800-462-6420

 Cooper Square Press

150 Fifth Avenue
Suite 911
New York, NY 10011